Family and Succession Law in the USA

Family and Succession Law in the USA

Fourth Edition

Lynn Dennis Wardle
William C. Duncan
Laurence C. Nolan

This book was originally published as a monograph in the International Encyclopaedia of Laws/Family and Succession Law.

Founding Editor: Roger Blanpain
General Editor: Frank Hendrickx
Volume Editor: Walter Pintens

Wolters Kluwer

Published by:
Kluwer Law International B.V.
PO Box 316
2400 AH Alphen aan den Rijn
The Netherlands
E-mail: international-sales@wolterskluwer.com
Website: lrus.wolterskluwer.com

Sold and distributed in North, Central and South America by:
Wolters Kluwer Legal & Regulatory U.S.
7201 McKinney Circle
Frederick, MD 21704
United States of America
Email: customer.service@wolterskluwer.com

Sold and distributed in all other countries by:
Air Business Subscriptions
Rockwood House
Haywards Heath
West Sussex
RH16 3DH
United Kingdom
Email: international-customerservice@wolterskluwer.com

Printed on acid-free paper

ISBN 978-94-035-0751-4

e-Book: ISBN 978-94-035-0752-1
web-PDF: ISBN 978-94-035-0753-8

Printed in the United Kingdom.

Dedicated to my wife, Marian, and our sons, daughters-in-law, parents, siblings, grandparents, grandchildren, aunts, uncles, and cousins, whose lives intertwined in the love and challenges of family relations have furnished zest for the study of this subject.—LDW

Dedicated to my wife Catherine and our children who inspire all of my efforts.—WCD

The Authors

Lynn Dennis Wardle is the retired Bruce C. Hafen Professor of Law at the J. Reuben Clark Law School at Brigham Young University in Provo, Utah, U.S., where he taught from 1978 to 2018. He received his B.A. from Brigham Young University (International Relations & Political Science), Utah, U.S. in 1971, and J.D. from Duke University School of Law in 1974. He served on the *Duke Law Journal* (editor & staff) and on the Moot Court Board. He clerked for Judge John J. Sirica, U.S. District Court for the District of Columbia, from May 1974 to September 1975, (during the Watergate cover-up trial and related cases), then practiced law as a trial attorney in Phoenix, Arizona until July 1978.

Professor Wardle has taught Family Law, Comparative Family Law, Children and the Law, Domestic Mediation, Constitutional Family Law, Conflict of Laws, Biomedical Ethics & Law, Origins of the Constitution, and other subjects. He was a Visiting Lecturer, China University of Political Science and Law (Beijing, summer 2004); Visiting Lecturer, Nanjing Agricultural University Faculty of Law (Nanjing, summer 2004); Visiting Professor at the University of Queensland T.C. Beirne Law School (Australia, summer 2000), Visiting Professor at Howard University School of Law (Washington, D.C., 1990–1991), a Scholar-in-Residence at the U.S. Department of Justice, Civil Division (Washington, D.C., 1989–1990), a Visiting Professor at Sophia University (Tokyo, Japan, 1988 summer), and a Visiting Research Fellow at the University of Aberdeen (Scotland, 1985 summer). Professor Wardle has served as President (2000–2002) of the International Society of Family Law (an international learned society), and remains a member of the Executive Council of the ISFL, is a member of the American Law Institute, and is the founding president of the International Academy for the Study of the Jurisprudence of the Family. He has served on the Juvenile Court Rules Committee and Child Support Guidelines Committee for Utah and on directing or advisory boards of Americans United for Life Legal Defense & Education Fund, National Right to Life Committee, University Faculty for Life, Canadian Journal of Family Law, Journal of Law & Family Studies, and other public interest organizations and scholarly journals. He is the coauthor (with Mark Strasser and Lynne Marie Kohm) of the casebook *Family Law from Multiple Perspectives* (2014) and fifteen other coauthored or coedited books and over 100 law review articles.

The Authors

William C. Duncan is the director for the Marriage Law Foundation. He formerly served as acting director of the Marriage Law Project at the Catholic University of America's Columbus School of Law, Washington, DC, U.S. and as executive director of the Marriage and Family Law Research Grant at J. Reuben Clark Law School, Brigham Young University, where he also served as a visiting professor. He teaches courses as an adjunct professor at BYU and the BYU Salt Lake Center.

Mr. Duncan has submitted briefs on constitutional and family issues in the U.S. Supreme Court, ten federal Courts of Appeals, eight state Supreme Courts, and other venues. He has presented expert testimony in the legislatures of seven states. His seventy-five scholarly articles have been published in the *Rutgers Law Review, Howard Law Journal, Journal of Legislation, Harvard Journal of Law and Public Policy, Stanford Law and Policy Review* and many other law journals.

Laurence C. Nolan is a retired Professor of Law at Howard University School of Law, Washington, D.C., U.S. She obtained her undergraduate degree (B.S.) at Howard University in 1961 and her law degree (J.D.) at the University of Michigan, Ann Arbor, Michigan, in 1974. Prior to joining the law faculty at Howard, she was an Associate Professor of Law at the Detroit College of Law. She taught and wrote about Family Law, Wills, Trusts and Estates, and the Law of Aging. Most of her publications were in the areas of family law and wills, trusts and estates, including the monograph, *Legal Status of Parent and Child* (1986). She also was the coauthor with Professor Wardle of a family law textbook, Fundamental Principles of Family Law (2nd ed., 2006). She was an active member of the International Society of Family Law and was a member of the bars of Michigan, Maryland, Washington, D.C., and the United States Supreme Court.

Table of Contents

List of Abbreviations

Admin.	Administrative or Administration
Ag.	Agency
Am.	American
Ann.	Annual
Annot.	Annotated
B.	Bar
Bio.	Biology
Biomed.	Biomedical
Bur.	Bureau
C.	College
Civ.	Civil
Co.	Company
Comp.	Comparative
Conf.	Conference
Cong.	Congress or Congressional
Const.	Constitution or Constitutional
Contemp.	Contemporary
Corp.	Corporation
Dep't	Department
E.	East[ern]
Fam.	Family
Fed.	Federal
Gen.	General
Gov't	Government
Hum.	Human
Inc.	Incorporated
Inst.	Institute
Int'l	International
J.	Journal
Jud.	Judicial

List of Abbreviations

Just.	Justice
Juv.	Juvenile
L.	Law
Law.	Lawyer
Med.	Medicine or Medical
N.	New or North
Nat.	Natural
Nat'l	National
Off.	Office
Para.	Paragraph[s]
Persp.	Perspective[s]
Phil.	Philosophy or Philosophical
Plan.	Planning
Pol.	Political
Pol'y	Policy
Prac.	Practical or Practice or Practicing
Prob.	Problems
Proc.	Proceeding[s], Procedure[s], Process
Prof.	Profession[al]
Pub.	Public
Q.	Quarterly
Rec.	Record
Reg.	Register, Regulation[s]
Rel.	Relations
Rep.	Report[s] [er]
Res.	Research
Resol.	Resolution
Rev.	Review
Rts.	Rights
S.	South[ern]
Sch.	School
Sci.	Science[s]
Sec.	Section
Soc.	Sociology
Soc'y	Society
St.	State
Stat.	Statistics
Symp.	Symposium
U.	University or United

U.L.A.	Uniform Laws Annotated
W.	West[ern]
Wk.	Week
Wkly.	Weekly

List of Abbreviations

Preface: 2018

Much has changed in the legal regulation of family in the United States since Professors Lynn Wardle and Laurence Nolan published the first edition of this monograph in 1997 (when I was a student and student assistant to Professor Wardle). These changes dovetail with important cultural changes that are still ongoing and promise even more change in family law going forward. Many of these changes represent the fulfillment of long-developing trends toward viewing the family as a site of personal fulfillment and the accompanying weakening of normative visions of an ideal family.

Recent changes, particularly in the law of marriage, demonstrate a revitalized role of constitutional litigation in reshaping the legal view of family in the United States. These changes are now trickling down to many other areas, particularly the legal understanding of who may be a legal parent. Additionally, the cultural retreat from marriage in favor of nonmarital cohabitation will likely presage further adjustments. Interestingly, that retreat has been particularly marked among those who lack financial and educational resources that might allow successful private ordering of family obligations. Thus, the emerging paradox of family law in the United States is that it may be a more important area of the law than ever even while it has lost a "voice" to influence family life as lived out in individual homes and relationships.

Developing trends relate to parentage (with pressure to broaden adults who may be designated as legal parents), family dissolution (with increasing emphasis on standardization of divorce processes), and, of course, marriage will be reflected in this update.

Despite significant changes in legal and cultural practice, the family is still a core concern of most people, and family law touches almost all lives. Continuity and change are likely to continue their interplay in U.S. law of the family and provide, if not stability, certainly interest and debate going forward.

William C. Duncan
June 2018

Preface: 1997

We accepted the invitation to write a monograph on *Family and Succession Law* in the United States in the belief that we could quickly write a 400-page manuscript and in hopes that writing it would help us attain a broader and more coherent general view of a subject that is too often fragmented in American legal scholarship. We also anticipated that the finished monograph would be of benefit to scholars, judges, and lawyers outside of the United States who may be bewildered by the confusing complexity of family law in a vigorous federal republic.

We were mistaken, of course, in believing that we could just quickly "dash off" the manuscript. Despite our many years of teaching, research, and writing experience in American family law, it took us more than three years to produce 200 manuscript pages apiece. When it came time to put pen to paper, we had the familiar experience of discovering how mushy and imprecise our general knowledge was, and ended up having to go to cases, statutes, and research sources to validate, clarify, and enhance our vague general understanding. In the process of research and editing, the service of our student research assistants was of tremendous value, and we express enormous gratitude to William C. Duncan (BYU Law School) and Amanda Castro (Howard Law School) especially for their great assistance.

We were not disappointed, however, in our hopes that doing the research and writing on this project, we would improve our strategic perception of the subject of Family Law in the United States. Indeed, it has enriched our understanding not only of details of specific threads in the subject but it has increased our vision of the overall pattern in the fabric of Family Law. The outline we were given and asked to follow, generally, was based on how the subject is conceived and taught, and how the laws are framed, in Europe (generally in civil law systems). Thus, for example, succession law, which is an entirely separate subject and discipline in the United States, is generally taught with and conceptualized as part of the subject of Family Law in Europe. Combining those subjects in this volume gave us a greater appreciation of the nexus of those subjects and other subjects like them. Likewise, the outline for the monograph provided by Kluwer reflected the categorization, division, and organization of topics and subtopics common in Europe, which, again, required us to rethink and reconceptualize some of the ways the subjects are usually presented in American legal education.

Preface: 1997

Whether our hopes that the monograph will be truly useful to give educators, scholars, judges, and practitioners in Europe and other countries abroad a valuable and worthwhile understanding of the subject of American Family and Succession Law remains to be seen. We hope the readers will not be disappointed.

Lynn D. Wardle
Laurence C. Nolan
December 1997

General Introduction

§1. General Demographic Background of the United States of America

1. The U.S. Census Bureau estimated the population of the United States of America in July 2017 as 325,719,178 persons.[1] Most Americans live in family households; in 2016, there were more than 77 million family households (of 117 million total households), more than 56 million were headed by married couples, and more than 7 million by unmarried partners. More than 28 million Americans in 2016 were divorced and more than 15 million were widowed. The average family size that year was 3.24.[2]

2. While most American families are marriage-based, the rate of the adult population that is married has dropped and the rate of divorce has increased in the last half-century.

3. Nonmarital cohabitation has also increased dramatically in recent decades.

4. Adoption peaked in the United States in 1972, when 148,701 children were adopted.[3] The following year, the Supreme Court of the United States legalized abortion-on-demand and the number of adoptions plummeted.[4] The most recent estimate is that about 105,000 children are adopted each year, about half by unrelated adults and about half by stepparents (the biologically unrelated new spouse of one of the child's biological parents).[5] In recent years, the number of adoptions slowly rebounded to a high of 22,911 in 2004, but since then the numbers have steadily dropped to 8,668 in 2012 (similar declines have occurred in most other nations, also).[6]

1. U.S. Census Bureau, *Quick Facts*, https://www.census.gov/quickfacts/fact/table/US/PST045216.
2. American Fact Finder, Selected Social Statistics in the United States, 2012-2016 American Community Survey 5-Year Estimates, https://factfinder.census.gov/faces/tableservices/jsf/pages/productview.xhtml?pid=ACS_16_5YR_DP02&src=p.
3. *1989 Adoption Factbook* 99 (National Council for Adoption, 1989).
4. *Roe v. Wade*, 110 U.S. 113 (1973).
5. *Ibid.*
6. L.D. Wardle, *Adoption: Upside Down and Sideways? Some Causes of and Remedies for Declining Domestic and International Adoptions*, 26 Regent U. L. Rev. 209, 215 (2013–2014).

5. The percentage of households with children has dropped slightly in recent decades, but it is still the norm in the United States; as of 2014, there were more than 115 million households in the U.S.; two-thirds of all children were living with their parents, about 93% of whom were married to each other.[7] That same year, nearly one-half (38.7 million) of all families (81.4 million) include children under age 18.[8] About 46% of all household families in 2010 had one or more children (down from 49% in 1990).[9] Seventy percent of the family groups with children had two-parents while 30% were headed by one parent (about 5:1 women:men).[10] The percentage of same-sex households is increasing; historically it has been just over 10% of unmarried couples; in 2010 the Census Bureau reported that for 2007, unmarried-partner households constitute 6.2 of 112.4 million households; 400,000 were two-male partners; 360,000 were two female partners; about 5.5 million were male-female unmarried households.[11] In raw figures, about 70% have biological children of both of the parents in the home; another 10% have biological children of the mother who are stepchildren of her husband; and another 10% have joint biological and stepchildren in the home.[12]

6. In 2012, there were 851,000 divorces and annulments in the United States, amounting to a rate of 3.4 per 1,000 total population; however, that data excluded data from California (a state with one of the most and highest rates of divorce, and five other states.[13] The numbers and rate of divorce have dropped steadily in recent decades in the United States but still are very high. For comparison,[14] the divorce rate was only 2.2 in 1960, 3.5 in 1970, 5.2 in 1980, 4.7 in 1990, and 4.1 in 2000.[15] However, some of the drop in the divorce rate may be attributable to the increase in cohabitation as the breakup of cohabiting couples is not reflected in the divorce data, and the previously cohabiting couples who marry appear to have about the same (not significantly higher) rate of divorce as persons who married without previously

---

7. Table C3. Living Arrangements of Children under 18 Years and Marital Status of Parents, *see* http://www.census.gov/hhes/families/data/cps2014C.html (seen Jul. 8, 2015).
8. Table F1. Family Households, by Tipe, etc., 2014, U.S. Census Bureau, *Families and Living Arrangements*, available at http://www.census.gov/hhes/families/data/cps2014F.html (seen Jul. 8, 2014).
9. U.S. Bureau of the Census, *Statistical Abstracts of the United States 2010* (U.S. Department of Commerce, 2008), at Table 65.
10. U.S. Bureau of the Census, *Statistical Abstract of the United States 2010* (U.S. Department of Commerce, 2010), at Table 67.
11. U.S. Bureau of the Census, *Statistical Abstract of the United States 2010* (U.S. Department of Commerce, 2010), at Table 71.
12. U.S. Bureau of the Census, *Statistical Abstract of the United States 1994* (U.S. Department of Commerce, 1995), p. 65.
13. CDC, *National Marriage and Divorce Rate Trends,* available at http://www.cdc.gov/nchs/nvss/marriage_divorce_tables.htm.
14. U.S. Bureau of the Census, *Statistical Abstracts of the United States 2010* (U.S. Department of Commerce, 2010), at Table 126; CDC, FastStats, Marriage and Divorce, available at http://www.cdc.gov/nchs/fastats/marriage-divorce.htm.
15. U.S. Bureau of the Census, *Statistical Abstracts of the United States 2070* (U.S. Department of Commerce, 2010), at Table 76. The U.S. government is very slow to compile and release divorce data; *see ibid.*

cohabiting.[16] The percentage of adult population in 1950 that was divorced was 1.9—and that included the increase from post-war divorces.[17] By 2008, the rate of divorce per 1,000 Americans was 3.5 (down from a high of 5.3 in 1981 but still much higher than the 2.0–2.5 rate of the early 1960s and before);[18] the rate of divorce per 1,000 population was 3.4 in 2009 (down from 4.7 in 1990). The number of children involved in divorces and annulments has risen from 299,000 in 1950 to 1,075,000 in 1990.[19] In 2009, the Census Bureau reported that 1,100,401 children were living with a parent who had divorced within the previous year.[20]

§2. Dual Sovereignty and the Multiplicity of Family and Succession Laws and Tribunals in the United States of America

7. In the United States, jurisdiction to determine laws regulating the family is shared between the national government and the states. The Constitution of the United States delegates to the national government the responsibility for national economic, defense, and international concerns, but "local" matters including most family law matters remain the responsibility of the individual states.[21] Thus, each family in the United States is regulated by two "sovereigns," operating simultaneously. This means there are really at least fifty-one separate sources of family law in the United States: each of the fifty separate states directly regulates domestic relations (marriage, divorce, paternity, adoption, custody, property division and alimony, for example) within their own jurisdiction, while the federal government regulates the federal law incidents of family (federal taxation, immigration, bankruptcy, etc.).

I. American Federalism and Family and Succession Law

8. Family and succession law is primarily "local" law—not directly within the scope of regulatory power allocated to the national government. Thus, family and succession law in the United States is predominantly a matter of state law. Most

16. CDC, Vital and Health Statistics, Marriage and Cohabitation in the United States: A Statistical Portrait Based on Cycle 6 (2002) of the National Survey of Family Growth Series 23, No. 28, February 2010) available at http://www.cdc.gov/nchs/data/series/sr_23/sr23_028.pdf (seen Mar. 3, 2010).
17. L.D. Wardle, *No-Fault Divorce and the Divorce Conundrum*, 73 B.Y.U. L. Rev. 139 (1991).
18. U.S. Bureau of the Census, *Statistical Abstracts of the United States 2012* (U.S. Department of Commerce, 1997), at table 78, at http://www.census.gov/library/publications/2011/compendia/statab/131ed/births-deaths-marriages-divorces.html (seen Jan. 26, 2016).
19. L.D. Wardle, *No-Fault Divorce and the Divorce Conundrum*, B.Y.U. L. Rev. 73, 142 (1991); and U.S. Bureau of the Census, *Statistical Abstract of the United States 1996* (U.S. Department of Commerce, 2-12), table 150.
20. U.S. Census Bureau, Marital Events of Americans: 2009 (August 2011), at Table 3. Characteristics of Children Who Live With a Parent Who Divorced Last Year: 2009, available at http://www.census.gov/prod/2011pubs/acs-13.pdf (seen Jul. 8, 2015).
21. *See* U.S. Constitution, amendment X; *The Federalist*, No. 10 (J. Madison); No. 17 (A. Hamilton); No. 45 (J. Madison); A. de Tocqueville, *Democracy in America*, ch. 8, 114 (Random House, 1945).

family and succession cases are heard in state courts; most of the government agencies that deal with families in crisis or posthumous transmission of property are state agencies; and most of the laws that regulate domestic relations and succession are state laws. Family law and succession disputes are the paradigmatic examples of the kind of "local" issues that state courts, rather than federal courts, are best suited to hear and decide.[22] The Supreme Court of the United States has declared that the "[r]egulation of domestic relations [is] an area that has long been regarded as a virtually exclusive province of the states."[23] Virtually all of the cases that normally are called family law or succession cases (e.g., divorce, child custody, child support, alimony, property division, paternity, adoption, abuse, neglect and dependency, juvenile delinquency, inheritance, intestate succession and probate) arise in state courts, not in the federal courts. Thus, family and succession law issues rarely arise in federal courts.[24] Despite this general principle, the United States Supreme Court can sometimes impose family law policies in the process of interpreting the Constitution. For example, in 2015 the Court in *Obergefell v. Hodges* interpreted the Constitution as requiring all states to allow same-sex couples to marry.[25]

9. Federal law, however, indirectly but substantially influences state family and succession laws. Even though the direct regulation of family relations and succession is not within the constitutional authority of the federal government, the federal government does have overlapping regulatory authority in many areas pertinent to family and succession law. Proper federal legislation dealing with matters clearly entrusted to the federal government such as commerce, defense, health, taxes, immigration, social security, and many other federal programs often have an indirect but very definite impact upon family relations. For instance, Congress allows married couples certain exemptions in filing federal income taxes; thus, the federal government has an interest in defining who is entitled to those benefits (e.g., who is considered "married" for purposes of federal income tax law). Likewise, certain relatives are entitled to preference in federal immigration laws, so Congress defines those relationships. It is possible that a couple may be deemed "legally married" for purposes of state law but not considered "married" for purposes of federal income tax law or federal immigration law. There has been a revival of congressional legislation in recent years defining domestic relationships and their incidents for purposes of federal law. Two distinguished Family Law scholars recently declared: "Probably one of the most significant changes of the past fifty years [in American family law] has been the explosion of federal laws … and cases interpreting them. As families have become more mobile, the federal government has been asked to

22. *Ankenbrandt v. Richards*, 504 US 689 (1992) (recognizing federal court abstention principle); C. Wright, A. Miller & E. Cooper, *Federal Practice and Procedure*, §3609 (West, 1984); M. Guggenheim, *State Intervention in the Family: Making a Federal Case Out of It*, 45 Ohio State L. J. 399 (1984).
23. *Sosna v. Iowa*, 419 US 393, 404 (1975); *see also Barber v. Barber*, 62 US (21 How.) 582 (1858).
24. For instance, in a federal case a question might arise regarding whether a witness may (or must) testify against a spouse, *see Trammel v. United States*, 445 US 40 (1980), or if a tort claim is asserted against an ex-spouse or parent. *Ankenbrandt v. Richards*, 504 US 689 (1992).
25. *Obergefell v. Hodges*, 135 S. Ct. 2584 (2015).

enact laws in numerous areas that traditionally were left to the states, such as ... domestic violence, and division of pension plans."[26]

10. The definition and protection of individual liberties listed in or covered by the Constitution (such as in the Fourteenth Amendment) also provide the basis for federal law to profoundly affect state family law. For example, some state laws regulating family relations have been invalidated, and state domestic relations rules and statutes modified or enjoined by or because they have been found to infringe upon federal constitutional liberties (such as the penumbral right of privacy) or because they impermissibly discriminate on the basis of certain classifications (such as race or gender) in violation of the federal Constitution.[27]

II. Similarity and Diversity of Family Laws in the American States

11. Family and succession law in the United States has developed separately within each state, by its own local courts and local legislature.[28] As a result, American family and succession laws vary significantly in both substance and procedure from one state to another. Of course, no state has developed its family law *entirely* independently. However, there are many homogenizing cultural influences in the United States that create a tendency for similarity, if not harmony and consistency. For example, persuasive sister-state judicial opinions, new legislation enacted in other states that proves to be effective or popular, proposals for uniform legislation, programs of the federal government providing support and incentives for states to take a particular policy position, federal constitutional standards, the national news and entertainment media, and special interests that operate nationally have produced many multi-state and national trends in the family laws of the various states. Due to these homogenizing influences, students and teachers of family law in the United States often look for—and find—trends, and general principles that are shared, and prevailing rules and practices in the fifty-four states and federal territories.

12. Notwithstanding many homogenizing influences, the various family laws of the American states remain remarkably diverse in policy and practice. Family law is a prime example of the "different laboratories" idea of how federalism usually

26. Linda D. Elrod & Robert G. Spector, *A Review of the Year in Family Law 2007-2008: Federalization and Nationalization Continue*, 42 Fam. L. Q. 713, 713 (2009).

27. *See*, e.g., *Pierce v. Society of Sisters*, 268 US 510 (1925); *Loving v. Virginia*, 388 US 1 (1967); *Stanley v. Illinois*, 405 US 645 (1972); *Wisconsin v. Yoder*, 406 US 205 (1972); *Zablocki v. Redhail*, 434 US 374 (1978); *Orr v. Orr*, 440 US 268 (1979); *Kirchberg v. Feenstra*, 450 US 455 (1981); *Pickett v. Brown*, 462 US 1 (1983); and *Idaho v. Wright*, 497 US 805 (1990).

28. L.D. Wardle, *Liberty Equality & the Quest for Family Justice in the United States*, in *Families & Justice* 208–229 (Marie-Therese Meulders-Klein ed., Bruylant 1997).

generates solutions to social problems much more quickly, how it preserves valuable cultural pluralism much more effectively, and how it fosters individual liberty much more fully than do centralized forms of governments.[29]

III. State Courts Hearing Family and Succession Law Cases in the United States

13. There are fifty-one different systems of family law in the United States, varying tremendously in substance, procedures, and organization.[30] Every state (as well as the federal territories, most importantly the District of Columbia) has its own, unique system of court organization and state court organization.[31] For instance, in New York, the "Supreme Courts" are the trial courts of general jurisdiction, and the highest Court of Appeal is the New York Court of Appeals. In most other states, the "Supreme Court" is the highest Court of Appeal; the trial courts of general jurisdiction are called "Superior Courts" or "District Courts;" and the "Courts of Appeal" are the intermediate appellate courts. But the size, composition, jurisdiction, procedures, and organization of the state court systems differ from state to state.

A. *Diversity of Court Systems*

14. Each state court system has its own unique judicial structure, with their own separate court systems, as do the federal territories (which function as states, but under congressional supervision). Also, there are six major territories—the District of Columbia and five other territories administered as insular territories of the United States (American Samoa, Guam, Northern Mariana Islands, Puerto Rico, and the U.S. Virgin Islands). Thus, in the United States of America there are fifty separate state court jurisdictions with fifty separate state judicial systems, plus six separate federal territorial judicial systems, each organized independently, in which family and succession law cases are regularly heard.

15. For many reasons (some historic, others functional, others political, others conceptual), most of the states separate family and succession cases from general

29. *See generally*, B.C. Hafen, *The Constitutional Status of Marriage, Kinship, and Sexual Privacy—Balancing the Individual and Social Interests*, 81 Michigan L. Rev. 463, 467 & 484 (1983).
30. L.D. Wardle, *Liberty Equality & the Quest for Family Justice in the United States*, in *Families & Justice* 208–229 (Marie-Therese Meulders-Klein ed., Bruylant, 1997).
31. *Want's Federal-State Court Directory* (1994) provides diagrams of the organization of state courts in all fifty states.

civil cases. Family law experts, social scientists, and many judges have recommended that states adopt a unified specialized court system to deal with the tremendously important and unique problems of children and families.[32] All states have set up special courts to hear and decide certain cases involving minors (usually called Juvenile Courts), especially cases involving alleged delinquency by minors or abuse and neglect of minors. Also, the establishment of Family Courts and Probate Courts to hear family law and succession law cases is common. However, many of the state courts that have jurisdiction over family law cases are not specialized courts.[33] In a majority of the states, at least some family and succession cases are heard by the ordinary civil courts (though often a separate division or department within the civil courts is created for at least some family-law cases). Some states have hybrid systems, with specialized courts and general civil courts sharing concurrent or partially overlapping jurisdiction in family and succession law cases. In some states, "Chancery Courts" have sole or concurrent jurisdiction in various family and succession law cases. In the past decade the expansion of specialized courts (such as "Drug Courts" and "Domestic Violence Courts") has increased.

B. Nonspecialist Judiciary

16. Most of the judges who hear family law cases in the United States are not trained as specialists. They are not usually required to have any special preparation, and they do not generally receive any specialized training in family or succession law. Thus, they rely, for the most part, on the knowledge and skills they bring with them and acquire on the job. When a separate family court, division, or department of the court of general jurisdiction is established, the assignment to the family division generally is a rotating assignment.

17. Judges in the United States are selected from among practicing lawyers. There is no separate educational track for judges. American law schools do not require any (or provide much) training in the special skills that lawyers and judges need to work with family law and relationship issues. However, many law students (and, therefore, lawyers) have obtained degrees (sometimes graduate and professional degrees) in psychology, family sciences, counseling, child development, social work, and other disciplines that provide excellent preparation for family law.

---

32. S.J. Messinger, *On Moving Toward a Family Court in Georgia Without the Need for Constitutional Revision*, 12 Georgia St. U. L. Rev. 667 (1996); S.N. Katz & J.A. Kuhn, *Recommendations for A Model Family Court: A Report From the National Family Court Symposium* 7 (National Council of Juvenile and Family Court Judges 1991).
33. In at least forty of the fifty states, at least some family law cases may be heard in courts of general jurisdiction (which hear a wide variety of civil cases), *Want's Federal-State Court Directory*, – n. 18, 121–173.

IV. Nonjudicial Regulation of Family Law Problems

18. The resolution of family law disputes in the United States often involves more intervention from nonjudicial than judicial agencies. In all states, many agencies have been created to support families in need. For example, state family or social services agencies offer special services to families with difficulties in parenting, especially for individuals with propensities for violence or abuse. Prenatal and perinatal care programs are offered to low-income pregnant women. Child protective agencies in all states receive and investigate reports of child abuse, neglect, and dependency.

19. Sometimes, family law litigation takes place as if in a vacuum. "Too often courthouse resolutions resolve only the legal conflicts, leaving unaddressed the underlying personal relationship and psychological disputes."[34] Courts are powerless to deal effectively with the core issues—usually nonlegal issues of finances, interpersonal skill, personal maturity, consideration, selfishness, love, etc. The resolution of these issues requires service from nonjudicial agencies and personnel.

A. *State and Local Nonjudicial Family Support Agencies*

20. Juvenile courts typically have some direct ties to specialized state agencies that work with delinquent youth to divert them from the adult penal systems. Often these include probation and counseling and rehabilitation services, job training, assistance in educational recovery, as well as connections to agencies that work with dysfunctional family members. All states also have special child support collection agencies to assist custodial parents in collecting child support from non-paying obligers. State adoption agencies supervise many adoptions. Other state agencies exist to provide protection to victims of spouse abuse.

21. Typically, personnel from at least three nonjudicial agencies are involved at least indirectly with many family law disputes. *Public school personnel* are often involved because they may discover and report evidence of child neglect or abuse, because they may provide valuable testimony about the effect of the child's relations with a particular parent-custody-contestant upon the child's academic and social life, or because they may be closer to a child and spend more time with a child at a particular time (especially during or following divorce) than any other adult whom the court can consult. Schools employ counselors who often work independently with children from dysfunctional or broken families. *Police* are often called to protect angry estranged spouses from each other, or to protect children from abusive parents. They do not always have to make arrests, and often can broker or mediate disputes and provide for informal resolution without making arrests or filing criminal charges. When arrests are made or criminal charges are filed, the police continue involvement by taking custody of the person (jail). Police officers are often called to testify in cases when violence or other forms of abuse or neglect

34. P.A. Williams, *A Unified Family Court for Missouri*, 63 UMKC L. Rev. 383, 384 (1995).

are alleged, relevant to custody battles, child abuse and neglect cases, and protective orders. *Social services personnel* are often involved because of their outreach programs for children and adults at risk of family violence or child neglect, because of their monitoring of a family or individual as a result of prior reports of abuse or neglect, because of their programs for pregnant women with financial needs, and because of child placement, foster care, and adoption programs. They may be valuable witnesses in court proceedings as well.

22. Health personnel (both medical and mental health workers) are often involved in family law cases. However, in the United States of America, most health services are provided through the private sector, not the public sector. Child psychologists are particularly influential in child custody disputes. Most American judges feel that they lack the wisdom and the resources and the information to make truly discerning judgments about which of two loving-but-estranged parents should be allowed to raise the child as the primary residential (custodial) parent. They usually defer to the recommendations of child psychologists who have interviewed the child or children. Most of these experts come from the private sector—paid by the parties. Custody cases sometimes become a battleground for contesting expert child psychologists. Some commentators believe that these experts may exert too much influence in some custody cases.[35]

B. Alternative Dispute Resolution

23. Because it gives the parties more control over the outcome, costs the parties and legal system less, results in more higher party satisfaction with the outcome, and usually results in speedier disposition, Alternative Dispute Resolution (ADR) is becoming a popular means of resolving family law disputes out of court.[36] Mediation is the most common form of alternative dispute resolution. Most states have enacted mandatory mediation statutes for child custody disputes and some other facets of family dissolution litigation.

In mediation, the parties meet with a third-party mediator, either together or separately, sometimes with an attorney present and sometimes without. The mediator attempts assist the parties themselves to work out a resolution to their legal issues, which can be presented to the court for approval without the necessity for trial. Mediated resolutions generally are more successful (leading to less subsequent litigation) than nonmediated judicial resolutions of family law disputes. Even when mediation does not result in settlement, it seems generally to result in at least narrowing the issues remaining to be resolved in court and thus reducing the length and costs of trial.

24. Mandatory mediation is now required in at least some family law cases in most states. That means that parties to contested cases involving specific (or general) divorce and related issues, especially custody and financial issues, must first

35. R.J. Levy, *Custody Investigations As Evidence in Divorce Cases*, 21 Fam. L. Q. 149 (1987).
36. *ADR in the USA*, in *Families & Justice* 534–540 (Bruylant, 1997).

go to a mediator to try to resolve their dispute by mediation before the court will hear their case. Thus, attorney mediation has been a growth industry within the family law bar in the past decade in most states. By 2015, over 19,000 attorneys belonged to the Section of Dispute Resolution of the American Bar Association.[37] Also, many non-attorneys (including individuals trained in counseling, psychology, family relations, and other related disciples) offer mediation services to parties in family law disputes. The most popular role-approach in American mediation is the facilitation approach—the mediators are seen as a neutral whose skills assist the parties to reach agreements that they seem to be unable to reach by themselves. Transformative mediation, to help the parties develop interaction skills of empowerment and competence is also common, and evaluative mediation to help the parties understand the strength and weaknesses of their position are also noted. There is a growing movement that focuses on reconciliation mediation, to help parties explore other alternatives solutions to their problems than divorce.

25. A variation of mediation is called "collaborative lawyering." In this technique, the parties on both sides and their attorneys agree to try to resolve the issues by mediation without litigation, and also agree that if that does not result, the attorneys will not be able to represent the parties in any ensuing litigation.[38]

V. Access to the Family Justice System in America

26. The legal system in the United States is primarily a private, adversarial system. That means that seeking judicial relief is usually a private choice, depending upon private initiative and private resources. For the most part, the government does not provide lawyers or funds for lawyers for parties to pursue civil actions.

27. Thus, most family and succession cases are considered private civil cases; the state is not a party in most of them. The parties usually hire private attorneys to file and prosecute the actions for them. For indigent persons, the government funds "legal services clinics" where some assistance is available. However, the demand for such services always exceeds the supply of services and attorneys.

28. All attorneys in the United States have the professional responsibility to aid in the provision of legal services to persons who cannot afford private legal representation *pro bono publico*. Thus, private representation of indigent clients without charging a fee is quite common, but it meets only a small fraction of the need, and ultimately all attorneys must charge enough of their clients to pay for overhead, salaries, etc. In other civil cases, representation often can be obtained by parties

37. *See ABA, Section of Dispute Resolution, Organization, About,* available at https://www.facebook.com/ABADisputeResolution1/info?tab=page_info (seen Jul. 8, 2015); *see generally* Ann L. Milne, Jay Folberg & Pater Salem, *The Evolution of Divorce and Family Mediation*, in *Divorce and Family Mediation* 4–7 (Guilford Press 2004).

38. *See generally* Stu Webb, Note, *Collaborative Law: A Practitioner's Perspective on Its History and Current Practice*, 21 J. Am. Acad. Matri. L. 155–169 (2008).

without liquid funds to pay for legal services by arranging to pay the attorney a contingency fee—a percentage of the amount recovered. If the suit is unsuccessful, there would be no fee owing to the lawyer. However, contingency fee arrangements in most family law cases (divorce and divorce-related) are considered unethical and unenforceable in most states because they appear to give the attorney a stake or interest in promoting the breakup of the family (the divorce, etc.). Thus, the provision of legal assistance in family law cases in the United States is still generally quite *laissez faire* and ad hoc.

29. The increase of computer-assisted divorce filing in the United States has been significant, especially since the year 2000. Now in many states, parties are able to use free computer programs or computer systems offered by the courts that assists them to "fill-in-the-blanks" in standard court forms and generates the forms and papers they need to file for or respond to divorce. The advantage is to eliminate (or reduce) the need for parties who have been married a very short time, who have no or very few assets, have no children, and no significant legal issues to hire lawyers to help them file for or represent them in seeking or responding to divorce petitions. The computer system allows them to proceed *pro se.* The disadvantage is that the computer systems allow parties who do have children, property, income, future interests or assets, or long-term marriages also to proceed *pro se* without consulting a legal advisor, by using the computer system, and that often complicates issues that often arise after divorce and may seriously prejudice one or both of the parties.

30. However, there are exceptions to this private adversarial model. The most prominent is to recover child support. Parents have the public duty to support their children, and when they cannot do so, the public must do so. Thus, the state has a vested financial interest in the recovery of sufficient child and spousal support to keep the child and dependant former spouse off public welfare rolls. Public attorneys provide assistance in the recovery of family support. An exception also exists for domestic violence. There is a public duty to not engage in violence and the public takes a great interest in preventing and punishing (criminally prosecuting and civilly enjoining or restraining) domestic violence. Public agencies exist in all states to assist in the collection of unpaid child support. These programs are encouraged or required to some degree by federal rules of which require states to have such agencies in order to be eligible for certain federal welfare funds.

§3. Sources of Family and Succession Law

31. There are four primary sources of family and succession law in the United States. They are constitutions, legislation, treaties, and common law.

I. Constitutional Law

32. Because of the dual sovereignty of American government, there are two kinds of constitutions that may provide law applicable in family and succession cases. They are the Constitution of the United States and the constitutions of each of the fifty states.

A. *The Constitution of the United States*

33. The Constitution of the United States is the "Supreme Law" in the United States of America, binding not only upon officials of the federal government but upon citizens and officials of all of the individual states as well. While the Constitution does not specifically mention families or any topic of family or succession law, and the government it created (the national, or federal, government) is not empowered to directly regulate matters of family or succession law, when its provisions and interpretations of them overlap with family law, they supersede conflicting provisions.

34. Until the twentieth century, there was very little resort to or application of constitutional doctrines in family and succession cases. However, during the twentieth century, especially the last one-third of it, the Supreme Court of the United States decided a significant number of cases invalidating laws regulating family relations as violative of the U.S. Constitution. Inasmuch as the Constitution is the supreme law of the land, these decisions effectively have established constitutional boundaries for the regulation of family relations by government units. To some extent, this has resulted in the judicial "constitutionalization" of family law, insofar as these decisions have set a few specific, national standards for the regulation of domestic relations and have speeded the nationwide acceptance of certain substantive and procedural values in family law.

35. Two influences, more than others, have been responsible for increased judicial scrutiny of family law under constitutional principles. They are the acceptance of substantive due process pertaining to social (noneconomic) interests and values, and the rejection under the Equal Protection clause of stereotyped gender discrimination.

1. Substantive Due Process and Privacy

36. The first significant U.S. Supreme Court decision regarding constitutional limits on family regulation was made in 1923, when the Court employed the doctrine of "substantive due process." This meant that the Court interpreted the national constitution to protect rights not specifically mentioned in the text of the Constitution, primarily economic rights like the ability of a private employer to set the terms of employment for the business free of government regulation. In *Meyer v.*

Nebraska,[39] the Supreme Court of the United States went beyond strictly economic issues to apply the doctrine of substantive due process to government regulation of education. The case involved a Nebraska law that prevented classroom instruction in German. In a challenge by a teacher and parents, the Court held that the authority of parents to rear their children without coercive interference from the state is one of the unwritten "liberties" protected by the due process clause of the fourteenth amendment. The Court emphasized that "[w]ithout doubt" among the undefined "liberties" protected by the fourteenth amendment are the rights "to marry, establish a home and bring up children" and that "[c]orresponding to the right of control, it is the natural duty of the parent to give his children education suitable to their station in life."[40] Two years later, in *Pierce v. Society of Sisters*,[41] the Supreme Court again focused upon parental rights when it affirmed that an Oregon law requiring parents of children between the ages of 8 and 16 to send their children to public school for instruction was unconstitutional. A religious order which operated an orphanage and private school, and a private military academy, successfully challenged the law in federal court. The Supreme Court again emphasized the rights of the parents of the children in vindicating the position of the private schools:

> [W]e think it entirely plain that the Act of 1922 unreasonably interferes with the liberty of parents and guardians to direct the upbringing and education of children under their control … . The fundamental theory of liberty upon which all governments in this Union repose excludes any general power of the State to standardize its children by forcing them to accept instruction from public teachers only. The child is not the mere creature of the State; those who nurture him and direct his destiny have the right, coupled with the high duty, to recognize and prepare him for additional obligations.[42]

37. The next major case was decided in 1944. In *Prince v. Massachusetts*,[43] the Court extended great rhetorical respect for parental prerogatives in child-rearing, but upheld the conviction of a woman under Massachusetts child labor laws who allowed her 9-year-old niece and legal ward to accompany her and join her in selling religious tracts on public sidewalks. The Court emphasized family privacy, stating: "It is cardinal with us that the custody, care and nurture of the child reside first in the parents, whose primary function and freedom include preparation for obligations the state can neither supply nor hinder … And it is in recognition of this that prior decisions have respected the private realm of family life which the state cannot enter."[44] But the Court also ruled that "the family itself is not beyond regulation in the public interest" and finding that there were substantial risks of physical and other harm to children from selling unpopular religious tracts on busy public streets the Court upheld the conviction.

39. 262 US 390 (1923).
40. 262 US at 399–400.
41. 268 US 510 (1925).
42. 268 US at 534–535.
43. 321 US 158 (1944).
44. 321 US at 166.

38. The extension of substantive due process to regulations of the family expanded in the 1960s, 1970s, and 1980s led by cases involving claims of "privacy" in which the Court invalidated laws restricting the distribution of contraceptives,[45] and overturned laws restricting abortion.[46] The "privacy" concept was applied to the family and produced a flurry of decisions in which the Court established the right of adults to regulate their family relations (and parents to raise their children) free from excessive government intrusion.[47] In the first decade of the new millennium, the Court declared unconstitutional state laws forbidding homosexual sodomy under an analysis that found such laws irrational.[48] The impact upon state law and family jurisprudence of federal court rulings is manifest by the fact that within less than five years thereafter, state Supreme Courts in Massachusetts, California, and Iowa had interpreted their state constitutions as requiring that same-sex marriage be legalized in those states (though California voters quickly overturned the ruling of the California Supreme Court by passing Proposition 8 just a few months later). In 2013, the U.S. Supreme Court ruled that the federal government had to recognize same-sex marriages that were legally performed in a state,[49] and in 2015 it controversially ruled 5-4 in *Obergefell v. Hodges* that the liberty and dignity protections of the Constitution require all states to allow same-sex couples to marry.[50]

2. Equal Protection

39. The Fourteenth Amendment forbids any state to deny to any person "equal protection of the laws." As interpreted by the modern Supreme Court, this means that a law or state action cannot use certain status-based classifications that result in a disadvantage to protected groups. In its most significant aspects the equal protection doctrine is a substantive constitutional doctrine because the outcome of a court's equal protection analysis will nearly always depend upon which legal analysis, referred to as a "standard of scrutiny," the court uses to assess the validity of a government classification. Justice White explained the equal protection tests as follows:

> The general rule is that legislation is presumed to be valid under the equal protection clause and will be sustained if the classification drawn by the statute is rationally related to a legitimate state interest ... When social or economic

45. *Griswold v. Connecticut*, 381 US 479 (1965); *Eisenstadt v. Baird*, 405 US 438 (1972); and *Carey v. Population Services Int'l*, 431 US 678 (1977).
46. *Roe v. Wade*, 410 US 113 (1973); *Planned Parenthood v. Danforth*, 428 US 52 (1976); *Akron v. Akron Center for Reproductive Health*, 462 US 416 (1983); and *Planned Parenthood v. Casey*, 112 S. Ct. 2791 (1992).
47. *Parham v. J.R.*, 442 US 584 (1979); *Zablocki v. Redhail*, 434 US 374 (1978); *Moore v. City of East Cleveland*, 431 US 494 (1977); and *Wisconsin v. Yoder*, 406 US 205 (1972). *See generally* L.D. Wardle, *A Critical Analysis of Constitutional Claims for Same-Sex Marriage*, 1 B.Y.U. L. Rev. 86–87 (1996).
48. *Lawrence v. Texas*, 539 U.S. 558 (2003).
49. *United States v. Windsor*, 570 U.S. 744 (2013).
50. *Obergefell v. Hodges*, 135 S. Ct. 2584 (2015).

> legislation is at issue, the Equal Protection Clause allows the states wide latitude, ... and the Constitution presumes that even improvident decisions will eventually be rectified by the democratic processes.
> The general rules gives way, however, when a statute classified by *race, alienage or national origin*. These factors are so seldom relevant to the achievement of any legitimate state interest that laws grounded in such considerations are deemed to reflect prejudice and antipathy – a view that those in the burdened class are not as worthy or deserving as others. For these reasons and because such discrimination is unlikely to be soon rectified by legislative means, these laws are subjected to strict scrutiny and will be sustained only if they are suitably tailored to serve a compelling state interest (...) Similar over-sight by the courts is due when state laws impinge on *personal rights* protected by the Constitution (...)

Legislative classifications based on *gender* also call for heightened standard of review. That factor generally provides sensible ground for differential treatment (...) A gender classification fails unless it is substantially related to a sufficiently important governmental interest (...) Because *illegitimacy* is beyond the individual's control and bears "no relation to the individual's ability to participate in and contribute to society," (...) official discriminations resting on that characteristic are also subject to somewhat heightened review.

Those restrictions "will survive equal protections scrutiny to the extent they are substantially related to a legitimate state interest.(...) We have *declined*, however, to extend heightened review to differential treatment based on age (...)."[51]

One way to summarize this approach is that the Court has established three basic levels of analysis. The most exacting, which the Court calls "strict scrutiny," applies to classifications based on race or similar categories. If the Court determines that a law or government action classifies on the basis of race, it will assume that the law or action is unconstitutional unless the government entity can show it has a compelling reason for taking race into consideration. Somewhat less exacting is "heightened scrutiny" which applies to classifications on the basis of sex and similar types of status. Here, the challenged law or action must be shown to advance an important state interest or it will be considered unconstitutional. Any other type of classification must only be shown to have a "rational basis," meaning that there is some conceivable valid reason for the state to employ the classification.

The lesson of *Murgia* is that where an individual in the group affected by a law have distinguishing characteristics that are relevant to interests the state has authority to regulate, the courts have been very reluctant, as they should be in our federal system with respect for the separations of powers, to closely scrutinize legislative choices as to whether, how and to what extent those interests should be pursued. In such cases the Equal Protection Clause requires only a rational means to serve a legitimate end.

---

51. *City of Cleburne v. Cleburne Living Center*, 473 US 432, 442 (1985) (emphasis added); *see also Romer v. Evans*, 116 S. Ct. 1620, 1627 (1996); and *Mills v. Habluetzel*, 456 US 91 (1982).

40. As noted above, classifications involving gender discrimination trigger the "intermediate" standard of scrutiny—a requirement that the classification serves an important government interest. In *United States v. Virginia*, the Supreme ruled that Virginia had failed to show sufficient justification for excluding women from its only state-run military academy. Some of the language used by the Court seemed to suggest that the Court was crafting a more stringent test for gender discrimination. It explained: "Parties who seek to defend gender-based government action must demonstrate an 'exceedingly persuasive justification' for that action. Today's skeptical scrutiny of official action denying rights or opportunities based on sex responds to volumes of history."[52]

41. It is interesting that the 1970s–1980s movement to adopt a constitutional amendment prohibiting legal discrimination on the basis of gender (the so-called Equal Rights Amendment or "ERA") ended in failure—with insufficient ratifications by the states within the allotted (and even the extended) time for ratification. If ratified, the ERA probably would have subjected all gender discrimination to strict scrutiny. The failure of that proposed amendment suggests lack of a constitutional consensus to completely prohibit by strict judicial scrutiny all gender discrimination—the sense of the *polis* that sometimes gender differences are real and relevant and do justify some legal distinctions.[53] The current "intermediate" standard of review for gender discrimination reflects a change of the prior law, but also appears to show respect for the will of the people in rejecting strict scrutiny. Equally interestingly, in ruling in 2015 that the Constitution requires all states to legally permit same-sex couples to marry, equal protection was not a significant aspect of the rationale of the Supreme Court.[54]

42. Since many laws regulating family relations are based upon or involve ideas about sex-roles, and since the gender-equality movement of the 1970s raised social consciousness about unnecessary, antiquated or inflexible sex-based stereotypes, the Equal Protection doctrine has assumed profound significance in determining the boundaries of permissible state-imposed gender-model compulsion and restraint.[55]

---

52. 116 S. Ct. 2264, 2274 (1996).
53. There is a possibility that the effort to enact a national Equal Rights Amendment may be revived, since two states have recently ignored the earlier deadlines and ratified the amendment. *See* Matthew Haag, *The Equal Rights Amendment Was Just Ratified by Illinois. What Does That Mean?*, A17 (N.Y. Times May 31, 2018).
54. *Obergefell v. Hodges*, 135 S. Ct. 2584 (2015).
55. *J.E.B. v. Alabama ex rel. T.B.*, 114 S. Ct. 1419 (1994) (Equal Protection Clause prohibits attorneys excluding men from a jury solely because of their sex); *Bowen v. Owens*, 476 US 340 (1986) (provisions of the Social Security Act authorizing payment of survivor's benefits to a widowed spouse who remarried after age 60, but not to a similarly situated divorced widowed spouse did not violate the Equal Protection clause; assumption that divorced widowed spouses are generally less dependent upon the resources of their former spouses than are widows and widowers is permissible); *Kirchberg v. Feenstra*, 450 US 455, 461 (1981) (affirming lower court ruling that Louisiana law that made husband "head and master" of property jointly owned with his wife, giving him unilateral right to dispose of such property without his wife's consent violated equal protection); *Orr v. Orr*, 440 US 268 (1979) (state statutory scheme providing that husbands, but not wives, may be required to pay alimony violates Equal Protection clause and cannot be validated on basis of state's preference for allocation of family responsibilities under which wife plays a dependent role); *Stanton v. Stanton*,

While its most frequent application has been in gender-discrimination cases, it has also been applied in other cases, particularly involving children born out of wedlock, to invalidate arbitrary classifications and unjustified disadvantages for children.[56]

B. State Constitutional Law

43. In recent years, as the Supreme Court of the United States has swung from liberal to moderate, some law reform advocates have turned to state courts to pursue their claims for judicial reform under state constitutional provisions. This is possible because the U.S. Constitution is deemed to set the floor, the minimum level of protection for certain rights, not the ceiling, or maximum level of protection.

44. Probably the most dramatic example of the potential for litigants to use state constitutional law to achieve law reform results they cannot obtain under federal law was in the field of same-sex marriage. Starting with *Baehr v. Lewin*,[57] several state courts ruled that the state constitution requires legalization of same-sex marriage. In Baehr, the Hawaii Supreme Court ruled that the Hawaii Constitution provided greater strength for both substantive due process claims and equal protection claims for same-sex marriage than the U.S. Constitution would provide. It ultimately rejected the due process (right to marry) claim, but revived and remanded

421 US 7 (1975) (invalidating Utah requirement that parents support boys until age 21, girls only until age 18); *Weinberger v. Wiesenfeld*, 420 US 636, 643, 648 (1975) (government must not rely on overbroad generalizations about the different talents, capacities, or preferences of males and females); and *Califano v. Goldfarb*, 430 US 199, 223–224 (1977) (Stevens, J., concurring in judgment).

56. *Clark v. Jeter*, 486 US 456 (1988) (Pennsylvania's six-year statute of limitations for paternity actions did not withstand heightened scrutiny under equal protection clause); *Pickett v. Brown*, 462 US 1 (1983) (same for Tennessee two-year limitations period); *Mills v. Habluetzel*, 456 US 91 (1982) (same for Texas one-year limitations statute); *Caban v. Mohammed*, 441 US 380 (1979) (New York Domestic Relations Law provision, which permits an unwed mother, but not an unwed father, to block the adoption of their child simply by withholding consent violates Equal Protection); *Trimble v. Gordon*, 430 US 762 (1977) (Illinois Probate Act which allowed children born out of wedlock to inherit by intestate succession only from their mothers, whereas children born in wedlock may inherit by intestate succession from both their mothers and their fathers, denied equal protection); *Jimenez v. Weinberger*, 417 US 628 (1974) (Equal Protection clause is violated by discriminatory laws relating to the status of birth where classification is justified by no legitimate state interest); *New Jersey Welfare Rights Organization v. Cahill*, 411 US 619 (1973) (New Jersey "Assistance to Families of the Working Poor" program were as indispensable to the health and well-being of illegitimate children as to those who were legitimate, and denial to illegitimate children benefits which were granted to legitimate children violated equal protection); *Gomez v. Perez*, 409 US 535 (1973) (state may not invidiously discriminate against illegitimate children by denying them substantial benefits accorded children generally, and that a state posits a judicially enforceable right on behalf of children to needed support from their natural fathers); and *Weber v. Aetna Casualty and Surety Co.*, 406 US 164 (1972) (Louisiana workmen's compensation statutes denying equal recovery to dependent unacknowledged illegitimates, in that unacknowledged illegitimates were relegated to lesser status in priority scheme, violated equal protection clause, for lack of significant relation to recognized purposes of workmen's compensation laws and unsubstantiality of claims that statutes served state interest in legitimate family relations and in minimizing problems of proof).

57. 852 P.2d 44, reconsideration granted in part, 875 P.2d 225 (Haw. 1993).

for trial the equal protection claim for same-sex marriage under the Equal Protection clause and Equal Rights Amendment to the state constitution. In 1996, the trial court ordered legalization of same-sex marriage, and the case was appealed to the Hawaii Supreme Court. Just a few months later the state legislature proposed a structural marriage amendment to the state constitution confirming the power of the legislature to limit marriage to a man and a woman. The state marriage amendment was approved by Hawaiian voters in 1998, effectively over-ruling the *Baehr* decision (the appeal of which the state supreme dismissed as moot).[58] Other state Supreme Courts later ruled that their state constitutions mandated recognition of same-sex marriage,[59] though California voters quickly overturned their state Supreme Court by adopting an amendment to the state constitution declaring that only marriage between one man and one woman would be valid or recognized in the state. As noted above, this issue was finally resolved as a national constitutional issue.

II. Legislation

45. Historically, most family laws are judge-made common laws. However, over the centuries those common law rules have been codified, revised, and supplanted in large part by legislation. Today, the first source of law to which a competent family lawyer in the United States will turn is to the statutes. Those statutes are still interpreted and applied by courts, so judge-made law still remains very important in American family law. But the main points and most of the critical details of the breadth of operative family and succession rules are legislated.

46. Most family and succession legislation is adopted at the state level. Thus, state legislatures are the primary sources of family and succession law policy in the United States. (That does not seem inappropriate in a constitutional democracy.)

47. Most state statutes or codes have a section dealing with "family law," but grouping, cataloguing, and indexing state statutes is not a highly refined science. Nor is it consistent from one state to another. Often, statutes regulating family relations are scattered throughout the code or statutes of a state, some in the family law section, others in the state welfare section, others in the general judicial or evidence code, etc.

48. In recent years the promulgation of uniform acts has become popular and has helped to promote a trend toward standardizing (somewhat) some discrete subjects of family law. The National Conference of Commissioners on Uniform State Laws

58. *See* David Orgon Coolidge, *The Hawai'i Marriage Amendment: Its Origins, Meaning and Fate*, 22 U. Haw. L. Rev. 19 (2000).

59. *See Goodridge v. Dep't of Pub. Health*, 798 N.E.2d 941 (Mass, 2003); In re Marriage Cases, 183 P.3d 384 (Cal. 2008); *Varnum v. Brien*, 763 N.W.2d 862 (Iowa 2009).

(NCCUSL) and the American Bar Association have promulgated a series of "uniform laws" which they have recommended for adoption by all states.[60] Nearly fifty of those proposed uniform laws deal with subjects of family and succession law.[61] Some proposed uniform laws have been very successful, and have been adopted by all of the states. For example, the Uniform Child Custody Jurisdiction Act has been adopted by all states,[62] and even a federal version (the Parental Kidnapping Prevention Act—regulating when states must give full faith and credit to custody decrees from sister states) has been enacted.[63] The Uniform Probate Act, covering some posthumous transfers of wealth, has achieved great respect and been adopted by

---

60. *Uniform Laws Annotated* No. 9 (West, 1988), pp. iii–iv.
61. "Uniform Probate Code" *Uniform Laws Annotated*, No. 8, (West, 1969), p. 22; "Uniform Absence as Evidence of Death and Absentees' Property Act" *Uniform Laws Annotated* No. 8A, (West, 1949), p. 1; "Uniform Ancillary Administration of Estates Act" *Uniform Laws Annotated* No. 8A, (West, 1949), p. 133; "Uniform Disclaimer of Property Interests Act" *Uniform Laws Annotated* No. 8A, (West, 1978), p. 149; "Uniform Disclaimer of Transfers by Will, Intestacy or Appointment Act" *Uniform Laws Annotated* No. 8A, (West, 1978), p. 161; "Uniform Disclaimer of Transfers Under Nontestamentary Instruments Act" *Uniform Laws Annotated*, No. 8A, (West, 1978), 179; "Uniform Disposition of Community Property Rights at Death Act" *Uniform Laws Annotated* No. 8A, (West, 1971), 191; "Uniform Disposition of Unclaimed Property Act" *Uniform Laws Annotated* No. 8A, (West, 1966), p. 207; "Uniform Durable Power of Attorney Act" *Uniform Laws Annotated* No. 8A, (West, 1979), p. 309; "Uniform Estate Tax Appointment Act" *Uniform Laws Annotated* No. 8A, (West, 1964), p. 331; "Uniform Gifts to Minors Act" *Uniform Laws Annotated* No. 8A, (West, 1966), p. 367; "Uniform Guardianship and Protective Proceedings Act" *Uniform Laws Annotated* No. 8A, (West, 1982), p. 439; "Uniform Interstate Arbitration of Death Taxes Act" *Uniform Laws Annotated* No. 8A, (West, 1943), p. 543; "Uniform Compromise of Death Taxes Act" *Uniform Laws Annotated* No. 8A, (West, 1943), p. 557; "Uniform Intestacy, Wills, and Donative Transfers Act" *Uniform Laws Annotated* No. 8B, (West, 1991), p. 1; "Uniform Multiple-Person Accounts Act" *Uniform Laws Annotated* No. 8B, (West, 1989), p. 165; "Uniform Nonprobate Transfers on Death Act" *Uniform Laws Annotated* No. 8B, (West, 1991), p. 191; "Uniform Probate of Foreign Wills Act" *Uniform Laws Annotated* No. 8B, (West, 1950), p. 239; "Uniform Simultaneous Death Act" *Uniform Laws Annotated* No. 8B, (West, 1991), p. 253; "Uniform Statutory Form Power of Attorney Act" *Uniform Laws Annotated* No. 8B, (West, 1988), p. 299; "Uniform Statutory Rule Against Perpetuities" *Uniform Laws Annotated* No. 8B, (West, 1990), p. 321; "Uniform Statutory Will Act" *Uniform Laws Annotated* No. 8B, (West, 1984), p. 746; "Uniform Succession Without Administration Act" *Uniform Laws Annotated* No. 8B, (West, 1983), p. 413; "Uniform Survival and Death Act" *Uniform Laws Annotated* No. 8B, (West, 1977), p. 441; "Uniform Testamentary Additions to Trusts Act" *Uniform Laws Annotated* No. 8B, (West, 1991), p. 451; "Uniform TOD Security Registrations Act" *Uniform Laws Annotated* No. 8B, (West, 1989), p. 479; "Uniform Transfers to Minors Act" *Uniform Laws Annotated* No. 8B, (West), p. 497; "Uniform Unclaimed Property Act" *Uniform Laws Annotated* No. 8B, (West, 1981), p. 567; "Uniform Veterans' Guardianship Act" *Uniform Laws Annotated* No. 8B, (West, 1942), p. 689; "Uniform Abortion Act" *Uniform Laws Annotated* No. 9, (West, 1973), p. 1; "Uniform Adoption Act" *Uniform Laws Annotated* No. 9, (West, 1997 Cumulative Supplement), p. 1; "Uniform Child Custody Jurisdiction Act" *Uniform Laws Annotated* No. 9, (West, 1968), p. 115; "Uniform Civil Liability for Support Act" *Uniform Laws Annotated* No. 9, (West, 1954), p. 333; "Uniform Divorce Recognition Act" *Uniform Laws Annotated* No. 9, (West, 1947), p. 355; "Uniform Interstate Family Support Act" *Uniform Laws Annotated* No. 9, (West, 1996, Cumulative Supplement) p. 195. *See generally* Uniform Law Commission at http://www.nccusl.org/Update/DesktopDefault.aspx?tabindex=2&tabid=60 (list of acts at official website of the NCCUSL).
62. *Uniform Laws Annotated* No. 9, (West, 1968), p. 115.
63. 28 USC. 1738A.

seventeen American jurisdictions.[64] On the contrary, the proposed Uniform Putative and Unknown Fathers Act was not adopted by any state and is no longer listed by the organization.[65]

49. Another distinguished national organization, the American Law Institute, also provides recommendations for uniform laws.[66] The American Bar Association and its topical Sections likewise sometimes prepares draft legislation or model rules dealing with family law.

50. Federal legislation indirectly affects family law. This influence may be most noticeable in the offering of federal funds to the states conditioned upon the state's adoption of legislation that conforms to a federal model or standard. For example, all states have enacted and regularly revise child support guidelines precisely because the federal government made that a requirement for eligibility to receive federal welfare assistance funds and keeps fine-tuning those requirements. Additionally, federal regulation of commerce, taxation, federal benefits, payments to federal employees, etc., often influence the way states formulate or interpret family law.

III. Treaties

51. Historically, international law, including treaties, has had very little influence upon the adoption, interpretation, and application of rules of family and succession law in the United States. Most inter-jurisdictional contacts were with the sister states so international rules of law were remote from the practical experience of most lawmakers and lawyers.

52. The availability of affordable and convenient means of international travel and the increase in international commercial transactions in the post-World War II era has produced some changes in that pattern. There is a greater need for regulation of international dimensions of family law disputes today than ever before.

53. The Hague Convention on the Civil Aspects of International Child Abduction is perhaps the best example of an international treaty which has been fully embraced and applied by the United States.[67] While it has not proven to be a flawless procedure for return of abducted children, it has had notable success in remedying international abductions and perhaps in reducing the incidences thereof (or at least influencing the nations into which the abducted children will be taken—favoring those that have not ratified the Abduction Convention.[68]

---

64. *Uniform Laws Annotated* No. 8, (West, 1969), p. 22 (includes intestate succession).
65. *Uniform Laws Annotated* No. 9B, (West, 1997, Cumulative Supplement), p. 82.
66. The ALI is presently preparing a project dealing with Principles of the Law of Family Dissolution.
67. Hague Conference on Private International Law, Convention of Oct. 25, 1980 on the Civil Aspects of International Child Abduction, available at http://www.hcch.net/index_en.php?act=convent ions.text&cid=24.
68. *See generally* L.D. Wardle, *The Merit of Modesty: Abduction, Relocation, and the Hague Abduction Convention*, 9 J. Compar. L. 89–110 (2014).

54. The United Nations Convention on the Rights of the Child (UNCRC)[69] is an example at the other end of the spectrum. Although it has been ratified by all but one other nation, the United States has thus far declined to ratify that treaty mainly because of three concerns: (1) concerns about loss of state control of sensitive family law policy issues and about increasing the power of the federal government and extranational bodies over issues of intensely local dimension; (2) concerns about controversial substantive policies that may be embodied in some of the provisions of the UNCRC that contradict values of the people in some states or in the United States generally, and about the potential of some vague or broad provisions to be interpreted and applied to invalidate some existing American legal policies; and (3) concerns about the effect that ratification would have to transfer family policy making from legislative bodies to judicial bodies, both within and without the United States.[70]

55. There are many other international treaties which, if the United States ratified, could significantly influence the way family law develops and applies in America. These include the Convention on the Elimination of All Forms of Discrimination Against Women,[71] the Hague Convention on Protection of Children and Co-Operation in Respect of Intercountry Adoption,[72] United Nations Convention on the Recovery Abroad of Maintenance,[73] the Hague Convention on the Law Applicable to Maintenance Obligations Towards Children,[74] the Hague Convention on the Recognition and Enforcement of Decisions Relating to Maintenance Obligations Towards Children,[75] Hague Convention on the Recognition and Enforcement of Decisions Relating to Maintenance Obligations,[76] Hague Convention on the Law Applicable to Maintenance Obligations,[77] and Inter-American Convention on Support Obligations.[78] The United States has not joined any of the existing conventions

69. General Assembly Resolution 44/25 of 20 Nov. 1989. By 1994, the UNCRC had been ratified or acceded to by 165 nations. S. Detrick, *"Family Rights" Under the United Nations Convention on the Rights of the Child*, in *Families Across Frontiers* 95 (Nigel Lowe & Gillian Douglas eds, Martinus Nijhoff 1996).
70. B.C. Hafen & J.O. Hafen, *Abandoning Children to Their Autonomy: The United Nations Convention on the Rights of the Child*, 37 Harvard Intl. L. J. 449 (1996).
71. 34 UN GAOR Supp. (No. 46) at 193, UN Doc. A/34/46, entered into force Sep. 3, 1981.
72. *See* G. Parra-Aranguren, *An Overview of the 1993 Hague Inter-Country Adoption Convention*, in *Families Across Frontiers* 565 (Nigel Lowe & Gillian Douglas eds, Martinus Nijhoff 1996).
73. 268 UNTS 32 (1957).
74. 510 UNTS 161 (1964).
75. 539 UNTS 27 (1965).
76. 11 ILM 1286 (1972).
77. The *Hague Convention of Nov. 23, 2007 on the International Recovery of Child Support and Other Forms of Family Maintenance* and the *Hague Protocol of Nov.23, 2007 on the Law Applicable to Maintenance Obligations, at* https://www.hcch.net/en/instruments/conventions/specialised-sections/child-support-and-family-maintenance *(seen Dec. 30, 2015); see* 21 American J. Comp. L. 596 (1973).
78. C. Bruch, *The 1989 Inter-American Convention on Support Obligations*, 40 American J. Comp. L. 817 (1992).

on international collection of family support obligations.[79] The teaching of international family law in American law schools is a matter of relatively recent origin and still is of comparatively limited enrollment.[80]

IV. Common Law

56. Judicial creation of family law doctrines is well established and unavoidable. It is well established because of the common law tradition what came with the early settlers and governments of the English colonies in North America. It is unavoidable because family cases are very fact-sensitive, requiring judges to consider questions the legislative rule drafters did not consider in contexts that the lawmakers did not imagine.

57. The American judiciary historically has been active and willing to participate in the process of establishing the rules it is created to interpret and to apply. In the last fifty years, the practice of "judicial activism" has won the American courts a lot of respect and prestige because of some courageous and ultimately popular policy-changing judicial rulings (especially in the field of civil rights). Those successes have stimulated both an increase in judicial activism and a counteraction to it by advocates of separation of powers (who argue that it is the legislative function to make law, and that the combination of the power to create the rules of law as well as to apply them allows a dangerous concentration of power in the judiciary). Nevertheless, the practice of judicial law-making (at least within certain style or procedural bounds), especially regarding interpreting of family law statutes and development of some family law doctrines in which historically much has been left to judicial discretion, is well-accepted in contemporary America.

58. Judicial law-making is especially unavoidable in family law cases because of the nature of the disputes and the diversity of family problems and issues. New questions and contexts arise at a pace that outstrips even the most active legislatures.

59. About one-third to one-half of all cases heard in state courts of general civil jurisdiction are family law cases. Thus, there are ample opportunities for judges to interpret and fashion family law doctrines.

---

79. M.S. Melli, *The United States and the International Enforcement of Family Support*, in *Families Across Frontiers* 715–716 (N. Lowe & G. Douglas eds, Martinus Nijhoff 1996).
80. *See*, e.g., J.L. Richards, C. Wei & L. dal Pezzo, *Practical Global Family Law* (Carolina Academic Press 2009); D.M. Blair & M.H. Weiner, *International Family Law* (Carolina Academic Press 2d ed. 2009).

§4. HISTORICAL BACKGROUND FOR FAMILY AND SUCCESSION LAW

I. English Law

60. The primary historical source of family and succession law in the United States is English law. That is because the original colonies were established by the English government and subject to English law. English common law was the most influential historical source of law. *William Blackstone's Commentaries on the Common Laws of England*[81] were published just a few years before the American Revolution, and were very influential in the first century of the fledgling new American republic. Thus, English common law, as summarized by Blackstone, became the touchstone for legal developments in virtually all of the American states.

61. Other bodies of English law and legal traditions were also influential. Many actions that we now denominate as family or succession law were heard in Chancery courts, where equity rather than common law prevailed. That is because the common law did not provide a sufficient remedy or because, historically, the type of action was considered an appeal for equity to the conscience of the King's Chancellor rather than a claim for justice under the explicit laws. Equity played a very important role in some schemes of property control for married women.[82] Thus, in early American colonies and states, marriage law cases were often heard in courts of equity rather than law courts.[83]

62. English Ecclesiastical law was also a major source of American family and succession law.[84] Ecclesiastical law was the law of the Church courts of the Church of England (and before that, the Roman Catholic Church). Matters that were deemed spiritual (including most prominently, matters pertaining to marriage, annulment of marriage, divorce, maintenance, and care of orphans and illegitimate children) were within the jurisdiction of the "courts Christian."[85] Decrees of those courts could be taken in some cases into the civil courts of England and there be enforced (or at least provide evidence in or provide the basis for civil claims).

II. Spanish and French Law

63. French law had some lasting influence on the family and succession laws of Louisiana, which was a French possession until purchased by the U.S. in 1803. By then, New Orleans was a substantial and well-established city and the deeply imbedded French legal traditions survived the absorption into the United States of

81. W. Blackstone, *Commentaries on the Common Laws of England* (3d ed., Cooley 1884).
82. B.M. Hoggett & D.S. Pearl, *The Family, Law and Society, Cases and Materials* 137–140, 184–187 (3d ed., Butterworths 1991).
83. H.H. Clark Jr., *The Law of Domestic Relations in the United States* 24 (2d ed., West 1988).
84. *Ibid.*, pp. 21–23, 125–131 & 405–412.
85. B.M. Hoggett & D.S. Pearl, *The Family, Law and Society, Cases and Materials* 249–250, & 568–570 (3d ed., Butterworths 1991).

America. Today, Louisiana is the only state to follow Civil Law (as well as common law), and its statutes are structured on a French Civil Law model.

64. Spain, another civil law country, provided the first laws and government for settlements in many of the states of the American southwest. When former Spanish territories became part of the United States (in the middle of the nineteenth century), they, too, brought their civil law traditions with them. Thus, in the laws of Texas, New Mexico, Arizona, California, and Nevada, (and to a lesser degree in Washington, and Idaho), there are some traces of Spanish civil law.

65. The most significant influence upon family and succession law from French and Spanish civil law is the community property system. All of the above-mentioned states (as well as Wisconsin by relatively recent legislation) have community property systems. Under community property laws, all property acquired during marriage by either spouse (or both spouses) is community property—owned equally and wholly by both spouses jointly as a community unit. The only exceptions are property acquired by gift, bequest, inheritance or devise.

66. Because married women retained significant property interest and (at least theoretically) control during marriage, the equity of community property has been very appealing to advocates of women's rights in this century. So popular has this concept become that today most common law (title) property systems follow a community property (marital property) approach to the disposition of property upon divorce (though not upon death or during the marriage).[86]

86. L.D. Wardle, C.L. Blakesley & J.Y. Parker, *Contemporary Family Law* Vol. 2, §12.01 (Callaghan 1988); and L.J. Harris, L.E. Teitelbaum & C.A. Weisbrod, *Family Law* 6–26 (Aspen 1996).

Part I. Persons

Chapter 1. The Status of a Person

67. The status of a person is concerned with the legal rights and capacities of recognized members and participants in a particular legal system. Though not as comprehensively important as in European law, an individual's personal legal status is significant in the law of the United States. Personal status is closely linked historically with family law, and in that area it is still the most relevant. Specifically, the personal status and capacity of persons affect marriage and childbirth decisions and creates important responsibilities for parents.

§1. Definition of a Person

68. The word "person" is a term of art in the law. A person is the holder of legal rights and responsibilities, and "personhood" is the status of holding legal rights and responsibilities.[87] In the law of the United States a "person" refers generally to a "human being ... though by statute [the] term may include a firm, labor organizations, partnerships, associations, corporations, legal representatives, trustees, trustees in bankruptcy, or receivers."[88] For purposes of family and succession law, the most important category of persons is "human beings." In 2011, voters in Mississippi (one of the most conservative states) rejected a proposed "personhood" amendment to the state constitution which would have legally redefined "personhood" to include all humans from the moment of fertilization. That development suggests both that "personhood" still is a subject of lively concern in some states, and that it is a complicated subject that evades ideological or political identification.

69. Under law, the categories of human beings who are considered legal persons have undergone some evolution and clarification over time. Two of the most important landmark shifts in personhood involved significant decisions of the Supreme Court of the United States. The first was the rejection of slavery. Slavery was legal in most of the colonies at the time of the American Revolutionary War, and though the drafters of the Constitution considered eliminating slavery as noted in some of

87. N.M. Ford, *When Did I Begin?* (Cambridge University Press 1988); and Sapontzis, *A Critique of Personhood* 90 Ethics 607 (1981).
88. *Black's Law Dictionary*, s.v. "person" 1028 (5th ed., 1979).

the most intense debates of the founding convention of 1787, ultimately they decided that it was beyond the immediate concern of the national government they were creating, and left each state to resolve that issue for itself. A slave had a unique status in American law—he or she was a "chattel personal"—having mixed status as property (primarily) and personhood (marginally, partially).[89] Slavery was part of the law of domestic relations in the sense that it was deemed a "domestic institution." Slaves were part of the household, though they had only semi-person status.

70. During the 1840s and 1850s, abolitionist sentiment grew and political controversy over slavery increased. In 1857, the Supreme Court of the United States decided *Dred Scott v. Sanford*,[90] ruling that slaves were neither citizens nor fully persons and invalidating a federal slavery law that prohibited slavery in certain new states and territories. The *Dred Scott* decision inflamed the slavery-abolitionist conflict; Abraham Lincoln (among others) campaigned for office on a platform repudiating and criticizing the decision; the related political and social animosity erupted into a Civil War. Shortly after the conclusion of the Civil War, the dead letter of *Dred Scott* was overturned explicitly when the Thirteenth, Fourteenth, and Fifteenth Amendments to the Constitution were adopted, which abolished slavery, granted certain basic rights to all "persons" in the country, and guaranteed the right to vote free of racial discrimination. Thus, it took a Civil War (costing more than 500,000 American lives) and three amendments that significantly restructured the Constitution to correct the judicial mistake of *Dred Scott* and the historical political-social-economic mistake upon which it was built, and to establish unequivocally the fundamental principle that *all* living human beings are "persons" in the eyes of the Constitution and the laws of the United States.

71. One hundred sixteen years after *Dred Scott v. Sanford* was decided, the Supreme Court rendered another incendiary decision that had at its core a controversy over the concept of personhood. In *Roe v. Wade*,[91] the Court ruled that state laws restricting abortion were unconstitutional because, in part, living but unborn children are not "persons in the whole sense." The Fourteenth Amendment, adopted after the Civil War to expand the rights and protections for rights of classes of human beings on the margins of concern for some influential classes or in some states, was the critical law in Roe. The Fourteenth Amendment expressly provides that states may not deprive any "person" of "life, liberty or property" without due process of law. Attorneys for a pregnant unmarried woman argued that a Texas law prohibiting abortions except when necessary to save the life of the mother infringed

89. J.C. Smith, Jr., *Justice and Jurisprudence and the Black Lawyer*, 69 Notre Dame L. Rev. 1077, Appendix (1994).
90. 60 US (19 How.) 393 (1857). *See generally* L.D. Wardle, *From Slavery to Same-Sex Marriage: Comity Versus Public Policy*, in *Inter-jurisdictional Recognition of Controversial Domestic Relations*, 2008 B.Y.U. L. Rev. 1855 (2008) (reviewing history of slavery recognition in the United States).
91. 410 US 113 (1973).

upon women's right of privacy, a liberty interest allegedly protected by the Fourteenth Amendment. The state responded that it had a compelling interest in protecting the "life" of the unborn child, but the Supreme Court ruled that unborn children are not "persons" for purposes of the Fourteenth Amendment, and suggested that no one knew whether they even had "life" (for purposes of the Fourteenth Amendment) before birth anyway. *Roe* was just the first of a long line of U.S. Supreme Court decisions—now totaling more than forty major cases directly defining the abortion right and its limits, as well as many additional peripheral case decisions indirectly concerning abortion. The scope of permissible regulation of abortion in the United States is still vary limited, and the legal doctrines are still based on the justification that unborn persons (fetuses) are not wholly "persons." For more than four decades since the *Roe* decision, the Court has been plagued by criticisms that *Roe* and its subsequent abortion decisions were unprincipled and illegitimate, merely the judges' personal preferences imposed on the country under the guise of "creative" constitutional interpretation.[92]

72. Ironically, when *Roe v. Wade* was decided in 1973, there was a growing movement in the states to expand access to legal abortion, which ended when the Supreme Court purported to resolve the issue for the entire nation. However, the Supreme Court decision in *Roe* provoked such strong objections on so many levels that the issue which probably would have been resolved politically in a short time with some degree of national consensus and equilibrium was reinvigorated, and the controversy about the abortion cases continues to plague the Court today. In June 2014 the Supreme Court decided two significant abortion cases. In *McCullen v. Coakley*,[93] the Supreme Court unanimously struck down a Massachusetts' law banning standing on a sidewalk within 35 feet of entrance to a reproductive health care facility, aimed at pro-life protesters but exempting clinic employees and agents. In June 2016, the Court struck down a Texas law increasing the health and safety standards abortion clinics were required to meet, saying that the specific requirements were not necessary to ensure women's safety and thus created and undue burden on the right to abortion.[94]

73. Both *Dred Scott v. Sanford* and *Roe v. Wade* were personhood decisions. That is, in both cases one critical question was whether the "marginal" class of human beings involved (African-American slaves and unborn children) were "persons" entitled to basic protections under the Constitution and laws of the United States. In both cases, the Supreme Court ruled that they were not, and in both cases an outcry from human rights advocates resulted. One of the lessons of both cases is that personhood is a very subjective concept; it has no fixed, absolute, constant meaning. Another lesson is that there is a very strong sentiment in America (perhaps stronger in the nineteenth century than in the twentieth) in support of the principle that all

92. J.H. Ely, *The Wages of Crying Wolf: A Comment on Roe v. Wade*, 82 Yale L. J. 920 (Yale University Press 1973); A. Bickel, *The Morality of Consent* 27–29 (1975); A. Cox, *The Role of the Supreme Court in the American Government* 113 (Oxford University Press 1976); and L.D. Wardle & M.Q. Wood, *A Lawyer Looks at Abortion* (Brigham Young University Press 1982).

93. 134 S. Ct. 2518, (2014).

94. *Whole Woman's Health v. Hellerstedt*, 136 S. Ct. 2292 (2016).

living human beings are persons entitled to basic protections—though not necessarily in the Court. Ironically, a majority of the justices of the Supreme Court—the institution designed to be the last protector of civil liberties—in both cases opposed the extension of "personhood" to marginal classes.

74. Because of the use of the term "person" in the Fourteenth Amendment to the United States Constitution,[95] the United States Supreme Court has had to determine what that legal term means in a number of cases. The Court has held that illegitimate children are persons for purposes of the Fourteenth Amendment,[96] and that aliens are included in that category as well.[97] The Court has also held that corporations (which are not humans, and have no tangible existence, but exist merely as legal organizational concepts) are "persons" for purposes of the Fourteenth Amendment.[98]

75. In recent years, feminists and critical race theorists have become interested in personhood issues especially as they relate to identity and membership theories, citizenship and immigration.[99] Thus, while personal status does not have the practical day-to-day legal significance in the United States that it has in many civil law countries, it is of importance in American legal theory and doctrine nonetheless.

§2. Capacity

76. In American law, "capacity" is the term used to describe a person's legal qualifications, capabilities, or competencies, his or her legal ability to be held accountable and to make valid, binding legal acts.[100] For most purposes, including capacity to sue, individual capacity is determined by state law.[101] Generally, the law of the individual's domicile (roughly where a person lives with an intent to stay for a period of time) governs his or her capacity.[102] While the rules of individual capacity are similar among the states, the details vary markedly from state to state.

77. The most important legal facet of capacity in American law may be the concept of legal age. A person must be of legal age to perform legally accountable,

95. U.S. Constitution, Fourteenth Amendment ("nor shall any State deprive any person of life, liberty, or property, without due process of law; nor deny to any person within its jurisdiction the equal protection of the laws").
96. *Levy v. Louisiana*, 391 US 68, 70 (1968) ("They are clearly 'persons' within the meaning of the Equal Protection Clause of the Fourteenth Amendment.").
97. *Plyler v. Doe*, 457 US 202, 210 (1982) ("Whatever his status under the immigration laws, an alien is surely a "person" in any ordinary sense of that term.").
98. *First National Bank of Boston v. Bellotti*, 435 US 765 at 780, n. 15 (1978); *Minneapolis & St. L. Ry. Co. v. Beckwith*, 129 US 26, 28 (1889).
99. *See*, e.g., M. Minow, *Not Only for Myself: Identity, Politics and the Law* (The New Press 1997); Y, Tirosh, *Adjudicating Appearance: From Identity to Personhood*, 19 Yale J. L. & Feminism 49 (2007); S.K. Katyal, *Exporting Identity*, 14 Yale J. J. & Feminism 97 (2002).
100. *Black's Law Dictionary*, s.v. "capacity", 188 (5th ed., 1979).
101. Federal Rules of Civil Procedure 17.
102. *Ibid.*; C.A. Wright, *The Law of Federal Courts* 455–457 (4th ed., West 1983).

valid, binding activities, such as to enter into a contract,[103] to marry,[104] to vote,[105] to consent to medical procedures without parental consent,[106] to be a party to litigation,[107] to engage in legal sexual relationships,[108] etc. The legal age of capacity to engage in particular activities may vary, depending upon the activity in question; that is, a state may set the age of legal capacity for driving at 16, for voting at 18, and for drinking at 21. There is also an age of general legal capacity (sometimes called "majority" or "adulthood") at which a person is deemed to have full legal capacity unless a law specifically provides otherwise. In Anglo-American common law, the age of general legal capacity was 21, but now it is 18 in virtually all of the United States.

78. The concept of legal capacity is especially important in U.S. family law because of the restrictions on entry into marriage. The legal age for marriage (and for most other issues of capacity) is 18 years old. Persons under 18 (who are referred to as minors) have limited capacity to contract a marriage (the most common limitation being a requirement of parental consent).[109] There are, of course, exceptions to the general principle of legal age, such as judicial bypass provisions which allow a judge to make an exception to the requirement that a minor (person under legal age) have parental consent before making certain decisions[110] and the possibility that a minor can be emancipated and therefore exempted from the requirement of parental consent to certain decisions.[111]

79. Despite movements to ameliorate the effects of legal age in international law, legal age remains an important concept in U.S. law.[112] Persons who lack capacity (generally minors and mentally handicapped persons) are still persons, but they are not able to exercise their own legal rights or fully accountable for their own legal duties. Guardians act for and in the name of persons who lack legal capacity. In American law, parents whose legal rights have not been modified or terminated are the "natural guardians" of their legal children. If an infant or incompetent person

103. *See* Ohio Statutes §3109.01 (1997).
104. *See* Idaho Code §32–202 (1997); and 43 Oklahoma Statutes Annotated §3 (1997).
105. United States Constitution, Amendment 26 (granting the right to vote to citizens over 18 years of age).
106. *See Lambert v. Wicklund*, 117 S. Ct. 1169 (1997)(*per curiam*)(validating Montana's statute requiring parental consent for an abortion performed for a "minor" [person not of legal age, generally under 18 years old] with judicial bypass provision); and Ohio Revised Code Annotated §2919.12 9 (1997) ("No person shall knowingly perform or induce an abortion upon a woman who is pregnant, unmarried, under eighteen years of age, and unemancipated").
107. Federal Rules of Civil Procedure 17; and C.A. Wright, *The Law of Federal Courts* 455 (4th ed., West 1983).
108. *See* California Penal Code §261.5 (1997).
109. *See* California Family Code §302 (1997); and N.Y. Domestic Relations §15 (1997).
110. *See* Massachusetts General Laws Annotated 207 §25 (1997); and Missouri Statutes 188.028 (1997).
111. *See* Alabama Statutes §26-21-2.1 (1987) (defining "emancipated minor"); and Virginia Statutes §16.1-334 (1997) (effects of emancipation).
112. *See* B.C. Hafen & J.O. Hafen, *Abandoning Children to Their Rights: The United Nations Convention on the Rights of the Child*, 37 Harvard Intl. L. J. 449 (1996).

has a legal representative, such as a general guardian or natural guardian, that representative may sue or defend on behalf of the incapacitated person (the ward).[113] Because the status of parent is so significant for parental standing and parental rights, some efforts have been made by various groups to expand the concept of parent which have received some academic interest. For instance, the American Law Institute proposed that the legal concept of "parent" be expanded to include "*de facto* parents" (unrelated adults who perform parental functions) and "parents by estoppel" (unrelated adults considered parents because they were treated as if they were a parent by one of the child's parents).[114] Nevertheless, such proposals have had very little acceptance.[115]

§3. ABSENTEES

80. Absentees are persons whose whereabouts are unknown "and it is impossible to ascertain whether [they are] alive or dead."[116] In family law, the concept of absentees is important because "the marital status of his spouse, [and] the paternity and legitimacy of children of his spouse's second marriage" may be in question due to the absence.[117]

81. Absentees are persons and entitled to legal protection. Their property may not be taken nor their liberties diminished without due process of law. Thus, they are entitled to notice of judicial proceedings affecting them or their legal interests.

82. An absentee is usually presumed to be dead after a given number of years. This allows a change in the status of his personal and property rights. The Uniform Probate Code specifies five years as the cut-off point for purposes of wills and inheritance.[118] A number of states have different presumptions.[119] In 1904, the United States Supreme Court upheld the Pennsylvania presumption of death statute against a due process challenge[120] and most states have followed the Pennsylvania statute's pattern.[121]

---

113. Federal Rules of Civil Procedure 17(c).
114. American Law Institute, Principles of the Law of Family Dissolution §§2.01–2.03 (2002).
115. *See* R.F. Wilson, *American Law Institute's Principles of the Law of Family Dissolution, Eight Years of Adoption: Guiding Principles or Obligatory Footnote?*, 42 Fam. L.Q. 573 (2008).
116. J.L. Carriere, *The Rights of the Living Dead: Absent Persons in the Civil Law*, 50 Louisiana L. Rev. 901, 902 (1990).
117. *Ibid.*, at 903.
118. "Uniform Probate Code" *Uniform Laws Annotated* §1-107(3) (1969).
(An individual whose death is not established under the preceding paragraphs who is absent for a continuous period of five years, during which he [or she] has not been heard from, and whose absence is not satisfactorily explained after diligent search or inquiry, is presumed to be dead. His [or her] death is presumed to have occurred at the end of the period unless there is sufficient evidence for determining that death occurred earlier).
119. Minnesota Statutes Annotated §576.141 (1997) (four years); West Virginia Code §44-9-1 (1966) (seven years).
120. *Cunnius v. Reading School District*, 198 US 458, 477 (1905).
121. J.L. Carriere, *The Rights of the Living Dead: Absent Persons in the Civil Law*, 50 Louisiana L. Rev. 901, 913 (1990).

83. A number of states have enacted "Enoch Arden" statutes, so-called after a famous romantic poem by the nineteenth century English Poet Laureate Alfred, Lord Tennyson, applying a presumption of death in the case of long absence for purpose of marriage. These statutes protect a spouse of an absentee; if the spouse remarries, she or he (and their new spouse) are covered by statutory protection from prosecution for bigamy should the absent spouse reappear. The application of such laws is quite rare in the twenty-first century but they remain in the statutes of many states.

84. In the past decade, there were some controversies about whether the same-sex partner of a biological father or mother could be (or had to be) listed on a birth certificate of the child. The June 2015 decision in *Obergefell v. Hodges*,[122] in which the U.S. Supreme Court ruled that all states must allow and recognize same-sex marriages, would seem to have resolved the controversy. Since same-sex couples can be married and enjoy the benefit of a "marital presumption" of parentage, and since the same-sex partner of a parent cannot claim the benefit of the biological parentage presumption the question has become one of marriage. In fact, the U.S. Supreme Court ordered the state of Arkansas to list the names of same-sex couples on the birth certificate of children born through artificial insemination.[123]

122. *Obergefell*, 135 S. Ct. 2584 (2015).
123. *Pavan v. Smith*, 137 S. Ct. 2075 (2017).

Chapter 2. Registration of Civil Status

85. In most civil law countries, registration of civil status is a significant legal process and results in a legal status of lifelong importance. In the United States, by contrast, there is no comparable registration of civil status. Civil records are kept, of course, and have legal significance, but even taken as a whole, those records provide no counterpart to the registration of civil status in civil law systems. When there is registration or recording of status in the United States it usually is governed by state law and deals primarily with the issuance of a birth certificate to a child at birth.

§1. Birth Certificates

86. Birth certificates are important in American law because they provide evidence of parentage. The biological father and mother are legally the parents of a child, and they have the legal rights and responsibilities of parentage. The birth certificate provides evidence (though not binding or conclusive evidence) of who the father and mother are.

87. Birth certificates also used to be important for the law of legitimacy. In English common law, a child born out of wedlock was given certain legal disabilities,[124] and while American law was never as severe, illegitimacy entailed significant legal disadvantages, especially regarding inheritance and succession. However, the legal distinction between children born in or out of wedlock has, for most purposes, been found to violate the Equal Protection clause of the U.S. Constitution, and the historic legal status of "illegitimacy" has largely disappeared as a significant legal distinction in American law.[125]

88. The health care provider who attends the birth of a child (and virtually all children in America are born with a health care provider in attendance) is generally required to file a birth certificate which provides evidence of maternity, but the birth certificates are for statistical and census purposes, and do not necessarily establish parentage.[126] It may be evidence of parentage, but it is not definitive.

89. The woman who gives birth to a child is presumed to be the legal mother of the child.[127] That has been perhaps the strongest presumption in Anglo-American

124. W. Blackstone, *Commentaries on the Laws of England* 446 (3rd ed., Cooley 1884).

125. *See* Part II, Chapter 4.

126. *See People v. Kelly*, 174 P.2d 342 (Cal. Ct. App. 1946). ("The fact that Louis John Holtz appears on the birth certificate is only prima facie evidence of the fact, was open to contradiction and must fall before the conclusive presumption above referred to.").

127. The parentage of the mother who gave birth is established in the Latin maxim "mater est quam gestatio demonstrat," which loosely translated means "she is mother who carries [and bears] the child." Both the Uniform Parentage Act (UPA) and the Uniform Status of Children of Assisted Conception Act (USCACA) adopt the biological "birth mother" or "gestational maternity" presumption. *Uniform Laws Annotated* No. 9B, (1987), p. 287, and *Ibid.*; (1994 Cumulative Supplement) p. 152.

common law for centuries. No documentation, registration, or legal proceeding is necessary.[128] Proof of giving birth (which is usually simple, since pregnancy and childbirth are hard to conceal) alone creates the maternity presumption.

90. Likewise, one of the strongest presumptions historically was the presumption that "every child born to a married woman is in law the legitimate child of her husband."[129] The presumption was most notably manifest in Lord Mansfield's rule of evidence which barred married persons from giving any evidence which would tend to bastardize a child born during marriage in most cases.[130] Lord Mansfield's Rule came to America with the common law. Even today, all states still presume that a married man is the father of all children born by his wife during the marriage. But that presumption is not as absolute or irrebuttable as it was at common law previously; contemporary American courts increasingly find that the marital paternity presumption is rebutted by evidence of biological paternity by a man other than the mother's husband, especially if that fact is coupled with something like the naming of the unmarried man as the father of the child on a birth certificate.[131] In the case of an unmarried woman who gives birth, the law in some states creates a rebuttable presumption of paternity if an unwed man allows his name to be placed on the child's birth certificate.[132]

91. Thus, the birth certificate provides prima facie evidence of maternity and (at least in the case of a married woman) paternity. In the case of a child born out of wedlock, the birth certificate may also provide an indication as to whom the mother believes to be the father of her child.

(Under the UPA, parental status for the "natural mother" may be shown "by proof of her having given birth to the child," or under the UPA [though no other provision of the UPA applies]. UPA §2.) (Under the USCACA, a woman who gives birth is deemed the "mother" of the child born. USCACA §2. *See also Burlington County Welfare Board v. McClain*, 458 A.2d 1348 (N.J. Burlington County Ct. 1983) ("[m]other" has an ordinary, well-understood meaning. It is defined either as one who gives birth to a child or a female who adopts a child); *A.v. X, Y, and Z*, 641 P.2d 1222, 1225 (Wyo. 1982) ("The woman carries the child through pregnancy. When born of her, the fact of motherhood is obvious.").

128. The health care provider is generally required to file a birth certificate which provides evidence of maternity, but the birth certificates are for statistical and census purposes, and do not necessarily establish parentage. *See People v. Kelly*, 174 P.2d 342 (Cal. App. 1946). ("The fact that Louis John Holtz appears on the birth certificate is only prima facie evidence of the fact, was open to contradiction and must fall before the conclusive presumption above referred to").
129. F. Pollock & F. Maitland, *The History of English Law* 398–399 (2nd ed., Cambridge University Press 1898 reprinted 1968).
130. In *Goodright v. Moss*, 2 Cowp. 591, 98 Eng. Rep. 1257 (1777), Lord Mansfield declared that "the law of England is clear, that the declarations of a father or mother, cannot be admitted to bastardize the issue born after marriage [unless] the husband was within the four seas at the time the child was born."
131. *See*, e.g., *McCarthy v. Estate of Krohn*, 16 So.3d 907 (Fla. 4th DCA, 2009).
132. *See* Lashanda Taylor, *Resurrecting Parents of Legal Orphans: Un-Terminating Parental Rights*, 17 Va. J. Soc. Pol'y & L 318, 341 n. 126 (2010).

I. The Registrar

92. Birth Certificates are filed with registrars whose existence and authority are provided for in state statutes. The Registrar is responsible for keeping vital statistics for the state, although specific duties may vary from state to state.[133]

II. Registers and Certificates

93. Birth Certificates are prepared at the place of birth of the child[134] and copies are issued by the Registrar, generally for a fee.[135] They contain the name of the child and the names of the parents as well as where the child was born.[136] When a child is adopted, a new birth certificate showing the adoptive parents as the legal parents may be issued.

94. Birth Certificates are used for a number of different functions depending on state law. For instance, birth certificates may be required to register to vote,[137] to receive a driver's license,[138] and to obtain a marriage license,[139] etc.

§2. Marriage Licenses and Certificates

95. The practice of licensing marriage grows out of the oldest formality required for marriage in Anglo-American law which is the requirement of public notice, traceable to the ancient practice of *banns*.[140] In all states, parties wishing to marry may obtain licenses to marry. In three-fourths of the states, licensing of marriage is mandatory. Nearly half of the American states require parties who intend to marry to file a formal application for marriage by or within a specified time period before the proposed marriage. The time periods range from twenty-four hours to five days.[141] (By contrast, in Las Vegas, Nevada, where marriage-tourism is a significant part of the tourism economy, the Marriage License Bureau is open seven days

133. *See* Michie's Alabama Code §22-9A-3 (1975); California Health and Safety Code §102175 (West 1997); Georgia Code Annotated §31-10-5 (1997); N.Y. Public Health Laws §4121 (Mckinney 1997).
134. *See* Maine Revised Statutes Annotated §2761 (West, 1997); and Louisiana Revised Statutes Annotated §40:45 (West, 1997).
135. *See* Florida Statutes Annotated §382.025 (West, 1997); and Iowa Code Annotated §144.13A (1997).
136. *See* Georgia Code Annotated §31-10-9 (1997); and Wisconsin Statutes Annotated 69-14 (West, 1997).
137. *See* Louisiana Revised Statutes Annotated 18:105 (West, 1997).
138. *See* S.D. Codified Laws §32-12-3.1 (1997).
139. *See* Louisiana Revised Statutes Annotated §9:225 (West, 1990).
140. L.D. Wardle, C.L. Blakesley & J.Y. Parker (eds), *Contemporary Family Law*, Vol. 1, §3:04, 3:07 (Callaghan 1988).
141. *State Policies to Promote Marriage: Preliminary Report*, U.S. Dep't of Health & Human Services Table 4 (March 2002).

a week from 8:00 a.m. to midnight, and open twenty-four hours on holidays; no blood test is required and there is not waiting period; and the fee is very modest.)[142]

96. Marriage licenses are issued in most states by the county clerk, town clerk, or some similar record-keeping official. In almost half of the states, at least one of the parties must reside in the jurisdiction, but most states do not impose that requirement. A nominal marriage license fee is charged. To obtain a marriage license, the couple must reveal their names and other relevant personal information such as birth date, prior marriage, and relationship to the proposed spouse.[143]

97. The Supreme Court's decision in *Obergefell v. Hodges*,[144] requiring all states to permit and recognize same-sex marriages, created a crisis of conscience for some employees of government offices and agencies that issue marriage licenses. While reasonable accommodation of their rights of conscience was both feasible and simple, the political dimensions of the issue led to some intransigence and reluctance to accommodate. Some government employees resigned rather than submit to requirements that they personally facilitate same-sex marriages.

98. Parties who marry under a marriage license (most marriages in the United States are by licenses) receive a marriage certificate upon completion of the wedding. Usually, the official solemnizing the marriage or the official issuing the license is charged with issuing the marriage certificate. Marriage records are public records, open to public inspection.[145]

99. Marriage certificates are often valued by the married couple and their families for sentimental reasons. They provide legal evidence of marriage, and so may be used to verify or establish a marital relationship, as, for instance, in a contested divorce case, or a will or succession dispute, or a life insurance proceeds contest.[146] But they are not of daily legal significance to most persons; only rarely are they used for legal effect.

---

142. Clark County, Nevada, Clerk, available at http://www.clarkcountynv.gov/depts/clerk/Pages/ContactUs.aspx.
143. *Ibid.*
144. 135 S. Ct. 2584 (2015).
145. *Contemporary Family Law* at §3:15.
146. *Spearman v. Spearman*, 482 F.2d 1203 (5th Cir. 1973).

Chapter 3. Personality Rights

100. The category of distinctive individual rights recognized in some civil law countries (particularly Germany and France) as "personality rights" is largely unknown in American law. In American legal literature, "personality rights" relate most prominently to the rights of artists, authors, copyrightists, and other creators of intellectual or cultural property, and there is very little legal use or recognition of the *droit moral* from which the civil law personality rights emanate.

101. However, there is a category of individual rights associated with protection against unwanted publicity and rights of autonomy. The latter kinds of rights have received some jurisprudential development in American constitutional and common law under the label of "privacy" rights. Additionally, stimulated by Justice Kennedy's reliance upon "dignity" in deciding some constitutional cases, a new dignity jurisprudence has been emerging judicially, intellectually and (perhaps) ironically.

102. The category of rights generally referred to as privacy or civil rights in U.S. law includes most of the familial or relational rights that might be considered "personality rights" in civil law countries—and more. Some of these rights are specified in the amendments to the United States Constitution (such as freedom of religion) but most are unenumerated "penumbral" rights, not explicitly mentioned in the text of the Constitution or its amendments but identified and defined by the United States Supreme Court in some of its constitutional interpretation decisions. The enumeration of these rights is potentially very large.

103. Some of the most significant constitutional privacy rights regarding family law are the rights of parents to choose what schools their children will attend,[147] and to determine to a great extent how their children will be raised;[148] the right of each adult person to procreate,[149] and to use contraceptives;[150] the right to engage in consensual sexual activity,[151] the right to marry including same-sex marriage;[152] and the right to have an abortion.[153] These rights are discussed in greater detail in other sections of this encyclopedia.[154]

104. Rights of privacy are both intellectually and operationally slippery because, for the most part, they are not textual rights and are grounded largely in the personal interpretations, instincts, or preferences of particular judges and courts. For this and other reasons, the Supreme Court of the United States in recent years has

147. *Pierce v. Society of Sisters*, 268 US 510 (1925).
148. *Meyer v. Nebraska*, 262 US 390 (1923).
149. *Skinner v. Oklahoma*, 316 US 535 (1942).
150. *Griswold v. Connecticut*, 381 US 479 (1965).
151. *Lawrence v. Texas*, 539 U.S. 558 (2003).
152. *Loving v. Virginia*, 388 US 1 (1967); *Obergefell v. Hodges*, 135 S. Ct. 2584 (2015).
153. *Roe v. Wade*, 410 US 113 (1973).
154. *See* Part II, Chapters 1 and 6.

preferred to use the language and jurisprudence of "liberty" to that of "privacy."[155] Nevertheless, the tradition of recognition of constitutional protection for some facets of family life is well established and very influential in contemporary law, even though not based on textual constitutional sources.

105. However, in the modern age of growing public and corporate intrusion upon and regulation of individuals' lives, the American public's desire for privacy may be growing. For example, in 1996, Congress enacted the Health Insurance Portability and Accountability Act (HIPAA) which legally mandates the protection of the confidentiality of most personal information of health care patients; rules implementing the privacy provisions of HIPAA took effect in 2003.[156] Despite medical industry objections to the bureaucracy of HIPAA,[157] it seems to have proven popular with the public.

155. *Planned Parenthood v. Casey*, 112 S. Ct. 1791 (1992).
156. *See* HIPAA Basics: Medical Privacy in the Electronic Age (Rev. January 2010), http://www.privacyrights.org/fs/fs8a-hipaa.htm. (seen May 12 2010).
157. *See* generally Nicolas P. Terry, *What's Wrong With Health Privacy?*, 5 J. Health & Bio. L. 1 (2009).

Chapter 4. Names

§1. Composition of a Name

106. "'At common law, a legal "name" consisted of a given name and of a surname or family name.' … . In western culture, people have traditionally used both a given name and a surname."[158] *Black's Law Dictionary* defines a name as follows: "A person's 'name' consists of one or more Christian given names and one surname or family name. It is the distinctive characterization in words by which one is known and distinguished from others."[159] Thus, most Americans have between two and four names; most have three names. Practically all persons have a given name and a surname; most have one middle name; some have two or more middle names.

107. It is very uncommon but not necessarily illegal for a person to legally change his name to only one name. Recently, a court in New York rejected a petition to change to just one name on the ground that: "a single name would cause too much confusion to society at large."[160] Another New York court rejected a name-change to a single name because: "The judicial approval of the use of a single name would be retrogression to antiquity, cause havoc and chaos in the proper identification and location of persons in this modern day and era, cause serious disruption of official records and lead to all kinds of complications in our economy, largely dependent on credit of easily identifiable persons. The judicial sanction of single names is as extinct as the Dodo bird."[161] However, a New Jersey court approved a name change for an artist to a single name finding that even though unusual, it would work no fraud and was not unduly confusing for the artist applicant to be legally known by one name only.[162] That would appear to be the emerging rule.

108. Because the United States is a melting pot, a wide variety of naming customs, styles, and names are present in the American population. While the English-European pattern of naming is probably the most common, many other naming patterns (especially Hispanic and Asian names and naming customs) are also common, so difference in name sound or pattern is not a matter of oddity or embarrassment, much less a legal problem.

109. Titles of nobility have no practical legal significance in the United States of America. They are rarely heard or used. Indeed, the Constitution of the United States declares that: "No Title of Nobility shall be granted by the United States … ."[163]

158. *In re Application of Ferner*, 685 A.2d 78, 81 (1996), citing *Petition of Dengler*, 246 N.W.2d 758, 760 (N.D.1976); and *In re Ritchie*, 159 Cal.App.3d 1070, 1072, 206 Cal.Rptr. 239, 241 (Cal. Ct.App. 1986).
159. *Black's Law Dictionary*, s.v. "name", 922 (5th ed., 1979).
160. *Matter of Miller*, 162 Misc.2d 527, 617 N.Y.S.2d 1024, 1026 (N.Y.C.Civ.Ct.1994).
161. *Application of Douglas*, 60 Misc.2d 1057, 304 N.Y.S.2d 558, 561 (N.Y.Sup.Ct.1969).
162. *Application of Ferner*, 295 N.J.Super. 409, 685 A.2d 78 (1996).
163. U.S. Constitution, Art. I, §9.

§2. SURNAME

I. Acquisition of the Surname

110. "The use of surnames is a relatively recent historical practice. 'In the early life of all races surnames were unknown, while given names have been used from the most distant times to identify and distinguish a particular individual from his fellows.'"[164]

111. Traditionally, in Anglo-American law, children received the surname of their father. That is still the most common pattern. That was the anticipated custom, but it was not a rule of law. With societal changes in the past decades, parents usually give the child a surname that connects the child to them but still there is no mandatory surname rule. Dual or hyphenated surnames historically were allowed, and today they are not uncommon, especially for married couples who wish to preserve in their names their nominal connection to the families of origin of both spouses.

112. As a general rule, both parents participate in selecting the name of the child. As a matter of legal technicality, however, the parent who is authorized to complete the birth certificate has the presumptive authority to name the child. When a child is born out of wedlock, the mother presumptively selects the name for the child. In the case of a disagreement, the state courts have the power to select the name of a child applying the "best interests of the child" standard—but that happens only rarely, and usually in cases involving paternity suits in which the name of the child is just one of many elements manipulated by the parties in their power struggle.

113. There have been statutes that required a certain surname be given to a child (i.e., the father's surname), but in recent years some of these statutes have not withstood constitutional attack for being gender-biased rules.[165] Others have been repealed as customs and social expectations have changed. One court did uphold a statute that required that a child born out of wedlock be given the mother's name when challenged by a father who wanted his child to have his surname.[166] In 1972, the U.S. Supreme Court summarily upheld Alabama's common law requirement that married women use their husband's surname on a driver's license application.[167] Because of developments in the Equal Protection Clause doctrine relating to

164. *Gubernat v. Deremer*, 140 N.J. 120, 126, 657 A.2d 856 (1995), citing *Smith v. United States Casualty Co.*, 197 N.Y. 420, 90 N.E. 947, 948 (N.Y.CT.APP.1910).

165. *Jech v. Burch*, 466 F. Supp. 714, 721 (D. Hawaii 1979) ("Plaintiffs have a Constitutionally protected right to give their own child any surname they choose."); *O'Brien v. Tilson*, 523 F. Supp. 494 (E.D.N.C. 1981); and *see generally* L.A. Foggar, *Parent's Selection of Children's Surnames*, 51 George Washington L. Rev. 583 (1983).

166. *Doe v. Hancock County Board of Health*, 436 N.E.2d 791 (Ind. 1982) ("This Court sees no reason to interfere with the legislative policies in handling statistical data.").

167. *Forbush v. Wallace*, 341 F. Supp. 217 (M.D. Alabama 1971), *affirmed* 405 US 970 (1972).

gender and stereotypes, that ruling may be of some doubtful validity today.[168] However, courts have recognized that states have a legitimate interest in promoting child welfare and public record-keeping that justifies a law requiring children to be given the surname of one or both parents.[169] Nonetheless, that requirement is not common to all states, and wider latitude in naming children seems to be the trend.

II. Change of the Surname

114. "The common law has long recognized the right to select and change names freely."[170] The most common example of name changes occurs when a wife takes her husband's surname at marriage (though this practice is only customary and not universal).[171] A marriage certificate is probably enough to prove the name change. It is also common for a name change to occur when a child is adopted, and often upon divorce. The procedure for changing a surname (as upon marriage) is simple; usually it consists of writing in the new surname upon the official form of the legal procedure.[172]

115. A civil action to change a name is usually advisable (in some cases required) for name changes other than in these somewhat common situations.[173] However, a person may acquire a name by common repute, without legal order. Indeed, "dba" or "doing business as" names and "aka" (also known as) names or aliases are not uncommon. Businesses assume business names just as authors assume *noms de plume*, and performers take stage names. Those are legal names, even if not obtained under court order.

116. The only significant requirement on changing a name is to avoid fraud or public confusion. A person may not have a name change that deceives creditors or customers or that creates confusion that operates to harm someone. As one court recently put it: "[A] person has a common law right to assume any name he or she lawfully chooses. At common law, any adult or emancipated person is free to adopt any name, except for a fraudulent, criminal or other illegitimate purpose."[174] However, adoption of a false name for the intent to deceive generally is illegal.

168. L. Kelly, *Divining the Deep and Inscrutable: Toward a Gender-Neutral, Child-Centered Approach to Child Name Change Proceedings*, 99 West Virginia L. Rev. 1, 13 (1996).
169. *Henne v. Wright*, 904 F.2d 1208 (8th Cir. 1990).
170. L.A. Foggar, *Parent's Selection of Children's Surnames*, 51 George Washington L. Rev. 583 (1983).
171. L. Kelly, *Divining the Deep and Inscrutable: Toward a Gender-Neutral, Child-Centered Approach to Child Name Change Proceedings*, 99 West Virginia L. Rev. 1, 13 (1996).
172. Office of the City Clerk, The City of New York, Marriage Bureau, available at http://www.cityclerk.nyc.gov/html/marriage/name_change.shtml.
173. *See* Delaware Code Annotated §5901 (1996); Hawaii Revised Statutes Annotated §574–5 (1996); Texas Family Code §3.64 (1997); Washington Code Annotated 4.24.130 (1997); and *Commonwealth v. Goodman*, 544 Pa. 339, 676 A.2d 234 (1996).
174. *Application of Ferner*, 295 N.J.Super. 409, 685 A.2d 78 (1996).

117. When a couple divorces, and a dispute arises about the name of the child (usually because the custodial mother wishes to eliminate her ex-husband's name from her life and the life of their child), courts generally have applied either a presumption favoring the existing name of the child (the status quo) or a custodial parent's right to name the child presumption, both operating within the framework of making a decision for the "best interests of the child." The name of the child may connect to or disconnect the child from the noncustodial parent (usually the father) and if it connects the child to the absent parent it may not only increase the likelihood of child support being paid but may also enhance the identity and relational development of the child by preserving at least a nominal relationship with the noncustodial parent. While some have criticized any rule that restrains maternal child-naming prerogatives, the courts generally put the child's interests above either parent's adult interests.[175] Gender-based and marital-status-based rules about naming children often receive unsympathetic review when challenged in courts.[176]

§3. Given Names

118. The given name of a child is the name given by the parents, who choose the name, and the name is recorded on the birth certificate.[177]

119. Given names can be changed by common repute or by judicial order. The procedures and standards for judicial change of given names are the same as for the change of surnames.[178]

175. M.H. Weiner, *"We Are Family": Valuing Associationalism in Disputes Over Children's Surnames*, 75 N.C. L. Rev. 1625 (1997).

176. *See*. e.g., *Brill v. Hedges*, 783 F. Supp. 340 (S.D. Ohio 1991); C.M. Durkin & A.M. Ordonez, *Naming Nonmarital Children: Birth Certificates and Name Change Petitions*, in *Paternity and the Law of Parentage in Massachusetts* Chapter 10 (P. Quirion, et al., eds, Mass. Continuing Legal Educa. Inc 2009).

177. *See* Florida Statutes Annotated §382.013 (West, 1997); Louisiana Revised Statutes Annotated 40:34 (West, 1997).

178. L.A. Foggar, Note, *Parent's Selection of Children's Surnames*, 51 Geo. Wash. L. Rev. 583 (1983).

Chapter 5. Nationality

120. Nationality in the United States may be acquired by birth in the United States[179] or birth to citizens of the U.S.,[180] or by naturalization.[181] The Fourteenth Amendment provides, in part, that: "All persons born or naturalized in the United States and subject to the jurisdiction thereof, are citizens of the United States and of the State wherein they reside."[182] Thus, nationality is constitutionally guaranteed to all persons born within the territorial jurisdiction of the United States.

121. The Fourteenth Amendment also guarantees national citizenship to persons naturalized in the United States. Congress sets the standards for naturalization. Generally, naturalization requires: some understanding of English, of the history of the United States, and of principles of U.S. government;[183] that the candidate must have no opposition to the U.S. government;[184] that the candidate must not be a deserter from the U.S. armed forces;[185] five years of residence in the U.S.;[186] and have obtained permanent resident visa.[187] Naturalization can also be given to a spouse of a citizen,[188] a child of a citizen and a non-citizen,[189] or a person who has served in the armed forces for three years.[190] Those who want to become naturalized citizens must file an application,[191] with photos,[192] submit to an investigation and examination,[193] take an oath in a public ceremony,[194] and receive a certificate of naturalization.[195] They thus receive the rights of citizens of the United States.

122. Laws using nationality (alienage) as a basis for awarding benefits or imposing special disadvantages have been scrutinized under close (heightened) judicial scrutiny.[196]

---

179. 8 United States Code §41 (1997). U.S. Constitution, amendment XIV.
180. *Ibid.*
181. 8 United States Code §§1421–1459 (1997); D.E. Telfeyan, *Obtaining Status as a Lawful Permanent Resident of the United States: Family-Based Immigration, Diversity Immigration, Miscellaneous Bases of Permanent Resident Eligibility and Consular Processing*, 408 PLI/Lit 61, 68 (1991).
182. U.S. Const., amendment XIV.
183. 8 United States Code §1423.
184. 8 United States Code §1424.
185. 8 United States Code §1425.
186. 8 United States Code §1427.
187. 8 United States Code §1429.
188. 8 United States Code §1430.
189. 8 United States Code §1431.
190. 8 United States Code §1439.
191. 8 United States Code §1445.
192. 8 United States Code §1444.
193. 8 United States Code §1446.
194. 8 United States Code §1448.
195. 8 United States Code §1449.
196. *Graham v. Richardson*, 403 US 365 (1971); *In re Griffiths*, 413 US 717 (1973); *Sugarman v. Dougall*, 413 US 634 (1973); and *Hampton v. Mow Sun Wong*, 426 US 88 (1976).

123. At common law it was said that a woman acquired the citizenship of her husband, but in American practice a woman who married a foreigner did not lose her U.S. citizenship unless she left the country to reside in his country.[197] A 1907 expatriation statute provided for the loss of American nationality upon marriage to a foreigner.[198] That statute was upheld by the U.S. Supreme Court in 1915,[199] but that provision was repealed in 1922,[200] and later Supreme Court decisions essentially overturned the 1915 decision.[201] The current American expatriation statute does not make marriage to a foreigner grounds for losing one's citizenship.[202] Traditionally, dual nationality was disfavored in American law, but "the law in more recent years has evolved to accommodate dual nationality in most instances." The importance of family relations as means to immigration and eventually American nationality are underscored by the significant litigation over such issues.[203]

124. For example, in *Miller v. Albright*,[204] and *Tuan Anh Nguyen v. I.N.S.*,[205] the U.S. Supreme Court upheld the requirement of § 1409 of the Immigration and Nationality Act, that unmarried U.S. fathers, but not unmarried U.S. mothers, obtain an official decree of parentage before the child reaches the age of majority in order for the child to qualify for American nationality, did not violate the Fifth Amendment and was not impermissible gender discrimination. The Court emphasized the government's need to assure that a real biological parent-child relationships exists, and the child and American parent have had the opportunity to develop a real parent-child relationship; the differences between mothers and fathers regarding both interests justified the rule. Some have been critical of the statute and of these decisions upholding it.[206]

---

197. *Shanks v. Dupont*, S.C., 28 US (3 Pet.) 242 (1830); and In re Fitzroy, 4 F.2d 541 (D.C. Mass. 1925).
198. *See* Act of 2 March 1907, Ch. 2534, S 2, 34 Stat. 1228.
199. *Mackenzie v. Hare*, 239 US 299 (1915) (American woman lost U.S. citizenship by marrying a British citizen).
200. Act Relative to the Naturalization and Citizenship of Married Woman, Ch. 422, 42 Stat. 1021 (1922).
201. *Afroyim v. Rusk*, 387 US 253 (1967); and *see also Vance v. Terrazas*, 440 US 252 (1980).
202. 8 U.S.C.A. §1481 (Weslaw 1998).
203. *See*, e.g., *Scialabba v. Cuellar de Osorio*, 134 S. Ct. 2191 (2014); *Lozano v. Alvarez*, 134 S. Ct. 1224 (2014); *see also "Preview" of Lozano v. Alvarez, No. 12-280*, 41 Preview of the United States Supreme Court Cases 139 (Dec. 2, 2013).
204. 523 U.S. 420 (1998)
205. 533 U.S. 53 (2001).
206. *See*, e.g., Kif Augustine-Adams, *Gendered States: A Comparative Constructions of Citizenship and Nation*, 41 Va. J. Int'l L. 93 (2000).

Chapter 6. Domicile and Residence

§1. Domicile

125. Domicile is the official legal home of a person. It consists of two elements, "residence in fact," which is actually living (physically residing) in a place, and an intention to make the place the home for a time.[207] These two elements must coexist simultaneously for domicile to be acquired. Domicile can be determined by looking at a number of factors, for instance, actual physical residence, ownership of property, place of employment, and participation in community activities.[208]

126. A person may have only one domicile at a time, and all persons have a presumptive domicile.[209] Ordinarily, the forum determines domicile according to its own rules. The intent needed to establish jurisdiction is not rigid. Thus, it is possible for a foreign visitor with only a temporary visa to have an intent to remain in a state if legally allowed to do so, sufficient to establish "domicile" in the state for purposes of divorce jurisdiction, even though she simultaneously has the intent to leave the state if not given legal permission to remain.[210]

127. Children have a domicile at birth—that is the domicile of their custodial parent(s). Since minors are incapable of legally recognized intent, their intent is exercised by their parents or guardians and minors take the domicile of their parents or guardians, or the domicile that their parents or guardians assign to them.[211]

128. An interesting scholarly debate is now raging in the United States regarding whether children born in the United States to illegal alien parents acquire citizenship. In part the debate turns on whether the Fourteenth Amendment requires, in addition to being born in the territory of the United States, that the parents are "domiciled" there, and whether that domicile requirement excludes illegal alien parents.[212] However, so far as the law goes, the historic rule that birth in the United States, alone, confers citizenship (regardless of parental domicile or greater mutual approval relationship).

129. At common law, married women had the same domicile as their husbands.[213] That is no longer the rule of law; married women, like unmarried women and married or unmarried men, are legally able to acquire their individual domicile

---

207. J.H. Friedenthal, M.K. Kane & A.R. Miller, *Civil Procedure* 30 (2nd ed., West 1993).
208. *Ibid.*
209. *Restatement, (Second) Conflict of Laws* §11 (1972).
210. *See Bustamente v. Bustamente*, 645 P.2d 40 (1982).
211. *Restatement, (Second) Conflict of Laws*, §22 (1972).
212. *See generally* Mark Shawhan, *The Significance of Domicile in Lyman Trumbull's Conception of Citizenship*, 119 Yale L.J. 1351 (2010).
213. A.L. Estin, *Family Law Federalism: Divorce and the Constitution*, 16 Wm. & Mary Bill of Rts J. 381, 386 (2007).

by choice—by residence in fact and intent to make it their home. However, the law presumes (rebuttably) that a husband and wife who live together have the same domicile.[214]

130. Once established, a person's domicile "continues unless and until a new one is acquired."[215] It is changed by residing (even briefly) in a new location with the intent to make it the domicile or home. Military personnel, prisoners, and other persons residing in a particular location by compulsion have been considered to possess the domicile they occupied before the compelled residence.[216]

§2. Residence

131. "Residence" and "domicile" are sometimes used interchangeably. To avoid confusion, it is best to distinguish between legal residence—domicile—and physical residence.

132. Physical residence is very simply the place where a person lives. A person may have more than one residence, unlike domicile, because residence denotes a place of abode whereas domicile is the one, more or less permanent home.

133. Residence is important as a legal concept in satisfying one of the requirements of domicile.[217] It is also important for a host of state and federal laws and programs ranging from taxation, to educational benefits, to drivers licensing, to voting to judicial jurisdiction.

134. For family law purposes, it is noteworthy that at common law, the husband determined the residence as well as the domicile of the marital union. Failure of the wife to reside where determined by her husband could constitute desertion, and in some states was ground for divorce.

214. *Restatement, (Second) Conflict of Laws*, §21 (1972); *ibid.*, (1988 rev.).
215. *Ibid.* §19.
216. *Ibid.* §17.
217. C.A. Wright, *The Law of Federal Courts* 161–162 (West 1994); and *Black's Law Dictionary*, s.v. "residence", 1176–1177 (5th ed., 1979).

Part II. Family Law

Chapter 1. Marriage

§1. The Nature of Marriage

I. Nature and Definition of Marriage

A. *The Core Concept*

135. Historically marriage has been and in most of the nations in the world still is the intimate, institutionalized, state-sanctioned relationship between a man and a woman that is the "gold standard" foundation of a family. The institution of marriage so defined is found in all societies and predates the state; indeed, anthropologically the State has been described as the outgrowth or extension of the marriage-based family. Marriage has long been regulated by religion and in recent centuries by the State as well. Marriage may be defined in different ways by the State, by religion, by psychologists or anthropologists, and by other subgroups of society. Of course, it is the *legal* nature and definition of marriage that is the focus of this work.[218]

136. Across time and across cultures, the core concept of marriage is the permanent consensual union of a man and a woman (or, in polygamous cultures, of a man and multiple women) of due age and competence who are unrelated within prohibited degree. Of course, the details of *how* permanent, *how much* and *what kind* of consent is needed, the *incidents* of the union, *what age* is considered competent for marriage, *what degree of kinship* is deemed improper for marriage, etc., have varied from culture to culture, and from time to time. And there have been rare transitory exceptions in which even the basic core elements have been briefly ignored. But the core concept of marriage as the voluntary, gender-integrating exogamous presumably permanent union of adults into family dyads (or small groups) has remained relatively constant for millennia.

137. Recently, the dual-gender aspect of marriage was the subject of major political and policy controversy in the United States, as in several other regions of

218. *See generally*, L.D. Wardle, *International Marriage and Divorce Regulation and Recognition: A Survey*, 29 Fam. L. Q. 497 (1995).

the world.[219] In the summer of 2015, the U.S. Supreme Court issued a 5-4 decision holding the nation's constitution requires all states to provide marriage licenses to same-sex couples and to recognize same-sex marriages contracted in other states.[220] That poses what is arguably the greatest revolution in the concept of marriage in the history of marriage, rivaled in that regard only by the movement from polygamy to monogamy and the movement from concept of marriage as nearly indissoluble to the adoption of unilateral divorce-on-demand in some countries.

B. The Constitutional Right to Marry

138. The U.S. Constitution (which is the oldest still-used Constitution in the world) contains no explicit reference to marriage. There is no explicit textual protection for marriage as an institution or of the rights of individuals to marry. However, the Fourteenth Amendment provides that no state may deprive any person of "life, liberty or property without due process of law," and the Fifth Amendment imposes the same rule upon the national government. The term "liberty" has long been interpreted to include those special rights and relationships which are "deeply rooted in this Nation's history and traditions."[221] Among those special relationships are marriage and the right of adults to marry.[222] The Constitutional cases have assumed, and in dicta some of the older cases have declared, that marriage is a dual-gender relationship. Whether the Constitution of the United States prohibits (or requires) legalization of same-sex marriage was addressed by the Supreme Court of the United States until 2013. In *United States v. Windsor*, the Court ruled that a federal law defining marriage as the union of a man and a woman for federal law purposes was unconstitutional, in part because it had been the practice of the national government to defer to state laws on the meaning of marriage.[223] Two years later, the Court ruled on the validity of state laws defining marriage as the union of a man and a woman and held that these laws, too, were unconstitutional.[224]

139. The United States Supreme Court has long extolled the importance of marriage to society, finding the relationship of marriage to be fundamental to the existence of society.[225] The Court has repeatedly ruled that marriage is a constitutionally protected relationship and that the State may not arbitrarily and irrationally restrict the right to marry.[226] For example, in *Loving v. Virginia*, the Court invalidated a Virginia anti-miscegenation law that prohibited interracial marriage, in part because the

---

219. *See* L.D. Wardle, *The Attack on Marriage As the Union of a Man and a Woman*, 83 N. Dak. L. Rev. 1365 (2007).
220. *Obergefell v. Hodges*, No. 14-556, 135 S. Ct. 2584 (2015).
221. *Moore v. City of East Cleveland*, 431 US 494, 503 (1979); *see also Washington v. Glucksberg*, 117 S. Ct. 2258 (1997); and *Planned Parenthood v. Casey*, 505 US 833, 849–850 (1992).
222. *Meyer v. Nebraska*, 262 US 390, 392 (1923); and *see also Maynard v. Hill*, 125 US 190 (1988).
223. *United States v. Windsor*, 570 U.S. 12 (2013).
224. *Obergefell v. Hodges*, 135 S. Ct. 2584 (2015).
225. *Maynard v. Hill*, 125 US 190, 210 (1888) ("[Marriage] is an institution, the maintenance of which in its purity the public is deeply interested, for it is the foundation of the family and of society, without which there would be neither civilization nor progress.").
226. *See generally*, W.P. Statsky, *Family Law* 158–159 (West 1991).

right to marry was so fundamental that restrictions based on race (which is irrelevant to any legitimate purpose the State may have for regulating marriage) could not be permitted.[227] Likewise, in *Zablocki v. Redhail*, the Court invalidated a Wisconsin law requiring men behind in child support to convince a judge that their child would not be a public charge before they could obtain a marriage license, again emphasizing the constitutional importance of marriage and the irrationality of the restriction.[228] In *Turner v. Safley*, the Court invalidated prison regulations which allowed prisoners to marry only in case of pregnancy or a child born out of wedlock or with warden approval, again emphasizing that marriage was a fundamental right and the restrictions were greater than needed for either marriage or prison policy purposes.[229] Thus, the right to marry is of constitutional significance in the United States and enjoys special judicial protection. But the authority of states to enact reasonable restrictions is also long-established and judicially respected.[230] The 2015 same-sex marriage decision relied on these cases and an expansive constitutional reference to "liberty" to hold that states must extend legal recognition to same-sex marriages.

1. Status or Contract

140. Marriage in American law is a contractual relationship insofar as the requirements for making a binding contract (capacity, consent, and consideration) must all be met. But marriage is "something more than a mere contract. It is rather to be deemed an institution of society founded upon the consent and contract of the parties ... ."[231] That is, marriage has some elements of status as well.[232] Thus, marriage may be the great example of what has been described as the movement in western law from status to contract and is the primary device for ordering human relationships.[233] Whereas marriage in the past may have been defined as a lifelong legal relationship between spouses, it has become more like a conventional contract between parties with rather simple procedures to abrogate the contract. Still, there are limits on the private ordering of marriage relationships and consequences from the relationship that distinguish marriage from ordinary contracts.

---

227. *Loving v. Virginia*, 388 US 1 (1967).
228. *Zablocki v. Redhail*, 434 US 374 (1978).
229. *Turner v. Safley*, 482 US 878 (1987).
230. *Zablocki*, 434 US at 393 (Stewart, J., concurring); *Ibid.*, at 399 (Justice Powell, concurring); *Windsor*, 570 U.S. 12 (2013).
231. J. Story, *Conflict of Laws* 193 (3rd ed., Little Brown 1846).
232. *Maynard v. Hill*, 125 US 190, 210 (1888) ("[M]arriage ... is something more than mere contract. Other contracts may be modified, restricted, or enlarged, or entirely released upon the consent of the parties. Not so with marriage. The relation once formed, the law steps in and holds the parties to various obligations and liabilities. It is an institution ... .").
233. H. Maine, *Ancient Law* 100 (E.P. Dutton 1917).

2. Duration

141. Historically, in the United States, as in most societies, marriage has been a legal relationship for the life of the parties. At the same time, all states have also long recognized some legal "escape valves" to allow parties out of marriages, at least when the minimum standards of marital responsibility and social decency are violated. Thus, divorce (or its legal equivalent, annulment) have long been recognized in all states on at least some grounds.

142. Marriage is still legally defined as a life-long status; when a marriage is created and until it is dissolved or nullified it is deemed to be a life-long relationship. Even if a marriage is terminated before death, it may have life-long legal consequences (such as alimony, or support of a family dependent).[234] Recent social trends associated with the adoption of unilateral no-fault divorce in the United States since 1970 have lessened the permanency aspect of the marriage relationship and the dissolution of marriage is much easier to achieve than it has been in the past. The rate and ratio of divorce soared during the 1970 and 1980s, but may now be leveling off.

3. Jurisdiction to Regulate Marriage

143. The power to regulate domestic relations in the United States, including marriage creation, relations, and dissolution, belongs almost entirely to the states. The federal (national) government has virtually no jurisdiction to regulate family law directly.[235] Thus, regulations regarding who may marry, what is required to establish a marriage, the effects of marriage and when marriages will not be recognized are almost entirely state-created. However, the indirect influence of federal law upon state marriage laws can be substantial, through federal income tax law, bankruptcy law, welfare laws, and a few specific constitutional protections (such as equal protection and due process guarantees).

144. Thus, the specific definition of marriage and the details of its regulation vary from state to state in the United States, sometimes markedly. But those variations exist within the parameters set by federal constitutional law and then influenced by the common culture and traditions of the American peoples. The constitutional limits are few and indirect, mostly relating to gender equality and the influence of the culture varies greatly. So there is wide latitude for states to define and regulate marriage as they prefer.

234. W.J. O'Donnell & D.A. Jones, *The Law of Marriage and Marital Alternatives* 149–165 (Lexington Books 1982); J. Singer, *Alimony and Efficiency: The Gendered Costs and Benefits of the Economic Justification for Alimony*, 82 Geo. L. J. 2423, 2435 (1994).

235. A.C. Dailey, *Federalism and Families*, 143 U. Pa. L. Rev. 1787, 1821 (1995).

§2. CAPACITY TO MARRY

I. Consanguinity and Affinity Restrictions

145. Certain marriage restrictions prohibit the marriage of persons related to each other within certain degrees by blood or by marriage. The former are called consanguinity restrictions; the latter affinity restrictions. All jurisdictions in the United States forbid marriages within a certain degree of consanguinity. All states prohibit marriages of persons related to each other as uncle-niece or aunt-nephew, or closer (brother-sister, lineal descendant-ascendant, etc.). More than half of the states also prohibit first cousin marriages. Half- or whole-blood, and legitimacy or illegitimacy are distinctions of no relevance to consanguinity restrictions. Likewise, relationships of adoption are treated the same as relationships of blood, except in some cases of the more remote forbidden relationships (such as first cousins) where the additional factor of adoption has been found in some cases to justify circumvention of the consanguinity rules.[236]

146. Affinity is not now the subject of the same regulation. For instance, a man is not prohibited from marrying a biologically unrelated daughter of his former wife and uncle-niece or aunt-nephew marriages are generally only forbidden if the marriage would violate rules against consanguinity, not if the relative is an in-law.[237] Likewise, foster- or step-relationships are not within the consanguinity proscriptions, because those relations are deemed affinal relations or relations of convenience, not full and bona fide legal parent-child relations.

147. The reasons for restricting the marriage of persons biologically related to each other are historic, moral, sociological, scientific, and cultural. Historically, consanguineous marriages have long been forbidden. They have long been deemed immoral and violative of religious codes of right and honorable conduct. Sociologically, they provide a haven in which vulnerable persons are free from the pressures of sexual competition. Culturally, the boundaries are always shifting but the existence of some boundary is a ubiquitous norm.

148. In addition to the restrictions providing that marriages among closely related persons will not be allowed, sexual relations (incest) is included as an offense in criminal statutes and common law, although different jurisdictions vary in considering it a felony or misdemeanor. Most of these criminal statutes' definitions of incest parallel the jurisdictions affinity and consanguinity prohibitions.[238] Some incest laws apply to persons outside the consanguinity marriage restrictions (such as stepparent and child sexual relations) for reasons similar to the reasons underlying consanguinity restrictions.

---

236. L.D. Wardle, C.L. Blakesley & J.Y. Parker, *Contemporary Family Law* §§2.04–2.08 (Callaghan 1988).
237. *Ibid.*, at §§2.09–2.10; *Nguyen v. Holder*, 24 N.Y.3d 1017 (2014).
238. *See* California Penal Code §285; N.Y. Penal Law §255.25; and Texas Penal Code §25.02.

II. Polygamy

149. In the United States, the policy in favor of only monogamous marriage is very strong.[239] Bigamy (being married to more than one spouse at a given time) is civilly prohibited and criminally punished in all states. This restriction obviously forbids a person marrying one spouse and then openly or covertly marrying another person while the former marriage is still in effect. The proscription of bigamy also can apply when a person remarries without completing the divorce process. Common law divorce is not recognized in any American state. Thus, even though a married couple agree to go their separate ways, or one spouse leaves the other, and they live separate lives for many years, or do not even know where each other lives, if formal divorce proceedings are not properly filed and finalized it is bigamous if either party subsequently enters into a new marriage. That is because there are two people to whom the remarried spouse is married at one time, even if only technically.[240]

150. While criminal prosecution in cases of technical (and, increasingly, open and notorious actual) polygamy is rare, the civil consequences (starting with invalidating the second marriage) are very common.

151. Polygamy, which is still allowed in a significant minority of nations, is strictly illegal in the United States. When a small religious group settled in the remote western territories in the nineteenth century attempted to revive the Old Testament practice in homogenous religious communities, Congress quickly outlawed polygamy in any federal territories, and the prohibition of polygamy was upheld by the Supreme Court of the United States.[241] That rule remains and polygamy is prohibited in all states by state law, and in the federal territories by federal law. However, while the status of marriage is unlikely to be extended to polygamous marriages, it is possible the particular incidents of marriage may be extended to polygamous spouses. In one well-known case, polygamous wives of an Indian marriage were recognized as surviving spouses for purposes of succession law because doing so in the circumstances of the case (foreign-residing wives of deceased) would not offend the public policy underlying the bigamy prohibition.[242] Changing social conditions such as increased nonmarital cohabitation, tolerance of adultery, the widespread practice of sequential-polygamy through divorce-and-remarriage, as well as glamorization of all kinds of extramarital sexual relations in the culture of the age have not yet produced any significant change in American attitudes strongly favoring exclusively monogamous marriage though at least one federal court has

239. H.H. Clark, Jr., *The Law of Domestic Relations in the United States* 64–69 (West 1988).
240. *Galbraith v. Galbraith*, 396 So.2d 1364 (La. App. 1981); *US v. Wisdom*, 320 F. Supp. 286 (E.D. Tenn. 1970); and *People v. Dunn*, 19 Cal. Rptr. 835 (1962).
241. *Reynolds v. United States*, 98 U.S. 145 (1878). While the Church of Jesus Christ of Latter-day Saints abandoned and then forbade the practice of polygamy shortly after the *Reynolds* decision, some small break-off or splinter groups persisted, and so small enclaves where polygamy is practiced underground can be found in several western states and in Canada.
242. *In re Dalip Singh Bir's Estate*, 188 P.2d 499 (1948).

questioned the validity of criminal laws prohibiting polygamy.[243] However, the growing influence of Muslim communities in America may create some pressure to reconsider the proscription of polygamy (as it has in the United Kingdom and Canada). For now, however, the predominant legal response to the practice of polygamy in those communities seems to be to ignore the practice until some scandal (such as child brides or welfare fraud) requires legal attention.

III. Mental Capacity

152. Marriage is a legal contract, so a requirement of legal marriage in all states is that the parties be mentally competent to consent to marriage.[244] If there is a lack of mental capacity there can be no marriage. Mental competency is not always easily defined, but it is clear that a complete knowledge of all the implications of the decision is not likely to be required to satisfy the requirement of mental capacity. Clearly a person who does not know what he or she is doing cannot contract a valid marriage, but all that seems to be required is a "general understanding" of the nature and significance of the relationship and of the fundamental legal duties it entails. It appears that the standard for capacity to enter a marriage contract is less technical, less intellectual, than might be applied to a person entering into a consumer contract. Marriage is said to be "of the heart, more than of the mind." And there is concern that an overly rigorous standard might invite overly exacting application and exclude many mentally less-gifted individuals from enjoyment of a fundamental, constitutionally protected relationship.

153. Theoretically, it is possible to lack capacity to contract marriage due to temporary incapacity, temporary insanity, or temporary intoxication. While there are cases in which marriages have been nullified because of temporary lack of capacity,[245] the presumption of capacity is very strong, the required degree of incapacity is very high, and skepticism of the "temporary incapacity" arguments is very great.

IV. Lack of Consent

154. A marriage cannot be validly contracted if there is no valid agreement to be married. Thus, lack of consent renders a marriage null and void in all American jurisdictions. In most cases, the lack of consent claimed is not lack of formal consent, but lack of informed and voluntary consent.

155. There are at least five situations where lack of consent has been found to make a marriage invalid. The first is marriage in jest. In this situation, a couple is

243. *Brown v. Buhman*, 947 F. Supp. 2d 1170 (2013).
244. W.J. O'Donnell & D.A. Jones, *The Law of Marriage and Marital Alternatives* 41 (Lexington Books 1982).
245. *Mahan v. Mahan*, 88 So.2d 545 (Fla. 1956); and *McNee v. McNee*, 237 P 534 (Nev. 1925).

married as a joke. Though these situations are clearly not common, there are sometimes situations where they do arise. An example might occur when a couple at a party is joking about marriage and decide that would be a clever way to shock their parents. Then after going through with the marriage, they of course, want out of their contract.[246] A few decades ago, the assertion of this situation might persuade a court to nullify a marriage, and theoretically it still could, but parties have been reluctant to assert or courts to accept this basis for nullification of marriage in any recent cases.

156. A second instance where lack of consent has been found to nullify a marriage is when there is a marriage for a limited purpose. This situation would occur, for instance, where a couple marries in order to secure a benefit for one of the spouses such as to secure citizenship, or to secure a benefit for a child born to the couple, as to allow the child to be born "legitimate."[247] The problem with this doctrine is that, conceptually, in order to obtain the benefit sought they had to be legally married, so the "limited intent" was still sufficient intent—that is, intent to have a legal marriage. These cases were common in immigration courts a few years ago; amendments to the U.S. Immigration and Nationality Act properly remedied the problem before the doctrine of marriage validity was damaged significantly.

157. Fraud and misrepresentation are more common examples of a situation where a marriage might be nullified because of lack of consent. In order for fraud to invalidate a marriage for lack of consent, historically it had to "go to the essentials of the marriage." In other words, there had to be some misrepresentation or concealment relating to procreative exclusivity of the parties' marital relationship. If the wife entered the marriage pregnant by another man, of if the husband married without intending to engage in sexual relations or live with the other spouse or procreate, that must be disclosed to the prospective spouse or there has been a misrepresentation which could potentially establish a lack of consent. But many states have lowered the standard to any "significant misrepresentation" and substituted subjective (the spouses') for objective (a reasonable person's) perspectives. Thus, if one of the spouses has lied about certain diseases (especially sexually transmitted diseases), a criminal record, prior marriage and children, or religious commitments, there may be a problem of lack of consent, the theory being that they might not have consented if they had known about the true, undisclosed facts. Other instances where misrepresentation may apply are mistaken identity, pregnancy, lack of love or religion (i.e., a potential spouse misrepresents their devotion to the religious beliefs of the other).[248]

158. Finally, lack of consent to marry may be found if there has been force, duress, or coercion. But the degree of duress must be substantial and usually

---

246. *Meredith v. Shakespeare*, 122 S.E. 520 (1924); and *Cronan v. Wartenberg*, 112 S.E. 234 (1922).
247. B. Stickney, *The Immigration Consequences of Divorce*, 13 J. Am. Acad. Matrimonial Laws. 271, 279–280 (1996); and J. Patterson, G.G. Palmer & E. Brandes, *IRCA, IMFA, and SDCEA: What Does This Immigration Alphabet Soup Spell?*, 39 Baylor L. Rev. 413, 453 (1987).
248. E.S. Fredricksmeyer, *Annulments in Colorado*, 22 Colo. Law. 2249, 2250 (1993); and *Bilowit v. Dolitsky*, 304 A.2d 774 (N.J. 1973).

illegal—a mere threat to file a legal, true report or lawsuit or complaint normally will not suffice. It must be external, not internal (subjective). It must be, as one court put it, "if there had not been a wedding, there would have been a funeral."[249] However, as tolerance of domestic violence is dropping and protection for individual autonomy is growing, it is likely that courts in the future will be more ready to invalidate marriage in cases where the degree of duress or coercion is less overwhelming.

V. Age Restrictions

159. All American states impose restrictions on the minimum age at which a party can marry. At common law, a man could marry at 14 years old, and a woman at 12 years of age. Today, the general minimum age for marriage is 18 years old. This usually means that a person over the age of 18 can marry without any type of permission being required of parents or the state (as long as other marriage requirements are met).

160. Many states also provide that youth over a minimum age can marry with the consent of a parent or state official or both. For example, in Utah a minor (under 18 years old) can marry with parental permission if 16, and if 15, with both parental and judicial approval.[250] Additionally, many states provide statutory exceptions to the general age restrictions for extraordinary circumstances, the most prominent example being when the underage potential spouse is pregnant.

161. In addition to the above requirements, most jurisdictions have some type of absolute minimum age before which marriage is not allowed at all. For example, Utah law provides that the marriage of a person "under 14 years of age" is "prohibited and declared void."[251] The criminal law also may come into issue in circumstances of underage marriage, as most states make sex with a minor under a certain age a criminal offense, and may make underage marriage criminally punishable.[252] Form of marriage (formal or informal) may impact upon the minimum age of marriage. For example, in 2006 the Colorado Court of Appeals addressed an interesting issue about age of marriage in *In re the Marriage of J.M.H. and Rouse.* [253] Colorado allows both licensed and unlicensed (common law) marriage. A Colorado statute set the age of sixteen as the minimum age to get a marriage license. When a state child protection agency petitioned challenging the validity of an alleged common law marriage entered into by a 15-year-old girl who was subject to a neglect and dependency proceeding, the trial court applied the statute and ruled that the marriage was not valid. However, the Court of Appeals held that the statute only applied to licensed marriages, correctly noted that the common law rule was

249. *Lee v. Lee*, 3 S.W.2d 672. 673 (Ark. 1928).
250. Utah Code Annotated §30-1-9.
251. Utah Code Annotated §30-1-2.
252. Arizona Revised Statutes §25-128 (1997).
253. 143 P.3d 1116 (Colo. Ct. App. 2006).

that girls 12-year-old and older could consent to marry, and held that in the absence of superseding statute, that was still the age of consent for females in common law marriages in Colorado. The next month, however, the Colorado legislature passed a law making age 18 (or 16 years with judicial approval) the minimum age for common law marriage as well for licensed marriages.

162. Evasive marriages by teenagers unable to marry in their home jurisdiction who travel to another jurisdiction where their marriage is permitted, marry there, and return home have long been sources of some passionate litigation throughout history. For many years—as late as the 1970s—those marriages were deemed to violate strong public policy enough to justify nonrecognition in the home state.[254] This issue arises less frequently today and such marriages might not always be found to violate strong public policy, though in some states and in certain cases that result might still be expected.

VI. Physical Incapacity

163. In order to form a valid marriage, it is expected that both parties will be able to engage in sexual relations with each other. Sexual consummation, not procreation, is the test. Absence of the ability to sexually consummate marriage—called impotency—may render the marriage voidable. Absence of ability to procreate (infertility) does not impair the legal validity of the marriage.

164. Physical incapacity may also arise where one spouse has a disease (again, often a sexually transmitted disease). Some jurisdictions have considered limiting the capacity to marry if one of the prospective spouses has AIDS, but this attempt has raised constitutional questions and will probably not ever become a valid regulation.

VII. Same-Sex Marriage

165. The prohibition of same-sex marriage could be said in one sense to have represented a matter of incapacity because it is based, at least in part, on the physical inability of the partners to engage in *vera copula* marital relations with each other.[255] It also represented one of the independent historic concepts of the meaning of marriage—that it is a gender-complementary, gender-integrating union of male and female.

254. Restatement of the Law, Conflict of Laws §283, cmnt j (1971).
255. W.J. O'Donnell & D.A. Jones, *The Law of Marriage and Marital Alternatives* 47–88 (Lexington Books 1982).

Between 1970 and 2015, dozens of cases were litigated in American courts over claims for same-sex marriage. The courts rejected most of the claims for same-sex marriage.[256]

VIII. Prisoners

166. A related issue of capacity to marry involves the rights of prisoners to marry. Conviction of a felony conceptually resulted in a "civil death" of the convict with respect to some rights and privileges. However, incarceration does not make a person incapable of contracting marriage. In fact, with some exceptions, prisoners have a constitutional right to marry. While recognizing the right of prison authorities to reasonably regulate inmates' marriages to preserve the discipline and security of the prison, the United States Supreme Court has invalidated rules generally forbidding or unnecessarily restricting marriages by inmates.[257]

IX. Choice of Law

167. The general rule regarding which jurisdiction's laws apply to regulate marriage is that the law of the state where the marriage was contracted applies to determine the validity of the marriage. This is expressed in the *Restatement, (Second) of Conflict of Laws*:

> A marriage which satisfies the requirements of the state where the marriage was contracted will everywhere be recognized as valid unless it violates the strong public policy of another state which had the most significant relationship to the spouses and the marriage at the time of the marriage.[258]

168. Thus, there is a strong, general presumption that a marriage that is valid where created will be recognized as valid in all of the states. The emphasis is on upholding marriages rather than finding them invalid.[259] The general exception, stated in the *Restatement*, allows for the nonrecognition of a marriage that violates the strong public policy of a strongly interested forum. Examples might include polygamous or incestuous marriages. When comity and strong forum public policy clash regarding recognition of controversial forms of domestic relations created and

256. L.D. Wardle, *A Critical Analysis of Constitutional Claims for Same-Sex Marriage*, B.Y.U. L. Rev. 1 (1996).
257. *Turner v. Safely*, 428 US 78 (1987); *see also Aliviado v. Kimoto*, Civ No. 12-00259 (U.S. Dist. Ct. Haw. 2012).
258. Restatement (Second) Conflict of Laws §283(2) (1971); and *see* W.P. Statsky, *Family Law* 77 (West 1991).
259. Note, *In Sickness and in Health, In Hawaii and Where Else?: Conflict of Laws and Recognition of Same Sex Marriages*, 109 Harv. L. Rev. 2038, 2049 (1996).

allowed in other jurisdictions, respect for forum public policy usually triumphs.[260] The recent controversy surrounding same-sex marriages included litigation over this issue until 2015 when the Supreme Court ruled in *Obergefell v. Hodges* that because each state must perform same-sex marriages, they must also recognize such marriages contracted in other states.[261]

169. Most states also have at least codified some rules limiting marriage recognition. One of the most common types of marriage nonrecognition statutes is called "marriage evasion" statues and applies when a couple seeks to avoid the requirements of the state where they are residents and where they are intending to live by traveling to another state and contracting a marriage solely to elude the requirements of the state where they live.[262] However, many marriage recognition rules are not codified and determination of which public policies are so strong that violation of them will result in nonrecognition of an otherwise valid foreign marriage must be made on a case-by-case basis.

§3. Formalities of Marriage

170. All of the jurisdictions of the United States allow formalization in marriage and most require certain formalities in order for a marriage to be legally recognized. These formalities generally include licensing, solemnization before witnesses, and a ceremony. However, the details of the formalities required vary from state to state, and exceptions to these general rules also exist.

I. Licensing

171. U.S. jurisdictions have varying requirements in order for a marriage to be licensed. All jurisdictions give marriage licenses and all encourage licensed, formal marriages. Moreover, at least forty states (all but the ten jurisdictions which still allow common law marriage) *require* licenses to be issued before a legal marriage is properly contracted. Marriage licenses are generally issued by the county clerks within the state (about half of the states designate the county of residence of either party or of the place of celebration as the appropriate place of licensing) and require the payment of a fee.

260. *See generally* L.D. Wardle, *From Slavery to Same-Sex Marriage: Comity Versus Public Policy in Inter-jurisdictional Recognition of Controversial Domestic Relations*, 2008 B.Y.U. L. Rev. 1855 (2008).

261. *See* L.D. Wardle, *International Marriage and Divorce Regulation and Recognition: A Survey*, 29 Fam. L. Q. 497 (1995); L.D. Wardle, *Non-Recognition of Same-Sex Marriage Judgments Under DOMA and the Constitution*, 38 Creighton L. Rev. 365 (2005). *See also* L.D. Wardle, *From Slavery to Same-Sex Marriage: Comity Versus Public Policy in Inter-jurisdictional Recognition of Controversial Domestic Relations*, B.Y.U. L. Rev. 1855 (2008).

262. R.F. Chase, *American Jurisprudence*, No. 52, *Marriage* §87 (2nd ed., Co-Operative Publishing 1970).

172. A license is obtained after some routine questions are answered by the applicants regarding citizenship, identity, and demographic data, etc. Some jurisdictions have considered using the licensing provisions to provide information on birth control or domestic violence. There are also various waiting periods attached to the licensing requirement.[263] For example, § 204 of the Uniform Marriage and Divorce Act (not widely adopted in particular but widely recognized as somewhat typical of state marriage laws generally) provides that a license becomes effective three days after issuance, and remains valid for 180 days. States charge fees to parties seeking marriage licenses, but as the state has a monopoly on legal marriage and since denial of a license on ground of poverty would be unconstitutional in most states (those without common law marriage, at least) waiver of the license fee presumably may be made for those who cannot afford to pay.

II. Solemnization

173. The requirements to solemnize a marriage are generally not extensive. Most requirements deal with identifying the person who may lawfully perform the wedding ceremony. Generally, any religious official and most civil authorities (such as judges, mayors, legislators, and county officials, etc.) may solemnize the marriage.[264] Some states have begun to create exceptions to the duty to solemnize marriages if the public official asked to perform the marriage objects for religious reasons.[265]

174. Most American jurisdictions do not extensively regulate the ceremony required for a marriage to be legal. Generally, all that is required is some sort of positive expression of assent by the bride and groom in front of the officiator and witnesses. Traditionally, this involved some sort of verbal assent but of course, exceptions are made when that is not possible.[266] This flexibility regarding ceremony makes possible accommodation of the broadest possible range of forms of solemnization. Practices from the simplest to the most complex, from the most hierarchical to the most egalitarian are all permitted, and the spouses and their families have great latitude to customize the wedding formalities (or lack thereof) to their own religious, ethnic, cultural requirements, sense of style, and propriety. Typically, states allow all ministers and equivalent religious officials (rabbis, priests, Islamic clerics, and other faiths leaders) to perform marriages, as well as judges, mayors and other government officials specifically named in the marriage solemnization statute.[267]

---

263. M. Closen, R. Gamrath & D. Hopkins, *Mandatory Premarital HIV Testing: Political Exploitation of the AIDS Epidemic*, 69 Tul. L. Rev. 71, 97 (1994).
264. R.F. Chase, *American Jurisprudence*, No. 52, Marriage §40 (2nd ed., Co-Operative Publishing 1970).
265. North Carolina General Statutes §51-5.5; Utah Code §30-1-6.
266. B.A. Allen, *Same-Sex Marriage: A Conflict of Laws Analysis for Oregon*, 32 Williamete L. Rev. 619, 639 (1996).
267. *See* Uniform Marriage and Divorce Act, § 206 (judge, certain public officials, and persons authorized to solemnize marriage by any religion of native American tribe).

175. An intriguing exception to the most common forms of marriage solemnization is proxy marriage. Here, at least one of the parties is physically absent from the place where the wedding is solemnized (although willing to be married, of course), but a proxy stands in for him or her and expresses the consent for the absent party. Proxy marriage appears to be explicitly authorized in at least four states (California, Colorado, Texas, and Montana), and traditionally appear to have been allowed in several others. Five states explicitly forbid proxy marriages. By 2010, the status of the law in the other jurisdictions is uncertain. Since proxy marriages are most common in times when transportation is very restricted (such as during war and among immigrants and their left-behind lovers), and transportation has never been more accessible than today, the dilemmas of proxy marriage are now uncommon.[268] Federal immigration law explicitly refuses to recognize for immigration purposes unconsummated proxy marriages.[269] Federal control of immigration may significantly impact marriage. For example, in *Kerry v. Din*,[270] the Supreme Court held that U.S. immigration regulations that barred the entry of an American citizen's foreign husband who was deemed to have supported terrorism did not unconstitutionally violate her constitutional or marriage rights.

III. Common Law Marriage

176. A common law marriage is one formed without licensing and usually without public celebration or solemnization. Common law marriages, which were widely accepted in the eighteenth and nineteenth centuries, have fallen out of favor with the law in the twentieth century. Today only ten states and the District of Columbia still allow common law marriages, for which no license or ceremony or formal solemnization is required. These states include Colorado, Iowa, Kansas, Montana, New Hampshire, South Carolina, Texas, and Utah. Other states (Florida, Georgia, Indiana, Ohio, and Pennsylvania) previously allowed common law marriage but recently prohibited common law marriages; however, they still recognize common law marriages that were contracted in the state before the date of prohibition. Opposition to common law marriages has mostly practical bases—that it renders the relationship too uncertain, it has the potential for great injustice to innocent, good faith spouses and children, and after the death or upon the breakup of the relationship, there will be an incentive to characterize the relationship in terms more noble and committed than the parties actually undertook during their joint lives, which courts have a difficult time evaluating. The recent explosion of nonmarital cohabitation has weakened some objections to common law marriage because the same kinds of problems afflict those relationships and yet society has accepted and the law has evolved to adequately deal with the litigated termination of those relationships.

268. *See* M. Possley, *Marry by Proxy Booming in Montana*, 32 Mont. Law. 32 (June/July 2007); W.J. O'Donnell & D.A. Jones, *The Law of Marriage and Marital Alternatives* 18 (Lexington Books 1982); *see also* S. H. Jackson, *Marriage of Convenience: International Marriage Brokers, "Mail-Order Brides," and Domestic Servitude*, 38 U. Tol. L. Rev. 895 (2007).

269. 8 USC § 1101(a)(35).

270. 135 S. Ct. 2128 (2015).

177. While the specific legal requirements vary from state to state, generally common law marriage requires three elements: an agreement between the participants to be married, cohabitation of the parties, and the parties holding themselves out as husband and wife.[271] The details and definitions of "agreement" and "cohabitation" vary from state to state, and upon such fine details do many cases turn. An unwritten factor in most cases in which a party seeks declaration of a common law marriage is equity—often the cases involve question of coverage of insurance, or of inheritance, turning upon the validity of the marriage.

IV. Choice of Laws

178. The rule regarding which jurisdiction's law applies to determine what formalities must be met to create a formal marriage is the same as that for determining which law applies to decide the capability to contract marriage. It is that the law of the state where the marriage is contracted applies unless it conflicts with the law of the state which has the most significant relationship to the contracting parties.[272] This rule is called *lex celebrationis* is reliable because rarely would a mere formality implicate such a *strong* public policy as to warrant ignoring the general rule upholding the validity of the marriage. Thus, even though most American states do not permit common law marriage within their own borders, if parties legally residing in another state in which common law marriage is allowed contract a valid common law marriage there, that marriage will be recognized as valid in all other states including those that do not permit common law marriage. However, when a strong forum public policy clashes with the presumption of comity in favor of foreign marriages that are highly controversial, forum public policy usually is given priority by the American state courts.[273]

§4. Effects of Marriage

I. Evolving Marital Rights and Responsibilities

A. Changing Marriage Incidents

179. The legal and economic effects of marriage are generally called the "incidents of marriage," and include both responsibilities and benefits. These have undergone significant change in recent years reflecting some of the major social and cultural shifts in American life and lifestyles such as the decline in the number of

271. W.P. Statsky, *Family Law* 159 (West 1991); C.G. Bowman, *A Feminist Proposal to Bring Back Common Law Marriage*, 75 Or. L. Rev. 709, 712–714 (1996); T.L. Lewis, Comment, *Standing in the Shadows: Honoring the Contractual Obligations of Cohabitants for Support*, 15 U. Puget Sound L. Rev. 171, 188 (1991).

272. *See* Restatement, 2d, Conflict of Laws § 283 (1971).

273. *See generally* L.D. Wardle, *From Slavery to Same-Sex Marriage: Comity Versus Public Policy in Inter-jurisdictional Recognition of Controversial Domestic Relations*, 2008 B.Y.U. L. Rev. 1855 (2008).

households with a single income and declining family sizes. The changing structure and orientation of the family have produced some significant changes in legal doctrines.

B. *Common Law Doctrine of Coverture*

180. Historically, the husband was responsible to provide monetary support for his wife, and the wife was responsible to provide homemaking services for her husband.[274] Blackstone summarized the common law of England (accepted in the U.S. as well):

> By marriage, the husband and wife are one person in law: that is, the very being or legal existence of the woman is suspended during the marriage, or at least is incorporated and consolidated into that of the husband; under whose wing/protection, and *cover*, she performs everything; and is therefore called in our law-French a *femme covert*, ... under the protection and influence of her husband ...; and her condition during her marriage is called her *coverture*. Upon this principle, of an union of persons in husband and wife, depend almost all the legal rights, duties and disabilities that either of them acquire by the marriage.[275]

Under the common law doctrine of married women's disabilities, married women also could not sue or be sued, could not testify as a witness for or against her husband (nor he for or against her), and her husband was entitled to all of her services.

C. *Married Women's Property Acts*

181. The common law doctrine of the legal unification of husband and wife was largely overturned by a series of statutes generally called "Married Women's Property Acts" that were passed in the United States beginning in the mid-nineteenth century. These Acts initially repealed the disability of married women to own real property, and to separately contract. Eventually, they and related legislation (including legislation giving women the vote), repealed all of the common law gender disabilities of coverture.[276]

D. *Equal Protection and Gender Equality*

182. Today the Equal Protection clause of the Fourteenth Amendment of the Constitution of the United States has been interpreted as generally prohibiting all laws which use gender classifications as the basis for extending or denying legal

274. L.J. Harris, L.E. Teitelbaum & C.A. Weisbrod, *Family Law* 6–13 (Aspen 1996).
275. W. Blackstone, *Commentaries on the Laws of England* 442–443 (3rd ed., Cooley 1884).
276. W. Wadlington, *Domestic Relations* 188–191 (3rd ed., West 1994).

benefits or burdens. Such laws will not be upheld unless that gender distinction is justified by a strong governmental interest that is not merely a gender stereotype.[277] Thus, it is settled that the Equal Protection Clause requires states to provide most (presumably all) marriage benefits and duties equally to husband and wife in America today.

II. Economic Rights and Duties of Marriage

A. Economic Support in General

183. At common law, the husband and wife could not make legally enforceable transactions with each other because they were one person. As noted above, in Blackstone's day the husband had full responsibility to support his wife, and the wife owed all of her service to her husband.[278] Today, each spouse is free to engage in his or her own employment and industry. However, both are deemed legally responsible for the economic support of the other. Husbands still are the principal provider for the economic needs of most families, and in many families the wife will devote her full-time efforts to homemaking and child-rearing; however, in most families most of the time the wife is only a part-time homemaker and mother, and devotes either full-time or part-time to her own paid employment.[279] Legally, however, both spouses are liable for the support of each other. The obligation of mutual support has been gender-neutralized. In some states, a presumption may exist that the husband is primarily liable for the economic support of the family, or that the primary income-earner is primarily liable for support, but the other spouse will be held liable if the primary earner/husband is unable to provide.[280] The law in this area seems to be moving away from a past treatment of married couples as unchangeably legally interdependent with the husband being the expected economic provider and the wife being the expected homemaker, and towards considering marriage as something of a limited partnership between individual actors each of whom may support him or herself and contribute also to the support of each other.[281]

184. Thus, the law imposes a mutual support obligation on the spouses in a marriage (although the general rule is that the obligation is more likely to be invoked against a husband). Thus both spouses are obligated to provide for one another's economic needs. This obligation is determined to some degree by their "station in life," meaning that the couple's circumstances generally determine what is appropriate to require for the support of each member.[282] While many different needs are covered by this doctrine (including food, clothing, housing, education, and legal

277. *Virginia Military Institute*, 116 S. Ct. 2264 (1996); and *Kirschberg v. Feenstra*, 450 US 455 (1981).
278. *See supra* para. 159.
279. U.S. Bureau of the Census, *Statistical Abstract of the United States 1996*, p. 400, Table 627.
280. Wardle, *supra* n. 86 at §12.02.
281. *See* J.B. Singer, *The Privatization of Family Law*, Wis. L. Rev. 1443 (1992).
282. S.L. Scheible, *Defining "Support" Under Bankruptcy Law: Revitalization of the "Necessaries" Doctrine*, 41 Vand. L. Rev. 1, 7 (1988); S. Cutler, Note, *The Taxation of Educational Trust Funds: Private Schools and Lessons*, 37 Tax Law. 205, 216–217 (1983).

expenses in some cases), the most important expense covered by the support obligation may be the obligation to provide for the medical needs of a spouse.[283]

B. Necessaries

185. Out of the duty to provide support has arisen the common law doctrine of "necessaries." This is the doctrine that the economic provider-spouse had the duty to provide the "necessaries" of life[284] (as opposed to the luxuries), defined in terms of the couple's income, history, lifestyle, and standard of living.[285] This doctrine authorized the dependent spouse (historically only the wife) to purchase "necessaries"—goods and services needed under the circumstances of their economic history and condition—and charge them against her husband's credit. With two earning spouses this, of course, is becoming a less-used and more-complicated doctrine. Generally, the obligation to provide necessaries and support depends first upon need and second upon ability to pay. While what may be considered a "necessary" for a two-income family may not be deemed a "necessary" for a one-income family. And what at common law was an exclusively a husband's duty has become a mutual and reciprocal obligation of both spouses in most states; both spouses have the same (and equal) duty to support each other in need.[286] However, the support obligations can be gender-equalized by denying them to both genders as well as by extending them to both.[287]

C. Agency

186. In marriage, spouses become limited agents who can act for one another in some circumstances. The most obvious example has already been mentioned: when a spouse that is not the primary financial contributor to the family makes a purchase against the credit of the primary earning spouse. This idea is really only applicable when the person who sold something or extended credit in reliance on agency wants to collect against the person whose credit was used.[288] Again, the importance of the rule has been abrogated by the change in social circumstances of many couples. The future of the agency rule in this day of aggressive individualism may be in doubt.

283. S.L. Rubenzer, *Necessaries and Family Purpose Debts*, 69 Wis. Law. 15 (1996).
284. H.H. Clark, Jr., *The Law of Domestic Relations in the United States* 265–266 (West 1988).
285. *Ibid.*, at 252–254.
286. *See generally* Thomas Oldham, *Changes in the Economic Consequences of Divorce, 1958-2008*, 42 Fam. L. Q. 419 (2008).
287. *See North Ottowa Community Hospital v. Kieft*, 578 N.W.2d 267 (Mich.1998).
288. M.L. Moxley, *North Carolina Baptist Hospitals, Inc. v. Harris: North Carolina Adopts a Gender-Neutral Approach to the Doctrine of Necessaries*, 66 N.C. L. Rev. 1241, 1247 (1988).

D. Separate and Community Property

187. In addition to the obligation to provide support, special rules apply to the acquisition of wealth and property during marriage. Before marriage each man and woman is the sole owner of the property he or she earns or acquires. In common law jurisdictions, that presumption continues even after marriage—the individual who acquires the property is deemed the sole legal owner of it. Nine American states have adopted community property as the regime of property ownership during marriage. In community property regimes, all property acquired by each spouse (except by gift, devise or inheritance) is deemed "community property" and owned equally by both spouses. While in some community property states the management of money earned by a spouse is within the presumptive control of the earning spouse, that presumption is rebuttable and covers only management, not ownership, and generally only personality, not realty.[289]

188. Some jurisdictions use a set of presumptions regarding the transfer of property of a married couple from one spouse to the other. These presumptions differ between separate and community property jurisdictions. In separate property jurisdictions, the presumption is that the husband intended to give property as a gift that he had transferred to them jointly or to his wife. However, if the wife purchased the property, it was presumed *not* to be a gift to the husband. In a community property jurisdiction, each spouse gets one-half of all the property that is considered to be community property (essentially what is not statutorily defined as separate property). There is no need for any gender-based presumption.

E. Miscellaneous Economic Benefits of Marriage

189. The marital status of individuals also has a number of other miscellaneous economic benefits for the spouses involved, particularly government benefits and some important government-regulated private benefits (particularly deferred-income type benefits). These include differences in tax treatment (such as filing jointly), social security benefits that are extended to spouses, the provision of worker's compensation benefits to spouses, unemployment compensation benefits, insurance benefits (both life and health insurance), retirement benefits, and death and survivorship benefits.[290] These benefits reflect the presumption that marriage creates an economic partnership for the lives of both spouses, and that one spouse ought not to have the power to destroy entirely the economic interests of the other. Increasingly, consent of both spouses is required to withdraw, transfer, or significantly change ordinary deferred-income benefits that are presumed by society to be for the benefit of both spouses.

289. L.J. Harris, L.E. Teitelbaum & C.A. Weisbrod, *Family Law* 6–13, 330–333 & 357–364 (Aspen 1996).

290. For Succession benefits, *see infra* Part IV Chapter 1.

190. Recent actions in a few jurisdictions had made some of these benefits available to unmarried cohabitating couples, but by and large they are still dependent on marriage.[291] That reflects the social presumption that married couples contribute something extraordinary to each other and to society that merits recognition, separate status and preference in law. Debates over the availability to unmarried couples of benefits provided to married couples have been ongoing for decades. The only significant changes in recent years relate to the success that same-sex couples have had in convincing lawmakers (judicial or legislative) to extend some (or all) benefits to them, since they could not marry in all states until 2015. The consequences of the *Obergefell v. Hodges*, changing the legal definition of marriage, for gendered marriage roles and spousal support obligations remains to be seen.

III. Non-economic Benefits

A. *Historical Disabilities*

191. At common law, three of the main non-economic effects of marriage upon the parties related to immunity, testimony, and discipline. The spouses were unable to sue each other, or to testify for or against each other, and:

> [t]he husband also (by the old law) might give his wife moderate correction. For, as he is to answer for her misbehavior, the law thought it reasonable to entrust him with this power of restraining her, by domestic chastisement, in the same moderation that a man is allowed to correct his apprentices or children .... But this power of correction was confined within reasonable bounds, and the husband was prohibited from using any violence against his wife ... [except] to use moderate chastisement) ... .[292]

B. *Contemporary Testimonial Privileges*

192. Today, there are two privileges applicable to married persons. The privilege against adverse spouse testimony is derived from the rule that the accused lacked the capacity to testify and the rule that the husband and wife were one person. At common law it applied to prevent either favorable or adverse testimony. Today this privilege against *adverse* testimony survives based on the need to protect the harmony of the marriage relations. In *Trammel v. United States*,[293] the U.S. Supreme Court held that such a privilege exists, but it is held by the testifying spouse who may voluntarily waive it and testify but may not be forced to testify involuntarily. The states vary, some having abolished the privilege entirely. In at

291. C.A. Bowman & B.M. Cornish, Note, *A More Perfect Union: A Legal and Social Analysis of Domestic Partnership Ordinances*, 92 Colum. L. Rev. 1164 (1992); *see also* W.P. Statsky, *Family Law* 57 (West 1991).
292. W. Blackstone, *Commentaries on the Laws of England* 443–445 (3rd ed., Cooley 1884).
293. 445 US 40 (1980).

least one the privilege is held by the other (nontestifying) spouse, and one source suggests that in most states the privilege is no longer recognized in civil cases.[294] In criminal cases, it survives in many forms; however, there are exceptions to the privilege in crimes against the family, such as domestic violence, child abuse or neglect, etc.

193. The other marital privilege is the privilege protecting confidential spousal communications. All states recognize this privilege by which either spouse may prevent the other spouse from revealing confidential communications. The key is the adjective "confidential." If the communication was not confidential (if it was made in the presence of a third person, for instance) it is not protected. This privilege can be waived; and, generally, there are exceptions when spouses are on opposite sides (as in divorce cases) and in criminal cases for crimes against the family (domestic violence, etc.) or if husband and wife jointly participated in a crime.[295] But still the spousal testimonial privilege in this spousal-witness-privilege-holder form survives and is robust in the twenty-first century.[296]

C. *Interspousal Immunity*

194. At common law complete marital immunity existed because the spouses could not sue each other. The woman could not sue her husband for injuries he inflicted upon her. And he could not be criminally prosecuted for sexually assaulting his wife. Gradually during the twentieth century (often in connection with adoption or amendment of women's property acts), the rule of total immunity began to erode. Initially, the rule eroded in the context of contract claims (repealed as part of married women's acts). Then the doctrine of interspousal tort immunity began to erode in automobile accident cases when the married parties were insured and one of them was injured by insured negligence of the other. The immunity doctrine also eroded (if it had ever existed) with respect to intentional acts of injury and violence. It has little vestigial remnant in criminal law but in specific contexts remains (in attenuated form) in civil context. Its survival (albeit in reduced form) attests to the continuing support for the notion that marriage entails some unity, privacy, accommodation, and trust between parties is valuable for the individuals and for society, such that holding spouses to the standards applicable to strangers may be inappropriate in some cases.

195. But complete abrogation of interspousal immunity was strongly opposed for many years. It was argued that: (1) Interspousal tort actions will destroy harmony in the marital relationship; (2) the doctrine of interspousal immunity helps preserve the unity of the husband and the wife; (3) the doctrine helps to prevent collusive and fraudulent claims; (4) that retention of the doctrine helps to prevent

294. Wardle, Blakesley & Parker, *supra* n. 74, at §§13:15–13:07.
295. *Ibid.*, at §13:07.
296. H.D. Krause & D.D. Meyer, *Family Law* 120–121 (4th ed., West 2009).

trivial claims; (5) that other types of actions such as divorce or criminal proceedings provide adequate redress to the injured spouse; and (6) if the doctrine is to be abrogated then it is the duty of the legislature and not the courts to effect the change.[297] Nevertheless, by 1985 more than half of the American states had at least partially abrogated the rule of general interspousal immunity in tort actions. That same decade saw the rejection of the "marital rape exception" whereby men could not be prosecuted for forcible sexual assault upon their non-separated wives. "Today, in about half of the states in the United States, the doctrine of spousal immunity to tortuous suits has been completely abolished … ."[298] It is presumed that there is no criminal or tort immunity; strong public policy reasons must be proven to establish a claim of interspousal immunity. But the rule of immunity remains in specific contexts. Today, "states still typically respect the 'subtle ebb and flow of married life.' To respect the 'ebb and flow', some states have [revoked spousal immunity] … only in certain circumstances that do not threaten family harmony, such as traffic accidents, cooking mishaps, and other domestic accidents."[299] One particular kind of inter-spousal suit that has split American courts concerns misrepresentation of paternity. Some courts allow a deceived husband to sue his (ex-)wife for damages from misrepresentation (both before and during marriage),[300] while other (most) courts refuse to allow such claims.[301]

D. Domestic Correction

196. The doctrine that a husband may give his wife "moderate correction" in the form of physical discipline is thoroughly rejected in America today. While parents still may use moderate and reasonable corporal punishment to train and discipline children, married women and men are not children and such interspousal behavior is universally considered unacceptable. Violence is generally inappropriate in society, and it is deemed particularly inappropriate within marriage. Laws in all states provide for restraining orders to be issued promptly, usually ex parte, at least initially, against an abusive husband who engages or threatens to engage in physical violence. Additionally, criminal laws apply to such behavior in all states, and are today (unlike earlier times) vigorously enforced.[302]

E. Name upon Marriage

197. At common law a married person (like a single person) could acquire by habit and repute any respectable name and it would be a de facto legal name. By

297. *See* McCurty, *Torts Between Persons in Domestic Relations*, 43 Harv. L. Rev. 1030, 1055 (1930).
298. B. Shmueli, *Tort Litigation Between Spouses: Let's Meet Somewhere in the Middle*, 15 Harv. Negot. L. Rev. 195, 215 (2010).
299. *Ibid.*
300. *Doe v. Doe*, 956 P.wd 887 (Wyo. 1998).
301. *Doe v. Doe*, 747 A.2d 617 (Md. 2000).
302. *See* L.D. Wardle, *Marriage and Domestic Violence in the United States: New Perspectives About Legal Strategies to Combat Violence*, 15 St. Thomas L. Rev. 791 (Summer 2003).

custom, most married men retained their family surname and most married women took the surname of their husbands. However, that was only the practice and custom; it generally was not a legal requirement in American states (though it may have been by statute or common law a presumption in a few states). Thus, wives were legally free to retain their pre-marriage family surname after marriage and a number of cases in the 1970s so established.[303] Statutes in some states and common law or custom protect that right (which exists not only at the time of marriage but at the time of divorce). Interestingly, only eight states appear to statutorily protect the right of a husband to take his wife's surname upon marriage; but equal protection would appear to require that even without a statute.[304] The use of hyphenated surnames by both spouses after divorce (including the wife's surname before and the husband's surname after the hyphen) is a common naming practice.

§5. Void and Voidable Marriages

I. The Concepts of Void and Voidable

198. When the regulations regarding the formalities of marriage or the capacity to marry have been violated, the issue of the effect of violating the rules becomes important. Jurisdictions provide the answer to this question by making certain nonconforming marriages either void or voidable. Void marriages are considered to never have had a legal existence because they controvert the strong public policy of a jurisdiction. At least in theory, void marriages are impossible to contract and are void *ab initio*. Voidable marriages are marriages against a lesser (although generally still important) policy of the state. The effect of a voidable marriage is that the marriage will be valid unless challenged, in which case it could be made void.

A. Void Marriages

199. Void marriages historically involved violation of the strong state requirements or policies. Examples of void marriages include incestuous relationships, bigamous or polygamous relations, marriage attempted when one person is not mentally capable, or (in some jurisdictions and some cases) attempted marriage to a person younger than the absolute minimum age for marriage.[305] Historically, a marriage void *ab initio* did not require judicial declaration; a party to such a void marriage could marry another without securing a judicial annulment. However, prudence has always suggested judicial annulment. When a marriage is void a party

303. *See generally* Petition of Hooper, 436 So.2d 401 (Fla. Dist. Ct. App. 1983); *Secretary of Com. v. City Clerk of Lowell*, 366 N.E.2d 717 (Mass. 1977); *Welcker v. Welcker*, 342 SO.2d 251 (La. Ct. App. 1977).

304. M.M. Frandina, Note, *A Man's Right To Choose His Surname in Marriage: A Proposal*, 16 Duke J. Gender L. & Pol'y 155 (2009).

305. R.C. Pyle, *Family Law* 88–94 (1994); and R.J. Resmini, *The Law of Domestic Relations in Rhode Island*, 29 Suffolk University L. Rev. 379, 390 (1995).

may get a declaratory judgment that the union is indeed void.[306] Even a nonparty to the marriage may challenge the validity of a void marriage, in some cases. There may be some protection for parties to a void marriage because of court-created doctrines granting privileges to some persons whose status resembles that of married people (which might include parties to a void marriage).

B. Voidable Marriages

200. Historically, canonical defects generally rendered the marriage voidable. Marriages often defined as voidable marriages include marriages by underage people without parental consent, marriages where one spouse has defrauded the other, or marriage in violation of formal requirements.[307] Voidable marriages generally may only be disputed by one of the parties.[308] This is important, because, unlike a void marriage, a voidable marriage has legal effect until it is voided at which time it becomes legally as if it had never happened.[309] Today, the kinds of legal defects that render marriages void are those representing a strong public policy, such as bigamy and incest.

II. Failure to Comply with Capacity Requirements

201. A marriage contracted in derogation of a capacity requirement is defective. The defect may render the marriage void *ab initio* or merely voidable. That depends upon how serious the defect is considered to be by the lawmakers of the particular state (or, if the legislators have not spoken, by the courts). Consanguinity, bigamy, and marriages of persons under minimum age to marry with parental and/or judicial consent generally render the marriage totally null and void *ab initio* regardless of the wishes or ratification of the parties; violation of the other marriage restrictions generally are deemed to render the marriage only voidable at the behest of one of the parties, and may be ratified or validated retroactively.

III. Non-compliance with Formalities

202. Non-compliance with marriage *formalities* will almost never render the marriage void *ab initio*. Non-compliance may, in some circumstances, however,

306. E.S. Fredricksmeyer, *Annulments in Colorado*, 22 Colorado Law. 2249, 2250 (1993); and J. McKnight, *Family Law: Husband and Wife*, 46 Southern Methodist U. L. Rev. 1475, 1511 (1993).
307. R.C. Pyle, *Family Law* 94–99 (1994); W.P. Statsky, *Family Law* 179 (West 1991); L.S. Love, Note, *The Way We Were: Reinstatement of Alimony After Annulment of Spouse's "Re-marriage"*, 28 Fam. L. 289, 290 (1990).
308. W.P. Statsky, *Family Law* 178–179 (West 1991).
309. R.C. Pyle, *Family Law* 88–94 (1994); R.J. Resmini, *The Law of Domestic Relations in Rhode Island*, 29 Suffolk U. L. Rev. 379, 390 (1995); and L.S. Love, Note, *The Way We Were: Reinstatement of Alimony After Annulment of Spouse's "Remarriage"*, 28 Fam. L. 289, 290 (1990).

render the marriage voidable. Generally, however, failure to comply with a marriage formality will not impair the validity of the marriage. The parties may be punished for violating the rule, but generally the validity of the marriage will be unimpaired. Some states have criminal penalties assessed for failure to obtain a license before marriage. If the marriage validity is impaired, it is generally deemed a voidable defect.

203. Common law marriage, generally categorizes as a formality, however, is unique. In most states that have outlawed common law marriage, the failure to get a marriage license and to properly solemnize the marriage will render the marriage voidable. Either underage party (and parents or guardians) may contest the marriage until the minor reaches the age of majority and of full consent to marry; thereafter, the marriage ripens into an incontestable, unimpeachable marriage. However, good faith belief in the authority of the person performing the ceremony to do so generally will validate a marriage solemnized by an unauthorized official; it is not void or voidable.

Chapter 2. Divorce

§1. Grounds

I. History of Divorce Law in the United States

204. Divorce was strictly regulated in England and the United States until quite recently. Historically (after the twelfth century, at least), marriage was a matter of canon or church law, which viewed marriage as essentially indissoluble. A defective marriage might be annulled (especially, if not exclusively, by the wealthy and influential), or a legal separation (called *divorce a mensa et thoro* or "divorce from bed and board") granted, but marriage-ending divorce as we know it (called then *divorce a vinculo matrimonii* or "divorce from the bonds of marriage") was not permitted.[310]

205. Divorce came into English law with the Protestant Reformation.[311] In cases in which an ecclesiastical court granted a *divorce a mensa et thoro* Parliament could grant a true *divorce a vinculo matrimonii*. However, that was very rare. One study reported that from the time of the Reformation to 1856 (a period of approximately two centuries) only 317 private Acts of divorce were passed by Parliament.[312] In 1857, the English Parliament adopted the Matrimonial Causes Act which permitted both husbands and wives to petition a court for true divorce on grounds of adultery (though wives had to supplement that allegation with evidence of cruelty, incest, sodomy, etc.). In the United States, divorce was obtainable long before this, however, on grounds that justified relieving one from marital obligations under the strict standards of marital integrity of the day—in essence, for breach of the fundamental terms of the marriage contract. The most common grounds for terminating marriage were adultery, desertion, abandonment, nonsupport, cruelty, habitual drunkenness or drug addiction, and imprisonment.[313] These came to be called "fault" grounds for divorce. During the nineteenth century, some states allowed divorce for the "no-fault" reasons of mental insanity and living separate and apart (usually under a decree of separation) for a statutory period of time (such as three or five years). Divorce on the grounds that the parties lived apart for a substantial period, in turn, may have evolved from "Enoch Arden" laws which allowed the spouse of someone who had been absent for a substantial time to remarry without fear of bigamy prosecution should the presumed-dead former spouse reappear.

310. L. Stone, *Road to Divorce* 1530–1987 (Oxford University Press1990).
311. M. Finer & O.R. McGregor, *History of the Obligation to Maintain*, quoted in B.M. Hoggett & D.S. Pearl, *The Family, Law and Society* 184–186 (Butterworths 3d ed., 1991).
312. B.M. Hoggett & D.S. Pearl, p. 186.
313. M.S. Brinig, *Divorce—Fault Grounds*, in *Contemporary Family Law*, Vol. 2, at §19:01 Chapter 19 (L.D. Wardle, C.L. Blakesley & J.Y. Parker eds, Callaghan 1988).

II. Modern No-Fault Divorce

206. The traditional "fault" model of termination of marriage lasted in the United States until the 1970s when the first wave of the post-World-War-II baby boom generation (like their parents) were struggling with marriage and marriage failures under the influence of an increasingly adolescent-dominated culture. In 1969, California enacted the first "modern no-fault" divorce law, replacing its prior conventional "fault" divorce laws with a new Family Law Act which provided that marriage could be terminated only upon the ground of "irreconcilable differences which have caused the irremediable breakdown of the marriage."[314] The next year an influential interstate commission proposed the Uniform Marriage and Divorce Act which totally eliminated fault grounds for divorce, replacing them with a provision permitting dissolution of marriage (the preferred euphemism for divorce) solely upon the ground "that the marriage is irretrievably broken."[315]

207. The idea of easy, no-fault divorce spread like wildfire. A new generation was anxious to be rid of legal constraints that could keep a marriage together after the spouses had concluded that the loving marital relationship was over, and lawyers and lawmakers hoped that the elimination of fault would reduce animosity, eliminate perjury, and more closely reflect prevailing notions about the mutually terminable nature of marriage and close the gap between the written (strict divorce) law, and the law in practice (liberal divorce).[316] By 1973, two-thirds of the states had enacted no-fault divorce laws, and by the end of the 1980s, all but one state had formally adopted some form of no-fault divorce in their laws (de facto no-fault divorce was in effect in all states by the end of the 1970s) and New York, the last state, formally adopted no-fault in 2012.[317]

208. Today, divorce law and practice in the United States of America is entirely no-fault (de facto if not de jure). Divorce is regulated at the state level, of course. Every state has adopted no-fault grounds for divorce, and the no-fault divorce idea is popular with divorcing parties because it fosters the illusion that no one will be hurt by the divorce, or that it will be simple and painless (though it seldom is either), and because it diverts attention from the very painful matrimonial failure that has caused them to seek to dissolve the marriage. And, the practicing matrimonial bar—the lawyers who specialize in divorce law—generally prefers no-fault grounds for divorce as well as the judges hearing divorce cases. Notwithstanding, there are still restrictions on how a marriage may be dissolved; changes in the law have made many requirements of marriage dissolution largely formal rather than substantive.[318]

314. California Civil Code §§4506, 4507.
315. Uniform Marriage and Divorce Act, §302(a) (2), *Uniform Laws Annotated* No. 9A (1987) p. 147.
316. L.D. Wardle, *No-Fault Divorce and the Divorce Conundrum*, B.Y.U. L. Rev. 79 (1991).
317. *Ibid.* 138, App. 1A.
318. J.B. Singer, *The Privatization of Family Law*, Wisconsin L. Rev. 1443, 1470–1472 (1992).

III. Emerging Reforms of No-Fault Divorce

209. Criticisms of the abuses and injustices of some aspects of no-fault divorce have grown for a quarter of a century. Among the earliest critics were feminists who pointed out that easy unilateral no-fault divorce had contributed to the "feminization of poverty" because the detrimental economic consequences of divorce of a marriage of significant duration with children were disproportionately borne by women and their custodial children.[319] That led to proposals for divorce law reforms that included both "tinkering" with minor adjustments and radical income-shifting proposals which focused upon the economic incidents of no-fault divorce without changing the fundamentals of the no-fault divorce system.[320] By the dawning of the twenty-first century, numerous public opinion surveys and other measures of social interest consistently reported that Americans believe that no-fault divorce is "too easy, especially divorce of couples with children."[321]

210. The first significant legislative reform of no-fault divorce was enacted in 1997 by Louisiana.[322] The legislation provides that parties may make a covenant marriage by executing a declaration of an intent to contract a covenant marriage and certifying by affidavit that they have undergone premarital counseling regarding the seriousness and nature of covenant marriage and that they acknowledge that divorce will only be possible where there has been a complete and total breach of the marital covenant. They must attest that full disclosure has been made before marriage of "everything which could adversely affect the decision to enter" a covenant marriage. By entering a covenant marriage they commit to take "all reasonable efforts to preserve our marriage, including marital counseling," and commit to remain married "for the rest of our lives." They may file this declaration of intent to contract covenant marriage at the time they apply for a marriage license; previously married couples may file a declaration to designate their existing marriage as a covenant marriage by filing a separate declaration and affidavit. By 2005 two other states, Arizona and Arkansas, had also adopted covenant marriage laws.[323] The impact of the "covenant marriage" concept upon the discussion or and perception of divorce across American was much broader and perhaps even more important than the impact on formal laws. There is a growing sense that marriages are not to be discarded lightly, and that spouses need to expect to encounter and try to work through marital problems that arise, for certainly problems will develop in all marriages.

319. L. Weitzman, *The Divorce Revolution* (1985); M. Fineman, *Implementing Equality: Ideology, Contradiction and Social Change, A Study in Rhetoric and Response in Regulation of the Consequences of Divorce*, Wisconsin L. Rev. 789 (1983); and Wardle, *supra* n. 74, 112–116.

320. *See* American Law Institute, *Principles of the Law of Family Dissolution: Analysis and Recommendations*, Preliminary Draft No. 6, 8 Aug. 1996.

321. L.D. Wardle, *Divorce Reform at the Turn of the Century: Certainties and Possibilities*, 33 Fam. L. Q. 783, 786 (1999).

322. Louisiana Act 1380 (1977) amending Louisiana Civil Code Arts. 102 and 103, and Louisiana Revised Statutes 9:234, 9:245, and adding 9:224(C), and 9:225(A) (3), 9:272-:275 and 9:307–9:309.

323. *See* Ariz. Rev. Stat. Ann. §§ 25-901 to -906 (2006); Ark. Code Ann. §§ 9-11-801 to -811 (2006).

211. The most significant difference between covenant marriage and ordinary marriage is that in covenant marriage, grounds for divorce are restricted. While other marriages can be terminated by proof of having lived apart for six months (or upon the historical grounds of adultery or conviction for a felony resulting in death or hard labor), covenant marriage cannot be terminated upon six months separation. Rather, covenant marriage may be dissolved only on six grounds: the other spouse has committed adultery, committed a felony resulting in a sentence of death or hard labor, abandoned the matrimonial domicile for one year, has physically or sexually abused the spouse or child of the spouse seeking the divorce, or the spouses have lived separate and apart for *two* years without reconciliation, or one year following a legal separation—(but if there are minor children legal separation must be at least 18 months unless child abuse was the basis for the legal separation). Legal separation is possible on the first five grounds above mentioned or because of the other spouse's habitual intemperance, cruel treatment, or outrages that are "of such a nature as to render their living together insupportable." Actions for legal separation in a covenant marriage are limited by procedures strictly narrowing jurisdiction, strictly limiting venue, and prohibiting summary judgment or judgment on the pleadings.

212. Thus, covenant marriage restores the explicit presumption that marriage is expected to be lifelong, and rejects the concept of "easy divorce," while retaining avenues for termination of marriage when there is seriously deficient behavior, or when the parties have shown an inability or unwillingness to live together for a significant period of time. However, it provides that model of marriage as an option, a choice that marrying parties make, not a public mandate. American family scholars have recently shown interest in reviving the "covenant" concept (the concept of greater-than-private interests) in marriage.[324]

IV. Divorce Tensions

213. No-Fault divorce laws vary, however, from state to state. Theoretically, important distinctions include exclusive or optional no-fault, unilateral or mutual no fault, and irretrievable breakdown, irreconcilable differences, or separation period no-fault. However, for most purposes these distinctions are of no practical significance.

A. Exclusive or Optional No-Fault

214. The first distinction is between those states that just added no-fault grounds to existing fault-grounds for divorce and those that abolished prior fault-grounds for divorce, replacing them with exclusively no-fault grounds. California led the way in abolishing fault-grounds for divorce, and about twenty states followed that model

324. M.F. Brinig, *Status, Contract and Covenant*, 79 Cornell L. Rev. 1573 (1994); C. Wolfe, *The Marriage of Your Choice*, First Things, 37 (February 1995).

of divorce law reform.[325] However, slightly more than half of the states have merely added no-fault grounds to existing fault grounds. On its face, this means that the basic philosophy of the written law regarding grounds for divorce varies tremendously from state to state. As a practical matter, however, the no-fault grounds are so heavily favored by divorce lawyers (and judges) in all states, that nearly all divorce filings in all states assert no-fault grounds. There has been little substantive change in grounds for divorce since the 1970s.

B. Unilateral or Mutual No-Fault

215. One of the strongest criticisms of no-fault is that it allows an irresponsible party to unilaterally terminate a mutual relationship, depriving the other party of valuable legal and social interests without just cause. The no-fault reformers of the 1960s and 1970s promoted no-fault divorce as a procedure to allow parties who mutually agreed that their marriage was over to end the marriage without unseemly accusations and undue hostility. Ideas of unilateral individualism did not drive the no-fault reforms.[326] However, many states (including California) adopted divorce reforms that created unilateral no-fault divorce—that is, that made no-fault divorce mandatory upon the allegation by just one of the spouses that the marriage was over. Of course, as a practical matter it takes both spouses to make a marriage work; if one wants to end the marriage he or she can usually do so regardless of the law. However, making divorce unilateral significantly altered the legal bargaining process that attends divorce, diminishing the bargaining position of the party who had invested the most in the marriage or had the most to lose from the termination of the marital status. Today, less than a dozen state no-fault divorce laws require mutual agreement for no-fault divorce.[327] "Unilateral" no-fault divorce remains the most common form of no-fault divorce in the American states; if either spouse seeks dissolution and alleges no fault grounds (typically "irretrievable breakdown" or "irreconcilable differences,") that are sufficient ground for the court to grant the divorce.[328] However, at least four states require "mutual consent" to no-fault divorce, meaning that both spouses must agree to dissolution of the marriage on no-fault grounds; otherwise, fault must be alleged and proven.[329]

C. Irreconcilable Breakdown or Irreconcilable Differences or Separation

216. "Irretrievable breakdown of the marriage" and "irreconcilable differences" are the most popular statutory descriptions of the grounds for no-fault divorce (with

325. *Ibid.*, p. 88; *ibid.*, p. 137, App. 1.
326. M.A. Glendon, *Abortion and Divorce in Western Law* 77 (1987).
327. Wardle, *supra*, p. 137, App. 1.
328. A. M. Parkman, *Good Intentions Gone Awry: No-Fault Divorce and the American Family* 13 (Rowman and Littlefield Publishers 2000).
329. G. L. Zborovsky, Note, *Baby Steps to "Grown-Up" Divorce: The Introduction of the Collaborative Family Law Center and the Continued Need for True No-Fault Divorce in New York*, 10 Cardozo J. Conflict Resol. 305, 306 n. 5 (2008).

about fifteen states using each of those formulations); "incompatibility" is the next most popular modern description of the no-fault ground. In ten states, living separate for a short period is the statutory no-fault ground, and in five states both living separate and one of the modern formulations is required. Several states have adopted multiple optional no-fault grounds, usually either living separate and apart or one of the modern no-fault formulations.[330]

217. In substance, the different formulations make little practical or conceptual difference. However, the different formulations may produce procedural differences. For instance, the living separate and apart ground imposes a period of delay in the divorce proceeding if the parties have not previously been living apart, or if they have not lived apart long enough. But those delays are relatively minor. However, as American divorce becomes increasingly bureaucratic and administrative and less judicial and legal, the cumulative effect of various procedures may result in delay and finalization of divorce that is not insignificant.

D. Remaining Fault Grounds

218. Most of the states did not completely abolish the traditional "fault" grounds for divorce, but merely supplemented them with no-fault grounds. Thus, in most states, divorcing parties can still file for divorce on grounds of fault (though few do so). When grounds for a divorce are permitted, the fault bases most commonly identified in the statutes are: adultery (which is often hard to prove), desertion (can be constructive if one spouse's conduct makes the other leave or if one spouse unjustifiably refuses sexual relations), physical cruelty (or a reasonable apprehension of cruelty), mental cruelty (a subjective test), and insanity (but this can also be a defense to a charge of fault, i.e., adultery).[331]

V. Defenses

219. A common criticism of fault divorce was the technical and sometimes conceptually silly common law defenses. For example, one defense was recrimination (if one spouse committed grounds for divorce in reaction to the other spouse committing grounds for divorce, both parties could block divorce by the other; neither party was eligible to seek divorce); another was reconciliation (if the parties had reconciled after the marital breach and by cohabitation indicated forgiveness, the forgiven act could not later be used as ground for divorce), etc.[332] Not surprisingly,

330. *Ibid.*, pp. 88–90.

331. Delaware Code Annotated Title 13 §1503(5) (1995) (defines "misconduct" and lists activities that constitute misconduct as a basis for divorce); *Defeo v. Defeo*, 605 N.Y.S.2d 202 (N.Y. Supreme Court 1993) (prisoner granted a divorce based on abandonment because wife refuses to visit or communicate); and *Rutherford v. Rutherford*, 414 S.E. 2d 157 (S.C. 1992) (reviews cases on whether mental impairment can be a defense to a charge of fault in a divorce).

332. M.F. Brinig, *Defenses to Divorce*, in *Contemporary Family Law*, Vol. 3, at §20:05 Chapter 20 (L.D. Wardle, C.L. Blakesley & J.Y. Parker eds, Callaghan 1988).

most states have abolished all of these common law defenses or by statute made them inapplicable to no-fault divorce. Where statutes have not eliminated the common law defenses, most courts have interpreted the old defenses as being inapplicable. However, in about 20% of the states, one or more specific traditional defenses has been retained as applicable to no-fault, with collusion and unclean hands being the most common.[333]

220. Under the "no-fault" divorce reforms, there is no substantive defense to a petition for no-fault dissolution in a state that allows unilateral no-fault divorce. If the petitioning spouse insists that he or she is unhappy in the marriage because of what he or she considers (subjectively) to be an intolerable situation, American courts accept that as sufficient evidence of an "irremediable breakdown" or "reconcilable differences" sufficient to dissolve the marriage, even over the objection of the other spouse.

221. Procedural defenses have replaced the traditional substantive defenses to modern no-fault divorce. Probably the most common is lack of jurisdiction—either because one or both of the parties is beyond the territorial jurisdiction (and the absence of one of the parties is not necessarily a jurisdictional defect), or because some factor in the description of the subject matter jurisdiction of the state court is missing. Time-of-residency requirements are the most common of these defenses.

222. The substitution of procedural for substantive defenses underscores a major shift in philosophy about marriage termination. Essentially, most states provide that there are no substantive defenses; if either spouse unilaterally (in most states) wants to end the marriage, the other party substantively can do nothing to stop the no-fault divorce.

§2. Divorce Procedure

I. Simplified Procedures

223. In some obvious respects, divorce procedures (and certainly legal policies toward divorce procedures) have been substantially simplified since the adoption of no-fault divorce. The prior policy of the law to discourage divorce was manifest somewhat in procedural requirements such as waiting periods, delays, and entry of interlocutory (rather than final) divorce decrees designed to give the parties opportunities and encouragement to reconcile. The no-fault philosophy that whether the marriage survives or ends is a private matter for the parties to resolve privately has undermined these procedures intended to encourage reconsideration, deliberation, and delay. In most states, these old delay procedures have been entirely repealed.[334]

333. L.D. Wardle & S. Starley, *No-Fault Divorce*, in *Contemporary Family Law*, Vol. 3, at §21:08 (L.D. Wardle, C.L. Blakesley & J.Y. Parker eds, Callaghan 1988).

334. L.D. Wardle & S. Starley, *No-Fault Divorce*, in *Contemporary Family Law*, Vol. 3, at §21:09–21:10 (L.D. Wardle, C.L. Blakesley & J.Y. Parker eds, Callaghan 1988).

Especially when there are no children of the marriage, no substantial property (or real estate) acquired, and short duration of marriage, divorce procedures are essential clerical in many states.

224. In other ways, ironically, no-fault divorce reforms have complicated divorce procedures. There probably is much more total procedure—more judicial procedures applicable to and regularly used in divorce cases—in divorce proceedings today than before the no-fault divorce revolution. Thus, divorce procedures in many states mandate the preliminary disclosures of financial and other information at the time of filing for divorce,[335] provide procedures and remedies for actual or threatened spousal violence that previously did not exist,[336] mandate counseling processes in some cases (especially when the divorcing parties have small children),[337] require mediation or other alternative dispute resolution procedures in some cases (especially when the divorcing parties have small children),[338] provide opportunities for more persons to participate in custody disputes (including grandparents and "psychological parents"), establish complex procedures for computing child support,[339] provide for much more intrusive monitoring of compliance with divorce decrees (particularly child support and alimony payment),[340] and provide extensive and sophisticated mechanisms for interstate enforcement of custody and support,[341] etc. Thus, it is remarkable and ironic that reforms that were intended to get government out of people's private lives by eliminating consideration of fault in divorce have resulted in more procedures for government regulation and involvement in their lives.

225. Moreover, no-fault divorce, and other social factors, both allowed and stimulated an increase in the number of divorce filings. The volume of divorce cases has led to a variety of measures to reduce the burden on state courts. Some have created positions like "commissioners" or quasi-sub-judges who make preliminary decisions of some issues in divorce cases. For example, by 2005 California state courts were using more than 400 subordinate (paid) judicial officers serving to hear

---

335. California Court Rules 1243 (1996); and Utah Code of Judicial Administration 4-912 (1996).

336. Utah Code Annotated §77-36-1 (1996) (criminal protections); §30-6-1 (civil protection); and C.F. Klein & L.E. Orloff, *Providing Legal Protection for Battered Women: An Analysis of State Statutes and Case Law*, 21 Hofstra L. Rev. 801, 882–885 (1993).

337. Pennsylvania Consolidated Statutes Annotated, Title 23 §3302 (1991) (where grounds for divorce is "indignities" to the spouse or where mutual consent is grounds for divorce); Utah Code Annotated §30-3-19 (1997) (mandatory mediation if child custody is in issue); and Utah Code Annotated §30-3-16.1 (mandatory counseling upon filing petition).

338. T. Grillo, *The Mediation Alternative: Process Dangers for Women*, 100 Yale L. J. 1545 (1991).

339. Utah Code Annotated §78-45-7.14 (child support guidelines); Utah Code of Judicial Administration 4-912 & App. G (1996) (child support worksheet); S.A. Roehrich, *Making Ends Meet: Toward Fair Calculation of Child Support When Obligors Must Support Both Prior and Subsequent Children*, 20 William Mitchell L. Rev. 967 (1994).

340. *Ankenbrandt v. Richards*, 504 US 689, 703–703 (1992) ("Issuance of decrees of this type not infrequently involves retention of jurisdiction by the court and deployment of social workers to monitor compliance.").

341. N.M. Raymond, Comment, *The Child Support Recovery Act of 1992—Is the Federal Government's Involvement in the Criminal Enforcement of Child Support at an End after* United States v. Lopez?, 101 Dickinson L. Rev. 417 (1997).

some issues regarding family and juvenile law matters. Moreover, local attorneys are sometimes asked to sit as judges-pro-tem in some family and juvenile cases.[342]

226. The effect of these contrasting developments has been to *reduce* procedures that are designed to discourage divorce and *increase* procedures that are intended to achieve a new constellation of moral goods through and in divorce. Overall simplification or complication of divorce procedures seem not to have been ends or goals in themselves, but simply means to achieving other ends (elimination of the old morality, establishment of the new).

227. Nevertheless, after a quarter-century of practically unrestricted unilateral divorce-on-demand there began to be some backlash, and some reform of the 1970s no-fault divorce reforms. In 1997, Louisiana (and shortly thereafter Arizona and Arkansas) enacted a new form of marriage called "covenant marriage" which cannot be easily terminated by simply living apart for six months, as standard marriages can be terminated, but which requires either a finding of seriously improper marital behavior or a two-year separation.[343] Additionally, a host of new, collateral procedural requirements is now applicable in divorce in nearly all American states including mandatory parenting education and/or divorce education (in all or parts of at least forty-six states), and mandatory mediation of at least some (usually custody-related) issues in nearly all states. These new procedures are designed to make divorce results fairer and less traumatic, especially for children, and to reduce some of the workload of the courts (and the public and private costs associated with litigation). A side effect of these new procedures is to make the process of divorce more lengthy and take more time.

II. Divorce Procedures Generally

228. Before the twentieth century, divorce was often a legislative matter, granted by a "private bill."[344] Today, it is entirely judicial (though usually applied in an almost administratively routine way) in all of the American states, and the statutory procedures prescribed must be strictly followed to obtain the judicial remedy of divorce.

229. The greatest variation among the divorce laws of the several states is in the procedures. Each state's procedural law has developed along its own, idiosyncratic

342. California Administrative Office of the Courts, http://www.courtinfo.ca.gov/courtadmin/aoc/ (last visited May 15, 2007).

343. Louisiana Act 1380 (1977) amending Louisiana Civil Code Arts. 102 and 103, and Louisiana Revised Statutes 9:234, 9:245, and adding 9:224(C), and 9:225(A) (3), 9:272-:275 and 9:307–9:309; K. Sack, *Louisiana Approves Measure To Tighten Marriage Bonds*, *New York Times*, (Jun. 24, 1997), p. A1.

344. *Maynard v. Hill*, 125 US 190 (1888); B.M. Hoggett & D.S. Pearl, *The Family Law and Society* 184–187 (Butterworths 3d ed., 1991).

lines. Thus, this reviews the kinds of procedures that generally are applicable in divorce cases in the United States; details as to the procedures in any particular state can be expected to vary significantly.

A. *Formal Proceedings*

230. Divorce is a formal, de jure procedure. While about one-third of the states permit common law marriage (self-help, nonformal, no direct official involvement) no state permits common law divorce. Divorce is a very formal, highly regulated procedure in all American states.[345]

B. *Adversary Proceedings*

231. Divorce cases are adversary cases, meaning that the parties appear as contestants competing against each other for the goods and awards of the court. The actual substantive ground for divorce is uncontested (indeed, in many states uncontestable) in no-fault divorce cases, but the ground for divorce is only a minor part of the overall divorce proceeding in which the court will identify and divide the property, income, rights, privileges, duties, legal interests, and parental responsibilities of the parties in a very adversarial process. Each party wins more by convincing the court to award the other less (or none)—of property to be divided, parental rights, etc.

232. Because the proceeding is adversarial and the consequences can be very significant, all parties who can afford lawyers, and most who cannot, seek the assistance and representation of legal counsel. That can be very expensive. Except for persons eligible for legal aid (those living at or below poverty level in the United States) the public only provides the judicial institutions to resolve the private legal dispute and, as a general rule it is for the persons who have a grievance to decide whether or not, and how, to use the legal system to resolve their grievances. However, in cases where there is perceived to be a substantial public stake, such as cases of alleged domestic violence and failure to pay child support (which often results in claims made upon the public treasury for welfare support), public legal assistance is often provided.[346] Many public (tax-funded) legal aid offices (that provide free legal services to impecunious parties) are over-burdened by and overwhelmed with requests for free legal assistance in divorce cases. Some legal aid offices have adopted restrictive policies limiting the availability of their services in divorce cases such as covering only cases in which there is an allegation of domestic violence.

345. California Family Code §3182 (West, 1994); Louisiana Revised Statutes Annotated §9:352 (West, 1991); and K. Rigby & K.S. Spaht, *Louisiana's New Divorce Legislation: Background and Commentary*, 54 Louisiana L. Rev. 19 (1993).

346. L.D. Wardle, *Liberty Equality & the Quest for Family Justice in the United States*, in *Families & Justice* 208–229 (Bruylant, 1997).

Monitoring the eligibility requirements for such aid is needed because so many persons misstate their income, resources, or make exaggerated claims of violence in order to obtain free legal services.

233. The dependence upon private attorneys results in some serious inequalities in the provision of legal services. The rich (families and individuals) are well-represented, while others are not so well-represented. The disparities between spouses on account of resources available to each (with disparate personal and family wealth or income) are not insignificant. While courts have authority to redistribute wealth and income during divorce proceedings to "level the playing field," most courts are reluctant to do so except in egregious cases. Increasing numbers of states have adopted or experimented with push-button divorce procedures; parties answer questions online which generates a divorce petition.

C. *Initiating the Proceeding: Pleadings*

234. Divorce cases generally are initiated by the party seeking the divorce filing (through his or her attorney) a petition or complaint for divorce. The petition or complaint is filed with the court and served with a summons (notifying the other party of the time—usually twenty to thirty days—within which a response must be filed) upon the other spouse. In some states the pleadings (complaint and answer) must be verified—certified to be true and accurate to the best of one's knowledge by the party on whose behalf it is filed, and not merely signed by the attorney.

235. At the time initial divorce pleadings are filed, other papers may be filed and immediate interim relief granted. For example, if there has been actual or threatened physical violence in the marriage, the filing party may also seek (and almost automatically obtain) a protective order or temporary restraining order compelling the other party to stay away from the party filing for divorce, or their residence, etc.[347] Sometimes, the parties are required to submit proposed plans for child custody with or soon after the pleadings are filed, if children are involved.

236. Most states have enacted mandatory (or have strongly encouraged) mediation processes.[348] At least thirteen states require that some issues in contested divorce cases be first heard by mediators before they can be brought to court (with rare exceptions, such as for domestic violence), and the "majority of the remaining states give judges discretion to order parents to enter into mediation."[349] The trend

347. C.F. Klein & L.E. Orloff, *Providing Legal Protection for Battered Women: An Analysis of State Statutes and Case Law*, 21 Hofstra L. Rev. 801, 882–885 (1993).

348. *See generally* J.C. Murphy & R. Rubinson, *Family Mediation: Theory and Practice* 1–10 (2009*); Divorce and Family Mediation* 3–25 (J. Folberg, A. L. Milne & P. Salem eds, 2004).

349. E. Kurse, Comment, *ADR, Technology, and New Court Rules—Family Law Trends for the Twenty-first Century,* 21 J. Am. Acad. Matrim. Law. 207, 209 n. 10 (2008) (citing Andrew Schepard, *Law and Children; Revisiting 1985 Law Revisions Report and Custody Mediation*, New York L.J. 3 (January 2005)). *See also* C. Tondo, R. Coronel & B. Drucker, *Mediation Trends: A Survey of the States*, 39 Fam. L. Rev. 431 (October 2001).

to require mediation before litigation has been consistent for the past dozen years, or more, and shows no sign of abating. Thus, both expansion of the number of states in which mediation is required as a prerequisite to litigation of divorce issues and refinement of those procedures is likely in the future.

D. Temporary Orders

237. Because court calendars may have long backlogs and delays of several years may occur before a divorce case is finally decided, it is often necessary for the court to enter an interim order awarding temporary custody and visitation pending the final resolution of the case, and awarding temporary support also. Technically, those awards are not binding and the court in its final order could rule just the opposite as it ruled in the temporary order. Nevertheless, experience shows that often the final orders entered closely resemble those temporary orders. Thus, the battles over the temporary orders are very intense. Usually, the temporary orders are based on less information, less-complete evidence, and much abbreviated hearings compared to the full trial upon which the final decrees will be based.

E. Disclosures and Discovery

238. Upon or shortly after filing for divorce, the parties in most states are typically required to make mandatory disclosure of their financial and property interests—since the parties' property and income are often the sorest points of contention in divorce proceedings. After both parties have had an opportunity to file their formal pleadings (complaint and answer), they may begin the *discovery* process in which they may serve written questions upon each other, demand production of documents, and take oral depositions (examinations by attorneys) of each other in an effort to discover facts that will help them present their case supporting or opposing the various claims to the court.

239. Among the most important witnesses are expert witnesses, especially experts in child psychology who may testify about which parent should be awarded custody of the children, and experts in valuation of nonliquid assets such as ongoing businesses, retirement plans, etc. These witnesses are generally paid for their time and expertise, and it can be very expensive to pay for their assistance (sometimes at USD 300–500 per hour) if it takes a lot of time for them to evaluate the situation or if their deposition takes a long time.

F. Bifurcation of Trial

240. A typical divorce case where there has been a marriage of significant duration will often involve six major issues: termination of the legal status and relationship of marriage (so the parties are free to marry other persons), allocating and dividing property acquired during the marriage, dividing and allocating the debts and obligations incurred during marriage, imposing spousal support (alimony) in favor of the economically dependent spouse, determining parental responsibility (custody and visitation), and determining how much child support will be paid by which parent(s). It is not uncommon for divorce courts to bifurcate the trial of these issues—that is, to divide up the trial into two or more stages. While comprehensive proceedings are often preferred, for practical reasons relating to the variety of situations in which parties seek divorce, split or bifurcated procedures are frequently used.

241. For example, since it is virtually impossible to contest grounds for divorce under no-fault, the court may grant the divorce (termination of marital status) before the other dimensions are tried. Likewise, the court may opt to try the property division and alimony claims separately from the child custody and child support issues.

G. Final Decree

242. Following the trial, the court will enter a final decree. If it has not done so earlier, the decree will terminate the marital relationship between the parties, and will resolve all legal issues, including all six identified above.

243. Courts prefer to defer to the parties' settlement of these issues whenever possible. That is, without abandoning the responsibility to independently evaluate the issue, especially concerning the welfare of children, the courts generally believe that the parties who know each other and their own circumstances the best are in the best position to know what is fair and workable (and that presumption even extends to matters concerning custody and visitation). Thus, pre-trial settlement of at least some (and usually all) of the issues in divorce cases in American courts is common.

H. Post-divorce Proceedings

244. Following entry of the final decree of divorce settling all issues in the case, it is not uncommon for the parties to return to court to request compulsory process to enforce provisions of the decree. Ongoing disputes over child custody have lasted for years, and efforts to force a reluctant obligor to pay outstanding child support or alimony are common. Likewise, post-decree motions to modify provisions of the prior decree may arise. The standard for modification generally includes substantial change of circumstances as one necessary element to obtain that relief.[350]

---

350. A.B. Laurence, *Child Custody and Relocation: A Constitutional Perspective*, 34 U. Louisville Family L. J. 1 (1995–1996).

III. No-Fault Divorce Procedures

A. Name of Proceeding

245. The proceeding to terminate a marriage has been known in Anglo-American law for centuries as a *divorce* proceeding. In some states, no-fault divorce proceedings are called *dissolution* proceedings or proceedings to dissolve a marriage.[351] Similarly, in some states the previous adversary style of "*Smith v. Smith*" has been replaced with "*In re the Marriage of Smith.*"[352] The new terminology reflects the no-fault philosophy just as the former term suggested failure and marital fault. However, both colloquially and professionally, the use of the term *divorce* is not only common but also predominant. Both terms are used interchangeably in this work.

B. Summary and Minimal Proceedings

246. Summary proceedings for termination of marriage are allowed in a few states in divorce cases involving minimal assets, time of marriage, and no children or real property.[353] The notion is that so little public interest is involved and so little of private value at stake that the court should let the parties divorce with minimal procedural restraints—essentially the parties give themselves a divorce. Another approach that is being tried in pilot programs in a few places is the use of "small claims court" procedures in uncontested cases, with inexpensive court fees, expedited hearings, expanded use of paralegals, and clients representing themselves.[354] There have been some reports that these *pro se* (self-representation) procedures seem to work well in uncontested cases. The trend in America is away from traditional divorce litigation and toward divorce by registration or summary dissolution proceedings, especially in marriages of short duration and/or when the parties have no children and/or limited assets.[355] This not only reflects greater respect for party

351. Arizona Revised Statutes §25-31-1 (1991); and California Family Code Annotated §2300 (1994); Kentucky Revised Statutes §403.130 (1984).
352. Arizona Revised Statutes §25-31-1 (1991); and California Family Code §2330 (1994); Minnesota Statutes Annotated §452.300 (1997).
353. *See* Alaska Statutes §25.24.200 (Supp. 1993); Colorado Revised Statutes §14-10-120.3 (1987); Florida Rules of Civil Procedure 1.611 (1993); Mississippi Code Annotated §93-5-2 (Supp. 1993); Nevada Revised Statutes §§125.181 et seq. (1993); Oregon Revised Statutes §107.485 (1993); 23 Pennsylvania Consolidated Statutes Annotated §2301 (1991); Tennessee Code Annotated §36-4-103 (1991); Washington Revised Code Annotated §§26.12.010 et seq. (West, 1986 & Supp. 1994); L.D. Wardle & B.N. Madsen, *Alternative "Dispute Resolution"*, in *Contemporary Family Law*, Vol. 3 §23:09 (L.D. Wardle, C.L. Blakesley & J.Y. Parker eds, Callaghan 1988).
354. J.C. Murphy, *Access to Legal Remedies: The Crisis in Family Law*, 8 B.Y.U. J. Pub. L. 123, 124 (1993); B.D. Sales, C.J. Beck & R.K. Haan, *Is Self-Representation a Reasonable Alternative to Attorney Representation in Divorce Cases*, 37 Saint Louis U. L. J. 553 (1993); and R.J. Gerber, *Recommendations on Domestic Relations Reform*, 32 Arizona L. Rev. 9, 11(1990).
355. S. Katz, *Family Law* in America 124–125 (2003).

autonomy (and the privatization of and the lessening of respect for the public interest in divorce) but also because the parties are more likely to "respect decisions in which they have had some input, or at least the opportunity to be heard … ."[356]

§3. EFFECTS OF DIVORCE

I. Distinguishing Divorce from Annulment and Separation

247. Divorce is the legal dissolution of a lawful marriage. Thus, there are three distinctive substantive elements of divorce in American law. Each of these elements distinguishes divorce from other remedies.

A. *Annulment Distinguished*

248. First, there must be a lawful marriage. If the marriage is determined to be unlawful and either void or voidable, the court will grant an annulment rather than a divorce. The annulment decrees that the marriage is void. If the defect is a very serious, fundamental defect (historically civil defects) that renders the marriage void, such as if the husband and wife discover that they are related as brother and sister, the annulment decree will be "declaratory" declaring the marriage *void ab initio*, meaning it was void from the beginning; the marriage is retroactively declared to never have been a valid marriage. The court decree does not make the marriage void; it is as a matter of law void and the court decree only recognizes a fact. Traditionally, if there was a defect rendering the marriage void, the parties did not even need to obtain an annulment; they could act as if the marriage had never existed because in the eyes of the law it never did exist. If the defect violates other basic requirements of marriage (historically canonical defects but not civil defects) and is voidable only, the annulment is sometimes called "constitutive," and the marriage is declared void retroactively but in the absence of a court decree it was and would continue to have been a valid marriage.[357] If the marriage was void, there is nothing for a court to dissolve and a divorce cannot be entered.

B. *Legal Separation Distinguished*

249. The second requirement for divorce is termination of the marital relation. If the judicial procedure does not result in complete termination—total dissolution—of the marital relation, it is not a divorce. Thus, the traditional relief to disaffected married parties granted by common law courts—*divorce a mensa et thoro*—was not a divorce by modern standards since it was only parting from bed and board. The modern equivalent of this traditional remedy is legal separation. It separates the parties from each other, ending some of the qualities of marriage, but

356. *Ibid.*
357. H.H. Clark, Jr., *The Law of Domestic Relations*, §3.1 126 (West 2d ed., 1988).

the marital relationship is not dissolved as a matter of law, but continues subject to the limitation of non-cohabitation, duty to separately support, etc. About half of the American states authorize legal separations, and in most of these states, living separate and apart under a decree of legal separation is one ground for divorce.[358]

C. Abandonment Distinguished

250. The third requirement for divorce is that the termination be "legal"—that is, it must comply with the substantive and procedural requirements for divorce. While ten of the states and the District of Columbia allow "common law marriage," without compliance with the formalities of ordinary civil licensed marriage, no state recognizes "common law" or de facto divorce.[359] Abandonment is not the same as divorce. However, it is not uncommon for estranged husbands and wives to simply abandon their partners, drop out of the marriage, leave without a trace, and disappear. Often these people establish "new" lives and marry other persons, even though the first marriage was never legally terminated. Generally, courts rule that the prior marriage, though dead as a practical matter and for many years nonfunctional, is still legally valid.[360] However, the law presumes that the last or latest marriage is valid; that presumption may be rebutted by proof of a valid former marriage and no record of any divorce in any jurisdiction in which either party to it was domiciled.[361]

II. Effects of Divorce: Relations with Ex-spouse

251. The effect of an annulment is to decree that the apparent marriage was not really a lawful marriage. The effect of a legal separation is to continue the marriage, restricted as to cohabitation, separate maintenance, etc. The legal effect of abandonment is to continue the marriage. The effect of a divorce is the termination of a valid marriage, the dissolution of a unique partnership. But, it is not always a "clean break." The consequences of the marital union may survive long after the marriage is legally ended.

252. Divorce directly affects both the horizontal spousal relationship and the vertical parental-child relationship. Both economic and non-economic relations are affected.

358. H.H. Clark, *ibid.*, §6.4, p. 268.
359. *Hilton v. Roylance*, 25 Utah 129, 69 p. 660 (1902).
360. H.H. Clark, *ibid.*, §2.6, pp. 64–70.
361. *Spearman v. Spearman*, 482 F.2d 1203 (5th Cir. 1973).

A. *Divorce Effects on the Spousal Relationship*

253. Divorce is designed specifically to affect spousal relations by ending the marital status of the husband and wife. However it does not completely end the legal relations of the spouses. It usually has a more complete, annihilating effect on non-economic relations between the parties than it has on their economic relations, as both property division and (especially) alimony (spousal support) may require ongoing post-divorce relations. Of course, the divorce normally will not preclude the need for post-divorce interaction and relations as co-parents. So while the legal marriage is effectively terminated, the relationships created during marriage are seldom fully extinguished by dissolution.

1. Non-economic Effects of Spousal Relations

254. The most obvious effect of divorce is upon the conjugal relationship between the spouses. They are no longer married to each other, no longer spouses, but former-spouses or ex-spouses. Each loses the right to cohabit maritally with the other. The marital community is terminated and the parties' marital status is ended. Each is legally free to marry another person. Historically, some states imposed restrictions on remarriage in some divorce cases (especially in the case of adultery), to encourage reconciliation, but those laws have been repealed.[362]

255. In cases when there has been domestic violence, the termination of the marital right to cohabit means that the abused spouse has even greater protection against the former spouse. The presumption of consent to and for cohabitation is terminated.[363] However, it is not rare for divorced parties to cohabit after dissolution, especially when the economy is difficult. But they cohabit as in the status of non-marital cohabitants.

256. Marriage emancipates a minor. A minor who has married and divorced while still a minor regains single (unmarried) status, but normally is not returned to the status of a minor.[364]

257. Upon marriage, it is customary (though not legally required) for the wife to assume the surname of her husband. Upon divorce, it is common (though not legally required) for the wife to reassume her former surname. However, if the marriage

362. M.F. Brinig, *Consequences of Divorce*, in *Contemporary Family Law* at §22:06, Vol. 2, Chapter 22 (L.D. Wardle, C.L. Blakesley & J.Y. Parker eds, Callaghan 1988).
363. M.F. Brinig, *ibid.* at §22:01.
364. C.N. Gardner, Note, *Don't Come Cryin' to Daddy! Emancipation of Minors: When is a Parent "Free at Last" from the Obligation of Child Support?*, 33 U. Louisville J. Fam. L. 927, 941 (1995).

was of long duration or if a child has been born of the marriage and will continue to bear the surname of the father, the wife not infrequently chooses to continue to be known by the marital surname.[365]

258. Married persons enjoy a privilege against giving adverse testimony against their spouses. Upon divorce, that testimonial privilege expires and former spouses may be called to testify against their ex-spouses over the objection of the former spouses, because the purpose of the privilege is to protect the relationship at the time of the testimony (trial) and if the marriage has ended, there is nothing for the privilege to protect. Confidential communications between spouses are also protected by a testimonial privilege, however, and this privilege survives the divorce since the purpose of the privilege is to protect the confidence that existed at the time of the communication.[366]

2. Economic Effects upon Spousal Relations

259. As a necessary part of divorce in all American states, the court must make an allocation of the property accumulated by the parties during the marriage (and sometimes property the parties brought with them to the marriage), must allocate responsibilities for the liabilities incurred by the couple during the marriage, and must determine whether alimony (called "maintenance" or "support" in some jurisdictions) must be awarded (and, if so, how much). Details vary considerably from state to state, yet there are some significant broad similarities and common principles.

260. First, the court must make equitable distribution of all marital or community property.[367] Marital or community property generally includes all property acquired during the marriage by either the husband or the wife except property acquired by gift, bequest, devise, or inheritance. Property acquired before marriage or by gift, inheritance or devise, and in some states any increase therefrom, is considered "separate" property and normally is not considered by the court in dividing property upon divorce.[368] In most states, the court is charged to make an "equitable" distribution of the marital or community property between the spouses.[369] The most common approach (codified or expressed as a judicial presumption in a few states, but the de facto unexpressed reality in most) is to make a roughly equal division of the property between the spouses. Nevertheless, most state property division laws identify a list of factors that the court should consider in making property

365. S.J. Kennedy-Sjodin, Note, *Keegan v. Gundahl: The Child's Surname as a New Bargaining Chip in the Game of Divorce*, 41 South Dakota Law Review 166, 177 (1995–1996).
366. M.F. Brinig, *ibid.* at §22:07.
367. This topic is addressed in greater detail in another chapter. *See infra* Part III, Chapter 5.
368. A few states' property division laws do not distinguish between separate and marital or community property. *See* Connecticut General Statutes Annotated §46b-81 (1995).
369. C.L. Blakesley & C. Curtis, *Property Division—Common Law*, in *Contemporary Family Law* at §30:04, vol. 2, Chapter 30 (L.D. Wardle, C.L. Blakesley & J.Y. Parker eds, Callaghan 1988).

division.[370] (One study counted thirty-eight factors mentioned in the various state property division statutes.)[371] Marital misconduct (fault) is considered a relevant factor in property division by about one-third of the states.[372]

261. Nonetheless, equal division of property acquired during marriage is the common rule and justified under the notion that the marriage is, among other things, and economic partnership (unless the parties have, by antenuptial, post-nuptial, or separation agreement provided otherwise). "California [and other states] replaced its equitable property distribution regime with a rule requiring equal division of marital property on the assumption that equitable distribution typically produced relatively equal awards for husband and wife."[373] However, ironically, there have been some unintended (and, arguably, unfair) results of the strict equal-division regime (and under the similar rigid ALI equal property division proposals, the equity gains by wealthy wives would be offset by the equity losses of women in less affluent marriages, of which there are many more).[374]

262. Liabilities and debts of the parties must be apportioned. In most states, debt is allocated on the same basis as property.[375]

263. Adjustment of economic relations not infrequently calls into question the validity of a pre-marital agreement (antenuptial contract) in which a negotiated economic provision is adopted by the prospective spouses, and one or both of the parties' property or spousal support and other economic claims are waived or limited. When enforcement of the pre-marital agreement would lead to significantly less economic advantage for one party than they could expect under generally applicable rules of property division and alimony, it is common for that party to contest the enforceability of the pre-marital agreement. The Uniform Pre-marital Agreement Act, adopted in most states, establishes some predictability by providing that such contracts will be enforced if made in writing and signed by the parties, unless (1) the agreement was not voluntary, or (2) it is shown that it was unconscionable when it was executed and that the party lacked "reasonable disclosure" and did not waive disclosure, and did not have (or have opportunity to have) "adequate knowledge of the property or financial obligations of the other party," or (3) it eliminates alimony and leaves a party so poor that he/she is "eligible for support under a program of public assistance … ."[376] Some courts attempt to circumvent and set aside such agreements in order to effectuate their judicial view of the equities of the case.

370. J.D. Gregory, P.N. Swisher & S.L. Scheible, *Understanding Family Law* 345–351 (1993).
371. American Law Institute, *Principles of the Law of Family Dissolution: Analysis and Recommendations*, Preliminary Draft, No. 2, §4.15, Rptr's Notes, Cmnt a (25 Sept. 1991).
372. D.J. Freed & T. Walker, *Family Law in the Fifty States: An Overview*, 23 Fam. L. Q. 495 (1990).
373. M. Garrison, *The Economic Consequences of Divorce: Would Adoption of the ALI Principles Improve Current Outcomes*, 8 Duke J. Gender L. & Pol'y 119, 123 (2001).
374. *Ibid.*
375. J.D. Gregory, P.N. Swisher & S.L. Scheible, *ibid.*, p. 350; Clark, *ibid.*, p. 606.
376. Uniform Premarital Agreement Act, §6.

However, judicial respect for premarital agreements is increasing. Similar principles apply to enforcement of post-nuptial agreements.[377] *See infra,* Part III, Chapter 1.

264. Finally the court must decide whether alimony should be awarded. This has become a source of much dispute in theory as well as in doctrine and practice. Historically, alimony was intended to be support given the separated wife who, though separated, was still married and as such still entitled to be supported by her husband. She was entitled to support because, but for her husband's egregious marital faults (which provided her with grounds for separation) she would still be living with and be supported by him under the lifetime commitment of marriage. However, now alimony is awarded after termination of the marriage, the marriage can be dissolved on no-fault grounds, and marriage is often not seen as a lifetime commitment to economically support the marital partner. Thus, the theoretical basis for awarding alimony is being reconsidered.[378] What at common law was exclusively a husband's duty has been gender-neutralized in most states; both spouses have the same (and equal) duty to support each other in need under modern alimony laws.[379] Today, husbands as well as wives may claim alimony if they have need for it and the other spouse have the resources and ability to pay.

265. As a matter of legal doctrine, alimony is still awarded in most states on the basis of the need of the financially dependant spouse (still usually the wife) and the ability to pay of the other spouse.[380] Thus, in marriages of short duration, and as more and more wives enter the paid workforce during marriage, there is less "need" for alimony upon divorce than once may have been the case. Traditionally, alimony was a permanent award—a monthly or other periodic payment lasting presumably as long as the dependant spouse lived (on the assumption that the economic dependency would last that long). Recently, however, it has become quite common for the courts to award a spouse "rehabilitative alimony" or alimony for a specific term (for two or three years, for example) to smooth the transition from integrated living on shared income to self-support. This is based on the finding that the need for financial help from the ex-spouse is temporary and transitional only.[381] American courts have the power and authority to account for the public values of marital stability and of protecting the investment of the home-making spouse (child-caretaking

377. *See* In re Marriage of Tabassum and Younis, 881 N.E.2d 396 (Ill. App. Ct. 2007) (post-nuptial agreement held valid and enforceable in Illinois).

378. *See* J. Carbone & M.F. Brinig, *Rethinking Marriage: Feminist Ideology, Economic Change, and Divorce Reform*, 65 Tulane L. Rev. 953 (1991); *see also* J. Eekelaar & M. Maclean, *Maintenance After Divorce* 15 (1986).

379. *See generally* J.T. Oldham, *Changes in the Economic Consequences of Divorce, 1958-2008*, 42 Fam. L. Q. 419 (2008).

380. C.L. Blakesley, *Alimony and Spousal Support*, in *Contemporary Family Law* at §32:02, Vol. 2, Chapter 32 (L.D. Wardle, C.L. Blakesley & J.Y. Parker eds, Callaghan 1988).

381. *Ibid.*, §32:08.1. *See also* American Law Institute, *Principles of the Law of Family Dissolution: Analysis and Recommendations*, § 5.03 (2002).

spouses, especially) in the family by means of awarding alimony, though most courts focus on the parties' private interests rather than public interests.[382]

266. Advocates of greater wealth-shifting upon divorce have proposed other theories for alimony that would shift it from its historic basis in the commitment of mutual support and reestablish it, grounded in a new presumed contract to share equally their economic resources during marriage and to share equally the economic consequences of the ending of the marriage. Alimony would be awarded to compensate a spouse for disproportionate losses incurred or to share disproportionate economic gains from the marriage.[383] But those proposals have not been widely embraced by lawmakers yet. For example, the proposals of the American Law Institute's *Principles of the Law of Family Dissolution* (2002) which provide for generous "compensatory spousal payments" have been criticized because they "transform alimony from need-based awards into entitlement-based compensation for specific economic losses caused by divorce. Although the ALI approved the Principles in 1997 [finally in 2000], no state has yet to formally adopt [those] Principles."[384] Indeed, a comprehensive 2008 review of the impact of the ALI Principles on family law in the states found that only one state has statutorily enacted any part of the ALI Principles, and the dozen of such cases each year (average) that cite the Principles do so as an "obligatory citation" but neither adopt nor rely upon its recommendations.[385]

267. While the action for divorce is pending, before a final alimony decree is entered, divorce courts in most states have authority to award temporary alimony *pendente lite*. This provides economic support while the divorce is being processed.[386]

268. Because alimony is periodic and because circumstances can change regarding either or both need and ability to pay, alimony can be modified. Courts maintain continuing jurisdiction to increase, decrease, or eliminate the alimony award upon a showing of substantially changed circumstances.[387] Among the factors which traditionally have been considered are changed needs and resources of the obligor and obligee, remarriage or cohabitation by the obligee (traditionally grounds for terminating alimony), and death of either party.[388]

---

382. L.D. Wardle, *Alimony on the Margins: Protecting Homemaking Services in the Public Interest*, in *Family Finances* 475 (Jan Sramek Verlag KG, Austria, B. Verschraegen eds, 2009).
383. American Law Institute, *Principles of the Law of Family Dissolution: Analysis and Recommendations* § 5.03 (2002).
384. David A. Hardy, *Nevada Alimony: An Important Policy in Need of a Coherent Policy Purpose*, 9 Nev. L.J. 325, 334 (2009).
385. *See* generally M.R. Clisham & R.F. Wilson, *American Law Institute's Principles of the Law of Family Dissolution, Eight Years After Adoption: Guiding Principles of Obligatory Footnote*, 42 Fam. L. Q. 573, 576 (2008).
386. J.D. Gregory, P.N. Swisher & S.L. Scheible, *ibid.*, pp. 250–251.
387. *Ibid.*, p. 255.
388. H.H. Clark, *supra*, pp. 656–671.

B. Divorce Effects on the Parental Relationship

269. While the legal focus and most immediate effect and purpose of divorce is upon marriage, divorce powerfully affects parent-child relations. Children are, after all, the innocent victims of divorce; they have no vote in whether their family will be broken up, yet they will usually suffer the effects of divorce more poignantly than either of the divorcing spouses because children have a profound need for the association, example, affection, training, and support of both parents.

1. Non-economic Effects upon Parental Relations

270. Theoretically, divorce does not terminate parent-child relations; it only ends the marriage and marital status of the husband and wife; it does not change the parental relationship in law or the parental status of either party to the marriage. Reality, however, does not draw such tidy distinctions. While the marriage exists, the husband and wife presumably cohabit and their children live with them. Since the parties will not cohabit after divorce, the children cannot continue to reside simultaneously and full-time with both parents. Thus, divorce mandates separation of the children from one of the parents.

271. If the child is old enough that his or her opinion regarding custody is sought by the court, the child will be put to a "Sophie's choice"—forced to choose which parent he or she prefers (to live with) and which to reject (as a custodian). Few traumas in the life of a person of any age can be greater than those experienced by children of divorce who are thus separated from and may feel forced to choose between their parents. Determining which parent will be given physical custody of the children is still one of the most difficult judicial tasks to be performed in divorce cases. They seems to be a disturbing trend of some American courts to avoid this difficult task by putting upon children of sufficient age the burden of making the choice of which parent they will live with after the divorce.

272. Procedurally, there have been some significant changes in custody and visitation law in the early years of the twenty-first century. Many states now required the divorcing spouses to prepare, file a proposed "parenting plan" which covers custody, visitation, and related issues. (i.e., the most—perhaps only—successful recommendation made by the American Law Institute's Principles of the Law of Family Dissolution, and the only section which has been adopted by a legislature—in the state of West Virginia.)[389] By court rule, many other states have adopted parenting plan requirements, as well. Since parental involvement and initiative in structuring a plan for future cooperation after divorce in the raising of children increases likelihood of success and reduction of conflict in implementation of

389. *See* American Law Institute, *Principles of the Law of Family Dissolution: Analysis and Recommendations*, Chapter 2 (2002); *ibid.* at §§ 2.10-2.12. *See also* M.R. Clisham & R.F. Wilson, *American Law Institute's Principles of the Law of Family Dissolution, Eight Years After Adoption: Guiding Principles or Obligatory Footnote*, 42 Fam. L. Q. 573, 576 (2008).

such plan, and since deference by the court to the parents in most cases is common, the efficiency and advantages of using parenting plans is apparent.

273. The ubiquitous legal standard for determining custody is "the best interests of the child." Most state statutes identify a number of factors which should be considered relevant to making that determination. Most are common sense factors including such things as the child's age, child's preference, siblings, stability, relevant behavior by the parents, etc.[390] But undergirding and often overriding those considerations are the effects of certain legal presumptions regarding custody. The most significant in recent years have been the natural parent presumption, the tender years presumption, and the primary caretaker presumption.

274. The right to raise one's child is a fundamental constitutional right, one of the liberties protected against undue state intrusion by the Fourteenth Amendment.[391] The association which other adults (especially unrelated persons) have with the child may be important, but does not rise to an equivalent constitutional level. Thus, for constitutional as well as for very pragmatic reasons American courts have long favored the biological parent over a nonparent (such as a stepparent) in custody disputes. This is still true today, though the strength of the presumption has waned mildly in recent years as the disintegration of the nuclear family and the increase in divorce-remarriage-divorce have resulted in more and more cases in which a biologically unrelated adult has acted *in loco parentis* and formed a parental bond with a child that is comparable to the natural bond between biological parent and child. The legal preference for the natural parent is still strong, though not as nearly absolute as it may have been three decades ago.[392] However, in the case of *Troxel v. Granville,* decided by the Supreme Court in the year 2000, the Court ruled that constitutional considerations mandate that states give substantial deference to and protection of the interests of a biological parent to control the custody and visitation of a biological child, even of the interests of well-meaning, caring biological grandparents.[393] With the increase of nonmarital cohabitation, artificial reproductive techniques (ART), and same-sex couple child-rearing, the prospects that a non-biological parent may contest and replace or supersede the parental rights of one (or both) biological parents is not insignificant today. In appropriate cases, it would not be unjustified by the best interests of the child to award custody of significant visitation to such quasi-parental caretakers of children. But the focus on best interests of the child, and the persistent survival of the presumption that biological parents are most inclined to act in the best interests of their children (as well as

390. Uniform Marriage and Divorce Act §402, *Uniform Laws Annotated* No. 9A (1970) p. 147; and E.M. Blackwood, Note, *Race as a Factor in Custody and Adoption Disputes: Palmore v. Sidoti*, 71 Cornell L. Rev. 209, 213 (1985).

391. *Meyer v. Nebraska*, 362 US 390 (1923).

392. J.D. Gregory, P.N. Swisher & S.L. Scheible, *supra.* p. 374.

393. 520 U.S. 57 (2000).

growing evidence that many children of ART and of adoption yearn to connect with their biological parents) are evidence that biological ties are not insignificant in parenting.[394]

275. Historically, at least in the twentieth century, the mother was preferred in law as the custodian of children of tender years.[395] This resulted in a maternal custody preference. Today, principles of gender equality and sexual homogenization have made most legislatures and courts uncomfortable with the explicit maternal custody presumption, and it has been explicitly abandoned in most American jurisdictions. Ostensibly gender-neutral standards for awarding child custody have been adopted instead of the old maternal presumption. Among the recent favorites is the "primary caretaker" presumption which gives custody preference to the parent who has been the primary caretaker of the child. However, while this standard is explicitly not gender-biased, as a practical matter it (like essentially all other custody standards) functions in a very gender-biased manner because culturally, child caretaking is still not a gender-neutral parental function; mothers spend more time in most families caring for children and fathers spend more time earning income for the family (some would argue that mothers (some) do both, while fathers (some) choose to do the latter only). However, there is some indication that courts in most states are more willing to abandon the old gender-biases and presumptions about parenting and custody today much more than they previously were.

276. Custody decisions can be modified. However, substantial change in circumstances is usually required. The law presumes that stability in the relationship between the child and the custodial parent is in the best interests of the child (the ultimate test), so motions to change custody must overcome that presumption.

277. Generally, following divorce, one parent is awarded custody and the other is awarded visitation rights. The noncustodial "visiting" parent usually is entitled to have the children reside with him (it is usually the father) on alternating weekends, alternating holidays, and a month or so during the summer.[396] Most states have adopted visitation guidelines that set forth default rules about when visitation will occur, presumptively applicable if the parties cannot agree upon a visitation schedule or whenever else the court deems it appropriate to adopt them in the custody and visitation order.

278. Joint custody is a popular term among American divorce lawyers and courts because it conjures up the vision of the divorcing parents both actively participating in the raising and daily lives of their children. In fact, joint custody usually means joint "legal" custody, a minor consolation prize for the parent who does not win physical custody of the child. It means that the parent legally is entitled to

394. L.D. Wardle, *Form and Substance in Parentage Law*, 15 William & Mary Bill of Rights J., 203 (2006).

395. M.M. Barry, *The District of Columbia's Joint Custody Presumption: Misplaced Blame and Simplistic Solutions*, 46 Catholic U. L. Rev. 767, 769 (1997); and R.L. Klaff, *The Tender Years Doctrine: A Defense*, 70 California L. Rev. 335 (1982).

396. *See* Utah Code Annotated §30-3-34 (custody guidelines).

obtain the information that parents can obtain (school records, etc.), and is entitled to give the consents that parents are entitled to give (for medical treatment, etc.).[397] Joint (or split) physical custody is also possible, but it usually functions like a more expansive form of custody and visitation, with the parents alternating custodianship for longer periods.[398] The benefit of the concept of "joint custody" is that it encourages both parents to continue to attempt to be parents for their children, to actively perform parental roles and functions as fully as they can following divorce.

2. Economic Effects upon Parental Relations

279. Upon divorce, if there are children of the marriage, a court must enter an order for the financial support of the children. Since 1984 much of the guess-work and judicial discretion for determining the amount of child support has been eliminated by the adoption in all states of child support guidelines. Those guidelines provide mathematic formulas and charts to objectify and equalize child support. The guidelines vary from state to state. Most child support guidelines are based upon an income-combining and relative-income-proportion standard for allocating the child support obligation. These guidelines and the standards for awarding child support are considered in greater detail in another section.[399]

397. C.L. Blakesley, *Child Custody and Visitation*, in *Contemporary Family Law* at §39:11, Vol. 3, Chapter 39 (L.D. Wardle, C.L. Blakesley & J.Y. Parker eds, Callaghan 1988).
398. J.D. Gregory, P.N. Swisher & S.L. Scheible, *supra*, pp. 387–389.
399. *See infra* Part II, Chapter 6.

Chapter 3. Cohabitation Without Marriage

§1. The Practice of Nonmarital Cohabitation in the United States

280. One of the most remarkable demographic developments in the United States in recent years has been the rise in nonmarital cohabitation. The number of nonmarital cohabiting couples rose 700% in twenty-five years from 523,000 in 1970 to 3,668,000 in 1995.[400] By 2006, the U.S. Census Bureau counted over six million unmarried couples living together in the United States, accounting for 5.4% of all households; and about 11%–12% of those cohabiting couples are same-sex couples.[401] As of 2012, there were 112 million unmarried Americans over age 18, constituting nearly 47% of the adult U.S. population; however, 40% of them have previously been married.[402]

281. However, nonmarital cohabitation by American couples seldom lasts very long.[403] Unfortunately, their marriages are not as stable as those of persons who did not cohabit before marriage.[404] A 2010 government report concluded that "[o]verall, first cohabitations were shorter-lived than first marriages," cohabitation lasting [at least] three years was only 31% for women and 24% for men; however, many cohabitation relationships transition to marriage," and "[o]verall, there was approximately a 65% chance that first cohabitations for men and women would transition to marriage within 5 years … ."[405] The report found that the rate of breakup within ten years of beginning the relationships is about 50% higher for couples who cohabit than for couples who marry without previously cohabiting (about 54% for couples who first cohabit versus 34% for couples who marry without prior cohabitation); though the rate of marital dissolution for cohabiting couples who later marry seems to be about the same as for couples who did not cohabit before marriage).[406]

400. U.S. Bureau of the Census, *Statistical Abstract of the United States 1994*, (1995), pp. 56 & 58; and U.S. Bureau of the Census, *Statistical Abstract of the United States 1996*, (1997), p. 56, Tables 61 & 62 and p. 58, Table 66.

401. Statistical Abstract of the United States, 2009, at Table 62.

402. Unmarried Equality, Statistics, available at http://www.unmarried.org/statistics/ (seen 6 Jul. 6, 2015).

403. L.J. Waite, *Does Marriage Matter*, 32 Demography 483, 485 (1995); Zheng Wu & T.R. Balakrishnan, *Dissolution of Premarital Cohabitation in Canada*, 32 Demography 521, 529 (1995).

404. W.G. Axinn & A. Thornton, *The Relationship Between Cohabitation and Divorce: Selectivity or Causal Influence*, 29 Demography 357 (1992); J.D. Teachman, J. Thomas & K. Pasch, Legal *Status and the Stability of Coresidential Unions*, 38 Demography 571 (1991).

405. Centers for Disease Control & Prevention, Vital and Health Statistics, Marriage and Cohabitation in the United States: A Statistical Portrait Based on Cycle 6 (2002) of the National Survey of Family Growth Series 23, No. 28, February 2010) available at http://www.cdc.gov/nchs/data/series/sr_23/sr23_028.pdf (seen 3 May 2010).

406. *Ibid.*

§2. Public Policy and Private Motivations

282. Nonmarital cohabitation has long existed, and for a variety of reasons. Some people want to marry but are legally unable to marry, so they cohabit instead. Some people are legally able to marry but do not want to sacrifice certain material benefits of nonmarital status. (For instance, some American tax laws and some government benefit programs impose a "marriage penalty" in the form of higher taxes or reduced benefits for a married couple than for two individuals who are unmarried).[407] Some people choose to cohabit without marriage in order to "make a statement" showing their rejection of the conventionality or social orthodoxy of marriage. Some people want to marry but their partners will not marry, so these people cohabit nonmaritally in the belief that it is the next best thing to (and hopefully a preliminary to) real marriage. But probably the major reason for nonmarital cohabitation in contemporary America is fear of the failure of marriage. The current young adult generation is the first generation of children of no-fault divorce to reach the marriage age. Having experienced abuse within or the breakup of their parents' marriage or their own prior marriage, many of this generation and their parents are wary of marriage as an institution.[408] Nonmarital cohabitation seems to offer an alternative to marriage, or a trial quasi-marriage, to some people who seek the benefits of marital intimacy without the risk of stifling marital obligations or the risk of formal divorce.

283. The practice of couples living together in civilized society without marriage probably has been discouraged as long as it has existed. While there are many ways that nonmarital cohabitation poses risks to individuals and to society, underlying all of the utilitarian arguments against it are fundamental concerns about human nature and social order. Although there are exceptions, human nature generally seems to require the kind of commitment associated with marriage in order to maintain and support the communitarian ideals associated with coupling. The practice of nonmarital cohabitation might undermine the commitment to marriage.[409] Casual or uncommitted coupling generally produces serious disorder for individuals and society—tragic consequences of broken promises, failed expectations, economic dislocation, and the abandoned semi-orphans and orphans. Children raised by cohabiting adults experience a socioeconomic environment closer to that of single-parent families than that of married families.[410] They are more likely to experience poverty in the nonmarital home, to be victims of child abuse, to be exposed to domestic violence, to drug use, and to alcohol abuse, and to experience the breakup of the family.

---

407. W. Bradford Wilcox, Joseph P. Price & Angela Rachidi, *Marriage Penalized: Does Social Welfare Policy Affect Family Formation?* Institute for Family Studies (2016).

408. W.G. Axinn & A. Thornton, *The Relationship Between Cohabitation and Divorce: Selectivity or Causal Influence*, 29 Demography 357 (1992).

409. W.G. Axinn & A. Thornton, *The Relationship Between Cohabitation and Divorce: Selectivity or Causal Influence*, 29 Demography 357 (1992).

410. *Economic Resources Lag Among Children Whose Parents Are Cohabiting*, 29 Fam. Plan. Perspectives 143–144 (1997).

§3. NONMARITAL COHABITATION IN LAW

I. Legality of Nonmarital Cohabitation

284. While nonmarital cohabitation has become widely accepted in the United States, at least among young adults, it is still not fully accepted in the law. While criminal laws that prohibit sexual relations (fornication[411] or adultery)[412] among persons who are not married are seldom (and arguably might never be constitutionally) enforced—usually only when there has been an outrageous breach of social tolerance. Some proponents of extramarital sexual relations assert that laws forbidding fornication, adultery, or cohabitation are unconstitutional,[413] though in several cases the Supreme Court or some of its justices have explicitly approved of such laws.[414] When the Supreme Court invalidated a Texas sodomy law, in *Lawrence v. Texas,* [415] it was careful to distinguish such matters as marriage, incest and adultery; since marriage remains available to most heterosexual couples who wish to live together, arguably heterosexual nonmarital cohabitation might be upheld, but in all states non-enforcement of fornication laws and other anti-cohabitation laws is the practice, if not the law and deference to the private sexual preferences of unrelated adults prevails.

---

411. Arizona Revised Statutes §13-1409 (1994) ("open and notorious cohabitation or adultery"); Colorado Revised Statutes Annotated §§18-6-201 to 203 (West, 1994) (crime of "bigamy" includes mere "cohabitation" while still married to another; "cohabitation" means living together "under the representation of being married"); Florida Statutes Annotated §798.02 (Harrison, 1991) ("lewdly and lasciviously associate and cohabit together"); New Mexico Statutes Annotated §30-10-2 (Michie 1978) ("Unlawful cohabitation consists of persons who are not married to each other cohabiting together as man and wife."); North Dakota Century Code §12.1-20-10 (1993) (living "openly and notoriously ... as a married couple without being married ... "); Virginia Code Annotated §18.2-345 (Michie, 1994) ("lewdly and lasciviously associate and cohabit together"); West Virginia Code §61-8-4 (1994) ("lewdly and lasciviously associate and cohabit together"); and M.E. Markey, *The Price of Landlord's "Free" Exercise of Religion: Tenant's Right to Discrimination—Free Housing and Privacy*, 22 Fordham Urb. L. J. 699, 752 (1995) (fornication is still a crime in approximately one-fourth of the states).
412. Alabama Code §13A-13-2 (1994) (sexual intercourse by married person with one not spouse and "lives in cohabitation" with that person); Florida Statutes Annotated §798.01 (Harrison, 1991) ("lives in open state of adultery"); Rhode Island General Laws §11-6-2 (1993); Utah Code Annotated §76-7-103 (1994); *State v. Thompson*, 31 Utah 228, 87 P. 709 (1906) (each act of sexual intercourse a separate offense); and West Virginia Code §61-8-3 (1994) (includes both adultery and fornication).
413. E. Kandoian, *Cohabitation, Common Law Marriage, and the Possibility of a Shared Moral Life*, 75 Georgetown L. J. 1829 (1987).
414. *Eisenstadt v. Baird*, 405 US 438, 448 (1972) (the state constitutionally may regulate extramarital and premarital sexual relations); *Ibid.* at 449 (state legislatures have "a full measure of discretion in fashioning means to prevent fornication"); *Griswold v. Connecticut*, 381 US 479, 498 (1965) (Goldberg, J., concurring) ("The State of Connecticut does have statutes, the constitutionality of which is beyond doubt, which prohibit adultery and fornication."); *Ibid.* at 505 (White, J., concurring) ("[T]he statute is said to serve the State's policy against all forms of promiscuous or illicit sexual relationships, be they premarital or extramarital, concededly a permissible and legitimate legislative goal.").
415. 539 U.S. 558 (2003).

285. While direct criminal prosecution of nonmarital cohabitation is rare and constitutionally dubious, the civil law continues to distinguish cohabitation from marriage. The legal recognition of nonmarital cohabitation agreements has been compared to the antiquated and discredited doctrine of "concubinage."[416] In only a few states may cohabiting couples claim economic rights deriving from the cohabitation relationship. In contrast, marriage confers a host of economic rights and claims upon the parties, including property division and alimony derivative from the relationship—as distinct from economic rights arising from contract or quasi-contract or some equitable doctrine such as unjust enrichment or quantum meruit. No American state extends full marital rights and benefits to cohabiting nonmarital couples.[417] Few states provide any benefits by statute specifically for unmarried cohabitants. Professor Margaret Mahoney has noted that "the relationships established between cohabiting, opposite sex couples are not regarded as family status relationships for most legal purposes."[418] Professor Tom Oldham has noted, in his review of the status of nonmarital cohabitation in the United States, that "because in most states cohabitants have no 'status'-like rights, regardless of the duration of the cohabitation or whether the relationship was childless or minor children were in the household, an 'unmarried' couple can cohabit for a long period and raise children and still have no rights or obligations (other than child support) when the relationship ends."[419]

II. Agreements among Cohabiting Couples

286. One way the law discouraged nonmarital cohabitation at common law was to deny enforcement to agreements regarding cohabiting arrangements, including agreements to share or co-own property, if any part of the agreement contemplated meretricious (i.e., sexual) relations. That rule has changed significantly in most states in the past forty years.

A. *The* Marvin *Rule*

287. In *Marvin v. Marvin*,[420] a woman who had lived for six years as the nonmarital cohabitant of a movie actor and then had been rejected by him asserted a claim against the actor for a share of his property based upon an alleged "oral agreement" to share equally all the property accumulated by the efforts of either of them. Because the cohabitation agreement was deemed to violate public policy, the trial court had ruled that as a matter of law the claim had to be rejected. The California

416. H.D. Krause, *Family Law in a Nutshell* 79 (West 3d ed., 1995).
417. *See*, e.g., M. M. Mahoney, *Forces Shaping the Law of Cohabitation for Opposite Sex Couples*, 7 J. L. & Fam. Stud. 135 (2005); A. L. Estin, *Ordinary Cohabitation*, 76 Notre Dame L. Rev. 1381 (2001); J. T. Oldham, *Lessons from Jerry Hall v. Mick Jagger Regarding U.S. Regulation of Heterosexual Cohabitants or, Can't Get No Satisfaction*, 76 Notre Dame L. Rev. 1409 (2001).
418. M. M. Mahoney, *supra* n. 417, at 160.
419. Oldham, *supra* n. 417, at 1411.
420. 557 P.2d 106 (Cal. 1976).

Supreme Court reversed, holding that express or implied contracts between nonmarital cohabitants were enforceable, and only those parts of such contracts (if any) that were directly founded upon the consideration of meretricious sexual relations would violate public policy, and further ruled that partnership, joint venture, tacit understanding, quantum meruit, or equitable remedies such as constructive or resulting trust could also provide the basis for a claim arising out of nonmarital cohabitation. Thus, claims for "palimony" were born.

288. The *Marvin* decision had a tremendous impact upon social perception of the legitimacy of nonmarital cohabitation—not only in California but throughout the United States. It was read by the general public as an endorsement of nonmarital cohabitation, and stimulated a mini-explosion of both the practice of nonmarital cohabitation and the filing of palimony claims throughout the country.

289. In actual practice, *Marvin* had very narrow doctrinal impact upon the law of California. For example, the plaintiff in the *Marvin* case was unable to establish at trial any of the possible claims suggested by the California Supreme Court, and recovered nothing in her suit against her former cohabitant. While the *Marvin* case is often cited, it is seldom successfully invoked as the basis for recovery of claims arising out of nonmarital cohabitation. The primary reason for this is that the facts needed to provide the basis for legal recovery (taking property away from a legal owner and giving it to someone else) are very hard to prove in the ambiguities and intentional informalities of nonmarital cohabitation. Since "heart-balm actions" (lawsuits for recovery after the ending of a romantic relationship) are unpopular (even outlawed in California) there is some suspicion of such claims. Nonetheless, in legal doctrine and theory a former nonmarital cohabitant may in some circumstances assert a claim for recovery of "palimony" arising out of nonmarital cohabitation or agreement in California.

290. The *Marvin* approach liberally allowing the assertion of "palimony" claims by former nonmarital cohabitants has been followed in several other states.[421] Thus, some states allow the assertions of "palimony" claims based on both express and implied contract, as well as on several theories or doctrines of equitable relief.

291. A few states have carried the *Marvin* approach even further. While *Marvin* rejected the notion that the nonmarital relationship itself gave rise to property or economic rights (a form of quasi-"common law" marriage which form of marriage the California legislature had firmly rejected and California case law had steadfastly denied), a few courts in other states have experimented with allowing such

421. *Boland v. Catalano*, 521 A.2d 142 (Conn. 1987); *Suggs v. Norris*, 364 S.E.2d 159 (N.C. App. 1988); C. Bruch, *Cohabitation in the Common Law Countries a Decade After Marvin: Settled In or Moving Ahead?*, 22 U. California at Davis L. Rev. 717 (1989).

economic claims based on the meretricious relationship.[422] The fairness of imposing a marriage-like obligation or duty upon parties who deliberately chose to avoid the formal status of marriage with its bag of legal duties and responsibilities has been questioned.[423]

B. The Hewitt *Rule*

292. Three years after *Marvin*, the Illinois Supreme Court reached the opposite conclusion in a case presenting a much more compelling case for granting a remedy in *Hewitt v. Hewitt*.[424] When they were students in college, a man and woman had sexual relations and the woman became pregnant. They agreed to live as husband and wife, the man telling the woman that no formal ceremony was necessary, and allegedly agreeing to share his life, future, earnings, and property with her. They lived as a conventional married couple for fifteen years, had three children, and the woman fulfilled the supporting role of wife and homemaker as well as assisting in his pedodontia office. When she filed for divorce, he responded arguing that they were not married and she amended her complaint to assert a *Marvin*-type palimony claim based on an alleged oral contract. The Illinois Supreme Court held that no property rights accrue as a matter of law to nonmarital cohabitants because the state legislature had outlawed common law marriage, that it would violate public policy to enforce a contract between cohabitants if sexual relations form part of the consideration, and that is up to the legislature to create the right of nonmarital cohabitants to recover based on equitable theories.

293. Thus, contrasting with the liberal, receptive *Marvin* approach of California, the Illinois approach in *Hewitt* was strict and strictly traditional. The quasi-wife plaintiff in *Hewitt* presented a much stronger case for judicial relief than the adulterous *paramour* plaintiff in *Marvin*. In more than one-fifth of the states, Mrs. Hewitt would have recovered as a common law wife, and in others she might have recovered on some theory of *estoppel*, reliance, contract, or unjust enrichment. The reason why she should not have been able to claim equitable relief was not clearly explained by the Illinois Supreme Court.[425]

294. However, the practical differences between the *Marvin* and *Hewitt* approaches are rather modest. Factually, the plaintiffs seeking recovery based upon nonmarital cohabitation ultimately lost in both cases—as a matter of law in Illinois and as a matter of fact in California. And the doctrinal separation between the cases is also modest; both states still refuse to enforce contracts which violate public policy, and it still violates public policy in both states to use meretricious sexual

422. *See Koher v. Morgan*, 968 P.2d 920 (Wash. Ct. App. 1998) (application of community property law to heterosexual couple who lived together seventeen years).

423. S. Lifshitz, *Married Against Their Will? Toward a Pluralist Regulation of Spousal Relationships*, 66 Wash. & Lee L. Rev. 1565 (2009).

424. 394 N.E.2d 1204 (Ill. 1979).

425. *Ibid.* (The court simply noted that it would invite many lawsuits in which very difficult factual questions (who is lying) would be raised).

relations as consideration for an agreement. In California, the void part of the contract is surgically separated from the rest of the contract and only the specific exchange for sexual services is unenforceable, whereas in Illinois the entire contract is tainted and rendered void if sexual services constituted any part of the consideration. Nevertheless, the *Hewitt* rule against enforcement of cohabitation agreements is generally presented as the conceptual opposite of the *Marvin* rule. In 2014, the Illinois Court of Appeals repudiated the *Hewitt* rule.[426]

C. *Intermediate Positions*

295. Most states have rejected both the *Marvin* and *Hewitt* approaches to claims for a share of property arising out of nonmarital cohabitation agreements or arrangements, and have adopted some intermediate position. They often are willing to award some share of property to the economically dependent former cohabitant, but they are cautious about establishing a narrow basis for recovery because of concerns about proof and about opening floodgates of (sometimes vindictive) litigation.[427]

296. Some states allow enforcement of a property sharing agreement between parties if based upon an express written contract;[428] others also enforce express oral contracts but not implied contracts or other claims.[429] Meretricious sexual consideration generally is severed, voiding the specific exchange but not the entire contract. Other states allow both contractual and some equitable remedies.[430] Other states extend quasi-marital or community property principles rejecting both Illinois' and California's strict rejection of common law marriage principles.[431] Massachusetts, for instance, recognized an agreement between nonmarital cohabitants if valid under normal contract principles and sexual services are not the dominant consideration for the agreement.[432]

§4. Recovery of Other Quasi-marital Legal Benefits

297. Property division is not the only valuable economic benefit flowing from marital status. However, it is the only significant benefit that nonmarital cohabitants have had widespread success in asserting (though not always in proving). Nonmarital cohabitants who have asserted claims to other economic benefits of marriage have achieved only limited and inconsistent success. The prevailing view is that

426. *Blumenthal v. Brewer*, 2014 IL App 1st 132250 (Ill. App. 2014).
427. J.D. Gregory, P.N. Swisher & S.L. Scheible, *Understanding Family Law* 20–22 (1993).
428. Minnesota Statutes §§513.075, 513.076.
429. *Tapley v. Tapley*, 449 A.2d 1218 (N.H. 1982); *Carnes v. Sheldon*, 311 N.W.2d 747 (Mich. App. 1981); and *Morone v. Morone*, 413 N.W.2d 1154 (N.Y. 1980).
430. *Watts v. Watts*, 405 N.W.2d 303 (Wis. 1987); and *Pickens v. Pickens*, 490 So.2d 872 (Miss. 1986).
431. *Suraleff v. Donnelly*, 817 P.2d 764 (Or. App. 1991); and *Eaton v. Johnston*, 681 P.2d 606 (Kan. 1984).
432. *See Wilcox v. Trautz*, 693 N.E.2d 141 (Mass 1998).

nonmarital cohabitants may not recover workers compensation benefits for injuries to their partners,[433] or for loss of consortium.[434] However, some states have allowed recovery for injuries to some relational interests.[435]

298. The critical question is whether nonmarital cohabitants acquire a legal status as cohabitants, arising from the relationship. Marriage is a status from which flows many legal rights, duties, and benefits. It is difficult to attribute status to informal relations between parties who choose not to marry, who reject the opportunity to assume marital status. Indeed, that might be seen as infringing on the parties' autonomy. Thus, most of the cases in which some quasi-marital status rights are obtained by nonmarital cohabitants involve the ad hoc, narrow extension of specific rights rather than the extension of status (and status rights) generally. The prevailing position in American states and courts is that nonmarital relationships do not create marriage-like economic rights, duties, and obligations. The only exception concerns duties to support (and corresponding non-economic right to establish and maintain a relationship with) nonmarital children.

§5. Same-Sex Quasi-marital Relationships

299. Persons of the same-sex who wish to cohabit on some long-term partnership basis are now able to marry in all states. Thus, they can acquire marital status and the benefits associated with it. Previous to this change in the definition of marriage, gay and lesbian advocates argued that they should be provided some equivalent legal status especially in the states that do not allow same-sex marriage.

300. Some courts had held that same-sex partners may obtain some particular benefits comparable to marital benefits. For an early example, in *Braschi v. Stahl Associates Co.*,[436] the New York Court of Appeals ruled that a long-term same-sex cohabitant partner of a deceased lessor of a rent-controlled apartment in New York City was entitled to statutory protection against eviction (or having to pay higher rent) as a member of the decedent's "family." The court emphasized the functional familial nature of the relationship, and that the parties' "relationship [was] long term and characterized by an emotional and financial commitment and interdependence."[437] In a few other cases, some courts in other states have recognized very narrow relational rights for same-sex partners in very fact-specific contexts.[438] The case did not create a general marriage-like status for same-sex cohabitants, despite

433. J.D. Gregory, *supra* at 24.
434. *Elden v. Shelden*, 758 P.2d 582 (Cal. 1988) (no consortium claim); and *Curry v. Caterpillar Tractor Co.*, 577 F. Supp. 991 (E.D. Pa. 1984) (no consortium claim).
435. *Dunphy v. Gregor*, 642 A.2d 372 (N.J. 1994) (engaged cohabitant may sue for emotional distress caused by witnessing death of cohabitant); and *Soto v. Montanez*, 578 N.Y.S.2d 758 (App. Div. 1991) (cohabitant may recover under dram shop act).
436. 543 N.E.2d 49 (N.Y. 1989).
437. *Braschi*, 543 N.Y.2d at 54.
438. *In re Guardianship of Kowalski*, 478 N.W.2d 790 (Minn. App. 1992) (guardianship to partner rather than parents).

the popularity of that notion with legal academics.[439] Other courts had refused to extend any significant relational rights to same-sex nonmarital cohabitants.[440]

301. Some legislative bodies created some sort of status for same-sex partners. That status is generally called "same-sex domestic partnership" or "civil union." These laws generally concerned employment benefits (such as health insurance, retirement benefits, etc.). Though very popular with legal writers,[441] they were not particularly popular with American lawmakers, who may be concerned about disproportionate costs. The number of American jurisdictions (states, counties, and cities) and private companies that offer domestic partnership benefits were increasing, though.

302. In 2015, the Supreme Court required each state to recognize same-sex marriages which may have the effect of limiting interest in the creation of quasi-marital statuses.

---

439. M.N. Cameli, Note, *Extending Family Benefits to Gay Men and Lesbian Women*, 68 Chicago-Kent L. Rev. 447 (1992).

440. *Coon v. Joseph*, 237 Cal. Rptr. 873 (Cal. App. 1987).

441. W.V. Vetter, *Restrictions on Equal Treatment of Unmarried Domestic Partners*, 5 Boston University Pub. International L. J. (1995); C.A. Bowman & B.M. Cornish, Note, *A More Perfect Union: A Legal and Social Analysis of Domestic Partnership Ordinances*, 92 Columbia L. Rev. 1164 (1992).

Chapter 4. Filiation

303. Historically, the legal status of the parent-child relationship was not primarily established upon the basis of biology, but on the basis of marriage between the child's parents. In the past, the legal status of a child at birth substantially affected the legal consequences of the parent-child relationship, especially between child and father. Today, the detrimental consequences have greatly lessened due to decisions rendered by the United States Supreme Court and to society's acceptance of childbirth out of wedlock.[442]

§1. Children Born in Wedlock

I. Definition of Legitimacy and Its Effect

304. The common law definition of a child who has the status of legitimacy is a child who was born to parents who were married to each other at either the time of the child's conception or the child's birth. This traditional definition continues to be valid unless modified by statute. All states have modified the common law so that a child born out of wedlock is legitimated if his parents marry one another after the child's birth and the father acknowledges the child. All states have also modified the common law so that children, who are born into marriages which are later annulled or are invalid, retain their legitimacy status. States may also have specific judicial proceedings for legitimation.

305. Unlike the common law, the current version of the Uniform Parentage Act (UPA 2000, amended),[443] as well as its previous versions, bases the legal parent-child relationship not on the marital status of the child's parents, but on the parent-child relationship itself, the biological relationship.

306. The status of legitimacy confers on the child all the legal rights and privileges of the parent-child relationship and imposes on the parent all the legal rights and responsibilities of the parent-child relationship.

II. Presumption of Legitimacy

307. One of the strongest presumptions at common law was the presumption that a child born to a married woman was presumed to be the legitimate child of the woman's husband. All states retain this presumption. Overcoming the presumption

442. The social and moral values of Americans continue to change. Nonmarital cohabitation continues to gain wide acceptance by society. The stigma of having a child born out of wedlock is disappearing, and more and more nonmarital couples are having and rearing children.
443. *Uniform Laws Annotated* No. 9B (amended 2002) p. 15 (Supp. 2008) (This Act is promulgated by the Uniform Commissioners of Law to encourage uniformity among the states as each state has jurisdiction over the law of filiation.).

was almost an impossible task at common law.[444] With the modern use of blood tests, however, the presumption may be more readily overcome. Statutes of limitations and equitable doctrines may still prevent the proof of nonpaternity by either the husband or wife. States that recognize same sex marriage or have enacted civil union laws or state domestic partnership laws would also apply the presumption to treat the child born to one of them as the legitimate child of the other.[445] The District of Columbia's "Domestic Partnership Judicial Determination of Parentage Act of 2009" automatically recognizes both members of a domestic partnership, whether heterosexual or same-sex, as parents of a child born to them and their names will appear on the birth certificate. If the mother, however under the District of Columbia law, was not married or in a domestic partnership at the time the child was conceived or born or between conception and birth, the other parent shall be entered on the birth certificate if they have signed a voluntary agreement. Issues regarding the establishment of parenthood because reproduction occurred with the assistance of technology are discussed under Assisted Reproduction. Whether the presumption of legitimacy and spousal parentage (or adoption) must extend to married same-sex couples has not yet been addressed by the Supreme Court. While the Court has mandated that same-sex couples must be allowed to marry (enter into a state relationship for adults) parenting is different than marriage, and the state interest in children being raised by a mother and a father when possible may justify a preference for or exclusive right of dual-gendered couple parenting.

§2. Children Born Out of Wedlock

I. History of Illegitimacy and Its Effect

308. The common law was very harsh in its treatment of a child born out of wedlock. The child was said to be *filius nullus*, the child of no one. The following reasons have been given for the common law's treatment of children born out of wedlock: (1) to provide certainty in the law as it pertains to paternity, (2) to avoid fraudulent claims of paternity, (3) to facilitate the administration of decedents' estates, (4) to protect the welfare of children by encouraging their parents to marry, and (5) to establish a preference for the institution of marriage.

309. The major detriments resulting from a child being born out of wedlock at common law affected the child's support and inheritance rights from his or her father. At common law, the paternity suit developed to provide support for the child by imposing the duty of support on the father once paternity had been established.

444. At common law, the presumption was said to be overcome only if the husband was beyond the seven seas. *See also*, *Michael H. v. Gerald D.*, 491 US 110 (1989).

445. *Adoption of a Minor*, No. SJC-11797 (Mass. 2015); *Gartner v. Iowa Dep't of Pub. Health*, 830 N.W.2d 335 (Iowa 2013).

II. Constitutional Requirements

A. *Constitutional Rights of Children Born Out of Wedlock*

310. The modern reasons for the law's discrimination against a child born out of wedlock are (1) to encourage marriage, (2) to avoid fraudulent claims of paternity, and (3) to facilitate the administration of decedents' estates.

311. Beginning in the 1960s, the United States Supreme Court, in a series of important decisions, held that as a general rule, it is unconstitutional under the due process clause and the equal protection clauses of the Fifth and the Fourteenth Amendments of the United States Constitution to discriminate against children on the basis of illegitimacy unless there are important state interests and the discrimination is narrowly tailored to accomplish those interests.[446] The Court has completely rejected the state interest of encouraging marriage because stigmatizing children is not a justifiable means to achieve that end, however proper it may be. The viability of the state interest to avoid fraudulent claims becomes more uncertain with the reliability of the scientific evidence in proving the probability of paternity. Similarly, the state interest of facilitating the administration of decedents' estates becomes less important if paternity may be readily proved.

B. *Constitutional Rights of Their Parents*

312. Although, originally at English common law, the child of unmarried persons was the child of "no one," the legal relationship between mother and child soon developed, where the child was the child of the mother and her relatives. As a general rule, the American states did not deny the child the full parent-child legal relationship between mother and child. The impact of the constitutional decisions, therefore, has had slight impact on the rights of mothers.[447]

313. Most states did not recognize the parental rights of fathers of children born out of wedlock prior to the decisions of the United States Supreme Court. That Court now recognizes that fathers of children born of out wedlock have constitutionally protected parental rights, protected by both the Equal Protection and Due

446. The Supreme Court has determined that illegitimacy is a suspect classification that is scrutinized under heightened scrutiny. This is an intermediate standard of review between the strict scrutiny standard accorded to race and the rational basis standard, which gives greater deference to the constitutionality of a statute.

447. Interestingly, the first two cases in which the Supreme Court held unconstitutional statutes discriminating on the basis of illegitimacy dealt with the unusual statutes discriminating against the mother-child relationship. *Levy v. Louisiana*, 391 US 68 (1968); and *Glona v. American Guarantee and Liability Insurance Co.*, 391 US 73 (1968).

Process Clauses under the Fifth and Fourteenth Amendments.[448] The states, therefore, must protect these rights as defined by the Supreme Court. The constitutionally protected parental rights of unwed fathers are predicated on their actual relationship with the child: the "mere existence of a biological link does not merit equivalent constitutional protection."[449] Even if unwed fathers have established a relationship with the child, the Supreme Court has upheld the traditional presumption of legitimacy that the father of the child is the wife's husband.[450]

314. Most states do not statutorily provide that the father of a child born out of wedlock or his relatives may inherit from the child unless the child is treated as the child of the father for inheritance purposes.[451]

III. Establishing Paternity

315. The child born in wedlock immediately has the advantage of having a presumptive legal father because of the presumption of legitimacy. The child born out of wedlock must establish paternity, however. Establishing paternity does not necessarily create the full legal parent-child relationship between child and father. Except for imposing the duty of support on the father and the right of the child to receive support, states vary as to the effect of establishing paternity on other rights, such as inheritance rights.

316. It has only been recently that establishing maternity has arisen as an issue with the advent of artificial reproductive technology (ART). Prior to the use of this technology, maternity was proved through the visible physical condition of pregnancy and a third-party witness identifying which woman gave birth to the child.

A. Legitimation

317. Legitimation is the process of legitimating a child born out of wedlock. This process varies among the states. The states may recognize one or more of these processes. Some states, for example, have a judiciary proceeding for legitimating a child. States may have specific rules to legitimate the child; such as, if the parents marry and the father orally or in writing acknowledges the child as his child. Legitimating a child creates the full legal parent-child relationship.

318. Over half of the states have adopted all or parts of the Uniform Parentage Act (1987)[452] or the Uniform Parentage Act 2000 (amended 2002)[453] Once the

448. Beginning with *Stanley v. Illinois*, 405 US 645 (1972), the Supreme Court of the United States has recognized that fathers have some constitutionally protected parental rights.
449. *Lehr v. Robertson*, 463 US 248 (1983).
450. *Michael H. v. Gerald D.*, 491 US 110 (1989).
451. *See*, e.g., Maryland Code Annotated, Estates and Trusts, §3-108 (Replacement Volume 2001).
452. *Uniform Laws Annotated*, No. 9B, (1987), p. 296.

father has been identified, this Act views all children on equal terms as to their legal relationship to their parents. The Act provides a scheme to identify the child's father, starting with the presumption that the husband is the father of a child born to a married woman.

B. Acknowledgment

319. The father may acknowledge paternity in writing. Acknowledgment does not necessarily mean the child has been legitimated. At a minimum, acknowledgment provides support and inheritance rights. Many states require the husband of a married woman to consent to such an acknowledgment.

320. The father may informally acknowledge the child if he has "openly and notoriously" recognized the child to be his.

C. The Paternity Proceeding: Procedural Requirements

321. The paternity suit is a judicial proceeding to establish paternity. Initially, the proceeding was to establish paternity for support purposes only. In some states, this proceeding may also be a method to legitimate the child or provide inheritance rights.

322. The proceeding is a civil proceeding although, in a few jurisdictions, it may still reflect quasi-criminal elements.[454] The court must have in personam (personal) jurisdiction over the father.[455] Most states require proof of paternity by the standard of the preponderance of the evidence. Others require the standard of clear and convincing evidence. A jury trial is allowed in many states. The judgment of paternity, at a minimum, establishes paternity and provides for support of the child. The judgment may also contain an order for payment of expenses connected with the pregnancy and the birth of the child as well as court expenses. The judgment may also contain provisions for custody and visitation.

323. The vast majority of paternity cases are commenced by the mother or a state child support agency on behalf of the mother. All states have enacted a statute of limitations of 18 years.

453. *Uniform Laws Annotated*, No. 9B (amended 2002) p. 15 (Supp.2008).

454. The paternity proceeding developed at common law to help the state put the burden of support on the child's father and not on the state. The proceeding originated as a criminal proceeding: the father was prosecuted for the crime of bastardy.

455. In a few cases, the father may have standing under paternity statutes to establish his paternity when the mother does not want to establish the child's paternity. Under such circumstances, the mother would be the defendant.

D. Scientific Evidence

324. Scientific evidence in the form of blood and other tissue tests is the most significant evidence in deciding paternity cases. The three traditional systems of testing were the traditional human blood and tissue typing system, the human leukocyte antigen (HLA) system, and the DNA system. The DNA system has emerged as the exclusive test used in deciding paternity. Courts accept the DNA testing system as reliable scientific evidence either under the theory that the procedure is generally accepted in the scientific community and is beyond the experimental stage or under the relevancy theory.

325. The DNA test is based upon the theory that the child inherits one-half of his or her genes from each parent. The test involves matching the child's genes with those of the mother and the putative father. The test provides information from which the experts may calculate the mathematical probability of a specific putative father's paternity in relationship to a child and the mother. Because these statements of the mathematical probabilities may be confusing to the jury, the court may deny their admission on the basis that the evidence will be prejudicial or confusing. This evidence may also not be admitted because the scientific testing for this specific case was not properly performed.

326. If the DNA test excludes the probability that the putative father is not the father, most jurisdictions hold that the exclusion is a conclusive presumption of non-paternity. If the putative father is not excluded, depending upon the strength of the statements of the mathematical probabilities, the court may admit such evidence. The United States Supreme Court has held that indigent fathers in paternity proceedings are entitled to blood testing at state expense. This Court has not held that they must be provided legal counsel at state expense. Some states, however, have held these indigent fathers are entitled to be represented by legal counsel at state expense.

E. Disestablishment of Paternity

327. Some states either by statute or by case law allow fathers to disestablish paternity, based usually on paternity fraud, when a former husband or nonmarital father learns through genetic testing that he is not the biological father. In the majority of such cases, courts will terminate future support payments, but are divided on whether to collect arrearages. No court has allowed the man to be reimbursed for support already paid.

IV. Support and Settlements

328. In order for parents or guardians to receive certain federal welfare funds, federal legislation requires the states enforce the parental duty of support when the parents are separated.[456] Paternity proceedings have greatly benefitted from this legislation. As a result, paternity proceedings are, more often than not, timely commenced and enforced.

329. The amount of support ordered should also be consistent with the amount ordered in a judgment of support for a child born in wedlock. The Supreme Court has held that states may not constitutionally discriminate against children born out of wedlock unless there is an important state interest.[457]

330. In the past, courts allowed settlement of paternity cases, where the accused father could settle the case for a lump-sum amount for the child's support and not have to admit paternity. Settlements were allowed because of the difficulty in proving paternity. They were also allowed in order to provide some support for the child by settling the case. Settlements for children born in wedlock are generally not allowed during their minority. Such settlements in paternity cases may, therefore, be unconstitutional since they are not allowed for children born in wedlock.[458]

§3. Regulating the Creation of the Parent-Child Relationship

I. Procreation Rights

A. *Right to Procreate*

331. The Supreme Court of the United States has dealt with the "right to procreate" more often in cases about "the right not to procreate," namely, in sterilization, abortion, and contraceptive cases. If one has the constitutionally protected right not to procreate, then logically one has the constitutionally protected right to procreate. In *Skinner v. Oklahoma*,[459] a sterilization case, the Supreme Court held that procreation was a basic civil right and strict scrutiny was the standard of review to determine the constitutionality of the statute.

332. If the Supreme Court's decisions regarding the constitutional use of contraceptives and abortion are also recognized as "the right to procreate" cases, then the right to procreate is an individual right of both married and unmarried persons. The right to procreate is one of the protected interests under the constitutionally protected right of privacy.[460] The Supreme Court's decision in *Lawrence v. Texas* held that adults could engage in private, consensual sexual conduct in the exercise of

456. *See*, e.g., The Family Support Act of 1988, Public Law 100-485, §103, 102 Stat. 2348 (1988).
457. *Gomez v. Perez*, 409 US 535 (1973).
458. *Dones by Dones-Carter*, 534 N.W.2d 221 (Michigan Court of Appeals 1995, appeal denied 552 N.W.2d 170 (Michigan 1996)).
459. 316 U.S. 532 (1942).
460. 316 US 535 (1942).

their liberty under the Due Process Clause of the Fourteenth Amendment when it held unconstitutional a Texas statute criminally prohibiting consensual same-sex sexual acts.[461]

B. Sterilization

333. Sterilization cases involve either involuntary sterilization, where the state's power to mandate this procedure is at issue; or, voluntary sterilization, where the state's power to deny an individual the right to choose this procedure is at issue.

334. The United States Supreme Court has held that sterilization of an individual involves an individual's right to procreation[462] and has also characterized that right as a basic civil right, subject to strict scrutiny. About a quarter of the states continue to have compulsory sterilization laws regarding mentally retarded persons.[463] Some courts have determined that they have jurisdiction over sterilization, without statutory authorization, under the court's inherent *parens patriae* power.[464] Courts usually do not have authority to order the sterilization of a mentally incompetent person on social and economic grounds, rather than on medical grounds.[465]

335. Courts have upheld an individual's right to choose sterilization if the individual is competent.[466] Sterilization for contraceptive purposes is legal in all states.

461. *Lawrence v. Texas*, 539 U.S. 558 (2003). " … the Due Process Clause gives them the full right to engage in their conduct without intervention of the government. It is a promise of the Constitution that there is a realm of personal liberty which the government may not enter. The Texas statute furthers no legitimate state interest which can justify its intrusion into the personal and private life of the individual."
462. In *Skinner v. Oklahoma*, 316 US 535 (1942), a statute requiring the sterilization of only certain types of criminals and not of others was challenged on equal protection grounds. The Court held that such statutes must be reviewed under the standard of strict scrutiny since the classification was based upon procreation, a basic civil right.
463. In an earlier case, where litigants challenged a statute mandating sterilization of an insane or retarded person, the Supreme Court held that the Constitution required only notice and a hearing, and that the sterilization was not arbitrary or punishment for a crime. *Bell v. Buck*, 274 US 200 (1927). After *Skinner*, it would seem that this case is overruled and the higher standard of review should apply.
464. *In re* Grady, 426 A.2d 467 (N.J. 1981).
465. *Frazier v. Levi*, 440 S. W. 2d 393 (Tex. Civ. App. Houston 1st Dist. 1969).
466. *Hathaway v. Worcester City Hospital*, 475 F.2d 701 (1st Cir. 1973).

II. Contraception and Abortion

A. Contraception

336. The Supreme Court of the United States has held that there is a constitutionally protected right of privacy. *Griswold v. Connecticut* [467] was the first case recognizing this right. In that case, the Supreme Court held that a married couple had a protected privacy interest in the use of contraceptives.

337. The United States Supreme Court has extended the constitutionally protected right to use contraceptives to unmarried persons[468] and to minors.[469] However, the court decision recognizing the right of minors to engage in sexual behavior outside of marriage and use contraceptives in that practice was only a plurality decision, and some uncertainty surrounds the extent to which unmarried minors have a constitutional right to engage in extramarital sexual behavior.

B. Abortion

338. The Supreme Court of the United States recognized that a woman had a right to have an abortion in *Roe v. Wade*.[470] A woman does not need the consent of the would-be father, even if he is her husband.[471] A minor child has the right to an abortion, without parental consent, if she is "mature."[472] The Supreme Court has, however, not clarified the meaning of "mature." The Supreme Court has also upheld parental consent and parental notification statutes requiring at least consent from one of the parents if there is an adequate "bypass" statute, allowing the minor to bypass the parent and obtain judicial consent.[473]

339. In *Roe v. Wade* [474] the Supreme Court held that a woman's right to have an abortion was rooted in the right of privacy. As such, the Court established a trimester scheme in delineating when the state may regulate abortion. During the first trimester, the abortion issue is left to the woman and her physician. After the first trimester, the state may regulate the abortion procedure to protect maternal health, but not the decision to have an abortion. After viability of the fetus, however, the state may not proscribe abortion except when necessary to protect the life or health of the mother. *Planned Parenthood of Southeastern Pennsylvania v. Casey* is the most recent case to uphold the central holding of *Roe*, that is, a woman's right to

---

467. 381 US 479 (1965).
468. *Eisenstadt v. Baird*, 405 US 438 (1972).
469. *Carey v. Population Services International*, 431 US 678 (1977).
470. 410 US 113 (1973).
471. *Planned Parenthood of Central Missouri v. Danforth*, 428 US 52 (1976); and *Planned Parenthood v. Casey*, 505 US 833 (1992).
472. *Planned Parenthood of Central Missouri v. Danforth*, 428 US 52 (1976).
473. *Planned Parenthood v. Casey*, 505 US 833 (1992).
474. 410 US 113 (1973).

have an abortion.[475] Nevertheless, this plurality decision rejected the trimester framework and imposed an "undue burden test," but retained the distinction between viable and nonviable fetuses.

340. Because access to abortion is deemed a matter of fundamental constitutional right, there are very few significant restrictions of abortion that have been upheld by American courts in recent years. Nevertheless, the following regulations of abortion, in addition to those mentioned above, have been upheld: informed consent requirements that doctors disclose to women adequate information on which they can make a reasonable decision whether or not to have an abortion,[476] including required disclosure of facts of fetal development;[477] restrictions on public funding of abortion;[478] restrictions on post-viability abortions;[479] restrictions limiting performance of abortion to doctors only,[480] and restrictions on a particular abortion procedure, partial birth abortion, and indicated for the first time the rationale that abortion restrictions protect women.[481] In a recent case, the U.S. Supreme Court held that state regulations on safety of abortion clinics were unconstitutional because they put an undue burden on a woman's ability to secure an abortion.[482]

III. Assisted Reproduction

A. *Introduction*

341. Non-coital reproduction is commonplace today because of medical technological advances, generally referred to as Assisted Reproduction Technology (ART). Non-coital reproduction allows infertile persons or persons who cannot bear children to have genetically related children or couples, where one of the partners, is infertile and cannot bear children, to have a child who is biologically related to one of them. It also has enabled gay and lesbian couples to plan and have children that are biologically related to one of the partners. Non-coital reproduction includes artificial insemination, in vitro fertilization, ovum transfer, embryo transfer, surrogacy arrangements, and posthumous reproduction. The legal problems which arise are difficult because they are novel and evade traditional law. Appropriate legislation is needed to determine the law. Moreover, assisted reproduction technology continues to remain largely unregulated by both federal and state governments.

475. 112 S. Ct. 2791 (1992).
476. *Planned Parenthood v. Danforth*, 428 US 52 (1976).
477. *Planned Parenthood v. Casey*, *supra*.
478. *Webster v. Reproductive Health Services*, 492 US 490 (1984).
479. *Ibid.*
480. *Mazurek v. Armstrong*, 520 US 968 (1997).
481. *Gonzales v. Carhart*, 550 US 124 (2007), upholding the constitutionality of the Partial Birth Abortion Ban Act, 18 USC § 1531 (2000 ed., Supp IV).
482. *Whole Woman's Health v. Hellerstedt*, 136 S. Ct. 2292 (2016).

B. Artificial Insemination

342. Artificial insemination describes the procedure by which a woman conceives a child by artificial means. Legal issues only arise if the donor of the semen is not her husband. If the woman is married and the donor is not her husband but the husband has consented to the procedure and it is to be performed by a licensed physician, the law treats the husband as the legal parent of the child in all states by statute or by the doctrine of equitable *estoppel* or by waiver. The donor of the sperm has no legal parental rights under these circumstances. If the husband, however, has not consented, the husband must rebut the presumption that states that the father of a child born to a married woman is presumed to be her husband. The success in rebutting the presumption depends upon the law in the various states.

343. If the woman is unmarried, states vary as to the rights of the sperm donor. Most states grant no legal rights to the donor if the artificial insemination procedure was done by a licensed physician. Statutes following the Uniform Parentage Act grant no legal rights to the donor unless he formally consents to the procedure with the intention to be the parent of the child.[483] If the state has not definitively declared the rights of the donor, the donor would then have parental rights as an unmarried father. Conversely, the woman would have the right to bring a paternity suit if the donor is known. One state would allow the state to seek child support from a known donor.[484]

344. Many donors of sperm are anonymous and wish to have no parental relationship with the child. Many of these anonymous donors deposit sperm in what is known as a "sperm bank" for a fee. The sperm bank, then, has the responsibility of providing the sperm to women or couples, who request sperm for artificial insemination. Along with the recent reform movement to allow adult adopted children to have access to their closed adoption records, more children conceived by artificial insemination are seeking to have disclosure of the identity of their sperm donor or have access to at least their donor's family medical history. Some donors are also agreeing to this disclosure or access to their medical histories. Moreover, some sperm banks are instituting procedures to facilitate access to this information. Women who wish to be single parents often use reproduction by artificial insemination, usually using sperm from an anonymous donor from a sperm bank. A large number of lesbian couples also use this reproductive technique.

C. In Vitro Fertilization

345. In vitro fertilization is the process whereby ova (eggs) are removed from a woman's uterus and fertilized by sperm in a laboratory. The fertilized ovum (embryo) may be re-implanted in the woman's uterus who donated the ovum, or it may be implanted in the uterus of another woman.

---

483. Uniform Parentage Act (UPA)(amended 2002), 9B U.L.A. 295, Section 703 (2001 & Supp. 2003).
484. *In re K.M.H.*, 169 P.3d 1025 (Kan. 2007).

346. With the development of in vitro fertilization, a variety of legal issues arise as to the parent-child relationship, depending upon who the donors and donees are and their legal relationships with each other. If the donors of the ovum and sperm are husband and wife and the fertilized egg is re-implanted in the wife, the child is their legitimate child. In all other husband-wife combinations, either one or both of the donors or the implantee would not be husband and wife.

347. When the implantee is the wife and she gives birth to the child, the child would be the couple's legitimate child under the following circumstances: (1) If the donor of the sperm was not the husband, then the law as it applies to artificial insemination should apply in this situation. (2) If the donor of the ovum is not the wife or the couple is not the donor of both the sperm and ovum, under traditional law, the woman who gives birth to the child is the legal parent and her husband is the child's father. With the development of in vitro fertilization, however, the birth mother may not necessarily be the genetic mother. The rights of genetically related donors of the ova are unclear in most states because there are few statutes governing these cases.[485] Lesbian couples also use all available artificial reproductive techniques, including in vitro fertilization. In some instances one partner may be the genetic provider and the other partner the gestational provider.[486]

348. The fertilized ova may also be frozen for later implantation. Legal issues arise as to their disposition at the donors' death or divorce. The law either is emerging or is non-existent among the various states. For example, one court balanced the rights of the donors in favor of the donor who wanted to avoid procreation when the other donor wished them to be donated.[487] Another court held that a husband's rights and control over the frozen fertilized ova were analogous to the abortion situation and ended with ejaculation.[488]

D. Surrogacy Arrangements

1. Same Gestational and Birth Mother

349. Surrogacy arrangements arise in circumstances where an individual or a couple enters into a contract with a woman.[489] The contract provides that for a fee, the woman will be artificially inseminated by the husband's sperm. When the child is born, she will release the child to the couple and will consent to the child's adoption by the wife. The contract between the parties is usually arranged by an intermediary, for a fee. The birth mother is termed the surrogacy mother although in fact she is the genetic mother.

---

485. *See infra* Chapter 4, s. 3, III (D), regarding surrogacy arrangements.
486. *See*, e.g., Amy Agigian, *Baby Steps: How Lesbian Alternative Insemination Is Changing the World* (Wesleyan University Press 2006).
487. *Davis v. Davis*, 842 S.W.2d 588 (Tenn. 1992).
488. *Kass v. Kass*, 1995 WL 110368 (N.Y. Supp.).
489. These arrangements may be used by men who wish to become parents and are frequently used by gay couples.

350. There are several objections to surrogacy contracts where the birth mother is artificially inseminated. Such contracts are viewed as contracts for the selling and commodification of babies, as exploitative of poor women, and as demeaning to women. A recent survey of surrogacy laws, including gestational carriers who were either the biological mother or a donor carrier, found that state laws were quite diverse, "ranging from laws banning any surrogacy arrangement as 'baby selling' to those which take an almost pure contract approach,"[490] but in many states the law is unclear as to their legal status and their enforceability. According to this survey, either by statute or by case law, twelve states explicitly allow surrogacy arrangements. In those states that prohibit the making and enforcing of surrogacy contracts where the gestational and birth mothers are the same, the birth mother either is given custody of the child or the court determines custody after the child is born. Several states permit surrogacy contracts based on a fee arrangement. A leading and influential case in shaping the law of surrogacy contracts, involved a birth mother who refused to honor a surrogacy contract. The highest court of New Jersey held that a surrogacy contract for a fee was against public policy as well as violating the adoption law.[491] The 2017 Uniform Parentage Act[492] approves surrogacy contracts.

2. Gestational Surrogacy

351. In vitro fertilization has created a phenomenon in nature, where the genetic mother and the gestational mother may be two different women. Under this arrangement, the fertilized egg is implanted in a woman who has not provided the egg. This situation is a true surrogacy arrangement. Both types of surrogacy arrangements have flourished regardless of the status of the law.

352. The law is sparse in this area as to parenthood when there are donors of either the gametes (sperm and eggs) or the gestational mother is not biologically related to the child or the intended parents may or may not have provided the gametes or a combination of these alternatives. For example, disputes may arise if the gestational mother plans to take custody of the child and the genetic providers renege and want the child, or *vice versa*. A few statutes give custody of the child to the gestational mother or the genetic mother. One court, deciding such a case, looked to the intent of the parties to the arrangement when the gestational mother refused to release the child to the genetic parents.[493] The intent theory seems to be the prevailing theory if courts make the decision.

490. Darra L. Hofman, *"Mama's Baby, Daddy's Maybe:" A State-by-State Survey of Surrogacy Laws and Their Disparate Gender Impact*, 35 William Mitchell L. Rev. 449 (2009).

491. *In re Baby M.*, 537 A.2d 1227, (N.J. 1988).

492. *Uniform Parentage Act (UPA)(amended 2002), 9B U.L.A. 295, Section 702 (2001 & Supp. 2003).*

493. *Johnson v. Calvert*, 851 P.2d 776 (Cal. 1993).

Chapter 5. Adoption

§1. Introduction

353. The concept of adoption is not of common law origin, but a "creature of statutory origin" in the United States. Adoption is, therefore, the process of creating the status of parent and child by statutory law. Beginning in the mid-nineteenth century, every state has enacted an adoption statute. The adoption process is a two-stage process. First, the legal relationship between the natural parent and the child is terminated. Then, the new legal relationship between the child and the adopted parent is created. This two-step process may be accomplished either in the same proceeding or in two different proceedings.

354. Adoption serves several social functions. Children who are in need of parents are provided parents. Couples, and now in many states single persons, who are childless or want more children, are able to become parents. Parents who are unable to rear their biological children are able to find parents for them. The state, which might be financially responsible for children in need of adoption, is able to find another source to bear such costs.[494]

355. In recent years, some people have challenged certain aspects of the adoption process, calling for reform. Many of these people have conflicting concerns. Biological parents[495] have challenged the time limits when their consent for adoption becomes final. They want a longer period of time. For them, adoption should be viewed as a process of last resort. Conversely, adoptive parents want shorter time limits in order to assure certainty and finality of the adoption process.[496] Adult adoptees, who were adopted as children, assert that adoption files that were closed when they were adopted and remain confidential should be open upon their request. They are in search of their biological identity. States are at various stages in responding to these reform demands. The Uniform Adoption Act, promulgated in 1994 by the National Conference of Commissioners on Uniform State Laws and also adopted by the American Bar Association in 1995, attempted to respond to these conflicting concerns. The promoters of the Act also seek to influence the various states to adopt this Act and bring uniformity of adoption law among the states.[497] One state has enacted substantial portions of the Act while others have enacted various provisions of the Act, either verbatim or in revised form.

356. Because adoption law is statutory and is in derogation of the common law, the judiciary strictly construes adoption law, especially as to its procedural requirements. If all procedural requirements have been satisfied, the best interests of the child is the pervasive standard for granting or denying adoption petitions.

494. J.H. Hollinger, *The Uniform Adoption Act: Reporter's Ruminations*, 30 Fam. L. Q. 345 (1996).
495. The terms biological parent, natural parent and birth parent will be used interchangeably.
496. J.H. Hollinger, *The Uniform Adoption Act: Reporter's Ruminations*, 30 Fam. L. Q. 346–347 (1996).
497. J.D. Tenenbaum, *Introducing the Uniform Adoption Act*, 30 Fam. L. Q. 333, 334 (1996).

357. All states prohibit the "sale" of a child for adoption purposes. Most states criminalize such conduct. Certain expenses are viewed as charitable expenses, rather than "buying" expenses, if they are not intended to influence the adoption process. Payment for actual and reasonable legal fees, maternity medical bills, medical expenses related to birth expenses, and necessary living expenses for the pregnant mother are examples of charitable expenses.

358. The typical adoption statute sets forth procedures for the following: the commencement of the adoption process, the court's investigation, the adoption hearing, the interim and final adoption judgment, the access to records, the consent and the revocation of the consent, and the revocation of the adoption. The statute also sets forth the legal effect of the adoption and whether the hearings and records are confidential and closed or are open.

359. Jurisdictional requirements require, first, that the trial court, adjudicating the adoption case, must have subject matter jurisdiction, and second, that proper notice of the adoption proceeding has been served on all the necessary parties. If the court does not have jurisdiction, the adoption judgment is invalid. It should not be recognized in other states and should be subject to collateral attack in another proceeding. If the adoption involves different states (interstate adoption) because the child and the prospective adoptive parents are in different states, the Interstate Compact on Placement of Children (ICPC) governs as to procedural requirements of placement of the children, not jurisdictional requirements. Some courts have interpreted the Uniform Child Custody Jurisdiction Act (UCCJA)[498] to govern not only child custody jurisdiction, but also adoption jurisdiction. The majority of states (now forty-eight states) have, however, enacted its replacement, the Uniform Child Custody and Enforcement Act (UCCJEA).[499] The UCCJEA specifically states that it does not apply to adoption cases.

§2. Adoption Placement

I. Adoption Agencies and Private Placement

360. Adoptions may be denominated as "agency" adoptions or "private or independent" adoptions depending on whether or not a state (or state-licensed) agency is involved. Historically, all adoptions were private or independent adoptions. In private or independent adoptions, the birth parents place the child directly with the adoptive parent. Private adoption often occurs in kinship adoption. Many states have banned independent adoption, especially between non-relatives.

361. State adoption agencies or state-approved private agencies are usually involved in the adoption process. When involved, the adoption agency usually acts

498. Uniform Laws Annotated No. 9 (1988) p.115. At one time all states had enacted some version of this Act to govern child custody jurisdiction.
499. *Uniform Laws Annotated* No. 9 (Pt. 1A) (1997), p. 649.

as the intermediary between the birth parents and the adoptive parents. The agency investigates the prospective adoptive parents as to their suitability, both to their personal and financial qualifications. Some states require that an adoption agency conduct this investigation even in private or independent adoptions. The adoption agency's decision is usually a terminal decision if the agency is acting as the intermediary and may not be challenged by the prospective adoptive parents.

II. Subsidized Adoption

362. Subsidized adoption provides financial assistance to adoptive parents to encourage adoption of children who are hard to place. These children are usually the older child and the mentally or physically disabled child. This subsidy may be paid on a regular basis. Most states as well as the federal government offer subsidies.[500] However, the overwhelming majority of adoptions in the United States are not subsidized adoptions. The only "subsidy" to most adoptions is that the federal government and most states for tax purposes will treat the costs of adoption as deductible to some extent from the taxable income.[501]

III. Open and Closed Adoptions (Postadoption Contact)

363. Beginning in the 1920s, adoption proceedings became closed and confidential. The adoption records were sealed. As a result, the identity of the birth parents and all information about them were unavailable to the adopted child. Similarly, the identity of the adoptive parents and the whereabouts of the child were unknown and unavailable to the birth parents. Statutes required the unsealing of the records only for shown good cause. Closed adoption protects the parental autonomy of the natural parents when they have been promised confidentiality. The opening of the records would breach that promise. Closed adoption also promotes the autonomy of the adoptive family, protecting that unit from interference by the birth parents.

364. With the recent strong movement by adult adoptees to unseal their adoption records, all states have amended the adoption law to allow adoption records to be unsealed in order to disclose to the adoptee the family health record and the social history of the birth parents, but not to identify them. Many states have also established registers allowing adopted children and birth parents to register so that they may exchange information anonymously or contact one another.

500. E.g., *Cesnik v. Edgewood Baptist Church*, 88 F.3d 902 (11th Cir. 1996) (federally subsidized adoption assistance payments available for children with special needs. 42 USC. §673 (1994)).

501. In 2001, the United States Congress enacted law to give incentive to adopt foster children by increasing the tax credit for all adoptions except for stepparent adoption, with a phase out provision for taxpayers at a certain level of adjusted gross income. Hope for Children Act, Pub. L. No. 107-16, 115 Stat. 38. A 2007 study revealed that the majority of adoptive parents who took advantage of the incentive were those adopting children privately or from foreign countries, but who were not in the foster care system.

365. Recently, there has been a movement to return to open adoption.[502] There are two types of postadoption contact: post adoption consensual agreement and court-ordered contact. In the former, both biological and adoptive parents cooperatively arrange to allow some level of openness between the birth parents and the adoptive family. At least twenty-one states have enacted statutes that provide the enforcement mechanisms for such arrangements.[503] As to court-ordered postadoption contact, a few states have enacted statutes allowing such visitation. Some states, however, specifically limit such visitation to stepparent, siblings, or relative adoptions. The standard in all court-ordered postadoption visitation is the best interest of the child.

366. When adoption occurs directly between the natural and adoptive parents, such arrangements are open to the extent that the birth and adoptive families know one another. Such knowledge would not, however, give the birth parents any more legal rights than if the adoption had been anonymous unless the adoption judgment provides for such rights.[504]

IV. Equitable Adoption

367. The doctrine of equitable adoption[505] is a potential remedy in intestate succession cases. The doctrine provides relief to persons, who were not formally adopted, so that they may inherit as a child of the foster parent. This situation may arise when a person has taken the child into his or her home and has reared the child without formal adoption. It may also arise when a person has agreed to adopt the child but did not finalize the adoption. Courts, generally, do not apply this doctrine to give relief in these situations unless they find an express or implied contract to adopt.[506] Outside of the intestate succession context claims for "equitable adoption" have rarely been asserted with success. Because adoption is a statutory procedure at variance with the common law, the statutory requirements must be fully satisfied for the legal effect of adoption to occur. Although equitable adoption evolved as a judicial doctrine, some states have codified the doctrine as well. Thus, in those states both the judicial and statutory doctrines exist.[507]

502. Social changes, for example, have reduced the perceived need for secrecy. The stigma attached to children born out of wedlock has greatly lessened. The psychological and emotional need of adopted children to search for their identity is recognized as important.
503. *See generally*, Cynthia R. Mabry & Lisa Kelly, *Adoption Law, Theory, Policy, and Practice*, Chapter 12 (Hein Publishing Company 2006).
504. *See supra* Chapters 5 & 6, regarding the legal effect of adoption.
505. *See supra* para. 855.
506. *See*, e.g., *O'Neal v. Wilkes*, 439 S.E.2d 490 (Ga. 1994).
507. Cal. Probate Code § 6455 (West 1993).

§3. Who May Be Adopted

368. Any minor child may be adopted. That is, there is no limitation or restriction regarding race, age, nationality, sex, etc. However, children that have two living parents whose parental rights are not terminated may not be adopted. Thus, any child without a parent or parents is eligible for adoption by an individual or couple, depending on the circumstances.

369. Adults may be adopted in many states as long as the adoption is not a sham or for fraudulent purposes. The proceedings are simple, requiring the consent of the adoptee and the adoptor.

§4. Who May Adopt

370. The qualifications of the adoptive parent vary among the states. The following qualifications are common among the states.

I. Marital Status

371. If a person is married, many states require both spouses to adopt the child as a couple. Many of these states will allow one spouse to adopt alone if the spouse is legally separated and the whereabouts of the other spouse is unknown, or, if the petitioner is the stepparent, or, if the court waives the requirement. Stepparent adoption accounts for over half of the adoptions in the United States. Preference for marital adult adopters is common in American adoption laws. As Professor Cynthia Mabry reports: "In all states, statutes provide that the following persons may adopt a child: single persons, a husband and wife together, and stepparents. In addition, a few state courts also allow unmarried cohabitants to adopt a child."[508]

372. Most states specifically allow single-parent adoption by statute although single persons adopt in all states. A few states allow unmarried couples to adopt as a couple regardless of sexual preference.[509]

---

508. Cynthia R. Mabry, *Joint and Shared Parenting: Valuing All Families and All Children in the Adoption Process with an Expanded Notion of Family*, 17 Am. U. J. Gender, Soc. Policy & L. 659, 661 (2009); *see also* Cynthia R. Mabry & Lisa Kelly, *Adoption Law: Theory, Policy, and Practice* 126 (2006).

509. *In re Jacob*, 660 N.E.2d 397 (N.Y. Ct. App. 1995).

II. Age

373. The adopting parent must be an adult although some states allow exceptions for good cause shown. Many statutes require a specific age span to exist between the adopting parent and the child in order to retain a semblance of the natural parent-child age span.

374. Younger-age adults are still generally preferred over older-age adults.[510]

III. Race

375. Traditionally, race has been considered a relevant adoption factor.[511,512] The United States Supreme Court has not clarified whether race may still be considered a factor and not violate the Equal Protection Clause of the Fifth and Fourteenth Amendments of the United States Constitution. It is clear, however, that race may not be the sole factor if adoption follows post-divorce custody cases.[513] In these cases, race may be considered if it is among a number of other factors considered as being in the best interests of the child. However, invidious use of race to discriminate against adoptive parents on account of their race or to discriminate against the placement of children on account of their race manifesting any belief in racial superiority or inferiority is clearly proscribed. However, to date courts are split upon the priority of using race as a relevant factor pertaining to the welfare of the child in adoption. Most courts allow that consideration as long as it is legitimate and not a mere subterfuge for racism. In 1996, the United States Congress enacted law (Interethnic Provisions Act) that prohibits states or other entities receiving federal funds to deny or delay adoption based on the child's or the perspective parents' race.[514]

IV. Religion

376. Some states allow religious matching, when possible, if religion is one of the factors considered in determining adoption. When such a statute has been challenged as unconstitutional under the Establishment Clause of the First Amendment

---

510. Discrimination on the basis of age does not receive higher constitutional scrutiny as does race or gender. Its standard of constitutional review is the minimum standard: the reasonable or rational standard. *See Massachusetts Board of Retirement v. Murgia*, 427 US 307 (1976).
511. *See* §8 of this chapter for the exception of Native American Children.
512. *In re R.M.G.*, 454 A.2d 776 (D.C. Ct. App. 1982).
513. *Palmore v. Sidoti*, 466 US 429 (1994), (holding that race as the sole factor in determining a post-divorce custody case is unconstitutional). Interracial adoption is controversial. However, Native American Tribes have exclusive jurisdiction over adoption of their children, domiciled on the reservation. Race may be a conclusive factor. *See* The Indian Child Welfare Act of 1978, 25 United States Code (§§1901-1023) (1994). *See* §8 of this chapter.
514. Pub. L. No. 104-188, § 1808.

of the United States Constitution, courts have traditionally upheld the statute so long as it is not the sole dispositive factor and so long as it legitimately pertains to the best interest of the child.[515]

V. Sexual Preference

377. With the changing of traditional values and mores and the change in the legal definition of marriage, all states now allow same-sex couples to adopt. A number of states allow a same-sex partner to adopt the other partner's biological child. This process is called second parent adoption, and it is deemed analogous to step-parent adoption. Legislation or appellate court decisions in some states and the District of Columbia permit same-sex partners to adopt, and in other states related judicial decisions suggest that that is likely to be the new policy when the issue arises.[516] Sexual behavior of a parent in most states may be one of many factors considered by adoption agencies and courts in determining whether a particular adoption placement is in the best interest of the child.[517]

VI. Disabled Persons

378. Physically and emotionally disabled persons may not be denied adoption on the sole basis of their disability. The disability is only relevant if it affects the disabled person's ability to parent.

VII. Financial Requirements

379. Many states require adopting parents to satisfy certain financial requirements.[518]

§5. Consent Requirements and Termination of Parental Rights

I. Parental Consent

A. Notice and Consent

380. The natural parents' parental rights and obligations must be terminated before adoption can be accomplished. Unless the parental rights of parents (father

515. *In the Interest of C.B.*, 583 N.E.2d 107 (Ill. App. Ct. 1991).
516. L.D. Wardle, *Comparative Perspectives on Adoption of Children by Cohabiting, Nonmarital Couples and Partners*, 62 Arkansas L. Rev. 31 (2010).
517. L.D. Wardle, *The Potential Impact of Homosexual Parenting on Children*, Illinois L. Rev. 601 (1997).
518. *See* Arizona Revised Statutes §8-105 (2009).

and mother) of children born in wedlock or of the mother of children born out of wedlock have already been terminated, these parents must be notified of the adoption and must give their consent to the adoption. It does not matter if the parents are divorced.

381. It is possible to conceive of adoptions in which new parental rights are created without the parental rights of the old parents being terminated. Thus a child might have three or more parents. Proposals to such effect have been made by advocates of quasi-parental rights or relationships of stepparents or nonmarital cohabitants of biological parents who are not living together. However, those proposals have been uniformly rejected. The historical and overwhelmingly prevailing model of parenting in the United States is that a child should have one father and one mother. Lesbian and gay couples who seek to adopt the biological child of their same-sex partner have challenged this pattern as well. Generally, the challenges have been rejected. However, in a few states, same-sex partners have been allowed to adopt without terminating the parental rights of the child's other biological parent.[519]

382. Historically, the consent of the father of children born out of wedlock was not required in adoption cases. However, the Supreme Court of the United States has held that fathers of children born out of wedlock have significant parental rights, which are protected by the Constitution. A state must respect these rights.[520] Nevertheless, there are constitutional differences among certain unwed fathers, such that their consent may not be necessary for adoption or that they may not even be entitled to notice of the adoption proceeding. For example, an unwed father, who has had the opportunity to establish a relationship with the child but who has not done so, does not have a constitutional right even to receive notice of the adoption, but he must be given that opportunity to form the relationship. The Supreme Court of the United States has not specified what evidence demonstrates he has been given that opportunity.[521] In *Adoptive Couple v. Baby Girl*, 133 S. Ct. 2552 (2013) involving the adoption by non-Indian couple of a part-Indian child, the Supreme Court held that the federal Indian Child Welfare Act did not protect the putative parental rights of an Indian biological father who had relinquished his parental rights and who never had custody of the child.

---

519. In *re Jacob*, 636 N.Y.S. 2d 716 (N.Y. 1995); *In re adoptions of B.L.V.B. and E.L.V.B.* 628 A.2nd 1271 (VT. 1993).

520. When a right is constitutionally protected, all states must follow the Constitution. States may, however, protect more rights than does the Constitution.

521. Some states have established certain procedures for putative fathers to follow in order to protect their constitutional right of notice. *See*, e.g., *Lehr v. Robertson*, 463 US 248 (1983) (New York had provided a "putative fathers registry" where notice would be sent to all putative fathers who had registered). More than thirty states have established these putative fathers registries in order to reduce the possibility of later litigation by fathers who argue they were not given the opportunity because he had no notice of the child's birth. The states have taken the position that nonmarital fathers are on notice of the possibility of a child's birth once they have had sexual relationship. Accordingly, the potential father will be given notice of an adoption if he is on the state's registry. The ongoing problems with registries are many. People are unaware of them. Second, the child may be placed for adoption in a state where the father did not register.

383. A noncustodial parent in divorce cases must be given notice and must consent to the adoption in stepparent adoption.

384. Of course, if the parent is dead no parental consent is needed for his or her child. Likewise, if parental rights have previously been terminated by judicial proceeding, notice, and consent requirements do not apply.

B. Involuntary Consent and Termination of Parental Rights

385. If the natural parent unreasonably withholds consent, the court may allow the adoption to proceed without the parent's consent if it is in the best interests of the child. Such cases usually involve parents who have willingly abandoned or willingly failed to support their children. The court, however, must still formally terminate the parent's parental rights. Because parental rights are fundamental rights under the United States Constitution, termination proceedings must observe all due process requirements.

386. Courts have had a tendency to find that it is in the best interests of the child to terminate parental rights and to go forward with the adoption in cases involving the consent of an unwed father, where the mother has already consented to the adoption. A few states seem more inclined to find that a noncustodial parent has abandoned or failed to support the child in stepparent adoption cases.

II. Non-parental Consent

387. Most states require the consent of the minor child if he or she has reached a specific age. This specific age varies from 10 years old to 14 years old.

388. The child's guardian, if he or she is not the natural parent, must consent.

389. If the adoption agency is involved, the agency must consent.

390. Grandparents are not required to consent to the adoption. States may, however, require that notice be given to grandparents and that they have an opportunity to be heard if it is in the best interests of the child.

III. Revocation of Consent

391. The procedures for giving consent must be strictly complied with for the consent to be valid and binding. Parental consent prior to the birth of the child is generally non-binding. There are conflicting views about how much time the birth parents should have to revoke their consent. Those who advocate a very short time argue that it is in the best interest of the child to have short time periods to assure stability and finality to the adoption. Others argue for longer time periods to take into account the psychological and emotional state of the birth parents. In such a mental state, it is unreasonable to require them to make such a significant decision in a short time frame.

392. A parent may revoke his or her consent under certain circumstances. If the consent was given under fraud, duress, or undue influence, the consent may be revoked. Historically, courts have been very reluctant to allow revocation of consent to adoption. In recent years, however, some courts have manifested a greater willing to do so in cases where there has been clear impropriety. Another issue arises when the parent is a minor child. May revocation be based upon the fact that the minor was not mature to give consent? While some courts allow consent by a minor, other states may appoint a guardian *ad litem* for the minor before consent is given or require the minor's parents give their consent or require another adult who is representing the minor's interest be present when the minor gives consent.

§6. Legal Effects of Adoption

393. The legal effect of adoption is virtually to replace the legal relationship of parent-child between the birth parents and the child with the newly created legal relationship of parent-child between the adoptive parents and the child. The adoptive parents become responsible for the custody, care, responsibility, and support of the child.

394. The child's birth records are typically reissued in the name of the adopting parents, but usually the child's birthplace, birth date, and other identifying information remain the same. The old records are usually sealed.

395. The state's incest laws apply to adoptive families. Law of consanguinity forbidding the marriage of persons closely related to each other also generally applies to persons related by adoption. Though in special circumstances, some courts have been willing to wave those requirements.[522]

396. All states treat adopted children as the issue of the adopted parents for intestate succession purposes. Most states treat adopted children as heirs of their adoptive parents' kin. The right of the adopted children to retain their right as heirs of their biological parents or through them is usually terminated at adoption, even though some states allow such inheritance. In stepparent adoption, however, most states allow the child to continue to inherit from the birth parent, if the birth parent died before the adoption or if the birth parent is the stepparent's spouse. The adoptive parents usually are the heirs of the adopted child.

522. In *Israel v. Allen*, 577 P.2d 762 (Col. 1978), the Supreme Court of Colorado held that its incest statute did not apply to adoptive children, who wanted to marry.

397. The adoption judgment may provide for continuous contact with the biological relatives.[523] For example, the judgment may provide for contact in the form of parental, grandparent, and sibling visitation arrangements.[524]

§7. Revocation of Adoption

398. Adoption judgments are usually not revocable unless there was a defect in the adoption process. The law favors finality as being in the best interest of the child. The adoption may be revoked if there was fraud, duress, or undue influence. Almost all jurisdictions have a statute of limitations for challenging the adoption judgment. The majority of revocation-of-adoption cases involve birth parents, who later challenge the validity of the adoption.

399. Adopting parents have sought the revocation of an adoption where the agency misrepresented the health of the child. Courts have denied such requests. A few courts, however, have recognized the tort of wrongful adoption, where the adoption agency has intentionally or negligently misrepresented the child's health.[525]

§8. The Indian Child Welfare Act

400. The Indian Child Welfare Act of 1978[526] provides in part that the Tribal Court has exclusive jurisdiction in deciding child custody cases of Native American children, who reside or are domiciled within the reservation of that tribe. This jurisdictional section of the Act was upheld as constitutional by the United States Supreme Court.[527] Even when state courts do properly have jurisdiction of Native American children for adoption, the Act also mandates their adoptive placement with a member of the children's family or tribe or other Native American families unless good cause to the contrary is shown.[528]

---

523. *See supra* Part II, Chapter 5, s. 2, Part II, (regarding open adoption).
524. *In re Adoption of Anthony*, 448 N.Y.S.2d 377 (N.Y. Fam. Ct. 1982).
525. *M.H. v. Caritas Family Services*, 488 N.W.2d 282 (Minn. 1992); and M.J. Blank, *Adoption Nightmares Prompt Judicial Recognition of the Tort of Wrongful Adoption—Will New York Follow Suit?*, 15 Cardozo L. Rev. 1687 (1994).
526. 25 USC. §§1901-19 (1983). The purpose of the Act seeks "to protect the best interests of Indian children and to promote the stability and security of Indian tribes and families by the establishment of minimum federal policy standards for the removal of Indian children from their families and the placement of such children in foster or adoptive homes which would not reflect the unique values of Indian culture, and by providing for assistance to Indian tribes in the operation of child and family service programs." (25 USC. §1902 (1978)).
527. *Mississippi Band of Choctaw Indians v. Holyfield*, 490 US 30 (1989). In that decision, the adoption was set aside because these jurisdictional requirements were not satisfied.
528. 25 USC.A. §1915(a) (1983).

§9. International or Intercountry Adoption

401. International or intercountry adoption by Americans of foreign-born children is governed by United States federal immigration law, state adoption law, and the foreign country's relinquishment for adoption laws. The following is a brief overview of the international adoption process. The child's country of residence governs the child's adoptability and the child's emigration from the country. American federal law governs the child's entry into the United States. The United States' Bureau of Citizenship and Immigration Services (BCIS) is responsible for implementing the federal law. This Bureau investigates both the child and the prospective adoptive parents and determines whether the child is eligible to enter the country. If the Bureau decides to allow the child to enter the United States, it issues a visa to the child. After the visa is issued, the state court of the prospective adoptive parents' residence must issue an adoption decree. If the child has already been adopted in the foreign country, the adoptive parents should petition their state court to recognize the foreign adoption decree under the doctrine of comity or petition for re-adoption.

402. Prospective adoptive parents use either the services of international service agencies or the services of foreign doctors, lawyers, or social workers to locate a child.

403. There are special rules applying to the adoption of foreign children that facilitate their entry into the United States, including the following. A child eligible for adoption must be under the age of sixteen at the time a petition is filed for entry into the United States. The child must be an orphan. The child is an orphan because of the death or disappearance of, abandonment or desertion by, or separation or loss from both parents. Or, the child is an orphan because the child's sole or surviving parent is incapable of providing the proper care and has in writing irrevocably released the child for emigration and adoption.[529] The terms defining orphan are further defined by federal regulations.

404. There are four methods that a child may follow to obtain a visa to enter the United States. They are: (1) to petition to have the child declared an "immediate relative;" (2) to petition to have the child declared a "special immigrant;" (3) to petition to have the child enter the United States under the Attorney General's discretionary parole authority; and (4) to petition to have the child to enter as an alien subject to the federal numerical limitations, which are allowed to the particular country.

405. If the child has been adopted in the foreign country, the child must still be lawfully admitted to the United States. The adoption of the child in the foreign country may facilitate this process. However, there are federal rules requiring the parents' presence in the foreign country during the adoption proceedings as well as

529. 8 USC. §1101(b) (1) (F) (2009).

the child still being required to meet the eligibility requirements for adoption. Adopted children usually are admitted as an "immediate relative."

406. Since 2001 with the enactment of the Child Citizenship Act of 2000, a child born outside of the United States automatically becomes a citizen of the United States if at least one parent is a citizen of the United States, the child is under eighteen, and the child is residing in the United States in the legal and physical custody of the citizen parent pursuant to a lawful admission for permanent residence.[530] Otherwise, when the child enters the United States and does not meet the requirements for automatic citizenship, the visa is voided and the child becomes a lawful "permanent resident," but not a citizen of the United States. The child must be formally naturalized. The naturalization process is simplified if the application for citizenship is made before the child is 18 years old and is still unmarried. No waiting period is required once the child is lawfully in the United States.

407. At all stages in the process of international adoption, the child must be eligible for adoption and the adoptive parents must be competent to adopt the child. These requirements at the international, federal, and state stages are not uniform. In 1993, the Hague Conference on Private International Law promulgated a new Convention to regulate international adoptions, which was to take effect in 1995.[531] In 1994, the United States signed the Convention. It was ratified by the United States Senate in 2007, but the legislation implementing the Convention was enacted by Congress in 2000. This legislation is the Intercountry Adoption Act of 2000 (IAA).[532]

530. *See* 8 United States Code §1431 (2000).

531. The Hague Conference on Private International Law, Final Act of the Seventeenth Session, May 29, 1993, 32 ILM 1134.

532. 42 United States Code § 14901 (2000).

Chapter 6. Parental Authority

§1. General Principles of Custodial Responsibilities

408. Parental authority over children derives from the traditional principle of parental autonomy, where parents are the primary decision-makers for their children, without interference from the state or from third parties. This principle of parental authority is also protected as a fundamental right under the United States Constitution,[533] and since 1965 has been described as part of the right of privacy developed in *Griswold v. Connecticut.*[534] Child-rearing responsibilities are considered the essence of the parent-child relationship. All states specifically provide that parents have the custody of their minor children and the responsibility for rearing them.

409. If parents are not available to care for their children, some other adult or the state must assume custody of the child and the rearing responsibilities. However, if a child has been properly emancipated, no adult need be appointed to exercise custodial rights or child-rearing responsibilities.

410. Furthermore, the law assumes that minor children are incapable of making decisions regarding their well being. Parents or some other adult must make most of their decisions until they reach the age of majority or are emancipated.[535] Minor children are, therefore, under certain disabilities. They cannot, for example, establish their own domicile. A child's domicile is the domicile of his or her parents, usually the father's if born in-wedlock, the mother's if born out-of-wedlock, or his or her custodian's.

411. Some states still follow the common law rule that the child's services and earnings are the property of the parents.[536] However, gifts and inheritances belong to the child. An adult must, nevertheless, be appointed to manage such gifts and inheritances because the child does not have the legal capacity to manage property.[537]

412. An unemancipated minor has the ability to make and enforce contracts, but the law allows a minor to disaffirm most contracts made during minority or within a reasonable time after reaching majority. Such contracts are voidable, not void. A

---

533. *See*, e.g., *Meyer v. Nebraska*, 262 US 390, 399 (1923) (among the liberties protected by the Fourteenth Amendment are the rights "to marry, to establish a home and bring up children").
534. 381 US 479 (1965).
535. "Most children, even in adolescence, simply are not able to make sound judgments concerning many decisions... Parents can and must make those judgments." *Parham v. J.R.*, 442 US 584 (1979).
536. At common law, however, the primary parent was the father.
537. Such management is accomplished through guardianship, custodianship, or trusts. *See infra* Part 2, Chapter 7 for guardianship, custodianship and Uniform Transfers to Minors Act, and Part 4, Chapter 3 for trusts.

minor is responsible, however, for contracts he or she enters into for articles and services necessary for his or her support if the parent cannot provide for them.[538]

§2. Limitations on Parental Authority

413. The state limits parental authority where the child is being harmed by the parent's decision or where there are other compelling public policies. Because of the importance of the concept of parental autonomy in American society, the limitations, when they are imposed, tend to be minimal intrusions.

I. Compulsory Education

414. Each state mandates that minor children be educated. The state sets minimum and maximum age requirements for compulsory school attendance and imposes a duty upon parents to enforce attendance unless there are statutory exemptions or exclusions. Typical exemptions include: the child is unable to attend school because of physical or mental disabilities, the child has completed the required grades, or the child has reached the minimum state employment age and is employed. Typical exclusions are suspensions or expulsions because of the child's conduct or because of the child's failure to be properly immunized.[539] If children are excluded from school attendance, this action must meet the requirements of the due process clauses of the United States Constitution. At a minimum, an exclusion requires some kind of notice and hearing.[540]

415. The state justifies its requirement of compulsory education under both its police powers and the doctrine of *parens patriae* (the concept that the state may intervene to protect a child as a matter of public policy).[541] The state has several legitimate interests regarding compulsory education. They include a belief that in a democratic society an educated citizenry is necessary for the common good of society, and a belief that an education is necessary for each citizen's own economic success.[542]

---

538. Parents are responsible for the support of their children and should provide the child with the child's "necessaries." If third parties, pursuant to a contract with the child, furnish those things or services necessary for the child's "necessaries," the parent is liable. The child is liable only if the parent is unable to provide the necessaries.

539. The Supreme Court has upheld claims by members of the Amish religion that Wisconsin's compulsory education laws interfered with their religious beliefs and practices under the First Amendment. *Wisconsin v. Yoder*, 406 US 205 (1972).

540. *Goss v. Lopez*, 419 US 565 (1975).

541. Education is not a fundamental right guaranteed to the individual under the United States Constitution. *See San Antonio Indep. School Dist. v. Rodriguez*, 411 US 1 (1973).

542. The Supreme Court has noted that education is an important state function and if children were denied an education, they could not be reasonably expected to succeed. *Brown v. Board of Education*, 347 US 483 (1954).

416. Each state provides a public education for the children of its residents. Parents are not required to send their children to a public school, but may choose alternative schooling, such as a private or religious school.[543] In the past thirty-five years, there has been a growing trend among some parents to teach their children at home, resulting in legislation authorizing home schooling as an alternative. Courts, however, have upheld the state's reasonable regulation of home schools as well as regulation of the other alternative schooling, especially in the area of teacher certification.

417. Parents continue to challenge state-imposed requirements. These challenges have been met with mixed results.[544] In public schools, parents have objected to such regulations as to sex-education programs, school prayer, and certain teaching materials. For example, parents have challenged sex-education programs as directly interfering with their prerogatives as to what to teach. Courts have upheld such programs if they provide for an exclusion of any child from the program at the parent's request. School prayers and religious meditations required by the state violate the First Amendment.[545] Teaching materials are valid so long as they do not require "the student to affirm or deny a religious belief or to engage or refrain from engaging in any act either required or forbidden by the students' religious convictions."[546]

418. Schools have the authority to discipline children. In public schools, this authority stems, first, from the fact that school officials are the state's representatives, and second, from the parents under the doctrine of *in loco parentis*. This doctrine allows one to stand in the place of parents when parents are not present.

419. Disciplinary measures in public schools must be constitutional.[547] Students may be suspended or expelled on the basis of their conduct, but such actions must meet with the due process requirements of the Constitution, requiring at a minimum notice and hearing.[548] Schools may use corporal punishment even if parents object, but it must be reasonable.[549] The current trend in many states is to prohibit the use of corporal punishment as a disciplinary measure. The Supreme Court has limited

543. In *Pierce v. Society of Sisters*, the United States found unconstitutional a provision in an Oregon statute precluding private schooling since the law "unreasonably interferes with the liberty of parents and guardians to direct the upbringing and education of children under their control." 268 US 510, 534–535 (1925).
544. The very first case challenged a regulation which prohibited the teaching of German. This case reached the Supreme Court of the United States, which held that the regulation interfered with the parent's liberty right to bring up his child. *Meyer v. State of Nebraska*, 262 US 390 (1923).
545. *Wallace v. Jaffree*, 472 US 38 (1985).
546. *Mozert v. Hawkins County Board of Education*, 827 F.2d 1058 (6th Cir. 1987), cert. den. 484 US 1066 (1988).
547. Non-public schools are not bound by all of the constitutional requirements as are public schools and may be much stricter in promulgating such regulations.
548. *Goss v. Lopez*, 419 US 565 (1975).
549. The Supreme Court held (1) that corporal punishment in public schools was not within the meaning of the Cruel and Unusual Punishment Clause of the Eighth Amendment and (2) that the Due Process Clause did not require notice and hearing before administering corporal punishment

public schools from regulating certain areas of student activities and conduct by protecting students' freedom of political expression,[550] their freedom of speech to use lewd and offensive language,[551] and their freedom from censorship of a high school newspaper.[552]

II. Parental Consent for Medical Care

420. As a general rule, parents must consent before their child receives any medical treatment, except in an emergency situation when the parent is not available. The states have also developed two additional exceptions, which may apply in certain circumstances. These are the "emancipated minor" and the "mature minor" exceptions.

A. Emergency Treatment

421. The emergency treatment exception was the first exception that the courts developed to modify the common law rule that parental consent was necessary when a minor child needed medical treatment. This exception applies when there is an emergency situation and the parents are not available. An emergency is typically defined as existing when the delay in treatment will endanger the life, limb, or mental well-being of the patient.[553] This exception is a common sense approach, based on the obvious fact that the parents are not available to consent and the child needs immediate care.

422. If parents are available, but will not give their consent for medical treatment to a condition that is life-threatening to the child, the law will override the parents' decision under its *parens patriae* power and act in the best interests of the child. Such cases usually arise when the parents' sincere religious convictions dictate against receiving such treatment.

423. Difficult medical decisions arise when children are born with severe handicaps. Parents, usually in consultation with the physician, make decisions regarding the withholding of life-sustaining medical treatment. If such cases reach the court,

because such punishment was limited by the common law "to inflict only such corporal punishment as is reasonably necessary for the proper education and discipline of the child; any such punishment going beyond the privilege may result in both civil and criminal liability." *Ingraham v. Wright*, 430 US 651 (1977). New Hampshire Revised Statutes Annotated §627:6(I) (2009) provides that "[a] teacher or person otherwise entrusted with the care or supervision of a minor for special purposes is justified on the premises in using necessary force against any such minor, when the minor creates a disturbance, or refuses to leave the premises or when it is necessary for the maintenance of discipline."

550. *Tinker v. Des Moines Independent Community School Dist.*, 393 US 503 (1969).
551. *Bethel School District v. Fraser*, 478 US 675 (1986).
552. *Hazelwood School Dist. v. Kuhlmeier*, 484 US 260 (1988).
553. *See*, e.g., Massachusetts General Laws Annotated Ch. 112, §12F (West, 1997).

the court usually applies the "substituted judgment" doctrine, which allows the parents to substitute their judgment for that of the child.[554] The federal government initially responded to these severely infant-handicapped cases by requiring hospitals receiving federal funds not to withhold life-sustaining support in most of these cases. The Supreme Court eventually found these regulations unconstitutional.[555] The current regulations encourage hospitals to establish an Infant Care Review Committee to assist in developing standards and require the posting of an informational notice that nourishment and beneficial medical treatment should not be withheld from handicapped infants solely because of the handicap.[556]

B. Non-emergency Treatment

424. All states have made exceptions to the general rule of parental consent for certain types of non-emergency treatment. These exceptions are for emancipated minors and for mature minors. The reason for the development of the exception for an emancipated minor is the recognition that an emancipated minor is no longer in need of adult decision-makers. On the contrary, there is also the recognition that certain unemancipated minors are "mature enough" to understand the nature and consequence of their decision for non-emergency treatment. Non-emergency treatment may include medical, surgical, hospital, dental, psychiatric, or other health services. State statutes are not uniform in defining non-emergency treatment or in deciding when the exceptions apply. State statutes are also not uniform as to whether parents must still be notified even when an exception exists.

425. Many of the statutes do not define "emancipated" except in terms of marital status. Many states allow minors who are married to consent to the medical treatment of their own child. Some of these states, however, still require parental consent for the minor parent's own medical treatment.

426. All states allow minors of a certain age to consent to the diagnosis and treatment of venereal disease. Most states have no age limit. Minors usually may consent for drug and alcohol abuse treatment although there is usually a minimum age requirement. In both types of treatment, the state has an interest in the welfare of the minor's health. The state also has other interests. For example, allowing minors to consent to treatment for venereal disease assists the public's interest for both the general welfare and the public health of the community in containing a contagious disease. Similarly, allowing minors to consent to treatment for alcohol and drug abuse aids the general welfare of the community in curtailing the devastation that alcohol and drug abuse costs the community.

---

554. *Custody of a Minor*, 434 N.E.2d 601 (Mass 1982); and *Care and Protection of Beth*, 587 N.E.2d 1377 (1992).
555. *Bowen v. American Hospital Association*, 476 US 610 (1986).
556. 45 CFR §84.55 (1992) (Procedures relating to health care for handicapped infants).

427. The Supreme Court has addressed a minor's right to an abortion with or without parental consent and with or without parental notice. The Supreme Court has held that a state, except in an emergency, may require an unemancipated minor, who wants an abortion, to obtain the parental consent of one of her parents if there is also a judicial "bypass" procedure if neither parent consents. This "bypass" procedure allows a court to determine whether to authorize an abortion on the finding either that the minor is mature and capable of giving an informed consent and has given an informed consent or that an abortion is in her best interest.[557] The Supreme Court has also found constitutional a state's requirement of notification of one parent that the minor wishes to obtain an abortion if there is also a judicial "bypass" procedure.[558] A state may not prohibit the distribution of contraceptives to minors.[559]

C. Mental Health

428. Historically, parents made all the decisions regarding the treatment of mentally disturbed children. The Supreme Court has held that a child has a liberty interest in not being unnecessarily confined to a mental institution and in avoiding the stigma of such confinement.[560] This liberty interest is, however, not the equivalent of an adult's, where a full commitment hearing would be required before commitment to a mental institution. In the case of a child, the parent may decide to voluntarily commit the child, against the child's wishes, as long as there is a thorough pre-commitment investigation by a neutral fact finder. The investigation includes a personal interview with the child, and if the child is committed, a periodic review of the child's confinement, including the same type of inquiry that led to the commitment.[561] The Supreme Court reasoned (1) that parents usually act in the best interest of their child, (2) that the law presumes that parents have what the children lacks in maturity, experience, and judgment, and (3) that the parent does not have absolute veto power.

III. Parental Discipline and Control

429. Parents may use reasonable discipline in the care, supervision, and control of their child. In some instances, a parent may no longer have the legal obligation of supporting a minor child if that child voluntarily abandons the home in order to avoid parental control.[562]

557. *Planned Parenthood v. Casey*, 505 US 833 (1992).
558. *See Ohio v. Akron Center for Reproduction Health*, 497 US 502 (1990); *and Hodgson v. Minnesota*, 497 US 417 (1990).
559. *Carey v. Population Service International*, 431 US 678 (1977).
560. *Parham v. J.R.*, 442 US 584 (1979).
561. *Parham v. J.R.*, 442 US 584 (1979).
562. *In re Parker v. Stage*, 371 N.E.2d 513 (N.Y. Ct. App. 1977); *Jennifer S. v. Marvin S.*, 568 N.Y.S.2d 515 (Fam. Ct. 1991); L.J. Harris et al., *Making and Breaking Connections Between Parents' Duty to Support and Right to Control Their Children*, 69 Oregon L. Rev. 689 (1990).

430. Some states have enacted statutes criminally sanctioning parents for contributing to the delinquency of a minor because they have failed to exercise reasonable supervision, care, or control of their child.[563]

431. Traditionally, reasonable corporal punishment is a parental disciplinary option. One court has stated that a "well-recognized precept in Anglo-American jurisprudence [is] that the parent of a minor child or one standing *in loco parentis* was justified in using a reasonable amount of force upon a child for the purpose of safeguarding or promoting the child's welfare."[564] Some states have codified this precept.[565]

432. The changing attitudes between those persons regarding corporal punishment as a parental disciplinary option and those persons believing the law should prohibit parents from using corporal punishment have raised issues regarding child abuse.[566] In such cases, the determining factors as to whether the punishment was parental discipline or whether it was abuse depended on the language of the statute defining child abuse and the requirement of "intentionally harming" the child as well as unofficially on the ideological preferences of the triers-of-fact for or against the concept of corporal punishment.

IV. Abuse of Parental Authority

433. The state intervenes under the doctrine of *parens patriae* when the child is in need of protection when the parent's care harms the child.[567] In order to protect children, whose parents have not provided them with the minimum level of care, all states have enacted laws on child neglect, dependency, and abuse. The state may have to intervene to the extent to remove the child from the home. The parent's conduct may require that parental rights be terminated. The Juvenile Court System usually has jurisdiction over these cases.[568]

434. The Supreme Court has held that the Due Process Clause of the Fourteenth Amendment of the Constitution does not require a state to protect a person's life, liberty and property against private action, only the state's action.[569] At times, the line determining whether the state is or is not obligated to act is difficult to define.

---

563. *Williams v. Garcetti*, 853 P.2d 507 (Cal. 1993).
564. *Bowers v. State*, 389 A.2d 341, 348 (Md. Ct. App. 1978).
565. New Hampshire Revised Statutes Annotated §627:6(I) (2009) ("[a] parent, guardian or other person responsible for the general care and welfare of a minor is justified in using force against such minor when and to the extent that he reasonably believes is necessary to prevent or punish such minor's misconduct.").
566. *In re Ethan H.*, 609 A.2d 1222 (N.H. 1992).
567. *See* L.B. Custer, *The Origins of the Doctrine of* Parens Patriae, 27 Emory L. J. 195 (1978).
568. The Juvenile Court system has jurisdiction over children who are delinquent because they commit crimes. This court has jurisdiction over certain conduct of a child, which would be noncriminal if done by an adult.
569. This ruling would also include the Due Process Clause of the Fifth Amendment. *DeShaney v. Winnebago County Department of Social Services*, 489 US 189 (1989).

For example, in cases where there is a reporting of possible neglect, dependency, or abuse, it is often a judgment call for the state to determine whether responding to the report would be the right call or whether responding would be an over-reaction, harmful to the child and the family.

A. *Child Dependency, Neglect, and Abuse*

1. Dependency and Neglect

435. A child is dependent upon the state for his or her care when there is no parent available or when the parent has failed to provide the minimum standard of care. Statutory definitions of dependency vary among the states. Similarly, the parent's neglect of the child places the child in need of the state's protection. Statutory definitions of neglect also vary among the states. Neglect and dependency proceedings are very similar as to the facts of the cases and the resulting sanctions. But, the difference between neglect and dependency proceedings centers on parental fault. In neglect proceedings, parental fault is at issue. The fault is not intentional but negligent. In dependency proceedings, parental fault is not at issue. Neglect proceedings may be either civil or criminal. Dependency proceedings are civil proceedings.

436. Parents who do not consent to lifesaving medical treatment for children may be found to be neglecting the child. If the child dies from lack of medical treatment because the parents have not provided such care, parents may be criminally liable for the child's death.[570]

2. Abuse

437. Each state has a child abuse statute, defining abuse. Abuse, unlike neglect, is the intentional injuring of a child. Abuse may be physical, mental, or sexual.

438. Each state has a child abuse reporting statute that may also include neglect. A reporting statute requires individuals who are in positions to notice abused children to report those cases to the proper state agency for investigation. Frequently, that agency is the Child Protective Services Agency, a local agency of the state's Department of Social Services. Typically, doctors, nurses, and teachers are such individuals, designated in the reporting statute.

439. The Child Abuse Prevention and Protection Act, 42 USCA §§5101–5106 (1984), was enacted by Congress to deal with child abuse as a national problem. The Act provides grants to the states to fund certain activities, such as for training, for

570. *Walker v. Superior Court*, 763 P.2d 852 (Cal. 1988).

research, and for providing clearinghouses for use in preventing abuse, and other related activities. The Act also mandates each state to enact reporting laws and procedures.

3. Evidentiary Issues in Dependency, Neglect, and Abuse Hearings

440. The Juvenile Court typically has jurisdiction over dependency, neglect, and abuse hearings. These hearings are usually confidential, closed to the public and to the press. They are usually civil proceedings. Neglect and abuse hearings may also be criminal proceedings. The juvenile court will not have jurisdiction when the accused person is prosecuted under the state's criminal code.

441. The standard for the burden of proof in civil child protective proceedings is the preponderance of the evidence. In criminal proceedings, the standard is beyond a reasonable doubt, a much higher standard of proof.

442. Many states allow expert witnesses to testify in child physical abuse cases that a child fits the pattern of a battered child as defined under the term, the "battered child syndrome." Such evidence is a type of scientific evidence that may aid the trier-of-fact in determining that abuse has occurred. The "battered child syndrome" describes "a clinical condition in young children who ha(ve) received serious physical abuse, generally from a parent or foster parent."[571] This syndrome, if accepted by a court, is useful in aiding in the proof of child abuse in appropriate physical abuse cases.[572] The evidence provided by the syndrome is relevant in showing that the child did not die by accident and that the act was intentional even though the evidence does not identify the abuser.

443. In sexual child abuse cases, some courts will allow an expert to establish that a child fits the pattern of the "child sexual abuse accommodation syndrome." This syndrome describes a pattern of behavior that is found to occur repeatedly in children who are victims of incest.[573] This behavior, however, is not found exclusively in victims of incest. Therefore, this syndrome is not probative as to substantive evidence of sexual abuse. Nevertheless, this testimony is helpful to the jury in explaining the contradictory behavior of a child who has been sexually abused.

444. The issue of the evidentiary hearsay rule arises in regard to the admission of a child's out-of-court statements. If admitted, the child's out-of-court statement must be corroborated. The standard for such admission and corroboration is more

571. Kempe et al., *The Battered Child Syndrome*, 181 JAMA 17 (1962). *See also* National Association of Adult Survivors of Child Abuse, Child Abuse Accommodation Syndrome (March 26, 2009) at http://www.naasca.org/2011-Articles/060111-ChildSexAbuseAccommodationSyndrome.htm.

572. *Estelle v. McGuire*, 502 US 62 (1991).

573. *State v.* J.Q., 617 A.2d 1196 (N.J. 1993); and J.E.B. Myers et al., *Expert Testimony in Child Sexual Abuse Litigation*, 68 Nebraska L. Rev. 1 (1989).

liberal in a civil proceeding than in a criminal proceeding.[574] In *Ohio v. Clark*, the Supreme Court held that admission of a statement made by a three-year-old to his pre-school teacher that the bruises on his body were caused by his mother's boyfriend did not violate the Confrontation Clause.[575]

445. A number of states have enacted statutes to lessen the potential trauma that a child may experience when testifying at trial in a sexual abuse case in front of the accused person. If the child will experience such traumatic distress that the child will not be able to reasonably communicate to the jury, these statutes allow alternative methods for the child to testify other than in open court. Alternative methods include videotaping the child's testimony under both direct and cross-examination prior to trial and using the video at trial as a substitute for the child's presence; allowing the child to present live testimony at trial, but not in the courtroom but through the use of a one-way closed circuit television, where the child's testimony is broadcast onto the monitor in the courtroom; and, through the use of a two-way closed circuit television, where both the child's image is projected in the courtroom and the child's testimony is broadcast into the courtroom.

446. In criminal proceedings, these statutes raise serious issues of denying the accused of his or her constitutional right to confront his or her accusers at trial as guaranteed by the Confrontation Clause of the Sixth Amendment of the United States Constitution.[576] The Supreme Court has set the following standard to determine the constitutionality of such statutes: the nature of the trauma that the child will suffer will impair the child's ability to communicate if the accused is present, but that the alternative method (as set forth in the statute) "ensures the reliability of the evidence by subjecting it to rigorous adversarial testing and thereby preserves the essence of the effective confrontation."[577] In 2004, however, the Supreme Court decided *Crawford v. Washington*, which held that admitting testimonial hearsay at trial, absent the availability of the declarant and a prior opportunity for cross-examination, violates the Confrontation Clause although the Court did not precisely define what is "testimony." It is unclear the impact of this decision on these state trauma statutes.[578] Two years later, in *Davis v. Washington*, the Supreme Court held that statements made during 911 calls seeking aid were not "testimonial" in nature and, therefore, were admissible.[579]

574. *In re Nicole V.*, 518 N.E.2d 914 (N.Y. Ct. App. 1987); and *Idaho v. Wright*, 497 US 805 (1990).
575. 135 S. Ct. 2173 (2015).
576. The Sixth Amendment to the U.S. Constitution provides in part: "In all criminal prosecutions, the accused shall enjoy the right...to be confronted with the witnesses against him."
577. *Maryland v. Craig*, 497 US 836 (1990).
578. 541 U.S. 36 (2004).
579. 547 U.S. 813 (2006).

4. Disposition

a. Disposition Options: Overview

447. If the juvenile court makes a finding of dependency, neglect, or abuse, the court has a number of alternative dispositions in deciding what sanctions should be imposed. The court may allow the child to remain in the home with court-imposed conditions. The court may remove custody from the parent and give custody to a private person, including a relative, to a child-placing agency, to the county or state welfare department, or to a private agency. The court may also place the child in a diagnostic facility or hospital, or in a county or state facility, or it may order medical or psychiatric services for the juvenile. The court may also emancipate the child or place the child in foster care. Finally, the court may terminate the parental rights of the parents.

b. Foster Care

448. Placing the child in foster care until the child can be returned to the parent or adopted is a common disposition in dependency, neglect, and abuse cases. The child may stay in foster care for long periods of time if the return to the parent or adoption does not occur. The increasing numbers of children in foster care for long periods of time is a problem of national scope. In 1997, Congress enacted the Adoption and Safe Families Act, 42 USC §629, which allows faster termination of parental rights for foster children so that they could be adopted and without the state having to use extreme efforts to reunite the child and biological parent. Ultimately, thirty-nine states and the District of Columbia developed subsidized guardianship programs to provide financial support to eligible relative caregivers of children as a result of that Act. Then the Fostering Connections to Success and Increasing Adoptions Act of 2008, 42 USC §§629, et seq., further enhanced foster placements, kinship guardianships, and adoptions, and encouraged sibling placements, educational continuity.

449. Foster parents are paid to provide appropriate care for the child if the foster home is licensed by the state.

450. Since foster children are in the custody of the state, the state must monitor foster care. Because of the large numbers of children living in foster homes and the lack of state funds to hire personnel, many state agencies do not properly monitor and investigate the foster homes.

451. Foster parents do not have constitutional due process rights before a foster child is removed from the home even when a close and loving relationship has developed between foster parents and foster children.[580] Contract law regulates foster care. The state contracts with the foster parent to care for the child and to relinquish the child upon request.

580. *Smith v. Organization of Foster Families for Equality and Reform*, 431 US 816 (1977).

452. In recent years, a new development has evolved regarding kinship care. Many grandparents have found themselves caring for their grandchildren because the grandchildren's parents (the grandparents' children) cannot care for them. Foster care statutes usually do not provide payments to relatives who care for children in situations similar to foster care although federal policy favors such placement. Many grandparents, who are part of this new phenomenon, find themselves in need of financial assistance from the state. They do not qualify because they are related to the children. Although several states provide financial assistance for kinship care, the debate continues over whether grandparents or other close relatives in such circumstances should be paid as if they were foster parents.

c. Termination of Parental Rights

453. The termination of parental rights should rank as the least favored disposition since the status between parent and child becomes that of strangers. Thus, the parent-child relation is permanently severed, causing the termination of all legal rights and obligations between the parent and child. A court usually considers termination proceedings if the rehabilitation of the parent is very unlikely or if the parent's conduct was extremely egregious. However, with the passage of the federal statute, Adoption and Safe Families Act, 42 USC §629, in 1997, to reduce the time that children spend in foster care, the time for parental rehabilitation has been greatly reduced.

454. The right to parent is a constitutionally protected right under the liberty clauses of the fifth and the fourteenth amendments of the United States Constitution. The procedures for the termination of this right must, therefore, meet constitutional standards. The Supreme Court has held the following concerning procedural standards. An indigent parent does not automatically require the appointment of counsel to represent him or her in a termination proceeding, but a court must determine on a case-by-case basis whether this particular indigent parent needs counsel.[581] If such counsel is needed, the state appoints and pays for the counsel. The standard for termination of parental rights is that of the best interests of the child. The standard of proof, however, that the state must meet in proving that it is in the best interests of the child to terminate parental rights is by clear and convincing evidence.[582] An indigent parent, who is appealing a judgment terminating parental rights, has a right to have the state pay for transcript preparation fees.[583]

455. However, the economic and social factors of the status of the parent are not relevant except as they bear upon the parent's ability to cease to harm the child.[584]

581. *Lassiter v. Dept. of Social Services*, 452 US 18 (1981). *See also Meyer v. Nebraska*, 262 U.S. 390 (1923); *Pierce v. Society of Sisters*, 268 U.S. 510 (1925); *Prince v. Massachusetts*, 321 U.S. 158 (1944); *Wisconsin v. Yoder*, 406 U.S. 205 (1972); *Troxel v. Granville*, 530 U.S. 57 (2000).
582. *Santosky v. Kramer*, 455 US 745 (1982).
583. *M.L.B. v. S.L.J.*, 117 S. Ct. 555 (1996).
584. *New Jersey Division of Youth and Family Services v. A.W.*, 512 A.2d 438 (N.J. 1986).

Similarly, mental illness or physical disability standing alone is not enough to terminate parental rights, but must bear upon the parent's ability to cease to harm the child.

V. Children Beyond Parental Control

456. The juvenile court system also has jurisdiction when parents cannot control their children. This court system was created in the nineteenth century to reform the common law's treatment of juveniles as adult criminals. The focus of the juvenile court system is on treatment and rehabilitation of juveniles, not on punishment. The state should act in its role as *parens patriae* and not in its role as prosecutor under its police powers.

457. Children beyond parental control include child delinquents and status offenders. Child delinquents are those whose offensive conduct would be crimes if committed by an adult. Child status offenders are those whose offensive conduct would not be crimes if committed by an adult.

A. *Delinquency Proceedings*

458. Each state has an age requirement, which brings the juvenile under the jurisdiction of the juvenile court. Each state defines what type of juvenile conduct constitutes delinquent conduct unless the state is barred by the Constitution or preempted by federal legislation. Therefore, because of the differences among the states in defining delinquent conduct, what may be defined as delinquency in one state may not be defined as delinquency in another state.

459. States have also enacted the Interstate Compact on Juveniles as a cooperative effort to return out-of-state runaways and delinquents. The Compact provides remedies and procedures that the various states contract to follow. These remedies and procedures are in addition to and not in substitution for other rights, remedies and procedures, which a state has already enforced.[585]

460. In delinquency proceedings, juveniles are afforded many of the same constitutional rights as are adults because these proceedings are now formal proceedings.[586] Juveniles must be afforded the following constitutional rights: "(1) Adequate written notice of the charge, with adequate time given to advise the juvenile and his parents of the allegations of misconduct; (2) the right of counsel; and

585. *See*, e.g., Delaware Code tit. 31 §5203 (2009).

586. With the emphasis of the reformers on treatment and rehabilitation, delinquency hearings were informal even though the child could be institutionalized for many years if adjudicated a delinquent. The United States Supreme Court held that informal court proceedings for juvenile delinquents were unconstitutional. *In re Gault*, 387 US 1 (1967).

if indigent, the right to have counsel appointed; (3) the right to confront witnesses; (4) the right to cross-examine witnesses; and (5) the right to invoke the privilege against self-incrimination."[587]

461. The standard of proof is beyond a reasonable doubt in the prosecution of juvenile crimes that would be crimes if committed by an adult.[588] The double jeopardy protection against a double conviction attaches when the juvenile is adjudicated delinquent in a juvenile proceeding that is then followed by a criminal trial in the adult court.[589] There is no constitutional right to a jury trial in delinquency proceedings, though a state may provide for a jury trial.[590]

462. Juvenile jurisdiction may be waived when the juvenile is charged with a serious crime as long as the juvenile's constitutional rights are protected.[591] The proceeding is then transferred to the adult criminal court. The juvenile has a constitutional right to receive a statement of the reasons for the transfer, a hearing on the transfer, and counsel. The counsel has a right to have access to the reports on which the transfer decision was based.[592]

463. After the juvenile has been adjudicated a delinquent, the dispositional phase of the case follows. The dispositions that the court may impose vary among the states. What is common among the states, however, is that this phase reflects and implements the philosophy of the juvenile court. The disposition should provide for treatment and rehabilitation instead of punishment. The disposition should be on a case-by-case basis: what is in the best interest of a particular juvenile. The most common disposition is probation in the parents' custody. The severest disposition is commitment to an institution for a period of years or until the age of majority. Juvenile records are usually confidential and sealed. In *Roper v. Simmons*, the Supreme Court held that it is unconstitutional to impose the death penalty upon person for crimes committed before they were aged 18.[593]

464. The Federal Juvenile Justice and Delinquency Prevention Act of 1974, 42 USC.A. §§5601–5751 (1974) created an agency, National Center on Child Abuse and Neglect, to administer and monitor grants to fund certain state delinquency prevention programs, provided that the state agrees to restrain juveniles charged with or convicted of a criminal act in secured detention or correctional facilities and not in adult jails.

---

587. L.C. Nolan, *Legal Status of Parent and Child* (U.S. Dept. of Health and Human Services, 1987), p. 327.
588. *In re Winship*, 397 US 358 (1970).
589. *Breed v. Jones*, 421 US 519 (1975).
590. *McKeiver v. Pennsylvania*, 403 US 528 (1971).
591. *See*, e.g., Virginia Statutes Annotated §16.1-269.1 (West, 1997).
592. *Kent v. United States*, 383 US 541 (1966).
593. 543 U.S. 551 (2005).

B. Status Offenders

465. Solely because of their status as minors, juveniles are prohibited from engaging in certain conduct that would not be prohibited if engaged in by an adult. In most states, typical categories of status offenses are incorrigibility, truancy, and running away. Parents are frequently the ones petitioning the court to take jurisdiction because the child is disobedient, truant, or a runaway. The states refer to status offenders under such labels as persons in need of supervision (PINS), child or children in need of supervision (CINS or CHINS), minors in need of supervision (MINS), juveniles in need of supervision (JINS), or youths in need of supervision (YINS).

466. The Federal Juvenile Justice and Delinquency Prevention Act of 1974, 42 USC.A. §§5601–5751 (1974), requires states, in order to receive certain federal funds, to remove status offenders from secured institutions where delinquents are housed and divert them from the juvenile court to other community programs. This Act also contains the Runaway and Homeless Youth Act, 42 USC. §5701 (1974). This Act establishes a national program to care for runaways in shelters and removes them to the jurisdiction of the Department of Health and Human Services.

467. Law enforcement is usually allowed to detain runaways in order to begin the process of returning them home. If runaways cannot be returned home, the juvenile court may take jurisdiction to find placement for them.

§3. Torts Between Parent and Child

468. The judicially created doctrine of parental immunity prevents a minor child, unless emancipated, from suing a parent for torts committed by the parent against the child. The underlying theories behind the doctrine are to promote family harmony and to prevent collusive suits in order to collect insurance benefits. Many states either have abolished the doctrine or have made exceptions to it. Typical exceptions extend to damages that are covered by insurance, such as automobile accidents, and cases of intentionally inflicted criminal abuse.

§4. Parental Liability for Torts and Crimes of Children

469. Although, at common law, children were liable for their torts to the person or property of third parties, their parents were not responsible for these torts unless the damages were directly attributed to the parents' action or non-action. The parents were, thus, responsible for their lack of supervision of the child. Most states have modified the common law rule and have enacted statutes making parents strictly liable for certain of their child's intentional torts. The typical statute is limited to property damage, and liability is limited to a minimum amount.[594] The purpose of these statutes is to create an incentive for parents to control their children's delinquent behavior. Under the family purpose doctrine, many states also impose liability on parents for the negligence of their child, especially when the child negligently drives the family car.[595]

470. Parents are not directly responsible for the criminal acts of their children. They may, however, be vicariously responsible under parental liability statutes for the following: contributing to the delinquency of a child if parents have failed to properly supervise the child;[596] or, if they have endangered the welfare of a child for failure properly to supervise the child;[597] or, if they are responsible under specific types of statutes.[598] The "endangering" statutes may apply to any adult. Violations of these statutes may result in fines, imprisonment, or probation.

§5. EMANCIPATION

471. The law assumes that minor children lack the legal capacity to make decisions regarding their care, supervision, and control. The law gives parents or some other adult that responsibility and disables the child from acting. The minor child, under these circumstances, is classified in the law as an unemancipated child.

472. Emancipation is a process, whereby a minor child is released from the legal disabilities before reaching the age of majority.[599] That is, the child is released from the parents' control and care, and the child takes responsibility for his or her own control and care. The release may be absolute or partial or revocable. If the release is partial, the parent still has the responsibility for the minor's care and control in those areas in which the child remains unreleased. Most emancipations are partial. Parental consent is required in most instances. Emancipation is usually reversible.

I. Operation of Law

473. A child may be emancipated by operation of law. Marriage and military enlistment were the two prevalent examples at common law. Many states have

594. *See*, e.g., Delaware Code Annotated §10-3922 (2009) (amount not to exceed USD 10,000.00).

595. *Madrid v. Shyrock*, 745 P.2d 375 (N.M. 1987); Annotation, *Modern Status of the Family Purpose Doctrine with Respect to Motor Vehicles*, 8 *American Law Reports, 3rd*, (1966), p. 1191 (1966).

596. *See*, e.g., Alabama Code §12-15-13 (2009); and North Carolina General Statutes §14-316.1 (2000).

597. *See*, e.g., New York Penal Law §260.10 (McKinley 1999).

598. E.g., California enacted the Street Terrorism Enforcement and Prevention Act of 1988 to combat gang violence, but it imposes criminal liability of a parent or legal guardian who does not exercise "reasonable care, supervision, protection and control over the minor child." California Penal Code §272 (West, 2008).

599. The age of majority in most states is 18. However, many states do not recognize the age of 18 for emancipating for all purposes. For example, the age requirement for purchasing alcohol in most states is above the age of majority. Several states still impose the parental duty of support to 21.

enacted statutes codifying the prevalent common law examples as well as including additional ones. Marriage emancipates a child in all states, either absolutely or partially. Most states require parental consent for such marriages. In many jurisdictions, the child remains emancipated even if the marriage ends during minority.

474. Enlistment in the military emancipates a minor, at least while the minor is in the military. Parental consent is required for the enlistment. Most states have lowered the age of majority from 21 to 18 years old. Lowering the age of majority has lessened the importance of military service for purposes of emancipation.

475. A state statute may provide the circumstances for emancipation. Statutory emancipation is usually for a specific purpose as listed in the statute. The minor is emancipated for that purpose while the other disabilities remain intact. For example, the typical statute allows certain minors to obtain certain medical treatment without the permission of parents.

II. Judicial Emancipation

476. The common law recognized certain factual circumstances under which a child became emancipated absolutely or partially. Since common law emancipation is determined on a case-by-case basis, this area of the law differs from jurisdiction to jurisdiction and may even be confusing within a jurisdiction. The emancipated child in judicial emancipation is usually the older, mature child, who is capable of living independently and being financially self-supporting. Parental consent is necessary unless the child has abandoned the parent. Under certain circumstances, a court may imply parental consent.

477. If a child has voluntarily abandoned the parent because the child refuses to obey the parent's reasonable discipline, the child is emancipated and the parent is relieved of support obligations.[600]

III. Judicial Declaration or Statutory Emancipation

478. At least nineteen states have enacted statutes creating a judicial proceeding for partial or absolute emancipation.[601] The purpose of these statutes is to clarify the law of emancipation. Such statutes delineate which circumstances emancipate the child and who may petition. The typical statute also provides notice to parents if they are not the petitioner. The standard for granting or denying emancipation is usually the best interests of the child standard.

600. *Parker v. Stage*, 371 N.E.2d 513 (N.Y. Ct. App. 1977); and *In re Jennifer S. v. Marvin S.*, 568 N.Y.S.2d 515 (N.Y. Fam. Ct. 1991).

601. *See*, e.g., 750 Illinois Compiled Statutes §§30/1–30/11 (West, 2003).

Chapter 7. Guardianship and Custody

§1. The Child Living in the Intact Family

479. In the intact family, both parents are entitled equally to the custody of their children without interference from the state or other third parties unless there is abuse of parental authority.[602]

§2. The Custody Decision

I. Introduction

480. When parents are living apart, the state, through the judiciary, under the doctrine of *parens patriae* determines the child's custody. The vast majority of custody cases arise from separation, divorce, and paternity cases. More cases are being litigated because of children being born through artificial reproduction techniques and children being born to same sex couples. The trial court enters an order granting custody to one or more of the litigants. This court has continuing jurisdiction to modify and enforce the order.[603]

481. The court does not generally interfere with the parents' custody decision if they have agreed upon the custody arrangement. The court's custody order usually reflects that decision.[604]

482. The losing party in a custody dispute may appeal the decision for appellate review. The appellate courts use either an abuse of discretion standard or a *de novo* standard. The majority of courts follow the abuse of discretion standard, which is a narrow standard of review, allowing the appellate court to affirm the decision unless there is a clear abuse of discretion.[605] The *de novo* standard allows the appellate court to review the evidence as if that court were hearing the evidence for the first time, although some weight must be given to the trial court's findings.[606]

483. The modern trend in disputed custody cases is the use of mediation or conciliation as an initial effort to help the litigants resolve the custody issue. Most states require litigants to mediate before judicial proceedings commence. Mediation involves the intervention of a third party (the mediator) whose role is to facilitate discussion between two adverse contestants (the parents) who are fighting over custody. Most mediators have some background in counseling, and increasingly some background in law as well. The mediator's role is not to decide the custody question for the parents but to help them reach a decision agreeable to both of them—to

---

602. *See supra* Part 2, Chapter 6, s. 2, Part IV.
603. *See* Part 2, Chapter 9, s. 5, interstate enforcement.
604. *See*, e.g., *Alanna M. v. Duncan M.*, 611 N.Y.S. 2d 886 (N.Y. App. Div. 1994).
605. *See*, e.g., *Carle v. Carle*, 503 P.2d 1050 (Alaska 1972).
606. *See*, e.g., *In re Marriage of Bowen*, 219 N.W. 2d 683 (Iowa 1974).

help them find a way to compromise and get along. Research has shown that mediated cases usually involve less cost, less hostility, and greater satisfaction with the custody decision.

484. A new method of resolving these cases without adversary is evolving as the process of collaboration. Under the process of collaboration the parties and their attorneys formally agree that the case will be resolved without court litigation. If one of the parties breaches the agreement, then these attorneys will not be part of the adversarial case. The parties must hire new attorneys. The point of collaboration is that the attorneys and the parties are acting in good faith to resolve any issues without litigation.

485. In disputed custody cases, the court may appoint an attorney to represent the child or a guardian *ad litem* to act in the child's best interests.

II. Best Interests Standard

486. Every state has adopted the "best interests of the child" standard to determine custody disputes. Inherent in this standard is the principle that each custody case should be judged upon its own facts to determine what is in a particular child's best interests. This standard evolved along with the maternal preference standard to displace the common law standard, which gave preference to the father.[607]

A. Major Criticisms of the Standard

487. The best interests of the child standard is criticized because it is both too broad and too narrow. It is too broad because it "provides little guidance for courts, given the resources actually available to them, to enable them to reach sensible decisions about how a child's interests will actually be best served."[608] It is too narrow because the child's interests may not be the only ones needed to be recognized.[609]

488. This standard has also been criticized because it is indeterminate. There are no consistent views as to what interests are in a child's best interests.[610] It is also indeterminate because it is really a prediction, a judgment call. The trial judge must predict which litigant, based upon past events, will serve the child's best interests for future events. The future events, however, will be different from those of the past.

---

607. At common law, the father had power and right over the child. The mother was "entitled to no power (over her children), but only reverence and respect." W. Blackstone, *Commentaries on the Law of England*, No. 1, (Cooley, 3rd ed., 1884), p. 453, quoted in *Ex Parte Devine*, 398 So.2d 686, 688 (Ala. 1961).
608. D.L. Chambers, *Rethinking the Substantive Rules for Custody Disputes in Divorce*, 83 Michigan L. Rev. 477 (1984).
609. *Ibid.*, 478, 499.
610. *Ibid.*, 479.

489. The standard of the best interests of the child is indeterminate. It is difficult to define the standard with any certainty. Its interpretation varies among the states as well as among judges within a given state.

490. The standard has also been criticized because in determining what is best for a particular child, it works against children in general. Searching for the best decision in every case delays the decision, produces more litigation, increases cost of the decision process, and when it is found, the decision may be out of date.[611]

491. The standard is frequently criticized because it gives too much discretion to the trial court.

B. Limiting the Discretion of the Judge

492. Although trial judges have discretion to determine custody, they do not have unlimited discretion. They must decide the case based upon the evidence before the court and the procedures established by law. Even so, this standard still gives much discretion to the trial judge when it is stated so broadly: "best interests." Such discretion may lead to decisions which are arbitrary or prejudicial, depending upon a judge's predilections.

493. There is a continuing debate whether "best interests" should continue as a broad discretionary standard or change to become a fixed rule.[612] Presumptions for custody, such as parental and maternal preferences, have been used to limit the judge's discretion. Various courts have delineated specific factors that the courts should consider in interpreting "best interests."

494. Many states have codified specific factors that the court must use to determine "best interests." Usually, no one factor is controlling. Such a statute requires the court to determine "best interests" after considering and weighing all the evidence against these factors. Even with such a statute, the trial judge still has much discretion as to how to evaluate and weigh the factors.

C. Factors Affecting the Interpretation of "Best Interests"

495. Courts use common factors in their interpretation of the "best interests" standard. They differ, however, as to how these factors should affect the decision.

---

611. J. Elster, *Solomonic Judgments: Against the Best Interest of the Child*, 54 U. Chicago L. Rev. 1 (1987).

612. Commentators have suggested that fixed rules are also beneficial because they would lessen custody litigation because parents would be informed of the probable outcome of such litigation. P.T. Bookspan, *From A Tender Years Presumption To A Primary Parent Presumption: Has Anything Really Changed? ... Should It?*, 8 B.Y.U. J. Pub. L. (1993).

Courts agree, for example, that a child's environment should be stable and permanent or that siblings, if possible, should not be separated. Even with these underlying principles, courts differ as to their interpretation of the "best interests" standard.

1. Natural Parent Versus Third Party

496. The best interests standard usually gives neither party an advantage in proving to the court how custody should be awarded. When the dispute is between a parent and a third party (a non-parent), however, the court must also consider that parents have a natural right to the custody of their children.[613] Most courts use a presumption that provides that it is in the best interests of a child for custody to be awarded to the parent unless the parent is unfit. Unfitness is usually found if the parent has abandoned or neglected the child or the parent is morally unfit.[614] The evidence needed to overcome the presumption depends upon the strength of the presumption. If the presumption for the natural parent is stated in terms of parental rights, the presumption is very strong and difficult to overcome. Some jurisdictions may use parental preference as only one of the factors to be considered in determining custody disputes.

497. Some courts may use the best interests standard without a presumption or preference to decide custody disputes between a parent and a third party. This standard gives neither party an advantage and the petitioner must show by a preponderance of the evidence that the best interests of the child will be served if custody is awarded to the third party. If the child has established a custodial environment with the third party, courts may be reluctant to change the continuity and stability of the child's environment when using the best interests standard.

498. Stepparents are usually treated as third parties when the child's parent and the stepparent divorce, and the stepparent seeks custody of the stepchild. However, if there has been a long-established relationship between the stepparent and the stepchild and if that relationship holds clearly the best potential for child-rearing, some courts have accorded both standing and some quasi-parental rights.

2. Gender and Age

a. The Tender Years Doctrine

499. The tender years doctrine, known also as the maternal preference doctrine, evolved in the nineteenth century to replace the common law standard, which gave preference to the father. At common law, the father had the primary right to custody unless he was unfit. The tender years doctrine awards custody of children of tender

---

613. *See supra* Chapter 6 §1.
614. *See* Lifestyles, Part II, Chapter 7; Sexual preference, Part II, Chapter 5.

years to the mother unless she is unfit. Its corollary, on the other hand, gives preference for a fit father to have custody of children who are not of tender years. Unfitness, both maternal and paternal, was commonly interpreted in terms of the parent's sexual morality.

500. Whether the tender years doctrine evolved as a separate standard or was part of the best interests standard, as that standard evolved in third-party custody cases, is still uncertain. When the courts in the nineteenth century began replacing the paternal preference standard with the maternal preference standard, courts spoke of it in terms of the best interests of the child.[615]

501. Most states have abandoned the tender years doctrine for a number of reasons, including: (1) the movement for the equality between the sexes, initiated by the women's movement; (2) the no-fault divorce laws, (paradoxically, resulting in more custody disputes); (3) the increase in the number of fathers seeking custody and attacking the doctrine; and (4) the U.S. Supreme Court's finding that discrimination on the basis of gender violates the Equal Protection Clauses of the Fifth[616] and Fourteenth Amendments of the United States Constitution. However, as a practical matter, most courts still award custody to the mother over the father in most contested cases reflecting a hard-to-erase cultural presumption. Additionally, some of the standards for child custody that have replaced the "tender years" presumption, such as the "primary caretaker presumption" are equally gender-biased because they identify as the linguistically gender-neutral factor which in reality favors one gender over the other in custody disputes. However, that may simply reflect the reality that child-rearing is still largely a gender influenced role.

b. Other Gender and Age Factors

502. There is some psychological evidence which supports an award of custody of a child of a certain age to the parent whose sex is the same as the child's.[617]

503. A court may consider as a factor the parent's age and "its potential effect on the welfare of the child."[618]

---

615. *Commonwealth v. Addicks*, 5 Binn. 520 (Pa. 1813) (children of tender years would be best cared for by the mother). *See generally*, L.L. LaFave, *Origins and Evolution of the "Best Interests of the Child" Standard*, 34 South Dakota L. Rev. 459 (1989). Early decisions which discussed the best interests standard without referring to the maternal preference rule did so in cases involving the natural rights of fathers to custody and third parties. *Chapsky v. Wood*, 26 Kan. 650 (1881).

616. The Fifth Amendment is interpreted by the Supreme Court as having an equal protection component although there is no written text.

617. D.L. Chambers, *Rethinking the Substantive Rules for Custody Disputes in Divorce*, 83 Michigan L. Rev. 477 (1984); Hetherington, Stanley-Hagan & Anderson, *Marital Transitions: A Child's Perspective*, Am. Psychol. 303 (1989).

618. *Phelps v. Phelps*, 446 S.E.2d 17 (N.C. 1994).

3. Psychological Parents

504. Sociological and psychological experts have advocated that in deciding custody cases, the determining factor should be in ascertaining to whom the child is psychologically and emotionally attached.[619] The best interest of the child will be served if custody is given to the person who has become the child's psychological parent, whether that person is the biological parent or not.

505. The psychological parent standard may be used more frequently to decide a custody dispute between a parent and third party in a reunification case. In reunification cases, the parent is attempting to obtain custody of a child, who is living with and is being cared for by a third party.

4. Primary Caretaker

506. The primary caretaker doctrine provides that the person who is the child's primary caretaker, if fit, should be granted custody of the child. West Virginia was the only state that adopted this standard, but the West Virginia legislature replaced this doctrine with the American Law Institute (ALI) Principle of allocation of custodial responsibility.[620] Other states, however, may use it as one of the factors to be considered.[621]

507. The primary caretaker doctrine resembles the tender years doctrine since the factors establishing who has the primary caretaker responsibility are still those which the mother traditionally performs more often than not.[622] This doctrine, however, is gender neutral and therefore is not constitutionally suspect.

619. *See*, e.g., Goldstein, Freud & Solnit, *Beyond the Best Interests of the Child* (1973); and Goldstein, Freud & Solnit, *Before the Best Interests of the Child* (1979).
620. The Supreme Court of West Virginia established this doctrine in *Garska v. McCoy*, 278 S.E. 2d 357 (W.Va. 1981), but the state's legislature replaced the doctrine with the American Law Institute principle of allocation of custodial responsibility, where the trial court allocates custody according to the "caretaking functions each parent performed for the child before their separation" (American Law Institute, *Principles of the Law of Family Dissolution* §2.09(1)(a) (2000). *See* West Va. Code §48-9-206 & 207 (2004).
621. *In re Marriage of Holcomb*, 888 P2d. 1046 (Or. Ct. App. 1995); and *Holmberg v. Holmberg*, 529 N.W. 2d 456 (Minn. Ct. App. 1995).
622. The West Virginia case used the following 10 factors: (1) preparing and planning of meals; (2) bathing, grooming and dressing; (3) purchasing, cleaning, and care of clothes; (4) medical care, including nursing and trips to physicians; (5) arranging for social interaction among peers after school, i.e., transporting to friends' houses or, for example, to girl or boy scout meetings; (6) arranging alternative care, i.e., babysitting, day-care, etc.; (7) putting child to bed at night, waking the child in the morning; (8) disciplining, i.e., teaching general manners and toilet training; (9) educating, i.e., religious, cultural, social, etc., and (10) teaching elementary skills, i.e., reading, writing, and arithmetic. *Garska v. McCoy*, 278 S.E.2d 357, 363 (W.Va. 1981).

5. Lifestyles

a. Heterosexual

508. In the past, a parent was usually considered unfit per se to have custody of a child if the parent was living in an unmarried heterosexual relationship (during or after marriage). With the change in society's acceptance of nonmarital relationships, a parent's sexual relationship becomes a factor in the custody decision only if it adversely affects the child. Generally, the perspective from which adverse impact on children is measured is very immediate, and long-range impact on child development is often overlooked.

b. Same-Sex

509. In the past, it was difficult for a LGBT parent to be awarded custody. Most courts held that a person who was LGBT was unfit per se to have custody. Now, however, most courts follow the general trend that the parent's sexual orientation is not a factor unless it adversely affects the child.[623] A small group of courts is in the middle of these two positions. Instead of finding a present detrimental effect, these courts are more willing, however, to find that a potential detrimental effect of the parent's orientation exists in the future and thus, they are more ready to deny or restrict custody than some other courts.[624] Again, in measuring adverse impact on children's development most courts focus on the immediate (is the child bleeding?) rather than long-term development. The effect of extramarital sexual behavior by parents on children may be less-than-immediate process though its consequences may be significant.[625]

510. In situations where a same-sex couple classifies themselves as co-parents of a child, the non-biological co-parent usually is denied standing as a parent when a custody dispute arises. However, there are increasing numbers of jurisdictions that recognize parental rights for the non-biological co-parent. Several jurisdictions have enacted statutes establishing criteria for standing for the non-biological co-parent. On the contrary, same-sex marriages, civil unions, or state domestic partnerships usually protect the standing right of the non-biological co-parent.

6. Race, Religion, and Culture

a. Race

511. Custody decisions, based on race, raise constitutional issues under the Due Process and Equal Protection Clauses of the Fifth and Fourteenth Amendments. Because race is a suspect classification, the government must show that the racial classification is necessary to accomplish a compelling governmental interest. The

---

623. *In re Marriage of Black*, 392 P. 3d 1041 (Wash. 2017).

624. *M.J.P. v. J.G.P.*, 640 P.2d 966 (Okla. 1982).

625. L.D. Wardle, *Parental Infidelity and the "No-Harm" Rule in Custody Litigation*, Catholic U. L. Rev. (2002).

Supreme Court has held that the parent's race may not be the sole factor in determining custody.[626] Even prior to this decision about race, other lesser courts generally did not use race as the sole criterion for awarding custody.

b. Religion

512. Custody decisions, based on religion, also raise constitutional concerns under the First Amendment of the Constitution. A state may not interfere with religious freedom and may not prefer one religion over another.

513. Under the strictest standard which gives the optimum protection to a parent's religious practice, courts may not consider a parent's religion as a factor in the custody decision unless there is an actual showing that the child is harmed by the practice.[627] Under a less strict standard, courts may consider religion as a factor if there is a showing of a reasonable or substantial likelihood of harm.[628]

514. Courts have taken religion into consideration as a favorable factor for the parent who has a religious preference over a parent who is anti-religious or nonreligious.[629] Courts have also considered religion as a favorable factor if a parent will continue the child's already-established religious training. Some courts will enforce a separation agreement, which contains the parents' agreement as to the religious training of the child.[630] Other courts will not enforce such agreements, which is the majority view in the United States.[631]

c. Culture

515. Courts have held that culture may not be the deciding factor in determining custody disputes between parties of the dominant American culture and a non-dominant one.[632] Some states have specifically provided culture as one of the factors.[633] Indeed, in *Adoptive Couple v. Baby Girl*, involving the adoption by non-Indian couple of a part-Indian child, the Supreme Court held that the federal Indian Child Welfare Act did not protect the putative parental rights of an Indian biological father who had relinquished his parental rights and who never had custody of the child.[634]

626. *Palmore v. Sidoti*, 466 US 429 (1984).
627. *Osier v. Osier*, 410 A.2d 1027 (Me. 1980).
628. *In re Marriage of Hadeen*, 619 P.2d 374 (Wash. Ct. App. 1980).
629. *Provencal v. Provencal*, 451 A.2d 374 (N.H. 1982).
630. *Perlstein v. Perlstein*, 429 N.Y.S.2d 896 (N.Y. 1980).
631. *Kendall v. Kendall*, 687 N.E.2d 1228 (1997).
632. The trial court was in error in awarding custody to an Indian mother who would be living in Juneau while the Indian father would be living in the village on the "hypothesis that it is necessary to facilitate the child's adjustment to what is believed to be the dominant culture." *Carle v. Carle*, 503 P. 2d 1050 (Alaska 1972). *See also*, *In re F.W.*, 870 A.2d 82 (D.C. 2005).
633. *See* Washington Rev. Code Ann. § 26.33.045(1) (2010).
634. 133 S. Ct. 2552 (2013).

7. The Child's Preference

516. A court may consider the child's preference for one custodian over another. Some states require that the child's preference be considered. When a child's preference is one of the factors, the court considers the child's preference and weighs it in determining custody according to the age and maturity of the child. As a general rule, the younger the chronological age of the child, the less weight the court will give this factor.

517. The child's preference is usually not given in a formal court proceeding. The judge may interview the child *in camera.* The judge may have a person, such as a social worker, either interview the child and inform the court of the child's preference, or interview the child in the judge's presence to obtain the child's preference. The court may appoint a guardian *ad litem* for the child for purpose of obtaining the child's preference. In order to remedy possible violations of the due process rights of the parents to hear and respond to evidence, some courts will have the parents' counsel present when the child's preference is sought and will also make a record of the proceeding. This record may become part of the trial court's record at the end of the proceeding, or it may become a part of the court's record only if an appeal is taken.

518. Little inquiry, if at all, has been sought as to any psychological harm that a child may suffer from having to voice a preference.

519. No state requires that the child be represented by independent counsel although many states provide for a discretionary appointment. Some states require that a guardian *ad litem* be appointed in contested cases.[635] The traditional role of the guardian *ad litem* is to make a recommendation to the court that reflects what is in the best interests of the child, not to act as an advocate representing a client.

8. Child Sexual Abuse and Domestic Violence

a. Child Sexual Abuse

520. Parental abuse and/or neglect of a child are critical factors in determining custody because they bear on the parent's fitness. The weight that the court gives these factors depends upon the degree of harm the child suffers from the abuse or the neglect. These factors may be determinative of the custody issue.

521. Recently, many more cases have arisen where one parent alleges that the other parent has sexually abused the child. Courts have, however, had great difficulty in determining the validity of these allegations.

635. Wisconsin Statutes Annotated §767.045 (West 1993 & Supp. 1994).

b. Domestic or Spousal Violence

522. In the past, the violence of one parent against the other parent rarely affected the custody decision. Since the 1980s, however, spousal abuse has been recognized as a chronic societal problem. As a result, spousal abuse has emerged as a determining factor in awarding custody to the non-abusing parent.[636] Many states have enacted statutes to include domestic violence as a factor in the custody decision.[637]

523. Some courts have adopted a presumption that a spouse abuser who murders the other spouse is an unfit parent even as to visitation.[638]

9. Custody Arrangements: Sole Versus Joint Custody

524. Until the mid-1970s, almost all custody arrangements were sole custody ones, where custody was awarded to one custodian, who had full decision-making authority over all aspects of rearing the child. With the increase of custody cases and the fathers' rights movement, joint custody has become the competing alternative to sole custody in all states. The concept of joint custody supports the principles that both parents need to be actively involved in the rearing of their child and that the child also needs their involvement.[639]

525. Joint custody usually means that both parents share the decision-making authority as parents do in the intact family. Joint custody may also mean that the parents share joint physical custody, where the child lives and spends equal time with them.[640] The majority of joint custody court orders provide for joint legal custody and sole physical custody.

526. Joint custody is distinguished from alternating or divided custody, where sole custody of the child is alternated between the parents. It is also distinguished from split custody, where each parent has sole custody of some of the children.

527. Some states raise a presumption of joint custody while others have a preference for joint custody, and still others allow joint custody as an option. Most courts agree that joint custody should be awarded only to parents who are friendly and can cooperate with each other.[641] Some opponents of joint custody fear that with a presumption of joint custody that it will be imposed involuntarily or a parent is

636. *In re Marriage of Brainard*, 523 N.W.2d 6ll (Iowa Ct. App. 1994); and *Gant v. Gant*, 892 S.W.2d 342 (Mo. Ct. App. 1995); *See*, Linda D. Elrod & Milford D. Dale, *Paradigm Shifts and Pendulum Swings in Child Custody: The Interests of Children in the Balance*, 42 Fam. L. Q. 381 (2008).
637. *See*, e.g., Arizona Revised Statutes Annotated §25-403 (2009); and Wyoming Statutes §§20-2-201 (209).
638. Massachusetts General Laws Annotated Chapter 209C §3 (a) (West 1999).
639. *Beck v. Beck*, 432 A.2d 63 (N.J. 1981).
640. *In Interest of S.D.J.*, 452 S.E.2d 155 (Ga. Ct. App. 1994); and *Darnall v. Darnall*, 657 So.2d 387 (La. Ct. App. 1995).
641. *Davis v. Kostin*, 617 N.Y.S.2d 229 (N.Y. App. Div. 1994).

fearful to oppose it because of the possibility of sole custody being awarded to the other parent or that it will increase the possibility of domestic violence because the parents must continually be in contact with one another in making decisions for the child.

10. Role of Experts

528. The social sciences, psychology, and psychiatry may be very helpful fields in determining custody cases.[642] First, their information on child development may be the basis of general principles applicable to custody cases.[643] Second, in a specific case, the psychological or psychiatric evaluation of the child and/or of the parents may be useful to the court.

529. The judicial system has been criticized for not utilizing available social science, psychological and psychiatric information.[644] Conversely, others have criticized the court's use of this information because psychology has not developed enough to be helpful in custody decisions and is too subjective and susceptible to bias and manipulation.[645]

530. In a specific custody case, the litigants may each have an expert testify, and/or the court may appoint an expert. The court determines what weight to give the expert's testimony.

531. The court may also appoint experts to make an investigation and report to the court. In some jurisdictions courts have an investigative staff to prepare a report. The court must be very careful how it uses these reports because they are not prepared with the rules of evidence in mind and may contain all sorts of information based on hearsay.

11. Disabilities

532. Courts may consider the parent's physical and mental disabilities in determining custody, but must not deny custody solely on the basis of the disability. The court must determine whether the handicap will in fact have "a substantial and lasting adverse effect on the best interests of the child."[646]

---

642. S.H. Ramsey & R.F. Kelly, *Using Social Science Research in Family Law Analysis and Formation: Problems and Prospects*, 3 Southern California Interdisciplinary L. J. 631 (1994).
643. *See*, e.g., Goldstein, Freud & Solnit, *Beyond the Best Interests of the Child*, (1973), M.L. Fineman & A. Opie, *The Uses of Social Science Data in Legal Policymaking: Custody Determinations at Divorce*, Wisconsin L. Rev. 107 (1987).
644. Sheperd, *Solomon's Sword: Adjudication of Child Custody Questions*, 8 U. Richmond L. Rev. 151 (1974).
645. Okpaku, *Psychology: Impediment or Aid in Child Custody Cases?*, 29 Rutgers L. Rev. 1117.
646. *In re Marriage of Levin*, 162 Cal. Rpt. 757, (Cal. Ct. App. 1980).

D. Visitation Rights

1. Noncustodial Parent

533. The noncustodial parent continues to have a right to have a relationship with the child. This right is an aspect of a parent's constitutionally protected right to have the care, custody, companionship, and management of his or her child. The grant of time to develop this relationship with the child is referred to as "visitation" or "parenting time" in all states. Visitation becomes part of the custody decision.

534. The best interests of the child is the standard to determine, limit, or deny visitation rights. Visitation must be awarded unless the child would be seriously harmed. Visitation may, however, be limited or supervised to the degree that it is not in the child's best interests. Many states now provide services for supervised visitation, where there may be constant supervision by a third party. Some states may also provide services only for the purpose of supervising the transfer of the child from one parent to the other for unsupervised visitation and the return of the child to the other parent after visitation.

535. The same factors that affect the award of custody also affect the grant of visitation.

536. There is no single model for the visitation order. A typical visitation order either states visitation in general terms of "reasonable visitation" or sets forth a visitation schedule. Typical time periods include weekends, weeknights, holidays, and summer vacation. An emerging form of visitation, started at the grassroots level, is virtual visitation, especially when distance separates the child and the noncustodial parent. Virtual visitation includes such internet tools as videoconferencing and webcams. Court-ordered telephone contact is the forerunner of the use of the internet.

2. Third Party

537. At common law, non-parents, including grandparents, did not have a right to have court-ordered visitation. Statutes that provide for visitation to non-parents are significant in that they infringe upon the parents' decision-making authority.

a. Grandparent Visitation

538. All states had enacted statutes, which, under certain circumstances, gave grandparents the right to petition the court for court-ordered visitation prior to the United States Supreme Court reviewing the constitutionality of such statutes as infringing upon parental rights. The majority of the statutes granted visitation rights in cases where the grandchildren's parents divorced or one of them had died. A few statutes allowed visitation in intact families. Most statutes used the best interests of the child as the standard for determining grandparent visitation. In 2000, the Supreme Court decided *Troxel v. Granville*, 530 US 57, reviewing the state of

Washington's grandparent visitation statute, which was an unusual statute because it granted visitation rights to *any* person under certain circumstances. The Court, in a plurality decision, did not hold grandparent visitation statutes unconstitutional per se, but found this statute unconstitutional as applied. The Court, noting that the statute was "breathlessly overbroad" in allowing anyone standing to request visitation and that the parents had not sought to cut off visitation, held that a court must give proper weight to a fit parent's decision regarding the best interest of the child as to visitation and not based visitation solely on the court's determination as to what is in the child's best interest. The Court left open as to what standard of review should apply to these statutes and did not agree as to the standard when the court could interfere with a fit parent's decision.

539. Both state courts and legislatures responded to *Troxel v. Granville*. Some found their statutes did not give due deference to a fit parent's decision; some determined grandparent visitation only if the harm standard is used or use best interest of the child test if the grandparent or third party had established a parent-child relationship. Others established a rebuttable presumption that the parent's decision is in the best interest of the child.

b. Stepparent Visitation

540. Stepparents may be awarded visitation upon separation and divorce. A few statutes specifically recognize the right of a stepparent to petition the court for visitation. A court, without a statute, under its *parens patriae* prerogative, may order stepparent visitation in appropriate cases. The best interests of the child is the standard for determining stepparent visitation. The court determines whether a bond exists between the child and the stepparent and further determines the quality of the bond between them. Usually, the court considers whether the stepparent has acted *in loco parentis* or has become the child's psychological parent. If such a significant bond has developed, the court applies the best interests standard to determine whether visitation should be granted.

c. Adoption

541. If a child is adopted, the termination of parental rights usually abolishes the visitation rights of all biological relatives. There is a trend in some states, especially those which allow open adoption, to allow the adoption judgment to provide for visitation with biological relatives.

542. Some statutes and court decisions grant visitation to grandparents of a child who has been adopted by a stepparent.

d. Other Third Parties

543. A few state statutes specifically allow other "interested parties" the right to petition the court for visitation. Courts without such statutes may also allow such third parties to petition for visitation. "Interested party" usually means a third party who has developed a significant bond with the child, especially if the third party and the child have lived in the same home. The best interests of the child standard is then applied.

E. Custodial Authority

544. Unless the custody order provides otherwise, the child's custodian usually has decision-making authority as to the child's upbringing. In joint custody arrangements, both parents jointly share custodial authority.

1. Education

545. The custodial parent has broad authority over the child's education. This authority will not be limited unless the child is harmed by the training or a state law is being violated.[647]

546. The custodial authority may be limited if the parents have agreed upon the child's education, and if this agreement is part of the custody order or the parents' separation agreement. If their agreement is only an agreement to agree, some courts will not enforce such an agreement. Under basic contract law, an agreement to agree is not enforceable.

2. Medical Treatment

547. The custodial parent's right to decide the child's medical treatment will be restricted only to the extent to protect the child from harm. Such cases often arise when the custodial parent's religious practice would prevent that parent from consenting to what a court perceives as standard medical care that would benefit the child. In order to protect the child from being harmed and to minimize the state's interference with the custodial parent's religious rights, the court may eliminate the custodial parent's need to consent[648] or order the noncustodial parent to make such decisions.

---

647. *Tersch v. Tersch*, 455 N.W.2d 130 (Neb. 1990).
648. *Levitsky v. Levitsky*, 190 A.2d 621 (Md. Ct. App. 1963).

3. Religion

548. The custodial parent usually has the right to control the child's religious training.[649] Courts may also require the child to be raised in the noncustodial parent's religion, if this arrangement is in the best interests of the child.[650]

549. The enforcement of religious restrictions also arises when parents enter into agreements regarding the religious training of their children. As a general rule, courts will not enforce these agreements. They defer to the custodial parent's decision and avoid the appearance of favoring one religion over another.[651] Conversely, a minority of courts will enforce these agreements.

4. Renaming Children

550. The problem of whether the custodial parent may change the surname of the child over the objection of the noncustodial parent usually arises when the custodial parent is the mother and the child has always used the father's surname. Courts generally follow the best interests of the child standard instead of either following the common law standard or custom, which gives the father a primary right to have the child bear his name, or using a rebuttable presumption that the custodial parent's decision should govern.[652]

5. Change of Residence by Custodial Parent (Relocation)

551. The most restricted area of custodial authority regards the custodial parent's decision to move with the child from one state to another state. The residential move usually interferes with the noncustodial parent's visitation rights. In order to protect the noncustodial parent's interest and to preserve the court's jurisdiction, most custody orders contain a provision that the child may not leave the jurisdiction of the court without its permission or the noncustodial parent's permission.

552. Courts use the best interests of the child standard,[653] but differ as to its interpretation. Relocation continues to be a frequently contested issue as the courts struggle to interpret the best interests standard for relocation matters. The following two interpretations are the prevailing ones, but with many variations. Relocation is

---

649. *In re Marriage of Gersovitz v. Siegner*, 779 P.2d 883 (Mont. 1989).

650. *Vazquez v. Vazquez*, 443 So.2d 313 (Fla. Ct. App. 1983). Paul, *You Get the House, I Get the Car. You Get the Kids. I Get Their Souls*, 138 U. Pennsylvania L. Rev. 583 (1989).

651. *In re Marriage of Heriford*, 586 S.W.2d 769 (Mo. Ct. App. 1979).

652. *In re Marriage of Schiffman*, 620 P.2d 579 (Cal. 1980).

653. This standard has been criticized because it ignores the custodial parent's constitutional rights regarding "travel, home, family, marriage, and autonomy." A.B. Laurence, Child *Custody and Relocation: A Constitutional Perspective*, 34 U. Louisville J. Fam. L. 1, 9 (1995–1996); Richard A. Warshak, *Social Science and Children's Best Interests in Relocation Cases*: Burgess *Revisited*, 34 Fam. L. Q. 83 (2006).

disallowed only if the noncustodial parent can show that the move is not in the child's best interests. Or, the move is allowed only if the custodial parent shows a good faith motive for the move.

F. Modification

553. The custody order is not a final judgment; it is modifiable. Custody orders are modifiable in order to protect the welfare of the child. Custodians as well as custody arrangements may be changed. The custody decision may also be modified to grant, deny, increase, or limit visitation.

554. The general standard for modification is the substantial change of circumstances standard. Substantial changes of circumstances must have occurred from the date of the entry of the custody order so that they warrant that it would be in the best interests of the child to modify the custody order. Some states will not allow a modification hearing if the current custody order has been in effect less than two years, unless there is a showing that the child is being physically or psychologically harmed. These standards are based on the principles of a child's perceived need for stability and continuity in the custody arrangement, of res judicata, and judicial economy.

555. Some courts have developed exceptions to the general standard of substantial change of circumstances if that standard cannot be met and the custodial arrangement is not in the child's best interests. One exception allows the modification proceeding to occur if there are facts, which the court did not consider at the time the custody decree was entered.[654] Other courts may allow modification hearings when the custody order was based upon the agreement of the parents or upon a default judgment.[655] Other courts either follow the best interests standard in all modification cases and not the substantial change of circumstances standard or use the best interests standard in compelling cases.

556. The changes of circumstances which courts find are substantial are similar to those in deciding the initial custody award. Such changes include the moral fitness of the custodial parent, the child's preference, and residential moves.

G. Enforcement of Custody and Visitation Orders

1. Intrastate

557. Custody and visitation orders are usually enforced by the contempt powers of the court, either civil or criminal contempt.[656] The penalties for contempt may

---

654. *Simons v. Simons*, 374 A.2d 1040 (Conn. 1977).
655. *Friederwitzer v. Friederwitzer*, 432 N.E.2d 765 (N.Y. Ct. App. 1982).
656. *Smith v. Smith*, 434 N.E.2d 749 (Ohio Ct. App. 1980).

range from incarceration to change of custody.[657] As a general rule, the self-help remedy of withholding of the child support is not a legal remedy for interference with visitation. Intrastate enforcement of custody and visitation orders usually concerns enforcement of visitation rights rather than enforcement of custody rights. The court is enforcing a custody judgment that it has rendered, which usually does not raise interstate custody issues.

2. Interstate

a. Introduction

558. In the past, states were not obligated to give full, faith and credit[658] to the custody judgments of sister states because they are modifiable and not final judgments. As a result, instead of enforcing a custody judgment already rendered by another state, the forum state had discretion to take jurisdiction, rehear the custody case if the child was in that state, and redetermine custody. The possibility of having another state redetermine custody led to unnecessary rehearing of custody cases and the "snatching" by parents of their children into other jurisdictions. The Uniform Child Custody Jurisdiction Act[659] and the Federal Parental Kidnapping Prevention Act[660] have brought both reform and stability to custody judgments. Most importantly, the Parental Kidnapping Prevention Act implements the Full Faith and Credit Clause of the Constitution to apply to custody judgments. In 1997, the National Conference on Commissioners on Uniform Laws, which proposed the Uniform Child Custody Jurisdiction Act, proposed the Uniform Child Custody and Enforcement Act to replace and modify the Uniform Child Custody Jurisdiction Act[661] and make it compatible with the Parental Kidnapping Prevention Act.

559. In 1968, the National Conference of Commissioners on Uniform Laws proposed the Uniform Child Custody Jurisdiction Act (UCCJA) to bring uniformity to the states' conflicting jurisdictional custody laws in order to stabilize custody judgments by discouraging multi-state relitigation and child snatching. All states have adopted a version of this Act. In 1997, however, the National Conference of Commissioners on Uniform Laws proposed the Uniform Child Custody Jurisdictional and Enforcement Act (UCCJEA) to replace and modify the UCCJA and to make it conform to the requirements of the federal Parental Kidnapping Prevention Act (PKPA).

---

657. Some states have innovative enforcement provisions. Example Michigan's statute provides for make-up visitation.

658. U.S. Constitution, Art. IV. s. 1. "Full Faith and Credit shall be given in each State to the public Acts, Records, and judicial Proceedings of every other State; And the Congress may by general Laws prescribe the Manner in which such Acts, Records and Proceedings shall be proved, and the Effect thereof."

659. *Uniform Laws Annotated*, No. 9 (pt.1A), (1999 & Supp. 2009), p. 261.

660. 28 USC.A. §1738A (1980).

661. *Uniform Laws Annotated*, No. 9 (pt.1A), (1999 & Supp. 2009), p. 649.

560. Congress enacted the Federal Parental Kidnapping Prevention Act (PKPA) in 1980 to respond to its findings that the conflict in state custody jurisdiction "contributed to the concealment and interstate transportation of children, the disregard of court orders, [and] excessive relitigation of cases" due to the "failure of such jurisdictions to give full faith and credit to the judicial proceedings of the other states."[662] The PKPA establishes the constitutional requirements for interstate enforcement of custody judgments. The PKPA also provides that if parental child snatching is a state felony in the state where the child was snatched, the Federal Fugitive Felon Act applies to the "snatching" parent. In all PKPA cases, the federal parent locator service is available to locate the "snatching" parent.

561. Since the PKPA implements the Full Faith and Credit Clause of the Constitution, the Act takes precedence, under the Supremacy Clause of the United States Constitution, when the Act conflicts with the UCCJA or the UCCJEA. These Acts establish the requirements for subject matter jurisdiction, for declining jurisdiction, for communicating between courts, and for enforcing or modifying another state's judgment. The UCCJA and UCCJEA also provide for the res judicata effect of the decree and the enforcement of judgments of foreign countries. UCCJEA also introduced expedited enforcement procedures. The UCCJEA has been adopted by forty-nine states and the District of Columbia; Massachusetts is the only State that has rejected the UCCJEA and still clings to the UCCJA.

b. Jurisdiction to Render the Initial Custody Order

562. The UCCJA confers subject matter jurisdiction in four categories of cases: the "home state," the "significant connection," "emergency," and "no other state has jurisdiction." The "home state" category permits jurisdiction if the state is the home state of the child. A state is a "home state" if the child has lived there since his or her birth if less than six months of age or has resided there with his parent for six months. A state is also a "home state" if it has been the child's home state within the six months period before the commencement of the custody case and the child is absent from that state because of removal or retention by a person claiming the child's custody. In either case, a parent or one acting as a parent must continue to live in the state.

563. The UCCJEA also confers subject matter jurisdiction in four categories: "home state" jurisdiction, "significant connection," "more appropriate forum," and "when no other state has jurisdiction." It also provides for "temporary emergency" jurisdiction. Unlike the UCCJA, the UCCJEA gives priority to "home state" jurisdiction, bringing it into compliance with the PKPA's priority of "home state" jurisdiction, and rejecting the UCCJA's equal treatment of "home state" and "significant connection" jurisdiction. The purpose of priority of "home state" jurisdiction should also reduce the number of states having concurrent jurisdiction, and thus reducing the number of custody orders by different state courts. Under the UCCJEA "home state" is defined as the state where the child has lived since his or her birth if less

662. P.L. 96-611, Sec. 7(a) (1980), *codified at* 28 USC.A. §1738A.

than six months of age or has resided there with the parent for a six-month period prior to the filing of the custody case or for a six-month period that is completed at any time within six months prior to the filing of the custody case and child is absent from this state, but a parent or person acting as a parent continues to live in the state.

564. The UCCJA's "significant connection" category permits jurisdiction if it appears to be in the child's best interest because the child and his parents or the child and at least one contestant have significant connection with such state other than mere physical presence, and there is available substantial evidence concerning the child's present or future welfare. The UCCJEA's "significant connection" jurisdiction permits a state to take jurisdiction if there is no home state or the home state declines jurisdiction if the child has sufficient ties to the state and substantial evidence concerning the child is available in the state. Although two or more states may have jurisdiction, the first state in which the custody case is filed has jurisdiction, but this state must communicate with another court if the case is also filed in that later state. The first state may now choose to defer to the second state. The UCCJEA eliminates the use of the phrase "best interests" to avoid a state's misuse of the phrase to provide grounds for awarding custody.

565. The UCCJA's "emergency" category permits jurisdiction if the child is physically present in the state and has either been abandoned or it is necessary to protect the child because there is an emergency. The UCCJEA clarifies that "emergency jurisdiction" is temporary only. It also expands "emergency jurisdiction" to include cases where a child, sibling, or parent is subject to or threatened with violence in another jurisdiction; however, unlike the UCCJA it excludes neglect cases. This exclusion makes the UCCJEA compatible with the PKPA.

566. The UCCJA's and the UCCJEA's "no other state" category permits jurisdiction if no other state has jurisdiction under the particular Act or has declined jurisdiction.

567. Because under the UCCJA more than one state may have jurisdiction, the Act requires a state to decline jurisdiction if another custody case is pending in another state. The state must decline unless (1) the other court is not exercising jurisdiction substantially in conformity with this Act, or (2) on the basis of forum non conveniens, or (3) under the Act's unclean hands provision if the petitioner has wrongfully taken the child from another state or has engaged in similar "reprehensible" conduct.

568. The third basis of initial jurisdiction under the UCCJEA is the "more appropriate forum," which permits jurisdiction when the "home state" and the "significant connection" states decline jurisdiction in favor of another state that is the more appropriate state because of inconvenient forum or unjustifiable conduct.

569. The Act makes no provision for the tolling of the home state period when a child is snatched and concealed. The home state would lose jurisdiction if an action were not commenced within that time period. However, some states have interpreted the Act to toll the home state period of time so that it would not lose jurisdiction.

570. A state's initial custody judgment should also conform to the PKPA's jurisdictional requirement so that the judgment will be enforced under the PKPA if interstate litigation occurs. The PKPA provides that the state rendering the initial custody judgment has jurisdiction to enter that judgment if the state had jurisdiction under its law (which would be its version of the UCCJA or the UCCJEA) and had jurisdiction under one of the five categories permitted under the PKPA. The first four categories of the PKPA are very similar to those of the UCCJA and the UCCJEA: "home state," "significant connection," "emergency," and "no other state." The fifth category permits jurisdiction where the rendering state has continuing jurisdiction. Unlike the UCCJA, UCCJEA is consistent with the PKPA with home state taking priority jurisdiction.

c. Jurisdiction to Enforce or Modify an Existing Custody Order

571. The UCCJA also applies to the enforcement and modification of a sister state's custody judgment (foreign judgment). Under the UCCJA, a state cannot modify a foreign judgment unless the rendering state no longer has jurisdiction or has declined jurisdiction and the forum state has jurisdiction. In addition, a state shall not exercise its jurisdiction if the petitioner has improperly removed the child from the physical custody of the custodian or improperly retained the child after a visit. The PKPA is also important in the modification and enforcement of custody judgments since it sets forth the requirement for subject matter jurisdiction for full faith and credit purposes so that a state must recognize the judgment. The UCCJEA, consistent with the PKPA, specifies that the state that entered the initial custody decree retains exclusive continuing jurisdiction for modification unless the initial decree court loses "significant connection" jurisdiction or the child, the child's parent, or someone acting as the child's parent no longer lives in the state.

572. The PKPA provides that a forum state shall enforce the rendering state's judgment if that judgment is made consistently with the provisions of the PKPA, unless the forum state has jurisdiction to modify the judgment and the rendering state no longer has jurisdiction or has declined jurisdiction. A judgment is made consistent with the PKPA if the rendering state had jurisdiction under its state law (UCCJA or UCCJEA) and under one of the five categories of cases under the PKPA. The UCCJEA conforms with the PKPA in giving priority to "home state" jurisdiction and in giving the initial state entering the custody decree exclusive jurisdiction for modification unless the initial decree court loses significant connection jurisdiction or the child, the child's parent, or someone acting as the child's parent no longer lives in the state. The UCCJEA also contains provisions for enforcement of custody judgments in order to bring uniformity among the states.

573. When the UCCJA or UCCJEA conflicts with the PKPA, the PKPA preempts the UCCJA. There is potential conflict because of the differences in the interpretation of the "significant connection" category in the two Acts. The UCCJA provides that a state (the forum state) shall not modify another state's (the rendering state) custody judgment unless it appears that the rendering state does not presently have jurisdiction under jurisdictional prerequisites substantially in accordance with the Act (the four categories) or has declined jurisdiction. Some states have interpreted this section broadly to mean that the rendering state continues to have jurisdiction under the "significant connection" category as long as one of the parents resides there. Other states have interpreted this section narrowly to mean that the requirements for continuous jurisdiction are the same as the requirements for initial jurisdiction. Unlike the UCCJA, there is no alternative under the PKPA where one state may have jurisdiction under "home state" and another under "significant connection." Under the PKPA, there can be jurisdiction under the "significant connection" category only if there appears to be no "home state." The UCCJEA, however, conforms to the PKPA regarding "home state" jurisdiction.

574. The PKPA does not preempt the UCCJA or UCCJEA simply if they conflict but if the conflict would undermine the PKPA. That is, the PKPA does not prevent states from giving greater full faith and credit to child custody decrees than it requires. Thus, if under the UCCJA a state would be required to respect and enforce a sister state child custody decree, even if it would not be required to do so under the PKPA, the UCCJA would require it to do so. In that sense, the PKPA would not "preempt" the UCCJA.

3. International

a. The Hague Convention

575. In 1985, the United States ratified the Hague Convention on the Civil Aspects of International Child Abduction and enacted its implementing legislation, the International Child Abduction Remedies Act.[663] The purposes of the Convention are "a) to secure the prompt return of children wrongfully removed to or retained in any Contracting State; and b) to ensure that rights of custody and of access under the law of one Contracting State are effectively respected in the other Contracting States."[664] The United States Supreme Court interpreted the treaty as treating a noncustodial parent's *ne exeat* rights as rights of custody rather than rights of access. Thus, under this interpretation of these terms under this treaty, the noncustodial parent has standing to invoke the treaty and litigate claim that the child was wrongfully removed from the country of habitual residence, which in this case was Chile.[665] This case is also the Supreme Court's first international family law case.

663. 42 USC. §§11601–11610 (1985).

664. Hague Conference On Private International Law: Convention on the Civil Aspects of International Child Abduction (14th Session, 25 Oct. 25, 1980), Art. 1.

665. *See Abbott v. Abbott*, 560 U.S. 1 (2010).

576. Each country has a "central authority" where the matter is initially filed. In the United States, the U.S. Department of State serves as the central authority. The U.S. Department of State will refer the matter to the appropriate jurisdiction.

577. The Convention applies to a child under the age of 16, who was habitually a resident in a contracting state immediately before any breach of custody or access rights.[666] "Rights of custody" includes "rights relating to the care of the person of the child and, in particular, the right to determine the child's place of residence."[667] "Rights of Access" includes the right to take a child for a limited period of time to a place other than the child's habitual residence.[668] The Convention also provides three affirmative defenses that the abducting parent can assert: (1) the child's caretaker was not actually exercising custody rights at the time of the removal or had consented to the removal; (2) there is grave risk that the return would entail physical or psychological harm to the child; and (3) the forum court, based on its discretion, finds that the child, who has attained an appropriate age and maturity, objects to the return.[669] The courts have generally construed these defenses narrowly so that the children are usually returned to the foreign country. Recent cases have raised the concern that abducting parents may be fleeing with the child because of domestic violence. Courts have usually construed that the domestic violence must be toward the child and not the parent.

578. The Hague Convention gives jurisdiction to the court at the place of the child's "habitual residence" to decide the merits of the custody issue. Thus, the court hearing the abduction claim has jurisdiction only to determine the merits of the abduction claim, not the merits of the custody issue. The contracting countries agree to the prompt return of children who are wrongfully removed or retained, unless the person or institution having care of the person of the child was not actually exercising custody rights at the time of the removal or retention, or the child will be physically or psychologically harmed or placed in an intolerable situation.

579. The Convention does not define "habitual resident." Some courts have concluded that there is no real difference between ordinary residence and habitual residence. It should not be confused with domicile or legal residence. It should refer to customary residence prior to the child's removal or retention. A child's habitual residence may only be altered by change of geography and passage of time.[670] A survey of recent federal court decisions indicate that about half the courts use the parents' last shared subjective indicators in determining of habitual residence. The other half use objective indicators.[671] In *Abbott v. Abbott*, 130 S. Ct. 1983 (2010), the Supreme Court held that a parent with a *ne exeat* right has a right of "custody" under the Hague Convention on the Civil Aspects of International Child Abduction

666. *Ibid.*, Art. 4.
667. *Ibid.*, Art. 5.
668. *Ibid.*, Art. 5.
669. *Ibid.*, Art. 13.
670. *Friedrich v. Friedrich*, 983 F.2d 1396 (Sixth Cir. 1993).
671. Tai Vivatvaraphol, *Back to Basics: Determining A Child's Habitual Residence In International Child Abduction Cases Under the Hague Convention*, 77 Fordham L. Rev. 3325 (2009).

(Convention) and the U.S. implementing statute, the International Child Abduction Remedies Act (ICARA), 42 USC §§11601 et seq.

580. The Hague Convention and its implementing legislation, the International Child Abduction Remedies Act, provide that the abductor shall reimburse the custodian for the necessary expenses incurred to secure the return of the child or children and which are not "clearly inappropriate," even if the abductor acted in good faith. [672] In *Lozano v. Montoya Alvarez*, the Supreme Court held that the one-year mandatory return provision in the Hague Convention on the Civil Aspects of International Child Abduction (Convention), October 25, 1980, was not subject to equitable tolling even with the abducting/retaining parent was concealing the child and her location.[673]

b. International Parental Kidnapping Crime Act and the Uniform Child Abduction Prevention Act

581. The International Kidnapping Crime Act[674] makes the international kidnapping of a child a crime when a person, with the intent to obstruct the lawful exercise of parental rights, removes a child from the United States or retains a child outside the United States who has been in the United States. The term "parental rights" is defined as (1) a right to physical custody of a child who is not 16 years old, whether in a sole or joint custody arrangement, or (2) a right to visitation of such a child. One of the purposes of the Act is to deter parents who would move the child to a country that is not a signatory to the Hague Convention. Thus, without this Act each non-signatory country would use its legal system to resolve the return of the child without regards to United States law.

582. Affirmative defenses include (1) fleeing from domestic violence, (2) acting within the provisions of a valid court order, that was issued pursuant to the Uniform Child Custody Jurisdiction Act and awarded custody or visitation to the defendant, and (3) failing to return the child because of circumstances beyond the defendant's control, but where the defendant made reasonable attempts of notification within twenty-four hours after the custody or visitation period had expired and returned the children as soon as possible. The Act provides that one who violates the Act shall be fined, or imprisoned not more than three years, or both.

583. The National Conference of Commissioners on Uniform State Laws promulgated the Uniform Child Abduction Prevention Act in 2006, to identify risk factors in domestic and international custody cases in order to help to prevent such abduction.[675]

672. *Currier v. Currier*, 845 F. Supp. 916 (D.N.H. 1994). Lynn D. Wardle, *The Merit of Modesty: Abduction, Relocation, and the Hague Abduction Convention*, 9 J. Compar. L. 89–110 (2014).
673. 134 S. Ct. 1224 (2014).
674. 18 USC.A. §1204 (1997).
675. 9 U.L.A. (pt. 1A) p. 40 (Supp. 2009).

§3. Children Born Out of Wedlock

I. The Unwed Mother

584. Under common law, the unwed mother had the right to the custody of the child born out of wedlock. The tradition continues in the United States although an unwed father may also obtain custody of the child. Furthermore, the unwed mother's right to custody is an aspect of her constitutionally protected right to parenthood. The constitutional protection of this right is comparable to the constitutional protection that is given to a married couple's right to parenthood.

II. The Unwed Father

585. Historically, the law has treated the unwed father's right to parenthood differently from that of the married father, who shares custody of the child with his wife. The United States Supreme Court has interpreted the unwed father's constitutionally protected right to parenthood in terms of his having established an actual relationship with the child.[676] A state may not deprive him of asserting his parental rights of custody and visitation if he meets this standard.

586. States may, however, limit or not recognize his rights if he does not meet this constitutional standard. The typical effect of not meeting the standard of having established an actual relationship with the child is that the unwed father is prohibited from establishing parenthood with the child.

587. If an unwed father has the right to assert parental rights and if paternity is established, states grant custody and visitation rights to unwed fathers, applying the best interests of the child standard.

§4. Guardianship

I. General Principles

588. When neither parent of a minor child is available to take custody of a child, the law in each state sets forth the procedure for appointing a guardian of the child's person. If the child has property, the court will appoint a guardian for the property.[677] The same person may be both the guardian of the child's person and the guardian of the child's property.

589. Guardianship is essentially a custody procedure. The best interests of the child is the standard for deciding guardianship cases. Many states have separate

---

676. *Lehr v. Robertson*, 463 US 248 (1983); *Stanley v. Illinois*, 405 US 645 (1972).

677. Although a parent is the natural guardian of the child's person, the court appoints a guardian of the child's property. *See* §5 on Conservatorship.

courts and separate statutes for deciding guardianship cases and for deciding custody in divorce and paternity cases. The guardian of the person of the child has custody of the child and assumes the child-rearing responsibilities, but does not assume the duty of support. Guardianship ends when the child reaches majority or is emancipated.

590. The court may appoint as guardian an individual, a state agency, or a private institution.

II. The Child's Preference

591. Most states allow a child of 14 or older the right to choose his or her guardian unless the court finds the person unfit. Several jurisdictions may require the court to find that the child has the mental capacity to make the choice. The court's willingness to allow the child's choice to be controlling in guardianship cases but not in divorce and paternity custody cases may be explained by the fact that guardianship cases do not involve disputes between parents, but rather, the choosing of an eligible adult to care for the child when his or her parents are not available.

III. Testamentary Guardianship

592. Both parents in the intact family have custody of their child. When one of the parents dies, the surviving parent has custody. This right of parental custody is also true in the case of the death of the custodial parent when parents are divorced or separated. The surviving parent has custody of the child.[678] When the surviving parent dies, that parent may use his or her last will and testament to appoint a person of his or her choosing to become the guardian of the person of the child. Although this appointment is subject to court approval, there is minimal investigation. Once appointed, that person will assume custody and rearing responsibilities. The surviving parent may also appoint in the will the guardian of the child's property.[679]

§5. Conservatorship

593. Although biological and adoptive parents are the natural guardians of their children, they are not the natural guardians of the property of their children. The law requires that a guardian be appointed for the child's property, that is, the child's estate. Guardianship of the child's estate is termed conservatorship in many state

678. Even though a child may be living with a custodial parent and stepparent, when the custodial parent dies, the noncustodial parent has the natural custody of the child. A stepparent may petition the court, arguing that it is in the best interests of the child that custody be awarded to the stepparent.
679. *See* §5 on Conservatorship.

statutes. A parent who dies often appoints the guardian of the minor's property in the will. Persons as well as institutions often act as the guardians of a child's estate.

594. A parent and others, while living or at death, who give property to children may avoid conservatorship by using a trust arrangement or using the custodianship arrangement under the Uniform Gifts to Minors Act or the Uniform Transfers to Minors Act or by trust.[680]

680. *See* Part 4, Chapter 2, s. 1, Part III, for tax consequences of gifts to children.

Chapter 8. Kinship and Relationship of Affinity

§1. Consanguinity Law: Incest

595. All states prohibit marriage within the immediate family, including ascendants, descendants, and siblings. The states vary as to prohibition of marriage between other blood relations and relations by affinity. The most common prohibitions among the states are marriages between aunt-nephew, uncle-niece, first cousins, stepparents and stepchildren, and adoptive parents and adoptive children. Kinship usually extends to half-blood relations. Prohibitions against marriage between relations by the affinity are rapidly ending, especially in circumstances where the relationship has ceased. States that recognize same-sex marriages or have enacted civil union or domestic partnership statutes have similar prohibitions for a woman marrying or entering into a civil union or domestic partnership with her mother, sister, niece, etc. as well as for a man marrying or entering into a civil union or domestic partnership with his father, brother, nephew, etc.

596. Incest occurs when persons who are closely related to each other have sex. It may be defined as a crime under state law. While both parties are guilty of incest, if one of the parties was under the undue influence of the other, it is generally the aggressor who is charged with the crime.

§2. The Extended Family: Kinship and Step-Relationship

I. The Extended Family: Kinship

597. In the American legal system the nuclear family is the operative unit and the focus of regulation, not the extended family. The traditional area in which the law has imposed rights on the basis of kinship extending to and beyond the nuclear family is in the area of dealing with succession and inheritance rights. A decedent's nearest surviving kin succeeds to the decedent's property if the decedent dies without a will. The nearest surviving kin may be a very distant collateral kin.[681] The grandparent-grandchild relationship generally does not confer any rights or impose any obligations, except for inheritance and succession purposes, unless there is a statute to the contrary. Recent statutes to the contrary are the grandparent visitation statutes, granting rights to grandparents to have standing to petition a court for court-ordered visitation with a grandchild.[682]

II. The Extended Family: Step-Relationship

598. The existence of the stepparent-child relationship does not usually confer any rights or impose any obligations. A few states have imposed an obligation for

681. *See infra* Part 4, Chapter 1, s. 3.
682. *See supra* Part 2, Chapter 7, s. 3, Part II (D).

support on the stepparent if the stepparent stands *in loco parentis* to the stepchild. An *in loco parentis* relationship is based upon the intent of the stepparent to enter into the relationship and assume the status of parent. This relationship is terminated when the marriage ends, or it may be terminated voluntarily by either the stepparent or the child. A few states statutorily impose support obligations on stepparents during the marriage.[683] States that have enacted domestic partnership and civil union laws usually treat the relationship between the non-biological partner and the other partner's child as a stepparent relationship.[684]

599. Unless there is statutory or case law to the contrary, a stepparent is treated as a third party in custody disputes between the stepparent and the child's biological parent.

600. Stepchildren are usually not included in intestate statutes for inheritance purposes. If stepchildren are included at all, they take in default of the *escheat* to the state.

§3. Family Expense Statutes

601. A fair number of states continue to impose a duty upon adult children to support parents, who are in need.[685] The purpose of the family financial responsibility statutes is to relieve the public of the financial responsibility and place it on the adult child. In some states, an adult child may raise as a defense that the parent abandoned and did not provide support for the child when the child was a minor. Similarly, many states also impose the duty of support upon the parent to support a needy adult child.[686]

683. *See*, e.g., Washington Revised Code 26.16.205 (2008).

684. *Ibid.*

685. Approximately twenty-eight states impose such a duty. *See*, e.g., Alaska Statutes §25.20.030 (West, 1997).

686. Approximately twenty-five states impose such a duty. *See*, e.g., Delaware Code Annotated tit. 13, §503 (West, 2010).

Chapter 9. The Child Support Obligation

§1. History

602. Apparently, at early common law there was no legal duty to support one's children except as a moral duty.[687] The English "poor laws" did impose a statutory civil support duty to protect the public from acquiring such an obligation.[688] Traditionally, in the United States, the father had the primary duty for support and the mother was secondarily liable. Today, both parents are equally responsible for the support of their children. Many states enacted statutes imposing such a duty on both parents before constitutional arguments were raised. The United States Supreme Court has held that distinctions based upon gender classification are unconstitutional under the Equal Protection Clause of the Constitution[689] if the classification does not serve important governmental purposes and is not substantially related to the achievement of those purposes.[690] Laws imposing the duty of child support only on fathers would most likely not meet this standard.

§2. Determining the Child Support Award

603. When husband, wife, and their child are living in an intact family, the law usually treats the support of children as a private matter under the theory of family autonomy.[691] Some jurisdictions, however, still recognize the common law doctrine of necessaries, where the husband would be directly liable to the merchant who furnished "necessaries" to the wife and children.[692] If the doctrine is applied only to husbands, the doctrine is likely to be unconstitutional because the classification is gender based. States that recognize same-sex marriage or domestic partnerships or civil unions would probably treat the couple and their child as an intact family in those states that provide that the child born during the union is the child of the union.

604. When parents live apart from their children, the state has jurisdiction to decide custody and support issues under the doctrine of *parens patriae*. The court has jurisdiction to enter an order, requiring the noncustodial parent to pay support to the child's custodian. Most court-ordered support cases arise from separation, divorce, and paternity cases. Though presently the number is small, such cases arise among same sex couples. The custodian usually has complete discretion as to how to spend the support money for the child's needs. Most child support orders do not provide for all of the child's needs.

687. W. Blackstone, *Commentaries on the Laws of England* No. 1, 447 (Cooley, 3d ed., 1884); H.H. Clark, Jr., *The Law of Domestic Relations in the United States* 187 (West 1968).

688. *Ibid.*

689. *See Reed v. Reed*, 404 US 71 (1971).

690. *Califano v. Webster*, 430 US 313 (1977).

691. The state will interfere if the parents do not meet the minimum standard of care under the neglect and dependency statutes. *See supra* para. 401.

692. *Also see* family expense statutes at *supra* Part 2, Chapter 8, s. 3.

605. In a child support proceeding, the trial court must obtain in personam (personal) jurisdiction over the parent, who is ordered to pay support. Personal jurisdiction may be obtained as follows: (1) if the parent is personally served with the appropriate process while the parent is physically present in the state, or (2) if the parent is domiciled in the state but is served in another state, or (3) if the parent consents to the court's jurisdiction, or (4) if the parent is a nonresident of the state, but has such minimum contacts within the state that so that he or she is deemed to be present in the state. This latter method is obtained by a statute specifically intended for such purposes, referred to as a "long-arm" statute. The Uniform Interstate Family Support Act (UIFSA) approved in 1992, amended in 1996, 2001 and 2008, has been enacted in all states as a result of federal law making its enactment by the states a condition of receiving federal funding for child support enforcement.[693] UIFSA specifically addresses the issues of obtaining jurisdiction over the nonresident obligor by providing factors for broad long-arm jurisdiction.

606. The child support order usually requires the obligor to pay support on a weekly or biweekly or monthly basis. As a general rule, since child support is for the benefit of the child and is a continuing obligation when owed, a parent cannot agree to a lump sum settlement of this obligation.[694]

I. Evolution from Discretionary Factors to Presumptive Support Guidelines

607. Traditionally, the trial court, on a case-by-case basis, used its discretion in determining the amount of support to be ordered. The court considered the needs of the child and the parent's ability to pay. The needs of the child were usually determined according to the parents' standard of living.

608. Prior to 1984, many states had enacted statutes patterned on the Uniform Marriage and Divorce Act[695] to guide the court's discretion in determining the amount of support.[696] These guidelines were general principles. Courts in a few states had developed non-binding guidelines as to the specific amount of support based upon the noncustodial parent's income level. Two primary purposes of the guidelines were to achieve uniformity and predictability.

609. Although each state has jurisdiction to determine its own family law, the federal government has taken an active role in influencing child support law among

693. 9 U.L.A. (pt. IB) 159 (2005 & Supp 2009).

694. *See supra* para. 300 for a possible exception in paternity cases.

695. *Uniform Laws Annotated* §309.

696. In a proceeding for dissolution of marriage, legal separation, maintenance, or child support, the court may order either or both parents owing a duty of support to a child to pay an amount reasonable or necessary for his support without regard to marital misconduct, after consulting all relevant factors including: (1) the financial resources of the child; (2) the financial resources of the custodial parent; (3) the standard of living the child would have enjoyed had the marriage not been dissolved; (4) the physical and emotional condition of the child and his educational needs, and (5) the financial resources and needs of the noncustodial parent. *Ibid.*

the states since 1975. Congress requires states to agree to certain conditions in order to receive revenue for their Aid to Families With Dependent Children programs (AFDC).[697] The Federal Child Support Enforcement Amendments of 1984 required all states to have child support guidelines as to the numerical amount of the support based upon the income level of the parents. The guidelines were not binding upon the judges.[698] In 1988, Congress revised this statute[699] and made the guidelines presumptive. Any deviation from them required specific justification, based upon criteria established by the state.[700] The effects of this legislation were to greatly curb the historical role of the trial court's discretion and to move from a case-by-case determination of support to a standardization of support for similar parental income levels. The trial judge must now presume that the numerical amount in the guideline is the amount to be ordered unless this amount would be unjust in a particular case. The determination of "unjust" is based upon criteria established by the state.

610. The states may establish the guidelines by statute or by judicial action or by administrative action.

II. Statutory Child Support Guidelines

611. There are no national guidelines. Each state develops its own guidelines. There are several purposes for requiring specific guidelines as to the amount of support. Guidelines attempt to establish an adequate amount for the child's support. They establish consistency among support orders in a jurisdiction. They are predictable, thus, leading to less litigation and more settlement.[701] Another important purpose of the guidelines was also to assure with some certainty that the child would continue as much as possible to live at the standard of living prior to the parents' separation.

612. Guidelines fall within three general patterns, but with much variation within the patterns.[702] The most typical pattern is the Income Shares Model. In this model, the incomes of the parents are combined. The state has already determined what the amount of support should be at this combined level of income. Each parent then pays his or her share of this amount, based upon the ratio of each parent's income to their combined income. The noncustodial parent's share becomes the amount in the child support order.

---

697. The federal provisions for the administration of child support to the states are being revised so that federal funds to the states are dispersed through block grants, and the AFDC programs are abolished. Personal Responsibility and Work Opportunity Act of 1996 (PL 104-103 (1996)).

698. P.L. 98-378 (1984).

699. The Family Support Act of 1988. Pub. L. 100-485, §103, 102 Stat. 2343, 2346 (1988) (*codified* at 42 USC. §667 (1988)).

700. Pub. L. 100-485, Title I. Subtitle A, §103, 102 stat. 2348 (1988).

701. Bureau of the Census, U.S. Department of Commerce, *Child Support and Alimony: 1987, Current Population Reports*, Special Studies, Series P-23, No. 167.

702. The state uses economic studies on the cost of rearing children. The studies by Thomas Espenshade have been influential. *See*, e.g., T. Espenshade, *Investing In Children: New Estimates of Parental Expenditures*, (1984).

613. The second pattern is the Percentage of the Noncustodial Parent's Income Model. The amount of child support that is ordered is a percentage of the noncustodial parent's income. The percentage varies, depending on the number of children. This pattern focuses on what percentage of the noncustodial parent's income should be designated as child support. This pattern assumes that a share of the child's support will be spent directly on the children by the custodial parent.

614. The third pattern is the Melson Formula Model. This model defines levels of subsistence support for parents and children. No support is ordered if the parent's subsistence level is not met. Income beyond the parent's subsistence level is applied to support the child's subsistence needs. Income beyond the subsistence levels is also allocated to additional child support in order to allow the child to benefit from the parent's higher income level.

615. Variations exist within each model. Income may be defined as gross or net. Net income may vary as to what is considered net. Typically, net income is gross income less federal, state, and city income taxes. Net income may also allow deductions for other child support orders or union dues. The models may allow for sharing of other child support expenses, such as child care and extraordinary medical expenses. Some guidelines may assign a specific amount as income to an unemployed parent based on that parent's potential earning capacity.

616. The guidelines may specifically deal with parents who have high incomes because if the guidelines were to apply, the amount of support would be far beyond the needs and comforts of the child. Some guidelines may place a cap of high-income levels. Others have no cap, and the trial judge decides the appropriate amount of support. Federal law also requires that the guidelines provide for child's health costs and coverage.

III. Separation Agreements

617. Parents who divorce or separate may settle incidents of the marriage in a private agreement, called a separation agreement. The separation agreement may contain provisions as to child support. Such provisions are rarely binding upon the court because under the doctrine of *parens patriae*, the court has jurisdiction to protect the child when parents are separated.[703]

618. If the agreement provides for expenses for higher education for the child, the court will usually enforce this provision under contract law.

703. *See supra* Part 2, Chapter 4, s. 2, Part IV for paternity cases and settlement agreements, which are not separation agreements.

§3. DURATION OF CHILD SUPPORT

619. Typically, the child support obligation terminates when the child reaches the age of majority, unless the state requires support for an adult disabled, dependent child. Support obligation may, however, terminate when the child is emancipated prior to the age of majority.[704]

I. Age of Majority

620. The age of majority in most states has been reduced from 21 years old to 18 years old. Some states have continued the support obligation after reducing the age of majority to 18 years old. For example, most states continue the support obligation to include children who have reached 18 years old but who are still completing high school until the first occurrence of the child either completing high school or reaching the age of 19. In many states, if a child becomes disabled during minority, a parent may still be obligated for child support when the child reaches majority. The age of majority in all states is 18 years, except in Alabama (19 years), Nebraska (19 years or marriage), and Mississippi (21 years).

II. Higher Education

621. Many courts have continued the support obligation for nonintact families while the child is attending college,[705] finding that the child is dependent and that college education is a necessity. The courts have justified this unequal treatment between intact and nonintact families on the basis of what is in the best interest of the child.[706] They reasoned that, in addition to supporting the principle of family autonomy, intact families are more willing to sacrifice for the child's well being and that children in nonintact families face more difficulties in pursuing higher education.[707]

622. If the court continues to enforce the support obligation, the order usually includes all or a portion of the actual cost of the higher education.[708] The order for support for higher education is made on the court's finding that the parent is financially able to contribute.

704. *See supra* para. 442.
705. These are cases in which there is no separation agreement. *See supra* Part 3, Chapter 2, s. 2.
706. The Pennsylvania Supreme Court held that a statute that required only divorced or separated parents to pay for their children's college education was unconstitutional under the Equal Protection Clause of the Fourteenth Amendment of the U.S. Constitution. *Curtis v. Kline*, 666 A.2d 265 (Pa. 1995).
707. *Childers v. Childers*, 575 P.2d 201 (Wash. 1978).
708. In *Ross v. Ross*, 400 A.2d 1233 (N.J. 1979), the noncustodial parent was ordered to continue the support obligation, while the daughter was a law school student, but did not order the noncustodial parent to contribute to the tuition expenses.

III. Death

623. At common law, the death of a parent terminated the duty of support. Many states follow the common law.[709] However, some modern courts allow the duty of support to survive the parent's death and be made binding on the parent's estate.[710] Many states, whether following the common law or modern view, allow the court to secure child support payments with a trust fund or life insurance policy for so long as the duty of support lasts, usually until the child reaches the age of majority.

§4. Modification

624. The standard for modification of the child support order is the proof of substantial change in circumstances from the date of the entry of the order. As a general rule, case law determines what changes are legally sufficient to be found to be substantial. The change must be continuing, not temporary, and must affect the needs of the child or the economic status of the parents or both. The Personal Responsibility and Work Opportunity Reconciliation Act of 1996 (PL 104–103 (1996)) also provides three bases that a state may review and adjust child support although the parent must request the review.

625. As a general rule, if the parent brings about the change of circumstance that would lower the support amount, courts in the past would not have recognized such a change as a valid change for modification. Such cases arise when parents remarry or have additional children, or voluntarily change jobs or professions with lower incomes. A few modern courts may be willing to consider additional children as a legal change in circumstance. A few courts will weigh voluntary change of jobs and professions against a good faith standard. A few may use a balancing standard or a best interest standard to soften the impact of the voluntariness standard.

626. As a general rule, the modification of child support is usually prospective. Courts will not, therefore, retroactively modify accrued arrearages. If there has been equitable reliance upon statements or conduct of the support recipient by the support obligor, however, some courts have been willing to make exceptions if retroactive modification is legally permissible in their states.

627. The trial court must obtain personal jurisdiction over the obligor in order to modify the support order. The Uniform Interstate Family Support Act distinguishes between initial jurisdiction to determine child support and jurisdiction to modify. The state that has initial jurisdiction retains exclusive and continuing jurisdiction over the child support order unless the obligor, obligee and the child no longer lives in the initial state or the parties consent to another state taking jurisdiction.

---

709. *Garney v. Estate of Hain*, 653 A.2d 21 (Pa. Super. Ct. 1995).

710. *Knowles v. Thompson*, 697 A. 2d 335 (Vermont 1997); *Kujawinski v. Kujawinski*, 376 Ne.2d 1382 (Ill. 1978).

§5. ENFORCEMENT

I. General Criminal and Civil Remedies

628. Almost all states have statutes making it a crime, usually a misdemeanor, for failing to pay support. These statutes are seldom enforced. In 1992, however, Congress enacted The Child Support Recovery Act of 1992 (CSRA), which makes the willful failure to support a child, living in a different state from the obligor, a federal crime.[711] CSRA does not create a private action for the custodial parent. In 1998, Congress amended CSRA, with the enactment of the Deadbeat Parents Punishment Act, making the willful failure to pay a support obligation for a child in another state a felony if the amount remains unpaid for more than two years or exceeds USD 10,000.00.[712]

629. Most child support orders are enforced through the court's civil contempt powers. The delinquent obligor may be found in contempt of court if he or she has the means to pay but does not pay. The obligor may be imprisoned until he or she responds and pays.[713] In civil contempt, the obligor has the means to pay but refuses. One may purge oneself of the contempt whenever compliance occurs. The jail sentence is, therefore, for an indefinite period. In *Turner v. Rogers*, the Supreme Court held that, due process does not require appointment for counsel in civil contempt proceeding for failure to pay child support when the other side is not represented by counsel and where the liberty, accuracy and other interests at stake are adequately protected by other procedural safeguards.[714] However, in the case at bar the absence of both counsel and procedural safeguards violated the obligor's right to due process of law.

630. An obligor who willfully disobeys the court's child support order may be found in criminal contempt of the court. Unlike civil contempt, whose purpose is to encourage compliance with the court order, criminal contempt is meant to punish noncompliance. In criminal contempt, the jail sentence is for a specific period.

631. With the encouragement of federal law, all states have enacted wage garnishment statutes, providing for the garnishment of the obligor's wages to fulfill the child support order. Wage garnishment statutes are very useful in enforcing and encouraging the timely payment of support. Child support is automatically deducted

711. 18 USC §228 (2006).

712. The Deadbeat Parents Punishment Act, 18 USC §228(a)(3) (2006). Lower federal courts are divided as to whether CSRA is unconstitutional. Courts finding this law unconstitutional based their analysis on not finding a nexus between criminalization of a parent's failure to pay support and inter-state commerce as required by *US v. Lopez*, 115 S. Ct. 1624 (1995). *See*, e.g., *US v. Schroeder*, 894 F. Supp. 360 (D. Ariz. 1995); *US v. Kerley*, 544 F.3d 172 (2nd Cir. 2008). Other courts have upheld its constitutionality. *See*, e.g., *US v. Hopper*, 899 F. Supp. 389 (S.D. Ind. 1995). The United States Supreme Court will ultimately have to decide this issue. During the 1996–1997 term, the Supreme Court refused to hear appeals from courts that have upheld the CSRA.

713. Imprisonment for failure to pay support does not violate the Constitution's prohibition against imprisonment for debt. *See Livingstone v. Superior Court*, 49 P. 836 (1897).

714. 131 S. Ct. 2507 (2011).

from the obligor's paycheck. Federal law now requires all states to provide procedures for the immediate withholding of wages by employers when a child support order is entered. There are other remedies, including the imposition of liens against the obligor's property or requiring the obligor to post bond to guarantee payments or tax refund interceptions or withholding, suspending or restricting licenses, such as driver's, professional, or occupational licenses.

II. Impact of Federal Legislation

632. Enforcement of support orders has long been recognized as a national problem, not just as a problem for each state to manage. Although collection of support continues to remain a national problem, federal Congressional action has at least resulted in the formation of a child support collection system in each state.[715] Federal legislation has created a cooperative effort between federal and state governments to enforce child support orders.

633. The federal government's initial entry in the area of child support, an area traditionally reserved to the states, occurred in 1935, when it provided states with funds to aid poor families with dependent children.[716] This program, as part of the Social Security Act, is known as Aid to Families with Dependent Children (AFDC). A family qualified if one of the parents was dead or absent.[717] In the case of an absent parent, the states were to collect the funds from the absent parent. By the 1970s, the states were very delinquent in even trying to collect the funds from absent parents. For the most part, the states had neglected even to have the proper court enter a child support order against the absent parent. Child support cannot be collected without an order from the court. Frequently, the most neglected cases in which child support orders were not obtained were the paternity cases. Additionally, the states were just as neglectful in enforcing support orders for non-AFDC cases. Federal funds are now dispersed through block grants and AFDC programs are abolished. (Personal Responsibility and Work Opportunity Act of 1994 (PL 104-103 (1996)). In *Astrue v. Capato*, the Supreme Court held that state intestacy law governs whether children posthumously conceived using the sperm of their deceased father are entitled to Social Security benefits.[718]

634. In 1975, Congress enacted the Federal Child Support Act of 1974, adding Title IV-D to the Social Security Act.[719] If a state wanted to continue to receive AFDC funds, this act required the state to create a public child support enforcement

715. *See* M.C. Haynes, *Supporting Our Children: A Blueprint for Reform*, 27 Fam. L. Q. 7 (1993).
716. Title IV-A of the Social Security Act. Codified at 42 USC. §§601–615.
717. The program was originally conceived to care for children when the primary wage earner was dead. Most of the children receiving aid are those whose father is living away from the children and failing to provide for their support.
718. 132 S.Ct. 2021 (2012).
719. Pub. L. No. 93-647, 88 Stat. 2348 (1975), *codified at* 42 USC.A. §651–667 (1982 & Supp IV 1986).

agency (IV-D agency), which would obtain and modify support orders, enforce support orders, establish paternity, and locate absent parents. The act has been amended several times to improve the enforcement of support.[720] The act and its amendments extend to both AFDC and non-AFDC cases. No state has opted not to participate because the federal government's contribution to the state's poverty program is essential.

635. The federal program focuses on providing the states with some of the means of efficiently enforcing support orders. For example, federal wages are no longer exempt from garnishment proceedings. Child support garnishment takes precedence over other types of garnishment. The procedure for wage garnishment automatically commences when the obligor is one month delinquent. The 1988 Family Support Act allows the states to require the immediate garnishment for all new or modified support orders of persons receiving AFDC funds unless the court finds there is good reason not to withhold the garnishment or if both parties agree in writing to alternative arrangements.[721] The state may also garnish wages when the obligor resides and works in a different state. Arrearages may be enforced through federal and state interception of income tax refunds.

636. Pursuant to federal requirements regarding the enforcement of support, states must enact legislation giving each state the mechanism to cancel professional licenses and driver's licenses of delinquent obligors.

III. Interstate Enforcement

637. Interstate enforcement of child support is very problematic, especially in a society as mobile as the United States. A state has difficulty in enforcing a child support order when the obligor has left the state. In the past, many states would not enforce another state's child support order because it was viewed as a non-final order since it could be amended. Only orders reduced to a final judgment were enforced. Even if they were reduced to a final judgment, the enforcing party would have to bring the enforcement action in the state where the obligor was present. States attempted to remedy these problems through uniform statutes. Each state enacts the uniform statute for the purpose of unifying the law among the states.

720. 1981 amendments in the Omnibus Budget Reconciliation Act, Child Support Enforcement Amendments of 1984, 1988 Family Support Act, the Child Support Recovery Act of 1992, and Full Faith and Credit for Child Support Orders Act of 1994.

721. The 1988 Family Support Act, USC.A. §666(b) (3) (A); The Personal Responsibility and Work Opportunity Reconciliation Opportunity Act of 1996.

A. *Constitutional Requirement*

638. The U.S. Constitution's Full Faith and Credit Clause has been interpreted to apply to final judgments.[722] Therefore, a state is not constitutionally mandated to recognize a sister state's nonfinal judgments. Though, under the principle of comity,[723] it may do so. A nonfinal judgment is modifiable. All child support orders for future support are modifiable. As to child support arrearages, most states recognize them as nonfinal judgments unless an accrued installment is final and not modifiable in the state where the judgment was rendered. As a result, unless the accrued arrearages were reduced to a money judgment, a sister state would not enforce the present child support order.

639. Congress enacted the Full Faith and Credit Child Support Orders Act in 1994[724] to alleviate the nonfinal-judgment interpretation of the Full Faith and Credit Clause as it applies to child support orders. Sister states must enforce child support orders if they meet the requirements of the statute.

640. The FFCCSOA also incorporated many of the concepts of the Uniform Interstate Family Support Act. In 1996, Congress amended FFCCSOA to make it consistent with the 1996 version of UIFSA. Congress mandated all states adopt the UIFSA in 1996. However, UIFSA was amended in 2001. Some states have enacted the 2001 version. Thus, there are different versions of the UIFSA. Most states have held, however, that if FFCCSOA and UIFSA conflict, then UIFSA takes precedent.

B. *Uniform Acts*

1. Uniform Reciprocal Enforcement of Support Act: Background for the Uniform Interstate Family Support Act (UIFSA)

641. The full faith and credit issue is not the only issue in the enforcement of child support. In most instances, once the obligor has left the state, which entered the support order, that state no longer has personal jurisdiction over the obligor to enforce its support order. States attempted to remedy the interstate enforcement problems through the enactment of uniform legislation. The purpose of the uniform approach was to encourage cooperation among the states in establishing and enforcing child support orders and to alleviate the need for the enforcing party to go to the state where the obligor was present in order to obtain personal jurisdiction over the obligor.

---

722. *Sistare v. Sistare*, 218 US 1 (1910).
723. *Scott v. Sylvester*, 257 S.E.2d 774 (Va. 1979).
724. 28 USC §1738B.

642. All states enacted some form of either the Uniform Reciprocal Enforcement of Support Act (URESA)[725] or the Revised Uniform Reciprocal Enforcement of Support Act (RURESA).[726] The Act has both civil and criminal provisions. The most used provision of the Act is the two-state civil enforcement provision. The Act essentially provides that an initiating state forwards a petition to a responding state alleging that a parent residing in the responding state owes a duty of support to a child in the initiating state. The responding state agrees to take jurisdiction over the parent and determine if a duty of support is owed. If such a duty of support is owed under the law of the responding state, the responding state will enter an order for support and enforce that order and forward the money collected to the initiating state. Hence, the states reciprocate in entering and enforcing child support orders of residents whose children live out-of-state.

643. The Act also provides procedures for the extradition of parents who are charged with the crime of nonsupport. The Act also provides for paternity proceedings if joined by a petition for support.

644. The adoption and interpretation of URESA and RURESA have not brought complete uniformity among the states. Some states enforce the collection of existing arrearages owed on orders of the initiating states. States, which enacted the revised version, allow existing orders of the initiating states to be registered and enforced in the responding state without the need for the responding state to enter an order.

2. The Uniform Interstate Family Support Act

645. The United States Commissioners on Interstate Child Support proposed the Uniform Interstate Family Support Act (UIFSA) in 1992 to replace the various versions of the Uniform Reciprocal Enforcement of Support Act. The Commission was responding to Congress' call to improve the establishment and the enforcement of interstate spousal and child support orders. In 1996, Congress mandated that all states adopt the 1996 version of UIFSA. Since that time, some states have enacted later versions of the Act. Thus, not all states have the same version of the Act.

646. This Act has similar provisions to URESA, but facilitates the initial state's jurisdiction over the out-of-state obligor. The very nature of URESA produces multiple support orders in a given case. The purpose of UIFSA is "to eliminate the possibility of multiple exercises of jurisdiction over support awards with attendant multiple, conflicting support awards from more than one state."[727] This purpose is accomplished by allowing one and only one state at a time to have exclusive child

725. Proposed by the Commissioners on Uniform State Laws and adopted by the American Bar Association in 1950.
726. The revision of the Uniform Reciprocal of Enforcement Act was adopted by the American Bar Association in 1968.
727. Uniform Law Commission, Short Summaries. 1992.

support jurisdiction through the use of long-arm statutes to obtain jurisdiction over an out-of-state obligor. The long-arm statute allows a state that had jurisdiction to enter the child support order to continue to have jurisdiction to enforce and modify that order as long as either the obligor or obligee or the child resides in the state.
All enforcement under UIFSA begins with the registration of the order in the responding state. These procedures are quite straight forward.

647. Unlike URESA, which required paternity proceedings to be joined with a claim for support, UIFSA provides that paternity proceedings need not be joined with a claim for support.

3. Uniform Enforcement of Foreign Judgments Act

648. The Uniform Enforcement of Foreign Judgments Act facilitates the interstate enforcement of sister states' judgments, that are subject to the full faith and credit clause. Almost all of the states have enacted variations of this Act. Such judgments are usually money judgments. A money judgment is enforced through attachment, sequestration, and garnishment proceedings. A state does not use its contempt powers to enforce money judgments. Child support arrearages may be reduced to a money judgment, and similarly enforced if the debtor resides in another state or has property in another state.

§6. Federal Income Tax Consequences

649. The Internal Revenue Code provides for the federal taxation of income. The code allows the taxpayer to reduce taxable income with dependency exemptions. A taxpayer's child qualifies as a dependent of a taxpayer not filing a joint return if the child lived with the taxpayer for more than half of the time in the taxable calendar year and the child did not provide more than half of his or her support. If the parents, however, do not file a joint return, the parent with whom the child resided for the longest period during the taxable year or if the child resided with both parents the same amount of time, the parent with the highest adjusted gross income takes the child as the dependent.[728]

650. If parents are divorced, legally separated, or live apart for the last six months of the calendar year, and if the child receives more than half of his or her support from the parents, the dependency exemption is automatically allocated to the custodial parent who has had custody of the child during the greater portion of the calendar year, unless the exemption is given in writing to the noncustodial parent and the noncustodial parent attaches the writing to his or her return.[729]

---

728. 26 USC.A. §152 (a), et seq. (2008).
729. Internal Revenue Code §§152(e) (1) (A) & (B) (2008).

651. Child support payments are not included in the custodial parent's income for federal tax purposes. These payments are not deducted from the noncustodial parent's income for tax purposes.

Part III. Matrimonial Property and Support Law

Chapter 1. General Economic Rights of Spouses During Coverture

652. In the United States of America, the regulation of economic relations between married persons is primarily controlled by state law. The economic relations between spouses concern three major subjects: control over property owned by the spouses, transactions, and transfers between the spouses, and the duty of spousal support during marriage. As to each of these three categories of regulation, laws vary significantly from state to state. In areas of economic activity that have national implication and which directly concern federal interests, federal regulation is constitutionally permissible. Thus, matters such as pensions, welfare benefits, and military and other federal government retirement entitlements, and federal taxes are regulated by federal law. It is important to emphasize that the principles discussed in this chapter apply only to persons who are in valid (or at least putative) marriages. They do not apply to nonmarital cohabitants. As Professor Mahoney has written:

> Notably, little development occurred in the law governing unmarried cohabitation between the time of the *Marvin* case in 1976 and the publication of the ALI Principles [in 2002], in spite of the continuing increase in the number of cohabiting couples during this period. Neither the enactment of "piecemeal legislation" nor the more comprehensive development of a new legal status. .., has been realized. The legal system extended little recognition to opposite sex cohabitants at the time of the *Marvin* case, and the same is true today.[730]

653. There are two different kinds of regimes of property ownership for married couples. The prevalent regime is the common law (title) system of property ownership, found in forty-one states. The remaining nine states adhere to the community property system. While the details and policy particulars of laws regulating spousal transactions and spousal support also vary substantially in the states, there is no fundamental conceptual division among the states, but in all states the laws

730. M. Mahoney, *Forces Shaping the Law of Cohabitation for Opposite Sex Couples*, 7 J. L. & Fam. Studs. 135, 137 (2005). *See also* Lynn D. Wardle, Mark P. Strasser & Lynne Marie Kohm, *Family Law from Multiple Perspectives* 735 (2014) (discussion of property division upon divorce).

are based upon similar underlying legal principles. There has been no major change of any state from one system to another for the past two decades, with one exception: In 1998, the Alaska legislature passed a community property act giving couples the option to "opt into" a community property regime.[731] However, the two different systems seem to be converging in their basic principles (with preference for the community property approach prevailing).[732] Moreover, in all states parties are free to arrange the terms of their spousal property ownership by contract, so presumably married couples living or couples marrying in a common law (title) property state could agree to community property ownership in their particular marriage, and vice versa.[733] As the Internal Revenue Service explains: "Common law is the dominant property system in the United States and has been adopted by 41 states. The theory underlying common law is that each spouse is a separate individual with separate legal and property rights. Thus, as a general rule, each spouse owns and is taxed upon the income that he or she earns."[734]

§1. The Common Law (Title) Marital Property Regime

654. Most of the American states (and before them the colonies) were settled by people from England who brought with them their English common law. Common law property ownership historically has been a separate property regime, i.e., based upon (and giving strong preference to) the concept of individual, not family, ownership of property. The common law also historically gave great preference for males (especially husbands and sons) and *primogeniture*.

I. Common Law Disabilities of Married Women

655. These influences combined in England and America to produce a system of property ownership in which the property rights of married women were suspended during marriage.[735] With a few complex exceptions, married women were legally incapable of independently owning property at common law. Any real property a woman owned at the time of marriage (and most of her personal property, except her "paraphernalia") became subject to her husband's possession and control. In return, the married woman obtained a "dower" interest in all real property owned by her husband during their marriage, which she alone controlled; her husband could not alienate his land without her consent. Blackstone summarized the disabilities and gave his opinion of the justification for them as follows:

731. Alaska Statutes Annotated §§ 34.77.010 et seq. (2010).
732. J.T. Oldham, *Changes in the Economic Consequences of Divorces, 1958-2008*, 42 Fam. L. Q. 419 (2008).
733. *See* Part III, Chapter 2, § 1, *infra* (discussion of antenuptial contracts).
734. IRS, Internal Revenue Manual, § 25.18.1.1.1 (02-15-2005) (seen Jul. 6, 2015).
735. C. Donahue, Jr., *What Causes Fundamental Legal Ideas? Marital Property in England and France in the Thirteenth Century*, 78 Michigan L. Rev. 59 (1979).

By marriage, the husband and wife are one person in law; that is, the very being or legal existence of the woman is suspended during the marriage, or at least is incorporated and consolidated into that of the husband, under whose wing, protection, and *cover* she performs every thing; and is, therefore, called in our law-French a *femme-covert, faemina viro co-operta*; is said to be *covert-baron*, or under the protection and influence of her husband, her *baron*, her lord; and her condition, during her marriage, is called her *coverture*. Upon this principle of a union of person in husband and wife depend almost all the legal rights, duties, and disabilities that either of them acquire by the marriage. I speak not at present of the rights of property, but of such as are merely *personal*. For this reason, a man cannot grant anything to his wife, or enter into covenant with her, for the grant would be to suppose her separate existence; and to covenant with her would be only to covenant with himself; and, therefore, it is also generally true that all compacts made between husband and wife, when single, are voided by the intermarriage. A woman, indeed, may be attorney for her husband, for that implies no separation from, but is rather a representation of, her lord. And a husband may also bequeath anything to his wife by will; for that cannot take effect till the coverture is determined by his death. … In criminal prosecutions, it is true, the wife may be indicted and punished separately; for the union is only a civil union. But, in trials of any sort, they are not allowed to be evidence for or against each other; partly because it is impossible their testimony should be indifferent, but principally because of the union of person; and, therefore, if they were admitted to be witnesses *for* each other, they would contradict one maxim of law, "*nemo propria causa testis esse debet*"; and if against each other, they would contradict another maxim, "*nemo tenetur seipsum accusare*". But where the offense is directly against the person of the wife, this rule has been usually dispensed with; … .

In the civil law the husband and the wife are considered as two distinct persons, and may have separate estates, contracts, debts, and injuries; and, therefore, in our ecclesiastical courts, a woman may sue and be sued without her husband.

But, though our law in general considers man and wife as one person, yet there are some instances in which she is separately considered, as inferior to him, and acting by his compulsion; and, therefore, all deeds executed, and acts done by her, during her coverture, are void; except it be a fine, or the like matter of record, in which case she must be solely and secretly examined, to learn if her act be voluntary. She cannot, by will, devise lands to her husband, unless under special circumstances; for at the time of making it she supposed to be under his coercion. And in some felonies and other inferior crimes, committed by her, through constraint of her husband, the law excuses her; but this extends not to treason or murder.

… .

These are the chief legal effects of marriage during coverture; upon which we may observe, that even the disabilities which the wife lies under are, for the most part, intended for her protection and benefit. So great a favorite is the female sex of the laws of England.[736]

While the justification for married women's disabilities may have been expressed in religious terms (marital unity), consistent with the prevailing norms of the day, the real reason and purpose for them may have been protective. Pollock and Maitland, for example, suggest that the common law simply created an economic guardianship for the wife, including high fiduciary duties of the husband.[737] Given the disabilities of women, both practical and legal, at the time, and given the social system of the time which looked to group representation rather than individualism, the strong legal preferences for the husband were as rational in the context of the time as they are appallingly unfair and discriminatory by modern standards.

656. The strictness of the common law disability of women stimulated the practice of making antenuptial contracts between women of means (and their families) and the men they wished to marry (and their families). It also stimulated the development of "trusts," "uses," and other equitable devices to circumvent the legal disabilities.[738]

II. Married Women's Property Acts and Estates by the Entireties

657. By the middle of the nineteenth century, "Married Women's Property Acts" were being adopted throughout America. These statutes repealed many of the common law disabilities of married women, particularly the property-ownership restrictions, and adopted in their place the general principle of separate (title) property ownership: property belongs to the person (married or single) who acquires (the title to) it.[739]

658. The common law created a unique form of property ownership for married couples known as tenancy by the entireties. It provided both husband and wife with equal, undivided interests in the property during the lifetime, with right of survivorship when one of the spouses dies. Neither party alone can alienate or encumber the tenancy. While the legal interests are completely equal, the husband's interest was deemed the managing interest.[740] About half of the common law property states today recognize tenancies by the entireties.[741] Since common law marriages are fully marriages, couples with common law marriages may enjoy tenancy by the entireties. One would assume that in states that allow same-sex marriage, same-sex married couples also my hold real property as tenants by the entireties; however, it

736. W. Blackstone, *Commentaries on the Law of England*, No. 1, (Cooley, 3d ed., 1884), 442–444.
737. F. Pollock & F. Maitland, *The History of English Law*, No. 2, (1898 ed., reprinted 1968), 405–406.
738. C.L. Blakesley & C. Curtis, *Property Division—Common Law*, in *Contemporary Family Law*, §30:01, Chapter 30 (L.D. Wardle, C.L. Blakesley & J.Y. Parker eds, Callaghan 1988).
739. H.H. Clark, Jr., *The Law of Domestic Relations in the United States* 289–291 (West 2d ed., 1988).
740. W.B. Stoebuck & D.A. Whitman, *The Law of Property* § 5.5 (3d ed., 2000).
741. J.D. Gregory, P.N. Swisher & S.L. Chewable, *Understanding Family Law* 57 (1993).

has been suggested that in the absence of direct legislation allowing same-sex marriage or modifying the real estate law, same-sex couples might not be free to hold title as tenants by the entireties, a result that seems quite illogical.[742] However, the Supreme Court decision in *Obergefell v. Hodges* interpreting the Fourteenth Amendment as requiring all states to allow same-sex marriage may result in some reconsideration of the property consequences of marriage as historically they were bound up with cultural understandings of gender roles that logically do not seem to apply to same-sex couples. Same-sex civil union couples in states that have statutorily given same-sex civil unions all of the "same" rights and benefits of marriage would be able to enjoy tenancy by the entireties.[743]

659. In states that do not recognize tenancies by the entireties, joint tenancy has been popular for married couples. It resembles the entireties estate insofar as undivided equal shares are held by the parties. The effect of death and conditions for and consequences of termination of the estate distinguish it from entireties.[744]

III. Recent Developments

660. While the common law and married women property act scheme of ownership works reasonably well in the case of unmarried persons, and when both spouses are satisfactorily employed, and in the case of married persons who remain married, in the case of a married couple who acquires significant property while the wife has been a full-time, nonearning homemaker-wife-mother and the husband has worked full-time, the separate (title) system creates a significant problem if there is a divorce (and possibly if there is a death). The problem is that all the property legally belongs to the spouse who earned it—typically (historically) the husband—and the other spouse, whose nonearning contributions to the marriage (and thereby to the acquisition of the property by the other spouse) may have been as great or even greater than those of the spouse with title, has no legally recognized interest in it.

661. The law has changed significantly in recent years in the context of divorce. Now no states apply the traditional "pure" common law scheme of property ownership upon divorce.[745] However, during marriage, the inequities remain. The significant expansion of employment opportunities in recent decades, and the increasing numbers of married women who have abandoned traditional homemaking careers for income-earning careers has alleviated the extent of the problem. However, "traditional" wives who limit or reject paid employment careers in order to pursue "traditional" wife-and-mother homemaking roles are left without legal recourse during the marriage if their economic interests are neglected by their

742. David E. Missirian, *Separate by Equal? Same Sex Couples in New England*, 35 Real Est. L. J. 558 (2007).
743. *Ibid.*
744. L.J. Harris, L.E. Teitelbaum & C.A. Weisbrod, *Family Law* 19 (Aspen 1996).
745. *See infra*, Part III, Chapter 3.

resource-controlling spouse. (Fortunately, nonlegal intra-family remedies effectively used by "traditional" wives for centuries are still available and somewhat effective, and the escape door of employment is open more widely to such persons today than it ever has been before.)

662. During the past half-century, the gender discrimination in the law has come under increasingly strict judicial scrutiny, and the male (husband) preference imbedded in the common law marital property regime has been shrinking under the persistent challenge.[746] The result has been the elimination of virtually all gender preferences in contemporary marital property regimes.[747]

663. "Private ordering" has always been allowed at common law. Indeed, as noted in the chapter on antenuptial contracts, parties have long been able to alter their economic relations in anticipation of marriage. Thus, the common law title system of marital property just provides the default or presumptive property regime during marriage for couples in common law states. However, the parties may alter their property relations as they deem appropriate, so long as they do not violate public policy. As it concerns economic relations, the major public policies are that married and formerly married persons should not become welfare charges on public assistance if their spouse or former spouse has the resources to support them both, and a (rebuttable) presumption that the spouses would want to give to each other and would expect to receive from each other some reasonable share of the economic increase produced by the efforts of each spouse during the marriage, unless something of value was exchanged for that expectation. Additionally, specific procedural and formal requirements (involving written agreements, public recordings, etc.) are typically imposed, which vary from state to state.[748] These technical requirements generally insure fair dealing and protect innocent third parties (especially creditors) who otherwise would assume that the property rights of the spouses are those associated with the standard marital property arrangement in the jurisdiction. Texas courts may not award more than USD 5,000 in child support per month (or a maximum of 20% of the payor's gross monthly income). The division of community property (usually 50%–50%) is deemed to minimize the need for substantial alimony.

664. Today, most states property regimes during marriage follow the principle that marriage turns the spouses into economic partners:

> If marriage ends, the fruits of both spouses' labor--the earnings accumulated by either spouse during marriage--are classified as marital [or community] property, subject to division at divorce. Assets acquired before marriage and gifts or inheritances received during marriage, on the other hand, generally

746. H.H. Clark, Jr., *The Law of Domestic Relations in the United States* 290–293 (West 2d ed., 1988).
747. *See generally Kirschberg v. Feenstra*, 450 US 455 (1981).
748. Arizona Revised Statutes Annotated §14-2207 (1995); and New Jersey Statutes Annotated §37:2-23 (1969).

> belong to each spouse separately. The classification of these assets as sacrosanct separate property means that they are sheltered from division at divorce. Thus, labor-generated property presumptively belongs to spouses as a unit, while premarital and luck-generated (gifted or inherited) property belongs to spouses as separate individuals.[749]

There remain significant policy differences between the states regarding the details of when and how the marital community property and the separate property will be classified and divided, but the general patterns of the schemes are remarkably similar.

For example, Texas has one of the strictest alimony laws in the United States. By statute, alimony generally may be awarded for no longer than five years, if the marriage lasted less than ten years and the court ordered maintenance because the paying spouse committed an act of family violence, or if the marriage lasted between 10 and 20 years long; for seven years, if the marriage lasted between 20 and 30 years long; and for ten years, if the marriage lasted 30 years or longer.[750]

§2. The Community Property: Marital Property Regime

665. Nine states (mostly in the west where Spanish law once prevailed) follow the "community property" system of property ownership during marriage. Additionally, Alaska gives couples the option to "opt into" a community property regime, if they wish to do so,[751] and parties by private agreement in any state may arrange their property relationship upon community property principles. The theory of community property is that both spouses contribute equally to the marriage, and they should enjoy equally the fruits of the marriage, as equal partners. Community property developed in the middle ages in countries where the power of and concern for family wealth (notably for this subject the wife's family of origin) overshadowed the concern for nuclear patriarchal or individual control, and where the aristocracy counterbalanced the power of the king, and where the tradition of communal cooperation was strong.[752] The states with community property are: Arizona, California, Idaho, Louisiana, Nevada, New Mexico, Texas, Washington, and Wisconsin.

666. The main doctrinal principle of community property is that all property acquired during marriage is "community property," except property acquired by gift, devise, bequest or inheritance. The latter property along with property acquired

749. Shari Motro, *Labor, Luck, and Love: Reconsidering the Sanctity of Separate Property*, 102 Nw. U. L. Rev. 1623, 1624 (2008).
750. Tex. Fam. Code §§ 8.051-8.056.
751. Alaska Statutes Annotated §§ 34.77.010 et seq. (2010).
752. C. Donahue, Jr., *What Causes Fundamental Legal Ideas? Marital Property in England and France in the Thirteenth Century*, 78 Michigan L. Rev. 59 (1979).

before marriage or after legal separation or divorce is deemed "separate property." Community property belongs equally to both spouses. Separate property belongs solely to the spouse acquiring it.[753]

667. During marriage, control and management may be problematic, because dual control could create inconsistent or inequitable dealings.[754] But most states provide for a presumption of control and management in one spouse upon a gender-neutral basis (e.g., the spouse who earned the income is presumptively entitled to manage it, etc.). Gendered presumptions once were common, but the general equality doctrine has negated such presumptions in recent decades. Upon death or divorce in a community property state, each spouse receives one-half of the community property (technically, each is entitled to one-half of each item of community property, but generally the courts try not to divide property, but award each item to the spouse most interested in it until both spouses have half of the total property).[755]

668. The community property states vary significantly in the details of many issues that may arise concerning the community property regime. These include issues of management, classification (of property as either community or separate—including recovery for damages, injuries, disabilities, goodwill, etc.), transmutation, commingled assets, tracing, income from property, increase in value of property, rights of creditors, treatment of any increase in and interest on separate property that accrues during marriage, etc.[756]

669. Under the Spanish civil law rule, the income from separate property of married persons was community property, but increase in the value of separate property was deemed separate property. The so-called "American rule" of community property, in contrast, provides that both increase and income from separate property is deemed separate property (unless the result of community labor—the labor of both of the spouses). Four community property states (Idaho, Louisiana, Texas and Wisconsin) follow the civil law rule, while the five remaining community property states (Arizona, California, Nevada, New Mexico, and Washington) follow the American rule.[757]

---

753. G. Scully and J. Scully, *Property Division—Community Property*, in *Contemporary Family Law*, §31:03, Chapter 30 (L.D. Wardle, C.L. Blakesley & J.Y. Parker eds, Callaghan 1988).
754. *Kirschberg v. Feenstra*, 450 US 455 (1981) (Louisiana statute allowing husband to encumber family home without notice to wife, but not *vice versa*, violates equal protection).
755. W. DeFuniak & M.J. Vaughn, *Principles of Community Property*, §227 (1971).
756. *See generally* K. W. Kingma, *Property Division at Divorce or Death for Married Couples Migrating Between Common Law and Community Property States*, 35 ACTEC J. 74 (2009) (American College of Trust and Estate Counsel).
757. W.A. Reppy & C.A. Samuel, *Community Property in the United States*, 11-1, (3d ed., 1991); Kingma, *supra* n. 756 at 76–80. *See also* American Law Institute, *Principles of the Law of Family Dissolution: Analysis and Recommendations* § 4.04 cmt. a (2002) (most community property and common law property states follow the "American Rule").

670. As mentioned in the preceding section on the common law (title) marital property regime, the marital property system just provides the default or presumptive property regime during marriage for couples in common law states.[758] In community property states, as in common law marital property states, the parties are free to alter their property relations, so long as they do not violate public policy (especially so long as the agreement does not cause one spouse to become a public welfare charge while the other spouse or former spouse has adequate resources to support them both). However, each state has its own technical requirements governing formalities that must be observed and other procedural and substantive requirements to insure that the parties are dealing in good faith, and that third parties (especially creditors) are not cheated by the arrangement.[759]

§3. Transactions Between Spouses

671. At common law, the husband and wife were deemed to be one and the same legal person (represented by the husband). Thus, transfers between spouses were prohibited. As Blackstone put it: "A man cannot grant anything to his wife, or enter into a covenant with her: for the grant would be to suppose her separate existence; and to covenant with her, would be only to covenant with himself."[760] Paternalistic (or guardianship) concern that the wife was not in a position to realistically resist the demand of her husband that she sign a particular contract may also have been a reason for the contractual disability.

672. The Married Woman's Property Acts largely eliminated the common law disability of spouses to contract with each other. Generally, they provided that married women could contract the same as if they were unmarried.[761] The fictive union of the parties was abolished and married women acquired separate legal personality. That was seen as a significant development in respect of and for the autonomy and independence of married women. That remains the starting point for much public policy today. For example in the realm of taxes on inter-spousal transfers, Congress treats such "transactions with favorable treatment. Congress has made it clear that inter-spousal transactions are to be income tax-free (*see* I.R.C. Section 1041), gift tax-free (*see* I.R.C. Section 2523), and are not to be subject to estate taxes (*see* IRS Section 2056)."[762] Thus, for federal tax purposes transfers between spouses generally are treated differently than transfers to other persons.

673. While the ideological impediment to interspousal contracting was rejected, the practical vulnerability of a less-educated, less-experienced, physically weaker partner in a marriage remained. Thus, contracts between spouses are often subject to closer scrutiny than contracts between strangers, because the husband and wife

758. *See supra, 627.*
759. *See supra* note Part 3, Chapter 1, s. 1.
760. W. Blackstone, *Commentaries on the Laws of England*, No. 1, (Cooley, 3d ed., 1884), *430.
761. H.H. Clark, Jr., *supra* at 299.
762. S. Stacy Eastland, *Family Limited Partnerships: Current Status and New Opportunities*, ALI-ABA CLE (SP023-ALI-ABA 429), Nov. 17-21, 2008, at III.G.1.

do not deal with each other "at arms length," but are in a reciprocal fiduciary relationship.[763] Each trusts the other and the relationship with each other is in some respects (at least by analogy) subject to trust principles. Some American courts still tend to be protective of women, especially those who do not have independent resources or higher education.

As the accompanying chapter dealing with antenuptial and separation agreement notes, contractual relations between spouses (or engaged, soon-to-be-spouses) have a higher standard of voluntariness, and lower threshold for duress than ordinary commercial contracts between strangers.[764] The law, in this manner, protects the right of married persons to trust each other, and supports the common assumption that spouses can rely on the good faith and fair dealing of the other. A recent series of rulings in California have held "that the presumption of undue influence is determinative if in conflict with the title presumption and the writing requirement for a valid transmutation. … [T]hese judicial decisions give renewed strength to the presumption of undue influence … ."[765] That seems to be the bell-weather development signaling the potential future trend. While hastiness to presume or find undue influence can undermine reliability and predictability necessary for prudent and reliable dealing with marital and community property, there are some good and realistic reasons for careful monitoring of inter-spousal transactions that benefit only one of the spouses.

674. The major limitation on the right of the parties to contract with each other is that the contract may not violate public policy. The duty of the spouses to support each other during marriage, for example, may not be contracted away. Public policy that a fundamental inalienable element of marriage is the reciprocal duty of support may not be waived.[766]

§4. General Principles of Spousal Support During Coverture

I. Common Law Spousal Support

675. The common law compensated for the suspension of most property-ownership rights of women during marriage by imposing a clear and specific duty upon husbands to support their wives. Conversely, the wife had the duty to render services to the husband in the home. Blackstone explained:

> The husband is bound to provide his wife with necessaries by law, as much as himself: and if she contracts debts for them, he is obliged to pay them; but, for anything besides necessaries, he is not chargeable. Also if a wife elopes, and

763. *In re Estate of Gab*, 364 N.W.2d 924 (S.D. 1985); and *In re Estate of Lemle*, 286 N.Y.S.2d 147 (N.Y. Cty Surr. Ct. 1967).

764. *See infra*, Part III, Ch. 2.

765. Christine Manolakas, *The Presumption of Undue Influence Resurrected: He Said/She Said Is Back*, 37 McGeorge L. Rev 33, 34 (2006).

766. *Kuder v. Schroeder*, 430 S.W.2d 271 (N.C. Ct. App. 1993); and M. Ploscowe, H.H. Faster, Jr. & D.J. Freed, *Family Law*, (2d ed., 1972), 829–831.

lives with another man, the husband is not chargeable even for necessaries; at least if the person, who furnishes them, is sufficiently apprised of her elopement. If the wife be indebted before marriage, the husband is bound afterwards to pay the debt; for he has adopted her and her circumstances together.[767]

676. The adoption of Married Women's Property Acts in the nineteenth century did not eliminate the other legal and extensive social disadvantages of married women in earning or ability to self-support. Thus, the common law duty to support the spouse continued to be the duty of a husband, and the benefit, not the duty, of a wife.

II. Modern Equal Support Duty

677. The equal protection revolution of the 1970s abolished the one-sided, gender-stereotyped duties of support-service.[768] Now, state "Family Expense Acts" or "Support" laws provide that each spouse is fully liable for the support of his or her spouse. For example, the widely adopted Uniform Civil Liability for Support Act provides, in section 3, that "Every father shall support his child; and every man shall support his wife when she is in need," and section 4 adds, "Every woman shall support her child; and she shall support her husband when he is in need."[769] Likewise, family expense statutes may obligate the property of married parties for the support of each other and their children. A typical statute provides: "The expenses of the family and the education of the children are chargeable upon the property of both husband and wife or of either of them, and in relations thereto they may be sued jointly or separately."[770] Since many wives (especially with young children) still do not work outside the home for significant periods during marriage, and since women still typically earn less than men when they are employed (they often seek more flexible employment conditions than men in order to accommodate homemaking, child-rearing and other domestic commitments and interests), these laws still primarily provide needed protection for married women; but men, too, may now use them.[771]

678. The gender-equalization of the duty of support does not mean that an economically wealthier spouse may refuse to support or may impose financially upon the resources of the economically poorer spouse. It is deemed to violate principles of gender equality protected by the Equal Protection Clause to codify a mere sexual stereotype of economic dependency or gender-based support duty.[772] To remedy the

767. W. Blackstone, *Commentaries on the Laws of England*, No. 1, (Cooley, 3d ed., 1884), *442–443.
768. *See generally Orr v. Orr*, 440 US 268 (1979) (alimony statute which provided that only husbands could be liable for and only wives could receive alimony violates equal protection).
769. Uniform Civil Liability for Support Act §§3, 4 (1954, 1988).
770. Utah Code Annotated §30-2-9 (1953).
771. *See generally* L.D. Wardle, *Alimony on the Margins: Protecting Homemaking Services in the Public Interest*, in *Family Finances* 475 (Jan Sramek Verlag KG, Austria, B. Verschraegen eds, 2009).
772. *Kirschberg v. Kirschberg*, 450 US 55 (1981).

gender-based disparity in the common law support obligation, states have adopted a number of gender-neutral approaches. Some have simply extended the same support obligation imposed by the common law on husbands to wives; others have created a gender-neutral rule requiring the spouse who incurred the debt to first assume the debt, and permitting collection from the other spouse only if the one who incurred the debt lacks sufficient funds to pay; but perhaps the most common approach is to adopt gender-neutral family expense statutes putting the spousal and child support obligations equally upon both husband and wife.[773]

679. The degree or amount of support required still depends upon the situation and circumstances of the parties, their relative and mutual status and conditions. At one time marital fault (such as desertion or adultery, etc.) would completely bar a spouse from recovering spousal support; but the extent to which such factors today are valid defenses to support claims has lessened.[774] Still, in at least thirty states, "fault" may be considered by courts in making alimony (spousal support) awards upon divorce, though in about one-fourth of those states the consideration of fault is uncommon.[775] Moreover, the flood of women into the workforce in the past few decades has reduced the need for alimony awards. Today, it is common for alimony awards to be of limited (not permanent) duration. They are viewed as transitional awards, to help the economically less-independent spouse to become self-supporting.

III. Family Autonomy and Necessaries Doctrine

680. Courts in the United States historically have been reluctant to interfere in an ongoing family. Thus, if the parties are not divorcing, filing for separate maintenance, or bringing some other clearly authorized action, courts have been reluctant to directly order a married person (usually a man) to provide a specific level of support for his spouse unless her life or health is in jeopardy.[776] There is probably less reluctance today than there was historically, but still the doctrine of judicial respect for family autonomy is alive and restrains judicial intervention in the ongoing family.

681. Courts historically recognized a legal doctrine that allowed for indirect provision of support for dependent family members. It was the "doctrine of necessaries." As a general rule, spouses are not legally the agents of each other, but based on the duty of the husband to provide adequately for his wife (and children), the

773. *See* R. E. Oliphant & N. Ver Steegh, *Family Law* 238–240 (2010); *see also* I.M. Ellman, P.M. Kurtz & K.T. Bartlett, *Family Law, Cases, Text and Problems* 92–94 (2d ed., 1991).

774. H.H. Clark, Jr., *The Law of Domestic Relations in the United States*, §6.1, (West 2d ed., 1988).

775. K.A. Portuan Miller, *Who Says Muslim Women Don't Have the Right to Divorce?—A Comparison Between Anglo-American Law and Islamic Law,* 22 N.Y. Intl. L. Rev. 201, 240 (2009).

776. *See McGuire v. McGuire*, 59 N.W.2d 336 (Neb. 1953); *see* C.L. Blakesley, *Family Autonomy,* in I *Contemporary Family Law* Ch. 1 (L.D. Wardle, C.L. Blakesley & J.Y. Parker eds, Callaghan 1988).

doctrine of necessaries allowed the wife, acting as the agent of necessity of the husband, to purchase necessaries from a merchant, and the merchant could then sue the husband to collect payment.[777] That entailed some risk, as only "necessaries," not discretionary items, were covered (and what is "necessary" depends upon the station and circumstances of each family and each case), and because the husband would have a defense if he had already provided necessaries, or money to purchase them, to the wife.[778]

682. The necessaries doctrine is still alive and well in American law. It is invoked with some regularity by health care providers seeking recovery for services rendered to the spouse of a patient who has failed to pay his or her bill for medical services.[779] When third persons like doctors, nursing homes, etc., provide services to a spouse that are deemed reasonably necessary for the support of that spouse, both spouses are liable for the costs of those services. In some states, "the spouse who actually incurs the debt may be deemed to be 'primarily liable', but both spouses are 'jointly and severally' liable to the third party under the necessaries doctrine."[780]

683. Failure of one having the ability to provide adequate support for his or her spouse and children is a crime. Criminal non-support laws in virtually all states penalize deliberate and knowing failure to support. For example, the 1980 Model Penal Code provides: "A person commits a misdemeanor if he persistently fails to provide support which he can provide and which he knows he is legally obliged to provide to a spouse, child or other dependent."[781]

§5. Homestead Rights

684. Homestead acts exempt certain family property from the reach of attachment, judgments, and forced sale to satisfy debt. Most states have enacted such laws, which vary tremendously in their provisions. While individuals may file and claim homestead protection, they were designed in recognition of the nuclear family unit which is the basic economic unit of society and the association in which most Americans live. These laws were enacted to protect families in times of economic distress, to preserve for them the bare necessities of life and, to let them carry on or start over without becoming homeless, without transportation, and without

777. *Branson Land Co. v. Guilliams*, 926 S.W.2d 534 (Mo. App. 1996) (an agency relationship does not exist merely because of marital relationship, and neither spouse is empowered to act as the agent for the other simply because they are married); and *Levine v. Levine*, 209 F. Supp. 564 (D.Del. 1962) (the obligation of a husband to support his wife and family is quasi-contract, founded upon public policy, not upon an implied contract).
778. H.H. Clark, Jr., *supra* §6.3.
779. I.M. Ellman, P.M. Kurtz & K.T. Bartlett, *Family Law, Cases, Text and Problems* 92–94 (2d ed., 1991).
780. *See*, e.g., Tex. Fam. Code § 3.201(a)(2); Thomas M. Fetherston, Jr., *The Necessaries Doctrine and Spouses Mutual Duty of Support* (2013).
781. American Law Institute, Model Penal Code § 230.5 (1980).

any family sentimental treasures.[782] The worldwide economic recession and mortgage crisis at the end of the first decade of the twenty-first century renewed interest in homestead exemptions as imprudent government and housing finance policies and optimistic private housing expectations left many in need of at least temporary protection.[783] Thus, homestead laws generally allow an individual to register a portion of his real and personal property as "homestead," thereby making that portion of his or her personal estate exempt from most claims of most creditors. The principle behind these homestead laws is the value of "preservation of the family farm, home, or other assets in the face of severe economic conditions."[784]

685. The main property protected, and the subject from which the exemption laws take their name, is the "homestead," the dwelling in which the family resides and the land under it. Typically, the exemption is for a minimum amount of value (set at a time when bare subsistence living was the acceptable norm). The amount of the "homestead" exemption varies dramatically among the states, from USD 5,000 to USD 100,000.[785] A typical protection law is the Utah Exemptions Act which protects the primary personal residence of an individual (USD 10,000) or couple (USD 20,000), and related water rights, from judicial lien, levy, execution or forced sale except for property tax liens, security interests in the property and purchase price judgment liens, child support and alimony liens, and consensual liens on mutual contract debts.[786] In 2005, shortly before the crisis erupted, Congress adopted a maximum amount of homestead exemption that debtors can claim in federal bankruptcy court.[787]

686. In addition to the family dwelling, homestead laws typically protect minor other categories of property whose sentimental value to the family far outweighs the commercial value of the property or its forced sale value to a creditor. Thus, for example, the Utah Exemptions Act protects, in addition to the homestead, a burial plot, health aids, disability or unemployment benefits, medical insurance benefits, veterans benefits, child support, one clothes washer and dryer, one refrigerator, one freezer, one stove, one microwave oven, one sewing machine, carpets, twelve months food and provisions, all wearing apparel excluding furs and jewelry, and all beds and beddings; art works produced by the debtor and his resident family, recovery for bodily personal injuries, retirement benefits and related qualified property divisions (QDRO) of retirement benefits, alimony, death benefits, pension benefits, up to USD 1,500 loan-value of life insurance, household furniture, personal books,

782. J.Y. Parker, *Economic Rights and Duties of Spouses*, in *Contemporary Family Laws*, §12:03, Chapter 12 (L.D. Wardle, C.L. Blakesley & J.Y. Parker eds, Callaghan 1988).
783. *See generally* M. Jennings, *From the Courts* 38 Real Est. L.J. 454 (Spring 2010) (noting that there is some possibility of making the homestead exemption applicable to mortgages).
784. Homestead Laws by State, available at http://homesteadlaws.uslegal.com/homestead-laws-by-state/.
785. Kentucky Revised Statutes Annotated §427.060 (1992) (USD 5,000); South Carolina Code Annotated Tit 34–61 (1996) (USD 5,000); and Massachusetts General Laws ch. 188, §1 (Supplement 1997) (USD 100,000).
786. Utah Code Annotated §78-23-3 (1997).
787. *See generally* J.P. Searcy, *Have the BAPCPA Amendments Solved the Problems Congress Intended to Solve:*, 57 Feb Law. 48 (Feb. 2010).

animals and musical instruments, heirlooms, professional tools of trade up to USD 3,500 and an automobile worth up to USD 2,500. The only claims that can be levied against exempt property are for taxes, alimony, child support, and one-month's wages, for purchase price of the object levied, and for mechanics liens. If property is jointly owned by a debtor and non-debtor, the creditor may levy against the interest of the nonexempt debtor and the purchaser of that individual's interest may have the property partitioned.[788]

788. Utah Code Annotated §§78-23-4 to -14 (1997).

Chapter 2. Antenuptial Contracts (The Marriage Settlement) and Separation Agreements

687. This chapter considers the voluntary economic settlements that are made by couples entering into and exiting from marriage. The former are generally called antenuptial contracts, or antenuptial agreements, or prenuptial agreements, or marriage settlements. The latter are generally called separation agreements or divorce settlements. Concern about enforcing agreements that might give one or both parties an incentive to divorce led courts in American jurisdictions to refuse to recognize such agreements for many years, at least to the extent they encouraged or were predicated upon divorce.[789] However, since about 1970 both kinds of agreements have not only be enforced but in most jurisdictions have been favored in the law because it is deemed to be in the parties' best interest and in the best interest of judicial economy and party autonomy to respect the right of the parties to control their own financial arrangements.[790]

§1. Antenuptial Agreements

I. History

688. Antenuptial contracts have a long and honorable history in Anglo-American law. At common law, a woman upon marriage lost most rights of property ownership. Her husband became the guardian of her property as well as her person. By marriage he acquired an interest (which he could alienate) in the rents and profits in land owned or acquired by her which would continue as long as she lived or, if a child were born of the marriage, as long as the husband lived. The wife, likewise, acquired an interest (dower) in the lands owned by her husband, a life estate in one-third of any land her husband owned in fee. Women and their families were interested in avoiding the wife's loss of control of property, and men and their families were interested in avoiding the encumbrance of the dower interest. The practice of creating trusts (jointure) to avoid this became so widespread that it led, in 1536, to the parliament enacting the Statute of Uses, which set strict requirements for avoiding endowment. Thus, the Statute of Uses is the oldest Anglo-American law regulating antenuptial contracts.[791] Likewise, the Statute of Frauds of 1677 regulated antenuptial contracts, requiring them to be in writing.

789. C.L. Blakesley & C. Curtis, *Property Division—Common Law* in *Contemporary Family Law*, §30:05, Chapter 30 (L.D. Wardle, C.L. Blakesley & J.Y. Parker eds, Callaghan 1988); L.D. Wardle, *Antenuptial Contracts*, in *Contemporary Family Law*, §5:02, Chapter 5 (L.D. Wardle, C.L. Blakesley & J.Y. Parker eds, Callaghan 1988).

790. *Posner v. Posner*, 233 So. 2d 381 (Fla. 1970), *rev'd on other grounds*, 257 So. 2d 530 (1972).

791. L.D. Wardle, *supra* at §5:02.

II. Modern Statutory and Case Law

689. Historically, most of the law governing the validity of antenuptial contracts was case law. Recently, however, case law regarding antenuptial contracts has been supplemented by statutes. Four model statutes or provisions are noteworthy. The most comprehensive and influential has been the Uniform Premarital Agreement Act (UPAA), promulgated the National Conference of Commissioners on Uniform State Laws (NCCUSL) in 1983, and adopted since then by one-half of the states.[792] That same year the NCCUSL also promulgated the Uniform Marital Property Act which, *inter alia*, provided for valid and enforcement premarital and postmarital agreements between spouses or prospective spouses to govern their marital property.[793] Likewise, the Uniform Probate Code also promulgated by the UCCUSL contains explicit provisions authorizing the advanced waiver of statutory rights by a surviving spouse.[794] Finally, the Restatement (Second) of Contracts contains a provision authorizing the enforcement of an antenuptial contract unless "it would change some essential incident of the marital relationship in a way detrimental to the public interest in the marriage relationship."[795] Today all states encourage and uphold premarital agreements, as a general rule.[796] Against this trend, the Principles of the Law of Family Dissolution proposed by the American Law Institute, take a grudging approach and view antenuptial contracts with suspicion and disfavor,[797] (which may account in part for the remarkable lack of adoption or implementation of the Principles in American states).[798] However, the policies in favor of upholding such agreements (in the absence of fraud) remains strong in most states for reasons relating to respect for party autonomy and general preference for private structuring of the economic consequences of marriage.

A. *General Validity*

690. Historically, there were two major common law restrictions on antenuptial contracts: they could not alter the essentials of the marriage relationship, and they could not "contemplate" or encourage divorce.[799] Additionally, agreements waiving

792. "Uniform Premarital Agreement Act," *Uniform Laws Annotated*, No. 9A, (1983), p. 369.
793. "Uniform Marital Property Act" §10, *Uniform Laws Annotated*, No. 9A, (1983), p. 121. (This Act, which embodies a form of community property, has been adopted only by the state of Wisconsin).
794. "Uniform Probate Code" §2-213, *Uniform Laws Annotated*, No. 8, (Supplement 1997), p. 144.
795. *Restatement (2nd) of Contracts* §190 (1981).
796. *See generally Prenuptial Agreements—An Overview, at* https://www.legalzoom.com/knowledge/prenuptial-agreement/faq/valid-prenuptial-agreements (seen Jan. 30, 2016).
797. American Law Institute, *Principles of the Law of Family Dissolution: Analysis and Recommendations*, Ch. 7 (2002).
798. *See generally Developments in the Law—The Law of Marriage and Family, Marriage as Contract and Marriage as Partnership: The Future of Antenuptial Agreement Law,* 116 Harv. L. Rev. 2075 (2003) ("the ALI Principles misses an opportunity ... "); D. Inkeles, *The Uniform Premarital Agreement Act: Taking* Castro *to a New Level for Prenuptial Agreements*, 81 Fla. B.J. 32 (2007).
799. L. Weitzman, *The Marriage Contract* 388–342 (1981); J. Younger, *Antenuptial Agreements*, 28 Wm. Mitchell L. Rev. 697 (2001).

or restricting spousal or child support, regulating intimate relations, or other provisions deemed contrary to public policy also generally have not been enforceable. Today, the general preference of most courts is to uphold premarital agreements in the absence of duress, deception, or violation of public policy against impoverishment of dependent former spouses and children.[800] In at least some states, marriage is required consideration for an antenuptial contract, so some courts have held that nonmarital cohabitants cannot enter into valid antenuptial agreements.[801] However, as nonmarital cohabitation increases, it is likely that most states will conclude that agreement to assume marriage-like duties will be sufficient consideration for such contracts between cohabitants. Professor Peter N. Swisher explains: "Drafting marital agreements ... is analogous to creating a 'private statute' between the parties which clearly enumerates their various rights and obligations."[802] Thus, the creative opportunities and responsibilities of the attorney are substantial.

B. Writing

691. More than three hundred years ago, the original English Statute of Frauds specifically required that an "agreement made upon consideration of marriage" be in writing and signed by the party charged to be legally enforceable.[803] Today, all American states have the same requirement.[804] The Uniform Premarital Agreement Act so provides, and further specifies that after marriage an antenuptial contract can only be modified by a signed written agreement.[805] Presumable an oral premarital agreement is unenforceable. However, where there has been part performance (other than marriage), equitable relief may be granted.[806]

C. Disclosure or Knowledge

692. Disclosure of material facts about financial condition of the party benefiting from the premarital agreement, or the effective equivalent of disclosure, is a common requirement. The Uniform Premarital Agreement Act provides:

> §6. a) A premarital agreement is not enforceable if the party against whom enforcement is sought proves that:
>
> 2. the agreement was unconscionable when it was executed and, before execution of the agreement, that party:

---

800. *Sogg v. Nevada State Bank*, 832 P.2d 781 (Nev. 1992).
801. W. A. Reppy, Jr., *Choice of Law Problems Arising When Unmarried Cohabitants Change Domicile*, 55 S.M.U. L. Rev. 273, 282 n. 44 (2002) (citing decisions in California and Wisconsin).
802. Peter N. Swisher, *Drafting Premarital, Antenuptial, and Cohabitation Agreements*, in Negotiating and Drafting Marital and Separation Agreements (Robert E. Shepherd, Jr. et al., 1984).
803. 29 Car. II, c. 3 (1677).
804. L.D. Wardle, *supra* at §5:04.
805. "Uniform Premarital Agreement Act" §§2, 5.
806. L.D. Wardle, *supra* at §5:04.

- was not provided a fair and reasonable disclosure of the property or financial obligations of the other party;
- did not voluntarily and expressly waive, in writing, any right to disclosure of the property or financial obligations of the other party beyond the disclosure provided; and
- did not have, or reasonably could not have had, an adequate knowledge of the property or financial obligations of the other party.[807]

Thus, mere nondisclosure of material facts about the property and financial obligations of the other party does not, alone, render the antenuptial contract unenforceable; it is unenforceable only if there was nondisclosure *and* no waiver *and* lack of adequate knowledge of such information *and* if the agreement was unconscionable when executed.

D. Adequate Provision

693. Generally speaking, either adequate provision or full disclosure (or equivalent knowledge) are alternative grounds for upholding and enforcing a premarital agreement. In some states, however, regardless of the reasonableness of provision, "full and complete disclosure" is an independent requirement for enforcement of an antenuptial contract.[808] In other states, either full and complete disclosure or adequate knowledge must be shown.[809] But those are minority positions.

694. Thus, in most states fair and adequate provision even without full disclosure or equivalent knowledge is enough to validate an antenuptial contract. Accordingly, the time for ascertaining adequacy of provision is critical. Many agreements that were fair and adequate when executed, on the eve of marriage, may not seem fair and adequate if judged in the context of circumstances that exist twenty years later when the parties divorce or one of them dies. The time at which fairness (conscionability) is assessed in ordinary contract validity disputes is the time of contracting, and that is the general rule applicable to antenuptial contracts, also. "[C]ourts have become increasingly reluctant to render antenuptial agreements unenforceable, especially on the ground of substantive unfairness at the time of an agreement's enforcement."[810]

695. However, there is a strong public interest in seeing that divorced and widowed spouses do not become public charges while their former spouses or his or

807. Uniform Premarital Agreement Act §6(a).

808. *DeLorean v. DeLorean*, 511 A.2d 1257 (N.J. Super. 1986).

809. *Gross v. Gross*, 464 N.E.2d 500 (Ohio 1984).

810. *Developments in the Law—The Law of Marriage and the Family, Marriage as Contract and Marriage As Partnership: The Future of Antenuptial Agreement Law*, 116 Harv. L. Rev. 2075, 2077 (2003) (interestingly, the student authors favor substantive fairness review at time of enforcement, reflecting the divide between youthful inexperience and the position taken by more experienced professionals in most courts and legislatures).

her other heirs enjoy economic surplus. For that reason, an antenuptial contract will be unenforceable as violative of public policy (at least under the UPAA) if it leaves the charged spouse so impoverished that she or he would have to receive public welfare assistance to survive.[811]

E. Independent Legal Counsel

696. Access to and opportunity to consult with independent counsel is closely related to disclosure or knowledge. The purpose of both requirements is to protect the right of the parties to make informed decisions. If one of the parties is particularly lacking in financial experience and understanding, the presence or absence of independent legal counsel may be a significant consideration if the validity of the premarital agreement is challenged. While actual consultation with a lawyer is clearly not required for an antenuptial contract to be valid and enforced, the absence of the realistic opportunity to obtain legal counsel before signing the contract may affect the validity of the agreement. The absence of an opportunity to get independent legal advice may be taken as evidence of duress or overreaching, or as breach of a fiduciary relationship, or as indicative of insufficient knowledge, depending on the circumstances of the case.[812] Due to the "unique relationships of the parties involved in a prenuptial agreement," independent counsel or, at least, opportunity and encouragement to obtain independent counsel, is important to protect both the parties and the process, as well as to protect the appearance of justice and the integrity and reputation of courts.[813] The more one-sided the agreement, the less likely a court will be to uphold it unless each party had independent legal counsel.[814] An attorney representing one party in drafting a premarital agreement risks personal liability for damages and for ethical misconduct if he or she does not encourage the unrepresented party to seek independent counsel.[815] "Due to the unique relationship of the parties involved in a prenuptial agreement, an attorney representing these parties has not only a different relationship but different responsibilities to the parties as well."[816]

811. Uniform Premarital Agreement Act §6(b).
812. N.R. Schembri, Note, *Prenuptial Agreements and the Significance of Independent Counsel,* 17 St. John's J. Legal Comment 313 (2003); J. Younger, *Antenuptial Agreements,* 28 Wm. Mitchell L. Rev. 697, 718 (encouraging lawyers to emphasize need for independent counsel to validate antenuptial agreements).
813. *See generally* N.R. Schembri, *Note Prenuptial Agreements, supra,* 17 St. John's J. Legal Comment, at 315–16.
814. N.R. Schembri, Note, *Prenuptial Agreements and the Significance of Independent Counsel,* 17 St. John's J. Legal Comment. 313 (2003); J. Younger, *Antenuptial Agreements,* 28 Wm. Mitchell L. Rev. 697, 718 (encouraging lawyers to emphasize need for independent counsel to validate antenuptial agreements).
815. *See generally* N.R. Schembri, *Note Prenuptial Agreements, supra,* 17 St. John's J. Legal Comment, at 332.
816. Nancy R. Schembri, *Prenuptial Agreements and the Importance of Independent Counsel,* 17 J. Civ. Rts. & Econ. Develop. 313, 315 (2003).

697. The critical element for validity of a premarital agreement is a real opportunity to consult independent legal counsel, not actual consultation with independent counsel. For example, in a case involving a famous American baseball player, Barry Bonds, the California Supreme Court upheld a premarital agreement in which both parties waived all interest in any earnings and property acquired by the other, even though the wife had not independent legal counsel. Barry, age 23, was born and raised in the United States, had three years of college, and had played professional baseball for three years, and had an attorney and a financial advisor, and was earning 106,000 per year. Susann, his nonmarital cohabitant and fiancé, was an immigrant from Sweden (conversationally fluent in English and French but a native speaker of Swedish) who had worked as a waitress, bartender and aspiring cosmetologist, and who testified that her English was quite limited but "out of pride" she did not tell anyone that she did not understand the agreement. Barry told Susann that he wanted to sign a pre-marital agreement two nights before they were to wed; the parties signed the premarital agreement the next day in the office of Barry Bonds' attorney, just one day before their marriage. Susann did not claim that she had evér considered not signing the agreement, or that she felt threatened, or that she wanted to consult an attorney of her own, or that she felt pressured to sign. The other persons present all testified that Barry's attorney had informed Susann of her right to independent counsel. When Barry filed for divorce six years later, he was earning USD 8 million per year, while Susann was a mother and homemaker without a paid job. The California trial court upheld the agreement, but the state Court of Appeals reversed finding the agreement to be invalid for want of independent legal counsel for Susann. The California Supreme Court reversed and upheld the agreement, holding:

> We conclude that although the ability of the party challenging the agreement to obtain independent counsel is an important factor in determining whether that party entered into the agreement voluntarily, the Court of Appeal majority erred in directing trial courts to subject premarital agreements to strict scrutiny where the less sophisticated party does not have independent counsel and has not waived counsel according to exacting waiver requirements.[817]

III. Limitations

698. The prevailing general rule that antenuptial contracts that comply with the above-noted form and procedural requirements are enforceable is not absolute. Some terms are suspect and some provisions in premarital agreements are still unenforceable. In a minority of states, such as Ohio, premarital agreements may not be modified after the parties have married.[818]

817. In re Marriage of Bonds (*Bonds v. Bonds*), 5 P.3d 815, 829 (Cal. 2000).
818. Sharon A. Skirbunt, *The Perils of Estate Planning and Divorce*, 17 Ohio Prob. L.J. 59 (2006).

A. Promotion of Divorce

699. Under the historic rule, American courts refused to enforce antenuptial contracts because they might tend to promote divorce, which was deemed contrary to public policy. Since the adoption of unilateral no-fault divorce (the de jure rule in less than half the states, but the de facto rule in all others), it is apparent that the public policy against divorce is not what it used to be. Almost every state court to consider the issue in recent years has disavowed the rule that antenuptial contracts made in contemplation of divorce are void against public policy.[819] However, in relatively recent times a few American courts have referred to and applied this public policy as the basis for refusing to enforce provisions in antenuptial contracts.[820] What seems to have changed is not so much the notion that it is against public policy to give married persons a strong economic incentive to seek divorce, or an economic death penalty for seeking a divorce even though the spousal treatment is intolerable. What has changed more is the recent recognition that antenuptial agreements usually do not constitute that kind of economic incentive. If, however, the facts of a case indicated that the premarital agreement was so economically egregious that it forced a person to live under intolerable conditions in the marriage, or that it gave one party an almost irresistible reward for filing for divorce, it is not unlikely that the provision would not be enforced under the public policy rationale.[821]

B. Child Support

700. Traditionally, terms setting or waiving child support were deemed unenforceable. The parties could not bind the court regarding child support. The court's *parens patriae* interest and duty to protect the welfare of children superseded the court's interest in respecting the autonomy of the parents to contract with each other.

701. The rule is essentially unchanged, even today. The Uniform Premarital Agreement Act provides: "The right of a child to support may not be adversely affected by a premarital agreement."[822] Note, however, that the rule does not absolutely bar child support provisions in antenuptial agreements, nor bar their enforcement. It nullifies them only to the extent that they "adversely affect[]" the right of the child to receive child support. Thus, parties may contract to provide greater child support than the state's child support guidelines would provide, and those provisions would be enforceable. However, an agreement that would result in the child

819. *Miller v. Ratner*, 688 A.2d 976 (Md.App., 1997); *Gordon v. Gordon*, 675 A.2d 540 (Md. Ct. App. 1996); *In re Marriage of Spiegel*, 553 N.W.2d 309 (Iowa, 1996); and *Smith v. Smith*, as: 656 So.2d 1143 (Miss. 1995).

820. *McAlpine v. McAlpine*, 637 So.2d 1163 (La. App. 1994), aff'd, 1995 WL 71495 (La. 1995).

821. *In re Noghrey*, 169 Cal. App. 3d 426, 215 Cal. Rptr. 153 (1985).

822. Uniform Premarital Agreement Act §3(b).

receiving less child support would not be enforceable. This appears to be a ubiquitous rule in all American states today.[823]

C. Alimony

702. Provisions restricting or waiving alimony historically were viewed with disfavor by American courts. The traditional rule reflected a paternalism and perhaps the economic realities of the times (limited self-employment opportunities for women).[824]

703. Today, both the economic situation and the policy of the law have changed. "The law on premarital agreements reflects shifting attitudes toward the family, marriage, family law, contract law, and gender equality. Over the past thirty years, there has been a shift in views about women and work. Women have increasingly been viewed as equals in society and are no longer considered to be at an economic disadvantage."[825] As a general rule, parties are free to contract about alimony, including to waive the right to receive alimony. The reason is that in the contest between principles of paternalism and autonomy, the people of most American jurisdictions prefer to let adults order their own affairs, even if the result is that sometimes they make bad bargains. However, there is an exception to the rule. If the effect of enforcing a waiver of alimony is that one of the spouses will be left so impoverished that she or he would become a public charge, that provision will not be enforced. For example, the Uniform Premarital Agreement Act provides that if the premarital agreement "causes one party … to be eligible for support under a program of public assistance" at the time enforcement of the agreement is sought, it is unenforceable.[826] In some states there are precedents indicating that the traditional rule against enforcing provisions regarding alimony might still be applied, at least in some cases.[827] While provisions waiving alimony are viewed with hostility by many American academics, and with cautious suspicion by some American judges, "[t]he majority of states that have looked at premarital agreements waiving spousal support have upheld them."[828]

D. Essentials of Marriage

704. It is generally stated that a premarital agreement may not "alter the essentials of the marriage relation."[829] But there is no clear agreement about what facets

823. *See* M.P. Strasser, *You Take the Embryos But I Get the House (and the Business): Recent Trends in Awards Involving Embryos Upon Divorce*, 57 Buff. L. Rev. 1159, 1224, n. 318 (2009).
824. L.D. Wardle, *supra* at §5:09.
825. S. Wolfson, *Premarital Waiver of Alimony*, 38 Fam. L. Q. 141, 142–143 (2004).
826. Uniform Premarital Agreement Act §6(b).
827. L.D. Wardle, *supra* §5:09.
828. S. Wolfson, *Premarital Waiver of Alimony*, *supra*, 38 Fam. L. Q. at 150 (2004).
829. L.D. Wardle, *supra* §5:10.

of marital relations constitute the "essentials of the marriage." Increasingly, American courts have been willing to allow the parties to alter customary social expectations of marital relations. Increasingly, courts have upheld the private ordering of marriage relations by the parties to the marriage.[830] However, that does not mean that parties are free to devise any terms and conditions, and that courts will automatically enforce them.

705. It is most accurate to state that American courts will not enforce provisions in premarital agreements that violate strong public policy. Thus, provisions that would violate criminal laws (for instance, agreement to engage in prohibited sexual or other felonious behavior, or to engage in a criminal conspiracy), or an agreement to submit to what amounted to slavery, or terms that left a party without any legal recourse for violation of basic human rights would not be enforced. However, in most states, while the same general contractual principles apply in drafting separation agreements between nonmarital same-sex (and cohabiting heterosexual) couples as apply to couples contemplating marriage, there are some substantive difference between cohabitation agreements and pre-marital agreements. For instance issues of consideration and tax consequences and other legal benefit may differ significantly between marrying couples and cohabiting couples.[831] Of course, the UPAA does not apply to nonmarital couples.

706. Among the most troubling are terms relating to religious practices. These include provisions agreeing to cooperate in obtaining a religious divorce or like decree, and agreements to raise the children in the religious faith of one of the spouses. The former have been upheld and enforced.[832] The latter generally have been not been given binding effect (underscoring the paramount *parens patriae* duty of the court which overrides even parental autonomy).[833]

IV. Procedural Issues

707. It should be apparent that antenuptial contracts are generally favored in American courts now. However, they are not absolutely enforceable. In fact, they are more easily deemed unenforceable than other kinds of (ordinary commercial) contracts. Judging from the reported cases, there is quite a lot of litigation upon divorce about the enforceability of premarital agreements. However, in recent years, the gist of the successful challenges has changed from challenges based on the fairness of the substance of the agreements to challenges based on the fairness of the processes by which the agreements were made. Thus, procedural issues in the court

830. J.B. Singer, *The Privatization of Family Law*, Wisconsin L. Rev. 1443 (1992); *Recent Developments: Family Law-Prenuptial Agreements-Pennsylvania Supreme Court Rejects Substantive Review Of Prenuptial Agreements*, 104 Harvard L. Rev. 1399 (1991).

831. P.F. Zupcofska, *When Couples Are Same Sex, Drafting Considerations Differ*, 32 Fam. Advoc. 18 (Winter 2010).

832. *Avitzur v. Avitzur*, 58 N.Y.2d 108, 446 N.E.2d 136 (1983); and *Goldman v. Goldman*, 554 N.E.2d 1016 (Ill. App. 1990).

833. *Kilgrow v. Kilgrow*, 107 So.2d 895 (Ala. 1958).

are not insignificant when the enforcement of an antenuptial agreement is in question. As noted above, opportunity to consult with independent legal counsel is perhaps the most important "procedural" issue.

A. Burden of Proof and Burden of Producing Evidence

708. The ultimate burden of proof lies with the party who has to plead a claim or defense. With respect to antenuptial agreements, as with other contracts, the party relying upon the contract must prove that the contract was made. Usually, introduction of the written agreement signed by the parties is sufficient to carry that burden. In some states, the party seeking enforcement of an antenuptial agreement has the additional burden of producing evidence that there was full disclosure or its equivalent, or (in some states) adequate provision. Absent such a showing, the contract will not be presumed valid.[834] But the general rule in most states is that the party challenging the validity of the premarital agreement bears the burden of proving as an affirmative defense that there was not full disclosure or its equivalent, or adequate provision.[835]

709. Once the prima facie case is made for the validity of the antenuptial contract, the burden shifts to the party seeking to avoid the contract. That party has the burden of presenting evidence to establish that the contract is invalid. That party must show duress, or fraud, or forged signature, or that there was not full disclosure, or its equivalent, or adequate provision. That is the prevailing American rule. Thus, the Uniform Premarital Agreement Act provides that "the party who alleges that a premarital agreement is not enforceable [must] bear the burden of proof as to that allegation."[836]

B. Choice of Law

710. Because there are significant variations between the states regarding whether and what disclosure is required, who bears the burden of proof, and waiver of alimony, choice of law questions regarding premarital agreements can be very important. Whether the law of one state or another applies may make the difference between enforcement or nonenforcement.[837]

711. As a general rule, the same choice of law rules applicable to other contracts are applicable to premarital agreements.[838] Thus, as a general rule, the law of the

834. *Friedlander v. Friedlander*, 80 Wash. 2d 293, 494 P.2d 208 (1972).

835. L.D. Wardle, *supra* §5:07.

836. Uniform Premarital Agreement Act §6.

837. *DeLorean v. DeLorean*, 211 N.J. Super. 432, 511 A.2d 1257 (1986).

838. J.H. McLaughlin, *Premarital Agreements and Choice of Law: "One, Two Three, Baby, You and Me"*, 72 Mo. L. Rev. 793 (2007); W. A. Reppy, Jr., *Choice of Law Problems Arising When Unmarried Cohabitants Change Domicile*, 55 S.M.U. L. Rev. 273, 282 n. 44 (2002) (citing decisions in California and Wisconsin).

place of contracting governs questions of validity, and the law of the place of performance governs questions of performance.[839] The Restatement, Second, of Conflicts suggests that the law of the state with the most significant relationship with the parties and transaction should apply.[840] Additionally, the parties are generally free to choose the state whose law will govern the antenuptial contract, so long as that state has some significant contact with the parties and their agreement.[841]

§2. Separation Agreements

712. The principles governing separation agreements are, for the most part, similar if not identical to the principles governing premarital agreements. The statute of frauds applies. Because the provisions will generally take effect shortly and the parties are considering the provision's effectiveness immediately, not just speculating about possible effectiveness at some point in the future, and because the separation or divorce is already in process, there historically has been less reluctance to uphold and enforce separation agreements than premarital agreements. Since the parties know their assets, obligations, needs, and circumstances best, and are more likely to be more satisfied by their own agreement than by a court-imposed property division, courts in America generally encourage the parties to settle their economic affairs and relations themselves, if possible. However, courts have long been sensitive to the potential for overreaching and exploitation of an emotionally and economically vulnerable spouse. Usually the court will incorporate the settlement agreement into the divorce or separation decree.[842] Additionally, the court may "merge" the agreement into the divorce decree. If the agreement is merged into the decree, the agreement has ceased to have separate and independent existence, but has been replaced by the decree of dissolution and is enforceable exclusively by means available for enforcement of judicial decrees, but no longer enforceable as a separate contract.[843] Only general contractual principles would apply in drafting separation agreements between nonmarital cohabiting couples.[844]

I. Modern Statutory and Case Law Regarding General Validity

713. Though only adopted by one state (Wisconsin) because of its incorporation of community property principles, the Uniform Marital Property Act (UMPA) represents the principles that are common if not prevailing in the American states. (Although adopted in only one state, the National Conference of Commissioners on Uniform State Laws considers the UMPA to be a "model act" which are influential

839. L.D. Wardle, *supra* §5:12.
840. *Restatement (2d) of Conflicts* §§6, 188 (1972).
841. *Ibid.* §187.
842. C.L. Blakesley & C. Curtis, *Property Division—Common Law*, in *Contemporary Family Law*, §30:05, Chapter 30 (L.D. Wardle, C.L. Blakesley & J.Y. Parker eds, Callaghan 1988).
843. *See Johnston v. Johnston*, 465 A.2d 436 (Md. 1983).
844. M. Mahoney, *The Law of Cohabitation for Opposite Sex Couples*, 7 J. L. & Fam. Studs. 135 (2005).

in many states.) The UMPA provides, in pertinent part, that a marital property agreement (including *both* premarital and separation agreements) must be written and signed by both of the spouses,[845] that it "may not adversely affect the right to child support,"[846] that the agreement may cover rights, obligations, control, management, and disposition regarding any of their property,[847] testamentary and trust provisions,[848] and alteration or total elimination of alimony (unless it would cause one spouse to be eligible for public support).[849] However, any provisions in violation of public policy or criminal statutes are not valid.[850] A marital property agreement executed during marriage (primarily separation agreements) is not enforceable if the spouse against whom it is to be enforced establishes that it was unconscionable when made, or was not executed voluntarily, or that there was not pre-execution: (i) fair and reasonable disclosure, (ii) equivalent notice of the financial assets or liabilities of the other, or (iii) waiver of disclosure.

714. Because of the difference in timing between premarital and separation agreements, there appears to be more willingness to overlook substantively unconscionable provisions in premarital agreements than in immediately effective separation agreements. According to the UMPA, mere unconscionability alone is enough to invalidate a separation agreement. That reflects particular and realistic concern for the vulnerability of parties during separation and divorce. The same concern underlies the requirement of fair and reasonable disclosure or equivalent notice of financial status. However, in the absence of substantial unconscionability, fraud, or duress the provisions of a separation agreement presumptively will be enforced.[851] The assistance of independent legal counsel is not required for validity of a separation agreement, but it covers a host of deficiencies, and goes a long way to satisfy a court that the agreement is a voluntary and fair bargain.[852]

II. Limitations

715. As noted in section I, normally child support provisions and spousal support provisions in separation agreements are not automatically enforceable. The child's right to support may not be adversely affected, nor may a spouse be left on public welfare. Those conditions are essentially identical to the limitations upon premarital agreements.

716. While the "promotion" of divorce is not a substantial restriction upon a separation agreement because the parties are already in the process of divorcing, the

845. Uniform Marital Property Act §10(a).
846. Uniform Marital Property Act §10(b).
847. *Ibid.* §10(c) (1–3).
848. *Ibid.* §10(c) (5–6).
849. *Ibid.* §§10(c) (4), 10(i).
850. *Ibid.* §10(c) (8).
851. J.D. Gregory, P.N. Swisher & S.L. Scheible, *Understanding Family Law*, §4.04, (1993).
852. *Williams v. Williams*, 508 A.2d 985 (Md. 1986); and *Radigan v. Radigan*, 465 N.W.2d 483 (S.D. 1991).

underlying public policy in supporting marriage is not entirely irrelevant. If the separation agreement "tends unreasonably to encourage divorce," it will not be enforced.[853] Likewise, if the parties reconcile it is generally held that the unperformed executory provisions are repudiated and invalid, while the executed provisions will be deemed valid.[854]

853. *Restatement (2d) Contracts* §190 (1981).
854. *Yeich v. Yeich*, 399 S.E.2d 170 (Va. Ct. App. 1990).

Chapter 3. Property Division upon Cessation of Marriage

§1. Property Division upon Divorce

I. General Principles

A. *Evolution of Marital Property and Equitable Distribution Principles*

1. Common Law Property and Community Property States

717. As noted previously,[855] most American states inherited their property distribution schemes from English *common law*. Because the common law suspended the legal personality of women during marriage, and for many other reasons, virtually all property acquired during the marriage (and even some property, that the wife had brought with her into the marriage) belonged to the husband.[856] Even after the nineteenth century Married Women's Property Acts eliminated many of the legal disabilities of married women, most property acquired during marriage was acquired in the name of the husband.

718. However, eight states with significant Spanish or French roots historically followed *community property* law rather than common law property law,[857] and a ninth state (Wisconsin) adopted similar principles in the Uniform Marriage and Divorce Act. Under the community property system all property acquired during marriage except that received by gift, devise, bequest or inheritance, was deemed to belong not to either party separately but by both parties together as a community of *acquets*. (Property acquired before marriage or after the termination of a marriage, and gifts, bequests, devises, and inheritances received anytime were deemed the *separate* property of the owning spouse.) The marital community was an entity in which both spouses held equal interests.

855. *See supra*, Part III, Chapter 1. *See generally* Lynn D. Wardle, Mark P. Strasser & Lynne Marie Kohm, Family Law from Multiple Perspectives 735–737 (2014).

856. "At common law, possession and control of the wife's realty and absolute title to most of her personal property vested in the husband by operation of marriage. [Upon divorce] the title of the H [to the chattels] being absolute, continued undisturbed." The same was true of choses reduced to possession, but W retained choses not reduced to possession. C. G. Vernier, *American Family Laws*, Vol. 2, §98, 220 (Greenwood Press, 1932, 1971 reprint).

857. *See supra*, Part III, Chapter 1. The eight traditionally community states are: Arizona, California, Idaho, Louisiana, Nevada, New Mexico, Texas and Washington. In 1986, Wisconsin adopted a modified form of community property when it adopted the Uniform Marital Property Act (proposed in 1983) applicable to property during marriage and upon death; and it retained its equitable distribution statute for division of property upon divorce. Wisconsin Statutes Annotated §§766.001-979.

2. The Title-Distribution Era

719. Property distribution upon divorce has gone through essentially three phases in the United States. The earliest phase was the *title distribution* phase of common law and community property. Historically, at common law, property was retained after divorce by the party who individually held title to that property. This put the wife at a severe economic disadvantage upon divorce in terms of property ownership. In the absence of statutory authorization to redistribute property (which historically did not exist at common law) courts had little authority to take property from the title owner and give it to another person, even a former spouse, even to prevent grave economic injustice. Judicial power to redistribute property was not widely authorized until this century.[858]

720. In community property states, upon divorce, both parties traditionally were entitled to all of the separate property and an equal share (one-half) of the community property—not as a matter of recognizing a mere inchoate expectancy (as the wife's dower or marital property interest in common law states could be described) but as a matter of recognizing the present, equal community property ownership interest of each spouse.[859] Thus, in the first phase of property division, property went to the title-holder in both common law and community property states, with women getting a much better result in community property states because they were deemed to have equal title to the community property.

3. Discretionary Distribution

721. The second phase can be called the *discretionary distribution phase*. In response to the substantial disparity in economic consequences of divorce for men and women in common law states, legislation authorizing judicial discretion to distribute some part of the property according to principles other than title began to be passed in the twentieth century. While the legislative schemes varied from state to state, typically they gave the divorce court tremendous discretion to divide any property held by either of the divorcing spouses. Often the statutes provided that the court was to make equitable division of property; hence, these property division statutes came to be known as *equitable distribution* laws. Even in community property states, equitable distribution of community property, in lieu of strictly equal division, was adopted by most of the community property states. While this afforded some relief from the inflexibility of the title-distribution system, discretionary distribution had other shortcomings. For example, while the notion of equitable distribution reflected a laudable aspiration for equity, these laws failed to define equity,

858. *Contemporary Family Law* §30:01 ff., Vol. 3, (L.D. Wardle, C.L. Blakesley & J. Y. Parker eds, Callaghan 1988); B.R. Turner, *Equitable Distribution of Property* §2.03 33–34 (2d ed., Shepard's/McGraw-Hill 1994); C. G. Vernier, *supra.* §96 ff; H. Clark, Jr., *The Law of Domestic Relations in the United States*, §7.1, 7.2 (2d ed., West 1988), 7.2.

859. L.D. Wardle et al., *ibid.*; B.R. Turner, *supra* §2.05 at 34–36; C.G. Vernier, *ibid.*; and H. Clark, Jr., *supra* §7.2.

or to identify the principles which, if followed, would produce equity. Judicial discretion gave room for nonlegal factors to play, including factors such as cultural or personal bias. Also, discretionary distribution could be very unpredictable, and the results could vary dramatically from judge to judge, or even from case to case.

4. Equitable Distribution of Marital Property

722. The third and present phase is the *marital property equitable distribution* phase. *Marital property* essentially is what property, that would be community property in community property states, is called in divorce proceedings in common law states. Under *marital property* principles, property acquired before marriage, or after termination of a marriage, or as gifts, bequests, devises and inheritances received during marriage, is deemed *separate* or *individual* property; all other property—basically all property acquired during marriage except that received by gift, devise, bequest or inheritance, is deemed *marital* property (still called *community* property in community property states). In marital property states, marriage is deemed at the time of divorce to have created a marital community of *acquets*, a partnership in which the spouses have interests that are presumed to be equal (at least for purpose of property distribution upon divorce).[860] "Today, equitable distribution of property upon divorce is applied in all fifty states and the District of Columbia."[861] In community property states, the spouses have equal legal interest in all community property both during marriage and upon divorce (subject to modification, unusually, by the court). In common law property states, the spouses have only an inchoate interest in the property acquired by the other during marriage, but upon divorce that ripens into an interest of variable scope and duration, depending on how the judge sees the equities of the case.

723. Upon divorce in marital (or community) property states, the separate property presumably will be awarded to the title-holding spouse, while the marital property will be equitably (re)distributed by the court. About thirty-five states (including seven of the nine states that presently adhere to community property law) plus the District of Columbia reportedly permit equitable division of marital (or community) property upon divorce.[862] Two community property states generally require equal distribution instead of equitable distribution, and in many (perhaps most) states there is a general (sometimes loose) presumption that the marital property should be split equally. All states allow exceptional redistribution to account for

860. In community property states, throughout marriage the law treats the spouses as equal partners, with equal present shares in the community of *acquets*. In common law states with marital property equitable distribution upon divorce, this equality only exists upon divorce (not during the marriage or upon death).

861. K. W. Kingma, *Property Division at Divorce or Death for Married Couples Migrating Between Common Law and Community Property States*, 35 ACTEC J. 74 (2009) (American College of Trust and Estate Counsel).

862. B.R. Turner, *supra* §§2.07; 5.02. This concept of divisible marital property conforms to the original version of §307 (and also to the community property version, §307, Alt. B) of the Uniform Marriage and Divorce Act, *Uniform Laws Annotated*, No. 9A, (1987), p. 142.

improper dissipation of marital property, and about one-third of the states allow consideration of other kinds of fault generally in making equitable distribution of marital property; a few states allow broader equitable distribution, not limited to marital property.[863] In all states the spouses are free to alter their property relations by premarital agreement or by separation agreement:

> Equitable distribution is based upon either the *all-property* model or the *dual classification* model …
> The *all-property* model of equitable distribution exists in fifteen states, fourteen of which are common law states and one of which is a traditional community property state [Washington]. In those states, courts may divide any asset owned by either spouse regardless of time or manner of acquisition. The precise division is left to the court's discretion, but there is an express list of factors that the court must consider. Several of those factors relate to spousal contributions to the marriage. The court, though, is required to consider property division in every divorce case.
> The *dual classification* model of equitable distribution exists in 27 common law states, the District of Columbia, the other seven traditional community property states, and the State of Wisconsin that adopted the Uniform Marital Property Act, for a total of 36 jurisdictions. Thus, a majority of equitable distribution jurisdictions follow some form of dual classification system. Under the dual classification system, the court begins the property division process by classifying each spouse's assets as either *marital* or *separate* property. *Marital property* is then divided *equitably* between the spouses, while *separate property* is divided according to *legal title*.[864]

5. Significance of Method of Cessation of Marriage

724. Historically, there have been three significant methods of cessation of marriage: annulment, separation, and divorce. The method of cessation could have great theoretical significance for property distribution. For example, since an annulment in the case of a marriage declared void *ab initio* legally declared that there had been no marriage, during the title-distribution era the wife's claim to recover property she owned at the time of the putative marriage theoretically might be enhanced, especially during the period when courts had little authority to adjust title upon divorce. Today, the method of cessation of marriage is usually not a significant issue regarding property division because courts exercise essentially the same power to adjust property ownership upon cessation of marriage regardless of the method of cessation. For example, the Uniform Marriage and Divorce Act sections authorizing

863. B.R. Turner, *supra* §§2.06, 2.07; L.D. Wardle et al., *supra* §§30:04, 31:29-:46; H. Clark, Jr., *supra* §7.2; American Law Institute, *Principles of the Law of Family Dissolution: Analysis and Recommendations*, Council Draft No. 34 (ALI, Philadelphia, 4 Oct. 1995), 1–11; L.W. Waggoner, *Marital Property Rights in Transition*, 59 Missouri L. Rev. 21, 28 (1991).

864. Kingma, *Property Division at Divorce or Death. Supra, 35* ACTEC J. 74. *See further* Lynn D. Wardle, Mark P. Strasser & Lynne Marie Kohm, *Family Law from Multiple Perspectives* 735–781 (2014).

courts to equitably apportion property upon cessation of marriage apply both "[i]n a proceeding for dissolution of a marriage, [or] legal separation … ."[865] Likewise, upon annulment, courts generally have divorce-like powers to adjust property, if needed. While the authority to allocate property generally is phrased most broadly in divorce states, for practical purposes the method of cessation of marriage is not of much significance for property division today.

B. What Assets are "Property"?

725. Under prevailing marital property equitable distribution principles, the first major issue that may arise upon property division is whether the disputed asset is "property." Few if any states' marital property division laws provide a definition of is the term *property*, but it is generally understood by the courts to include all assets of value to which a legal ownership interest may attach, including any interest acquired by the parties to the marriage through the use of marital funds or the efforts of the spouses. Transferability, marketability, and capability of valuation are all factors in determining whether an asset is "property" (though none absolutely essential in all cases).[866]

1. Traditional Property and "New Property" Distinguished

726. Traditional forms of wealth, such as land, money, bank accounts, securities, jewelry, vehicles, etc., are recognized forms of "property" and rarely are questions about their property-status raised. The "new property," however, not infrequently poses definitional dilemmas. The term "new property" comes from a famous 1964 *Yale Law Journal* article, "The New Property," by Professor Charles Reich, in which he suggested that employment income, benefits, and pensions were the primary form of wealth for most people, and for the poor, government benefits were the primary form of wealth.[867] Professor Reich proposed that both forms of wealth should be treated like new forms of property and that they "must be surrounded with the kinds of safeguards once reserved for personalty."[868] Later, Professor Mary Ann Glendon observed that one of the most significant developments in marital property law in the recent decades was the expansion of the definition of property subject to distribution to include these relatively intangible, but highly valuable forms of "new property."[869] Among the most important forms of new property considered upon divorce are pensions, business and professional goodwill, educational licenses and professional licenses, and workers' compensation awards, personal injury recovery, and disability benefits. Increasingly, intangible interests

865. Uniform Marriage & Divorce Act §307 [Alts. A &B], *Uniform Laws Annotated*, No. 9A, (1987), p. 156.
866. B.R. Turner, *op cit.* §5.01 at 122; §5.03 at 125; and §5.06 at 129.
867. C. Reich, *The New Property*, 73 Yale L. J. 733, 738–739 (1964).
868. *Ibid.*
869. M.A. Glendon, *The New Family and the New Property* 2, 67 (Butterworths 1981).

that have significant value are being brought before divorce courts and made subject to division upon marital dissolution, if those interests are capable of realistic and reliable valuation and fair division, and if they meet the other requirements noted below for property division.

2. Skills and Capacity Distinguished from Property

727. The prevailing rule in American law is that skills, earning capacity, and personal attributes are not property. Rather, skills and earning capacity are personal characteristics inseparable from the core of individual identity protected by the Fourteenth Amendment and over which the state generally has no power to dictate or control.[870] As the Colorado Supreme Court stated in *In re Graham*, concluding that an educational degree or professional license lacks the essential characteristics of property because:

> [i]t does not have an exchange value or any objective transferable value on an open market. It is personal to the holder. It terminates on death of the holder and is not inheritable. It cannot be assigned, sold, transferred, conveyed, or pledged. An advanced degree is a cumulative product of many years of previous education, combined with diligence and hard work. It may not be acquired by the mere expenditure of money. It is simply an intellectual achievement that may potentially assist in the future acquisition of property. In our view, it has none of the attributes of property in the usual sense of that term.[871]

However, assets that are transferable generally are deemed to be property. Thus, most courts have concluded that pensions, business and practice goodwill, disability payments, personal injury awards, and workers' compensation awards are "property" for purposes of division upon divorce, but educational degrees, professional licenses and personal talents are not. These topics are described in further detail below.

3. Debt

728. In most states, marital debt is treated just like property and apportioned according to the same principles, with one exception. Statutes that require a court to divide property upon divorce have been interpreted in some states as requiring division of debts also. In most states, however, the division or allocation of marital debt is not a requirement, but discretionary.[872]

---

870. American Law Institute, *Principles of the Law of Family Dissolution: Analysis and Recommendations, Preliminary Draft No. 4*, (ALI, Philadelphia, 9 Sept. 1993), §4.08 at 207–208.
871. 194 Colo. 429, 574 P.2d 75, 77 (1978).
872. J.D. Gregory, *supra* at 350.

C. Is it "Marital" Property?

729. Once an asset is determined to be property, it must be classified as marital or separate. (For practical purposes, marital property amounts to a civil-jurisdiction imitation of community property, and the division of marital property is based on similar principles to the division of community property.) Generally, courts only have authority to divide marital property upon divorce. Marital property often is generally defined as all property acquired during marriage that is not separate property (defined as above). This definition gives the benefit of doubt in favor of marital property. It is generally presumed that all property acquired during marriage is marital property.[873] As a general rule, all returns on labor performed by either spouse during marriage are marital property, including deferred returns on labor performed during marriage for which payment or benefit is to be received after marriage.[874] Thus, time of acquisition is the key determinant of marital property.

730. With respect to the "new property," the task of separating the "return on labor performed during marriage" from "skills, earning capacity, and personal attributes" may be quite complicated. The "new property" consists primarily of labor-exchange assets, including various forms of protection of the "future" value of labor exchanges. Income-replacement future benefits are a particularly difficult kind of "new property" for courts to characterize. Many kinds of valuable assets have been acquired in part during marriage and in part before marriage or after divorce. Most states treat these assets as part marital and part separate, in the proportion that they were acquired with labor or resources that were marital or separate. Examples are provided below.

D. Valuation of the Property

731. A critical variable in property distribution is valuation of the property. Typically, one party will keep an item of property, and pay to the other party a proportionate share (usually one-half) of the court approved value of the property. If the valuation is lower than the actual market value of the property, the person keeping the property has received a windfall; if the valuation is higher than the actual market value, the person keeping the property has received a shortfall. Thus, while on paper the parties may be awarded equal amounts of property, in reality the property division may be quite unequal if the valuation is inaccurate.[875]

732. Valuation is a question of fact, for the finder of fact to decide. Moreover, in many cases (especially items for which there is not a robust market, intangibles, and "new property") valuation is simply a guess, speculation, an approximation. Thus,

---

873. B.R. Turner, *supra* §5.03 at 125; §5.06 at 129, §5.13 at 189.
874. American Law Institute, *Preliminary Draft No. 4 supra* 4.08 at 229.
875. H.H. Clark, Jr., *The Law of Domestic Relations in the United States* §15.4 (West 2d ed., 1988).

there will normally be hard swearing on both sides, with the property-keeping party's experts insisting on a low valuation, and the other spouse's experts pressing for a high valuation.[876]

733. There are many different methods for valuation of property. The methods that are accepted or approved for valuation of property upon divorce vary depending upon the type of property involved and the state in which the issue is being litigated. Perhaps the best reference is to current market price—that is, the actual price paid recently for the same kind of property similarly situated. But in some cases (as when valuating an investment, an heirloom, an unfinished item, a future interest, or a type of property not commonly on the market) another measure of value may be preferred. In times of economic volatility, especially, determining the date of valuation is a very important factor in the valuation of property to be divided upon dissolution.[877] In many states the "law does not set a definitive date upon which to value the marital assets, and trial judges are left with the discretion to fix the date of valuation after due consideration of all of the circumstances. Additionally, valuation dates may be different for each item of property at issue."[878]

E. Distribution of the Divided Property

734. The goal of property distribution in most cases is to facilitate a "clean break" when that is reasonably fair. That is, since the parties are unhappy living with each other, dealing with each other usually is unpleasant as well. Thus, it usually is deemed best to divide the property in a manner that allows both parties to walk away from the marriage with no ongoing or future required economic ties to or relations with each other.

735. However, a "clean break" is not always possible. It is not uncommon for courts to defer property division of some types of property. That is not a preferred tactic, but a tactic of economic necessity in some cases. The court may exercise "continuing jurisdiction" of the parties and the property until some future event (such as the youngest child leaves home or turns 18, or the spouse retires, or the property vests), at which time the court reopens the property division and divides the property that was deferred. Deferred division or distribution of property "awards the nonowning spouse a stated equitable portion of the marital share of each future payment, if, as, and when received."[879]

---

876. J.D. Gregory, P.N. Swisher & S.L. Scheible, *Understanding Family Law* §9.11 (1993).

877. D.L. Manz, *Choosing A Valuation Date of Marital Assets in Dissolution of Marriage Cases: Permutter and Its Permutations*, 81 Fla. B.J. 49 (May 2007); J.D. Ary-Hogue, *Peace on Earth, Goodwill in Divorce: Revising Traveis in Light of Oklahoma's Revised Ethical Rule Allowing the Sale of Law Practice Goodwill*, 61 Okla. L. Rev. 585 (2008).

878. J.D. Ary-Hogue, *Peace on Earth*, *supra*, 61 Okla. L. Rev. at 608.

879. *See* Deferred Distribution of Retirement Benefits: Retroactive Awards, 2004 National Legal Research Group, available at http://www.divorcesource.com/research/dl/pensions/04apr66.shtml (seen Jul. 6, 2015).

736. Lump-sum property division awards whereby the employee spouse is awarded the entire marital property and the wife's share is "bought out" by awarding her an offsetting portion of other marital property, or the employee spouse trades some of his separate property to the other spouse to compensate for her share of the particular "new property" asset are preferred. However, in most divorces the parties do not have sufficient other property for the employee to "buy out" the nonemployee's portion of the disputed asset all at once.[880]

737. Thus, deferred distribution or deferred division are often used in cases involving nonwealthy divorcing spouses with interests in some form of investment or "new" property that will pay potentially valuable sums in the future. For example, the court can order a specific amount to be paid when the benefit is received (e.g., upon retirement). Another alternative (apparently now the preferred alternative) is to award the non-employee spouse a percentage of the indefinite future benefits (usually in the form of periodic installments) to be paid whenever the benefits are paid.[881] Another alternative is for the court to simply postpone dividing the "new property" until it begins to pay benefits or a liquid value can be fixed. However, this increases the costs (financial and temporal) to the judiciary, and in the years between divorce and retirement, memories may dim, so this is not the preferred alternative.[882]

II. Equitable Division of Traditional Property: In General

738. The Uniform Marriage and Divorce Act provides a fair example of the basic standard for property division. It provides that:

> the court, without regard to marital misconduct, shall … apportion between the parties the property and assets belonging to either or both however and whenever acquired, and whether the title thereto is in the name of the husband or wife or both. In making apportionment the court shall consider the duration of the marriage, any prior marriage of either party, any antenuptial agreement of the parties, the age, health, station, occupation, amount and sources of income, vocational skills, employability, estates, liabilities, and needs of each of the parties, custodial provisions, whether the apportionment is in lieu or in addition to maintenance, and the opportunity of each for future acquisition of capital assets and income. The court shall also consider the contribution or dissipation of each party in the acquisition, preservation, depreciation, or appreciation in value of the respective estates, and the contributions of a spouse as a homemaker or to the family unit.[883]

---

880. B.R. Tucker, *supra*, §6.11 at pp. 346–366. Where it is not feasible for one spouse to buy out the other with one lump-sum payment, some courts permit a schedule of payments over a relatively short time period. *Ibid.* §4.08 at 245.
881. ALI Draft No. 4, *supra* §4.08 at 236, 239.
882. B.R. Tucker, *supra*, §6.11 at pp. 346–366.
883. Uniform Marriage and Divorce Act §307(a).

It appears that more divorcing spouses (and more often both spouses) have substantial property to divide upon divorce, so equitable distribution has become a significant issue in divorce, and in the future will have greater impact in lives than in the past.[884] Many factors can influence the distribution of assets and liabilities upon divorce, including such things as "the duration of the marriage, each party's circumstances (financial and otherwise), tax consequences that might occur, employment or any other factors which could impact the finalized distribution."[885]

A. *Fault*

739. The UMDA provision set out above does not permit a court to consider non-economic misconduct or unjust behavior by the spouses in dividing property. Likewise, the America Law Institute's Principles of the Law of Family Dissolution recommends that fault not be considered in property division.[886] However, about one-third of the American states still permit courts to consider "fault" in dividing property upon divorce.[887] It is the preference of most commentators, and perhaps the trend of cases in recent years to disallow the inclusion of fault as a factor in property division.[888]

740. Nevertheless, there are some good reasons to continue to allow consideration of fault. For example, Professor Robin Fretwell Wilson suggests three reasons why fault is still relevant, and important, in marital dissolution proceedings. They are:

> first, that the transaction costs of showing fault may be worth it financially or emotionally to the party who has been wronged; second, that deeply unfair results can arise in the absence of an inquiry into fault in the divorce; and third, if we trust judges and juries to determine what is and is not acceptable behavior in the criminal and civil contexts, then why not trust them to make similar determinations about fault in the context of family law?[889]

---

884. J.T. Oldham, *Changes in the Economic Consequences of Divorces, 1958-2008*, 42 Fam. L. Q. 419, 434 (2008).

885. Division of Property in a No-Fault Divorce, May 20, 2013, available at http://commonlegalquestions.com/index.php/2013/05/30/division-of-property-in-a-no-fault-divorce/ (seen Jul. 6, 2015).

886. American Law Institute, *Principles of the Law of Family Dissolution: Analysis and Recommendations* (2002).

887. L.D. Wardle, *Beyond Fault and No-Fault in the Reform of Marital Dissolution Law*, in *Reconceiving the Family* 9 (R.F. Wilson ed., 2006). *See also* American Law Institute, *Principles of the Law of Family Dissolution: Analysis and Recommendations*, at 43–49 (2002).

888. *Ibid.* at §4.15, cmnt e.

889. R.F. Wilson, *Beyond the Bounds of Decency: Why Fault Continues to Matter to (Some) Wronged Spouses*, 66 Wash. & Lee. L. Rev. 503, 504 (2009); *see also* L.D. Wardle, *Beyond Fault and No-Fault, supra*, at 9–22.

741. Even most states that do not generally allow noneconomic "fault" to be considered during property division allow various kinds of economic fault to be considered. For example, the UMDA specifies that "dissipation" of property may be considered in dividing property. There is some confusion over what "dissipation" means, but generally it refers to using, wasting, or transferring assets when divorce is impending for the purpose of depriving the spouse of his or her share of the asset.[890]

B. All Property or Only Marital Property

742. The UMDA provision set out above allows a court to divide all of the property belonging to married parties, regardless of whether it is separate or marital. However, a substantial number of states limit the power of property division to marital property only (at least in the absence of some extraordinary case or exception). However, to the contrary, in a few states, such as Utah, courts have power to equitably divide all property of the married parties upon divorce, regardless of the nature, characterization (as marital or separate), and source of the property (unless superseding federal law applies).

C. Choice of Law

743. Americans move around a lot, and it is not uncommon for the parties to have lived in different states, gotten married in another state, lived as a married couple in two or three other states, and end up residing in yet another state when they or one of them files for divorce. The general rule is the law of the parties' domicile at the time of acquisition of the property governs the marital property regime and the characterization of the property as separate or community. However, when spouses move with property from a state with a common law marital property regime to a state with a community property marital property regime, and there file for dissolution of marriage, complicated questions of how to treat that property can arise.[891] Some community property states have adopted statutes that treat such property as "quasi-" property of the kind it would have been if acquired in the latter

---

890. *Robinette v. Robinette*, 736 S.W.2d 351 (Ky. Ct. App. 1987); and J.D. Gregory et al., *supra*, at 347.
891. *See generally* K. W. Kingma, *Property Division at Divorce or Death for Married Couples Migrating Between Common Law and Community Property States, 35* ACTEC J. 74 (2009) (American College of Trust and Estate Counsel).

state.[892] The common law property states have not yet adopted a coherent scheme for dealing with such property.[893]

D. Antenuptial Agreements and Separation Agreements

744. If a premarital agreement or a separation agreement was signed by the parties and is valid, it will generally be enforced, absent duress, fraud, etc. Public policy favors letting the parties settle their property division disputes.[894]

E. Factors That Must or May Be Considered

745. Most equitable distribution statutes require a court to consider a host of factors and to make an "equitable" (i.e., a fair) distribution. "One survey lists 38 different factors found in the various state statutes as bearing upon the equitable division of property, but nearly all are a specific application of the need or contribution principle."[895] "Economic circumstances" at time of divorce, "contribution" and "length of the marriage" are the three most commonly listed considerations. Faulty behavior theoretically may affect property distribution amounts in fifteen or sixteen states (apart from exceptional economic abuse, such as dissipation of the assets, a fault-consideration that all states accept).[896] Property division often considers only economic factors in making equitable redistribution. That may operate to the detriment of homemakers, whose major contributions to the marriage may have been noneconomic (at least no wage was contributed, though her labor undeniably had economic value to the marriage). Some states have followed the lead of the UMDA and added homemakers' noneconomic contributions to the list of factors to be considered in property division.[897]

F. Equal or Equitable Division of Property

746. Given the many potentially relevant factors and the subjectivity of the standard (i.e., "equitable" distribution), inconsistency and unpredictability have long

892. *See* W. Reppy, Jr., *Louisiana's Proposed "Hybrid" Quasi-Community Property Statued Could Cause Unfairness*, 13 Commun. Prop. J. 1, 3–4 (1986); J.T. Oldham, *What IF the Beckhams Move to L.A. and Divorce? Marital Property Rights of Mobile Spouses When They Divorce in the United States*, 42 Fam. L. Q. 263, 274, 279 (2008); *see also* D. Rosettenstein, *Comity, Family Finances, Autonomy, and Transnational Legal Regimes*, 23 Int'l J. L. Pol'y & Fam. 192, 204 (2009); S.Symeonides, *The Conflicts Book of the Louisiana Civil Code: Civilian, American, or Original?*, 83 Tul. L. Rev. 1041, 1057 (2009).

893. J. J. Sampson, *Uniform Family Laws and Model Acts*, 42 Fam. L. Q. 673, 677 (2008).

894. *See* Part III, Chapter 3.

895. ALI, Preliminary Draft No. 4, *supra* §4.15, Rep. Note a, p. 262.

896. ALI, Council Draft No. 3, *supra* at pp. 1–10.

897. ALI, Preliminary Draft No. 4, *supra* §4.15, Rep. Note c, at 264.

been problems with equitable distribution. One solution to that problem is the adoption (formally or informally) of an equal division presumption. Equal distribution is the rule or presumption in most community property states. It is a de jure legal presumption in some equitable distribution states, and a de facto presumption in many others.[898] The prevailing rule of equitable distribution seems to include a general presumption of equal division of assets, at least in cases of long marriages. Today, equal division of marital or community property acquired during marriage is the standard American rule and reflects the currently prevailing concept that the marriage is, among other things, an economic partnership (unless the parties have, by agreement provided otherwise). "California [and other states] replaced its equitable property distribution regime with a rule requiring equal division of marital property on the assumption that equitable distribution typically produced relatively equal awards for husband and wife."[899]

G. Marital Home

747. For many divorcing couples, the only major asset is the family home. When possible, the court will award the house to one party and order that party to pay a portion (usually one-half) of the value of equity in the house to the other party, or the court will order the house to be sold and the proceeds split between the spouses. Sometimes, the cost of buying or renting another house (or the cost of home mortgages) has risen so much since the family home was purchased that it would be impractical, uneconomical, or impossible for the parties to simply sell the house and split the proceeds, especially if children were born and need housing comparable to the current home. If the parties have children, it is common to award the house to the party getting custody, and order the house to be sold when the youngest child leaves the home or the custodial parent moves, whichever first occurs.

H. Modification of Property Division

748. While alimony and child support are reasonably modifiable, property division generally is not modifiable. As a Georgia family law attorney succinctly put it (in words that would apply equally in most other states):

> Georgia law is clear concerning the modification of a final judgment concerning an equitable division of property in a divorce case. It cannot be done. Although some final orders, such as those for alimony, child custody, child support and visitation may be modified based on a change in circumstances, a change in circumstances does not allow for the modification of a final property division order.[900]

---

898. ALI, Preliminary Draft No. 4, *supra* §4.15 and 263–266.

899. M. Garrison, *The Economic Consequences of Divorce: Would Adoption of the ALI Principles Improve Current Outcomes*, 8 Duke J. Gender L. & Pol'y 119, 123 (2001).

900. *See*, e.g., N. Ghertner, *Modification of Property Division in Divorce*.

Support orders are deemed to be ongoing; property division is intended to be once-for-all. Consistent with the "clean break" concept that is the vague ideal of property division, courts are very reluctant to revisable property division. That is a general rule in all American states.[901] Indeed, in some states it has been decided that to modify a prior property division decree is "beyond the power of the divorce court."[902] However, evidence of serious fraud or concealment of property (especially if the parties could not have discovered it by reasonable diligence before the property division award) generally may result in the reopening of the property division award. Property division awards are not dischargeable in general Chapter 7 bankruptcy liquidation.[903]

III. Equitable Division of the Most Significant "New Property"

749. Among the most important and contested types of "new property" are pensions, goodwill, degrees and licenses, and recovery for disability, workers' compensation or personal injury awards. The rules for equitable distribution of these different forms of new property differ from one variety of property to another.

A. *Pensions*

1. Significance of Pensions

750. Historically *pensions* were gratuitous allowances given in recognition of valuable services, bounties which a generous employer might grant to a loyal servant, not as a matter of right but of discretion, and which could be withdrawn and withheld by the grantor at will.[904] Today, a *pension* is usually considered to be a contractual system of deferred compensation for services previously rendered; paid by the employer to the employee after retirement to provide a source of post-retirement income.[905] It has been said that in many families, the pension and the house are the only assets of substantial value. Since at least two-thirds of all employees in the United States have pensions, the characterization and division of pension benefits upon divorce is a subject of frequent concern in American divorces.[906]

---

901. *See* K. McClure, *Top 10 Things Every Woman (and Her Husband) Should Know Before Filing for Divorce*, 49 The Advoc (Tex) 55 (Winter 2009).
902. *See generally* J. W. McKnight, *Family Law: Husband and Wife*, 62 S.M.U. L. Rev. 1149, 1191 n. 414 (2009), citing Tex. Fam. Code § 9.007 (Vernon 2006).
903. *See generally* Janet Leach Richards, *A Guide to Spousal Support and Property Division Claims Under the Bankruptcy Abuse Prevention and Consumer Protection Act of 2005*, 41 Fam. L.Q. 227 (2007).
904. *Black's Law Dictionary* 1291 (West Publishing Co. 1968).
905. ERISA, 29 USC.A. §1002(2) (A).
906. M.A. Glendon, *supra*, p. 174. *But see* L. Weitzman & M. Maclean, *Economic Consequences of Divorce, The International Perspectives* 133(Clarendon Press 1992).

2. Vesting and Maturation

751. Pension benefits or rights may be *vested* or *unvested*. They are vested if the employee's right to receive benefits is fixed and would survive termination of employment. Otherwise the pension is deemed "unvested." It usually takes a substantial period of employment for a pension to vest. A pension is *matured* if the employee has an unconditional right to immediate payment; usually that happens upon retirement. Thus, many pension rights vest after a certain period of employment, but do not mature until retirement and election to begin drawing benefits.[907]

752. For example, under the pension plan offered by the one employer retirement benefits are vested upon completion of certain number of years of service (the number depends upon the age of the employee), but the earliest age at which one may begin to draw retirement benefits (early retirement) is 55, and normal retirement is at age 65.

3. Defined Contribution and Defined Benefit Pensions

753. The simplest kinds of pensions to value and distribute are called *defined contribution* pension plans. These kinds of pensions consist of contributions made by or on behalf of the employee, plus income from the employer, which are used to purchase an annuity for the employee. The more common kind of pension is a *defined benefit* pension plan, in which there is no separate retirement account for any particular employee. Employees contribute nothing. The employer provides the pension, often establishing a fund from which all employee pensions are drawn. The pension benefit is determined by a formula (usually a certain amount per period of time) that has no necessary connection to any amounts set aside during employment.[908] Since pensions often account for three-fourths of the value of the total estate of the marital parties, distribution of the pension upon divorce is of profound significance.

4. Pensions as Property

754. Because pensions historically were matters of discretion, not legal right, early cases declined to treat pensions as property divisible upon divorce. Arguments against treating pensions and retirement benefits as property emphasize their uncertainty (both in ascertaining the scope of benefits to be paid in advance and in determining how long they will be paid—death varies) and the nontransferability of the benefits (comparing them to educational degrees or professional licenses). Divorcing employee spouses have argued that they are similar to future inheritances, which

907. H. Clark, *supra* §15.6 p. 613; and B.R. Turner, *supra* §6.02 pp. 288–289.
908. ALI, Draft No. 4, *supra* §4.08 at 235; and B.R. Tucker, *supra* §6.02 at 289, §6.10 at 336.

are not divisible on divorce.[909] Moreover, pensions are not merely deferred payments for past services, but are intended to replace future [including post-divorce] earnings.[910] In the last forty years, courts in all states have come to treat *vested* pension or retirement benefits as divisible property upon divorce. Most states view vested pension benefits as deferred compensation—like money earned during the marriage but put in the bank and saved for retirement—or note that the financial contributions of the employee spouse that earned the pension benefits were marital property.

755. Because of contingencies that could prevent realizing any benefits, unvested pensions were the source of much debate and disparate decisions in the courts for many years. Initially, some courts distinguished unvested pensions as not divisible property. However, today the issue has been resolved in favor of treating unvested pension benefits as marital property in nearly all states.[911] The leading case to establish that unvested pensions are divisible marital (community) property is *In re Marriage of Brown*,[912] decided by the California Supreme Court in 1976. The California Supreme Court distinguished unvested pensions from "mere expectancies" such as future inheritances, characterizing pensions instead as "part of the consideration earned by the employee."[913] Unvested pension rights are contractual chosen in action, the court reasoned, which are divisible community property. While ripening of unvested pensions is contingent on continued employment, "when community funds or efforts are expended to acquire a conditional right to future income, the courts do not hesitate to treat that right as a community asset."[914] If payment is received it is remuneration for services performed during marriage by a spouse, and therefore it is community property.

5. Federal Pensions as Divisible Property

756. Special mention must be made of the pension and retirement benefits of federal employees. In two significant cases decided in 1979 and 1981 the Supreme Court ruled that federal laws regulating retirement-related benefits, especially those provided by the federal government to certain employees, preempt state property division divorce laws. In *Hisquierdo v. Hisquierdo*,[915] the Supreme Court of the United States held that the federal railroad law preempted state community property and property division law, and that the federal law made railroad employee

909. B.R. Turner, *supra* §6.09 at 328.
910. G.G. Blumberg, *Marital Property Treatment of Pensions, Disability Pay, Workers' Compensation, and Other Wage Substitutes: An Insurance, Or Replacement, Analysis*, 33 U. California at Los Angeles L. Rev. 1230, 1265–1266 (1986).
911. *See generally* R. E. Oliphant & N. Ver Steegh, Family Law § 13.21 at 291–292 (3d ed., 2010). For example, Alabama, Indiana, and Arkansas continue to allow only vested pensions to be divided upon divorce. *See* J.E. Kirschner, *Division of Military Retired Pay*, 43 Fam. L. Q. 367, 384, n. 68 (2009); *ibid.* at 421.
912. 15 Cal. 3d 838, 544 P.2d 561, 126 Cal. Rptr. 633 (1976).
913. 544 P.2d at 565.
914. 544 P.2d at 566.
915. 439 US 572 (1979); and B.R. Turner, *supra* §6.03 at 290–292.

retirement plan benefits the separate benefits of the employee, exempt from division upon divorce. The Court held that Congress intended to protect such pensions uniformly in all states, considering them to be more like social welfare benefits than private contractual rights, and it interpreted the nonassignment clause of the federal act to override state property division laws. Two years later, the U.S. Supreme Court dropped an even bigger bombshell. In *McCarty v. McCarty*,[916] the Supreme Court interpreted the federal law regulating military retirement benefits and held, again, that Congress intended that they preempt state laws and not be subject to state community property or property division laws. The U.S. Supreme Court found that Congress intended the retirement pay of military service personnel "be the personal entitlement of the retiree," free from all claims of creditors and others (except for child support and alimony). That decision meant that state courts could not equitably redistribute or divide as community property military retirement benefits (typically, the most substantial benefits acquired by military couples). When federal law addresses a subject that is also regulated by state divorce law, federal law continues to preempt state law to the extent that the two laws conflict.[917]

757. When Congress passed the Railroad Retirement Act and the military retirement laws, it did not intend to provide protection for spouses. Indeed, since those laws originated before "marital property" was widely recognized, in the days of the predominance of the title theory of property division upon divorce, the law that such retirement benefits belonged to the earning (title-holding) spouse reflected the prevailing beliefs of the traditional property system of the day. Between passage of those laws and the time *Hisquierdo* and *McCarty* were decided, the property system had substantially changed in most states to reflect partnership (marital property) rather than trusteeship (paternalistic) notions. However, Congress had not revised its statutes to keep up with those changes.

758. The unpopular Supreme Court rulings in *Hisquierdo* and *McCarty* put pressure on Congress to update these laws. *Hisquierdo* was legislatively overruled when Congress amended the railroad retirement law to create two tiers of railroad retirement benefits. One tier is divisible under state law; the other tier is separate and nondivisible.[918] Likewise, the year after the Supreme Court decided *McCarty*, Congress enacted the Uniformed Services Former Spouses Protection Act of 1982 (USFSPA),[919] which declared that subject to certain qualifications, state courts "may treat disposable retired or retainer pay [of retired military personnel] … either as property solely of the member or as property of the member and his spouse in accordance with the law of the jurisdiction." Because of the number of persons who serve in the military, the USFSPA is of great importance to family lawyers in all states,

916. 453 US 210 (1981).
917. *See Astrue v. Capato*, 132 S.Ct. 2021 (2012); *Kennedy v. Plan Adm'r for DuPont Sav. & Inv. Plan*, (2009); *Egelhoff v. Egelhoff*, 532 U.S. 141 (2001); *Boggs v. Boggs*, 520 U.S. 833 (1997).
918. B.R. Turner, *supra* §6.06 at 319; and 45 USC. §231m(b) (2) (1986).
919. 10 USC. §1408 (1983 & Supp. 1995).

and military pension controversies remain a matter of significant litigation relevance upon divorce.[920] Thus, as a matter of federal law, division of military pensions upon divorce is governed by federal (not state) law if it conflicts with state law. "It is now well settled that entitlement to retired pay, based upon uniformed service, creates a marital or community asset to be dealt with upon ending a marriage. All fifty states have accepted the authority conferred by the United States Congress in the Uniformed Services Former Spouses' Protection Act passed in 1982 [to divide such assets upon divorce]."[921] Nevertheless, "there is no uniform treatment among the fifty states for pensions in general or for military retirement in particular."[922]

759. Statutes regulating the Federal Employees Retirement System (FERS),[923] and Foreign Service Pension System (FSPS),[924] also provide that state courts may treat *federal civil service* and *foreign service* retirement benefits as divisible marital or community property subject to equitable distribution upon divorce. Thus, it is now clear that virtually all federal retirement pension benefits may be (and are) deemed by state courts to be marital property, subject to division or equitable distribution upon divorce.

760. Social security benefits are a special form of pension or retirement benefit, provided by the federal government as an old/age, retirement survivors, and disability program funded by a special tax. Social security benefits are governed by federal law. Most courts have ruled that social security benefits may not be divided as marital property upon divorce, but there are a few contrary opinions.[925] More importantly, divorce courts in most states that have faced the issue have ruled that they may consider the value of social security benefits payable to one spouse in dividing property, and award a disproportionate share of other property to the other spouse to compensate for the disparity in asset allocation that otherwise would result from equal division of the other assets but non-division of the social security; however, a minority of states bar consideration of social security by the court in awarding property upon divorce.[926] As a matter of federal preemption, that rule seems to be the most correct interpretation, but state courts tend to prefer to give priority whenever possible to state domestic relations law (with which they are most familiar and which reflect more closely their own notions of fairness) and that explains the majority rule.

920. J.E. Kirschner, *Division of Military Retired Pay,* 43 Fam. L. Q. 367 (2009).
921. J.E. Kirschner, *Division of Military Retired Pay,* 43 Fam. L. Q. 367, 367 (2009).
922. J.E. Kirschner, *Division of Military Retired Pay,* 43 Fam. L. Q. at 368.
923. 5 USC. §8345(j) (1) et seq. (1980); B.R. Turner, *supra* §6.06 at 316.
924. 22 USC. §4054, 4069 (1990); B.R. Turner, *supra* §6.06 at 317.
925. H. Clark, Jr., *supra* §15.6 at 612; R.L. Brown, *supra,* p. 901; and B.R. Turner, *supra* §6.06 p. 317.
926. R.E. Oliphant & N. Ver Steegh, Family Law, § 13.22 at 292–293.

6. Valuation of Pensions

761. Pensions are among the most difficult of assets to value and distribute upon divorce.[927] The simplest kinds of pensions to value and distribute are *defined contribution* pension plans. The contributions of or for a particular employee are (or easily can be) segregated into a separate retirement account for the specific employee. The value of these kinds of pensions can be computed with accuracy—the amount contributed (by employer and employee) to the employee's retirement account during the marriage, and the accrued interest, constitutes marital property.[928]

762. Valuation of *defined contribution plan* pension benefits is simple. The proportion of the pension contributions acquired during marriage (called the *coverture factor*, where the numerator is the years of marriage during employment and the denominator is the total years of employment), is calculated then divided equally (presumably) or equitably.[929] For example, if Husband (H) has been employed for twenty years at Acme Company which has a defined contribution pension plan to which H and Acme have been contributing, and if H was married to Wife (W) during that entire time, the coverture factor would be one (20 over 20), meaning all of the pension would be marital property, and the court would equitably distribute all of it, presumably awarding one-half to W. If H and W had been married only twelve of the twenty years during which the pension was accruing, the coverture factor would be 60%, meaning only 60% of the pension would be marital property, and the court would presumably award one-half of that portion (30% of the total pension) to W.

763. However, valuation of *defined benefit* pension benefits is much more difficult because in a *defined benefit* pension plan, there is no separate retirement account for any particular employee. The pension benefit is determined by a formula (usually a certain amount per period of time) that has no necessary connection to any amounts set aside during employment.[930] One method of valuation is to use the amount the earner spouse would be entitled to take from the fund at the time of divorce—the *liquidation value*. That is the simplest and clearest, but least inclusive. The other method is to determine the value the pension will have when payable, and reduce it to *present value* by discounting for mortality and vesting contingencies.[931]

764. The *present value* of the pension earned to the time of divorce is the preferred method of determining value of a *defined benefit* pension plan. To determine present value, the court must estimate the amount of retirement benefits the owning

927. *Encyclopedia of Matrimonial Practice*, (R.L. Brown ed., Prentice Hall 1993) at 901.

928. ALI, Draft No. 4, *supra* §4.08 at 235; and B.R. Tucker, *supra* §6.10 at 336.

929. B.R. Tucker, *supra* §6.10 at 336; ALI, Draft No. 4, *supra* §4.08 at 237–238. Profit-sharing pension plans are treated like defined contribution plans because separate accounts are maintained and the precise value of the benefits can be easily mathematically calculated. M. Snyder, *The Actuarial Approach to Valuing Pensions Upon Divorce*, in R.L. Brown, *supra*, p. 996.1.

930. ALI, Draft No. 4, *supra* §4.08 at 235; and B.R. Tucker, *supra* §6.02 at 289, §6.10 at 336.

931. B.R. Turner, *supra* §15.6 at 616.

spouse will receive, discount it to present value taking into account also mortality and forfeiture risks. That dollar amount is split proportionately according to the period of employment during which the parties were married (the *coverture fraction*), and that portion is divided between the parties. However, estimating the value of defined benefit pensions, unlike defined contribution pensions, entails substantial guess-work. Multiple factors influence the value of a pension, including retirement age, life expectancy, amount of pay, annual benefit accrual rate, and rate of interest. Expert financial assistance in ascertaining pension value may be helpful. The difficulty of estimating life-expectancy, future cost-of-living increases, and selection of retirement payout options makes ascertaining present value very subjective. For these reasons, when large amounts are at stake, future division of defined benefit pensions is preferred.[932] But that creates other problems. One flaw in the popular coverture formula is that it uses time rather than value to assess the respective shares. Thus, if a man with a pension plan is married to Wife 1 for fifteen years while employed during which his average income was USD 30,000, they divorce, and he marries Wife 2 and stays married for fifteen more years of employment with the same employer, during which his average income was USD 50,000, then he retires (or dies), with a benefit owing of USD 40,000 per year, the share of Wife 1s interest in the benefits will be ½ x ½ of the value using the coverture (time-based) formula (USD 10,000 per year). However, as the amount of money (value) accumulated during the second marriage will be much greater (earnings in the last half of one's employment life generally are much greater than earnings in the first half of the employment life– because of experience, maturity, and seniority). So using the coverture formula results in a significant windfall to Wife 1 (in this case approximately USD 2,500 per year). A value-based formula would be much more accurate and arguably fairer. Nevertheless, the time-based coverture formula is the standard approach used in American courts to determine a non-employee spouse's interest in the pension or retirement benefits of the employee spouse.

7. Distribution of Private Pensions and QDROs

765. Since 1974, the federal Employees Retirement Income Security Act (ERISA) has regulated employer-sponsored pension and retirement plans in the United States. If an employee benefit plan "qualifies" under ERISA, employer contributions to it are tax deductible, and investment earnings are exempt from immediate taxation. Thus, employers make great effort to see that their pension plans qualify under ERISA. For ten years after ERISA was enacted, the law prohibited the assignment or alienation of an employee's pension benefits. That made it difficult for a divorced spouse of an employee to obtain property division of the pension benefits. Courts and agencies disagreed over whether a state court in a divorce case could divide or offset the pension in the process of dividing marital property.

766. In 1984, Congress enacted the Retirement Equity Act (REA) to clarify the matter. It authorized the assignment of part or all of an employee's retirement or

932. ALI, Draft 4, *supra*, at 235.

pension benefits if done under a Qualified Domestic Relations Order, known as a "QDRO." A QDRO is an order, decree, or judgment made pursuant to state domestic relations law that creates or recognizes an alternative payee's right to receive some or all of an employee's benefits under an employee benefit plan. The key requirements of a QDRO are that it identify the employee, the alternate payee (spouse, former spouse, child, or other dependent), the benefit plan, the amount or percentage of benefits to be paid to the alternate payee, the time period during which the alternate payee is to be paid, that it relate to division of marital property, or payment of alimony or child support, and the order may not alter the amount, form, or other provision of benefits payable under the pension plan.[933] An order for property division of pension benefits that complies with the requirement as a QDRO is enforceable against a qualified pension plan, and direct payment of a portion of the pension benefits directly to the ex-spouse of the employee is permitted under the REA for QDROs. The importance of direct payment of retirement benefits to a former spouse can hardly be overstated because it provides certainty that payments will be made.[934] The REA also created two types of survivors benefits for spouses.

767. When ERISA provisions conflict with state divorce laws, ERISA preempts state law and ERISA controls.[935] For example, in a notable 2009 case, the decedent named his wife as his beneficiary of an ERISA-regulated employee benefit plan. The couple subsequently divorced, and the divorce decree explicitly divested the wife of any interest in the benefit plan. However, the husband failed to execute a document changing the beneficiary of the benefit plan (perhaps relying erroneously upon the decree to effect the beneficiary change). When he died, his daughter (the administratrix of his estate) asked the benefit plan administrator to disburse the plan benefits to the estate, according to the divorce decree, not to his former wife, according to the ERISA, which requires payment according to the benefit plan documents. The daughter sued raising both state divorce law, divorce decree and fairness arguments, but the Supreme Court held that the plain language of ERISA governed and it required disbursement according to the plan documents, not the divorce decree. In another case, *Egelhoff v. Egelhoff ex rel Breiner*,[936] the U.S. Supreme Court held that ERISA preempts conflicting state law wills doctrines. In that case, the deceased husband's benefits would have passed to his two children of a prior marriage if the state estate law had applied, but since the Court ruled that ERISA preempted conflicting state laws, the former wife also received the pension plan benefits even though she had previously received her share of the marital property in the divorce agreement.[937]

933. G. A. Shulman, *Qualified Domestic Relations Order Handbook* (John Wiley & Sons: New York, 1993), §1.1, pp. 3–4, §1.7 p. 708; §1.9 at 9. ERISA is 29 USC. §1001 et seq. The Regiment Equity Act of 1984 is 29 USC. §1056 and IRC, 29 USC. §401, created the QDRO.

934. ES Fierst, *The Federal Retirement Systems in Divorce*, in R.L. Brown, *supra*, Ch. 10, p. 912.

935. *See Kennedy v. Plan Adm'r for DuPont Sav. & Inv. Plan*, 555 U.S. 285 (2009); *Egelhoff v. Egelhoff*, 532 U.S. 141 (2001); *Boggs v. Boggs*, 520 U.S. 833 (1997).

936. 582 U.S. 141 (2001).

937. *See* Katherine A. McAllister, *A Distinction Without A Difference? ERISA Preemption and the Untenable Differential Treatment of Revocation-o-Divorce and Slayer Statutes*, 52 Boston Coll. L. Rev. 1481 (2011).

768. As amended in 1993, ERISA requires employment-based health plans to provide health coverage to the children of parent-employees who are divorced. A Qualified Medical Child Support Order (QMCSO)—usually issued in connection with divorce—provides such health coverage to a child or children of an employee through his or her employer's group health or health insurance plan. However, the QMCSO may not require the health benefit plan to provide any type of benefit not otherwise provided under the plan.

8. Distribution of Federal Pensions

769. Distribution of federal pensions is governed by a different set of federal laws (for the most part) than governs distribution of private (nonfederal) pensions. The three major federal retirement plans are called Civil Service Retirement System, the Federal Employees Retirement System, and the Civil Service Offset plan. For *Civil Service*, disability retirement benefits are treated the same as retirement for age and service; no time of service or limit on award is imposed. 5 USC. 8345(j). *Foreign Service* requires marriage for ten years during creditable service for the former spouse to get a share, presumed to be 50% of the retired pay earned during the marriage, but the amount may be less or greater by agreement or court decree. 22 USC. 4054(a). *Military* retirement benefits of up to 50% of the member's disposable retirement pay are payable to a former spouse if there was marriage for ten years during military service. For less than ten years, direct payment is not authorized, but alimony may be 10 USC. 1408. The retirement payment stops upon death of either the service member or former spouse.[938] A "Court Order Acceptable for Processing (COAP)" is the federal governments' equivalent of a state QDRO. As with drafting QDROs, care must be taken in drafting COAPs because "[a] slight change in verbiage can mean tens of thousands of dollars in favor of one or the other spouse."[939]

770. As noted earlier, most courts have ruled that Social Security benefits are not divisible property. However, by statute social security benefits are payable to non-earning spouses married to an earning spouse for at least ten years before divorcing (though a spouse or former spouse may not get in full both survivor benefit and social security, to preclude dual payment based on same earnings). The nonearning spouse may get up to one-half of the ex-spouse's benefits unless she would be entitled to more on the basis of her own status as an earner. However, "A majority of courts have found some mechanism or theory to compensate the nonmilitary spouse for the economic impact of the waiver of retirement pay."[940]

---

938. ES Fierst, *supra*, pp. 912–922; E. U. Fierst, "Sharing Military Retirement Pay" in R.L. Brown, *supra*, Ch. 10, p. 922.16. *See further* Katherine A. McAllister, *A Distinction Without A Difference? ERISA Preemption and the Untenable Differential Treatment of Revocation-o-Divorce and Slayer Statutes*, 52 Boston Coll. L. Rev. 1481 (2011).

939. Tim Voit, *Federal Pensions in Divorce*, Divorce Magazine, Aug. 27, 2012, available at http://www.divorcemag.com/articles/federal-pensions-in-divorce (seen Jul. 7, 2015).

940. *Military Retirement Pay—Postdivorce Elections*, 1999 National Legal Research Group, available at http://www.divorcesource.com/research/edj/military/99apr37.shtml (seen Jul. 7, 2015).

B. Goodwill

1. Definition of Goodwill

771. Another intangible type of property is the "goodwill" associated with a going economic enterprise. Goodwill is the label accountants give to a part of the market value (or sale price) of a business enterprise in excess of the assets. "Goodwill" is commonly defined as "the amount by which the market value of a going concern exceeds the total value of its assets ('asset value'), without regard to the reason for the excess."[941] Goodwill is tied most closely to the expected income flow, and may reflect many variables such as location, reputation, etc. It may reflect the spouse's personal skill, labor, and earning capacity as well as the age, reputation, and location of the enterprise and other business assets.[942] Accounting conventions usually ascribe no goodwill to a business until it is sold. Upon sale, the excess value over tangible assets is listed as goodwill in the buyer's balance sheet. While most going enterprises operating by divorcing parties are not sold at that time, most courts try to ascertain the "goodwill" value of a going business for purposes of property distribution upon divorce.

2. Goodwill as Divisible Property

772. Since goodwill may derive from both property and nonproperty factors characterization may be complicated; if it results from the spouse's personal skill, labor and earning capacity it should not be deemed property; if it results from location it should be property.[943] The prevailing rule is that, if acquired during marriage, goodwill is divisible property to the extent it has value not attributable to the value of the spousal earning capacity and spousal skills.[944] However, courts have begun to recognize that goodwill may contain both marital and personal (non-divisible) components.[945] It is said that "[a] majority of states hold that individual goodwill is not property, and therefore that it cannot be considering in valuing the practice for purposes of property division."[946]

---

941. ALI, *supra* §4.07 at 215. "Goodwill reflects the ability of a business to earn a profit that is higher than average for that industry." M. E. Kline, *Law Practice Goodwill: an Evolving Concept*, in R.L. Brown, *supra*, p. 889; and F. E. Lieber, *Personal/Professional vs. Practice Goodwill*, in R.L. Brown, *supra*, p. 896.
942. ALI, Preliminary Draft No. 4, *supra* §4.07 at 215–216.
943. *Ibid.*
944. *Ibid* §4.07 at 215; and H, Clark, *supra* §15.5, p. 606.
945. J.D. Ary-Hogue, *Peace on Earth, Goodwill in Divorce: Revising Traveis in Light of Oklahoma's Revised Ethical Rule Allowing the Sale of Law Practice Goodwill*, 61 Okla. L. Rev. 585 (2008).
946. *Goodwill and Spousal Support*, 2005 National Legal Research Group, available at http://www.divorcesource.com/research/edj/alimony/05jun61.shtml (seen Jul. 7, 2015).

3. Valuation of Goodwill

773. Valuation of business or practice goodwill is also a matter of conjecture and appraisal. Goodwill is only property to the extent that it is realizable. If the business is not being sold at the time of divorce, proving the amount that would be realized if the business were sold is not a matter of mathematic precision. Actual sales of comparable businesses in the area are the best indicator of the goodwill value, but expert testimony may suffice or buyout agreements may indicate value.[947] In many cases, the question of valuation is the major contested issue in dividing professional or business goodwill.[948] Deference to the trial court valuation is common.

4. Division of Goodwill

774. The key to division of goodwill seems to be realizability—value that can be "realized" on the open market. Thus, the starting point is that goodwill must be transferable (realizable) to be divisible. Proof of the goodwill portion of the sales prices of similar businesses is the key to proving realizability.[949] Unrealizable (unsellable) goodwill presents a much more difficult problem, and that is the situation with respect to professional practices. Most professional licenses are heavily regulated by the state and may not be sold. The state courts are split over whether professional goodwill is divisible. Some compare professional goodwill to a professional license itself, which all states except New York have ruled is not divisible property. Others disallow division of professional goodwill on the ground that it may result in double-valuation. On the contrary, some states find that even though professional goodwill may not independently be sold, it has value in conjunction with other assets that can be sold, and it may be treated as divisible property. The prevailing rule appears to be that professional goodwill is divisible property if it has value independent of the reputation or other personal characteristics of the professional-spouse.[950] Thus, professional goodwill must be separated into two components: practice goodwill and personal/professional goodwill. Generally, practice goodwill is deemed divisible property, but the personal/professional goodwill is not.[951] As a Texas court explained:

> to the extent that goodwill exists in the professional practice separate and apart from the professional's personal ability and reputation, that goodwill has a commercial value and is community property subject to division upon divorce. Further, in order to determine whether goodwill attaches to a professional practice that is subject to division upon divorce, the goodwill must be determined to exist independently of the personal ability of the professional spouse and if

947. B.R. Turner, *supra* §6.22, pp. 420–433.
948. *See generally* L. L. Taylor, *Family Law Update*, 46 The Advoc. (Tex) 1, 4–5 (2009).
949. B.R. Tucker, *supra*, §6.22, pp. 422–424.
950. M.G. Heyman, *Goodwill and the Ideal of Equality: Marital Property at the Crossroads*, 31 U. Louisville J. Fam. L. 1, *10 (1992–1993).
951. F. Lieber, *supra*, p. 897.

> such goodwill is found to exist, then it must be determined whether that goodwill has a commercial value in which the community estate is entitled to share.[952]

In dividing assets, especially intangible assets, it is important to avoid "double dipping"—that is, paying a former spouse twice for a single asset (a in property division and calculation of alimony.[953] Unlike valuation of goodwill based on past earnings in a business sale, upon divorce the valuation of goodwill focuses on future potential. Appeals courts usually defer to trial courts.

C. Educational Degrees and Professional Licenses

1. The "Degree Dilemma"

775. The "degree dilemma" is the dilemma that arises when one spouse devotes herself to supporting the other spouse in acquiring an educational degree of professional credential that would allow that spouse to earn a very comfortable living. The idea was that the degree or license would be used to support both spouses. But then, shortly after the degree or license is obtained, there is a divorce. Since the degree or license traditionally has not been treated as divisible property, that meant the supported spouse would have sole enjoyment of an asset to which both significantly contributed, and the supporting spouse would be left with little financial value (since usually the parties in those circumstances had very few other assets to divide). The inequitable outcome in such cases is the essence of the "degree dilemma."

2. The *O'Brien* Rule of New York

776. In 1985, the New York Court of Appeals held in *O'Brien v. O'Brien*,[954] that a divorcing man's license to practice medicine, earned while he was largely supported by his wife who sacrificed her own career and educational opportunities to put her husband through medical school, was "property" subject to equitable division upon divorce. The basis for the *O'Brien* holding was very specific language in the New York Equitable Distribution Law declaring that the court must consider in making equitable distribution "contributions [of] … a spouse … to the career or career potential of the other party" and must ignore the claimed difficulty of valuation of "any interest in a … profession."[955]

---

952. *See generally* L. L. Taylor, *Family Law Update*, 46 The Advoc. (Tex) 1, 4–5 (2009).
953. Gabrielle Hollingsworth, *Double-Dipping and Goodwill in Divorce*, available at http://www.legalmatch.com/law-library/article/double-dipping-and-goodwill-in-divorce.html (seen Jul. 7, 2015).
954. 489 N.E.2d 712 (N.Y. 1985).
955. 489 N.E.2d at 716, citing N.Y. Domestic Relations Law §236[B] [5] [d] [6], [9]. *See* Timothy Tippins, New York Matrimonial Law and Practice § 5:28. *O'Brien v. O'Brien and its progeny* (Nov. 2015).

3. Degrees and Licenses as Property in Other States

777. Many commentators expected that many other states would follow New York and treat professional licenses and educational degrees as "property" divisible upon divorce. However, no other state legislature in America has adopted such a broad definition of "property" for purposes of equitable distribution, nor has any other state Supreme Court followed the *O'Brien* approach.

778. There are two reasons why the *O'Brien* rule that licenses (and degrees) are property has been unanimously rejected. The conceptual reason, explained in *Graham, supra,* focuses on the fact that a license or degree is quite distinguishable from traditional forms of property, and is much too inseparable from individual talent, skill and effort to be comfortably classified as property. The practical reason for the unanimous rejection of *O'Brien* has to do with the experience of New York since *O'Brien.*[956] For example, in *Elkus v. Elkus,*[957] *O'Brien* was applied to the career of an opera singer, awarding her husband a share of her future earning potential because of her career development during marriage. In *Golub v. Golub*, the actress-wife's career was deemed marital or community property.[958] In another case, a New York court applied *O'Brien* to hold that the value of a divorcing government lawyer's license to practice law included the potential income the attorney-spouse could earn as a private attorney, not just the lower-paying job he had as an attorney employed by a government agency.[959] In yet another case, the court applied *O'Brien* to the promotions a husband-policeman had received during marriage after acquiring a college degree.[960] Treating professional licenses and educational degrees as property puts the New York courts onto a slippery slope that no other courts have wanted to slalom down.

4. Other Solutions to the "Degree Dilemma"

779. While the prevailing rule is that licenses and degrees are not property, that does not mean that there is no remedy for the "degree dilemma" of supporting spouses abandoned by the degree or license acquiring partner. Other remedies for the non-degree supporting spouse include disproportionate compensatory distribution of the marital property (if the parties have enough property to make that feasible), award of traditional alimony, award of reimbursement alimony (reimbursing for the value of the contribution the supporting spouse made the degree-receiving spouse), award of some form of restitution alimony (again providing restitution for

956. B.R. Turner, *supra* §6.21 at 413–419.
957. 169 A.D.2d 134, 572 N.Y.S.2d 901 (1991).
958. 139 Misc. 2d 440, 527 N.Y.S.2d 946 (Sup. Ct. 1988).
959. *Cronin v. Cronin*, 131 Misc.2d 879, 502 N.Y.S.2d 368 (Sup. Ct. 1986).
960. *Alloco v. Alloco*, 578 N.Y.S.2d 995 (Sup. Ct. 1991).

loss incurred or loss of investment made by the supporting spouse), award of rehabilitative alimony, or equitable restitution.[961] While some restitutionary award is certainly fair, most of the claims for property division of degrees and licenses echo of claims for loss of windfall and seem inconsistent with other aspects of dissolution law and practice. That may explain in part why so few states allow property division of interests in licenses or degree.[962]

D. Disability Benefits, Workers Compensation, and Personal Injury Awards

1. Loss of Future Earning Capacity Due to Injury

780. Courts have not been consistent in their treatment of compensation for loss of future earnings or earning capacity. However, there are some clear patterns. Three different forms of compensation for loss of future earning capacity caused by accident or injury have caused much consternation in the courts. *Disability pay* is an employment (contractual) benefit provided by an employer as a form of private insurance to replace the income a disabled employee may lose as a result of sickness or injury. *Workers' compensation* is a state (statutory) system of no-fault recovery for work-related injuries. The employee gets a certain amount according to a schedule (a scheduled amount for the loss of one finger, another amount for the loss of two fingers, etc.) rather than damages tailored and individualized to his or her specific circumstances and injuries, avoiding the uncertainties and expenses of tort litigation. *Personal injury* awards are obtained through private settlement or judicial resolution of tort claims for damages suffered as a result of someone's tortious misconduct (often negligence).

781. All of these schemes share at least one common characteristic: Each is intended, at least in part, to compensate an injured worker for damage to or loss of his or her present ability to generate income—a marital property factor. But all also contain an element of recovery for loss of future (including post-divorce) ability, skill, or capacity—a personal factor. Thus, all of them are hybrid forms of "new property" that may or may not be treated as divisible marital property at the time of divorce. In all three cases, courts are split between two different approaches: a mechanical or mechanistic approach and an analytical approach. The application of these approaches differs.

---

961. B.R. Turner, *supra* §6.20 at 405–409. *Hubbard v. Hubbard*, 603 P.2d 747 (Okla. 1979); *Mahoney v. Mahoney*, 91 N.J. 488, 453 A.2d 527 (1982); In re *Marriage of Olar*, 747 P.2d 676 (1987); and *Downs v. Downs*, 154 Vt. 161, 574 A.2d 156 (1990).

962. J.T. Oldham, *Changes in the Economic Consequences of Divorces, 1958-2008*, 42 Fam. L. Q. 419 (2008). *See also* L. L. Loeb & M. K. McCann, *Dilemma v. Paradox: Valuation of an Advanced Degree Upon Dissolution of a Marriage*, 66 Marquette L. Rev. 495 (1983).

2. An Insurance Analogy

782. A common judicial tactic is to compare these types of benefits, especially disability awards, to personal injury recoveries—which usually are classified as separate property.[963] That is consistent with how insurance proceeds are characterized. Insurance benefits take the same character as the assets they replace. Since disability pay is really a form of insurance for the earnings of the employee, disability pay should be characterized the same way as earnings—marital property to the extent it replaces post-marital earnings, and separate to the extent it replaces post-divorce earnings.[964] Disability pay may continue after retirement, if the retiring person so chooses. To avoid double-payment, the retiring employee usually must give up retirement pay equal to the amount of disability pay he receives after retirement. Some states separate retirement-replacement disability pay from true-disability pay, classifying the former as retirement benefits (marital property).[965]

3. Disability Payments

783. States are split over whether disability pay is marital or separate property, with some following what has been called a *mechanical* approach, and others following an *analytical* approach. States that follow the mechanical approach look solely to the date the right to disability pay was acquired. If it was acquired during marriage, since it is not a gift, devise, bequest, or inheritance, it is deemed marital property; if it was acquired before or after marriage, it is deemed separate property. States that follow the analytical approach are divided between those that look to the source of the benefit (marital labor) and those that look to the nature of the wages replaced (to the extent the disability recovery replaces post-divorce wages, it is separate). In *Hillman v. Maretta*, the Supreme Court held that the former spouse still named as beneficiary of Federal Employees' Group Life Insurance Act of 1954 (FEGLIA) was entitled to the proceeds of that life insurance and not the later wife who was married to the covered employee at the time of his death.[966]

4. Federal Disability Benefits

784. Federal law preempts state law regarding whether federal employee disability pay is divisible upon divorce. In 1989, in *Mansell v. Mansell*,[967] the U.S. Supreme Court held that federal disability pay may not be divided upon divorce as marital or community property. The case arose (like *Hisquierdo* and *McCarty*) in California, where a state court ordered a retired military man to give his former wife 50% of his combined military retirement and disability pay. After *McCarty* was

963. B.R. Turner, *supra* §6.16, pp. 384–387.
964. ALI, Preliminary Draft No. 4, §4.08, p. 240.
965. B.R. Turner, *supra* §6.16, pp. 384–387.
966. 133 S. Ct. 1943 (2013).
967. 490 US 581 (1989).

decided, and after Congress passed the USFSPA, the man asked the court to allow him to keep all of his retirement and disability pay. The veteran's disability law contained a broad anti-attachment clause. The California courts ruled that the disability pay was community property. The Supreme Court reversed. The case turned on whether in enacting the USFSPA Congress intended merely to establish that military retirement pay can be treated as divisible marital or community property, or whether it intended broadly that all military benefits, including veterans' disability pay, can be so treated. The Supreme Court opted for the narrow reading, finding no clear congressional intent to do anything other reverse the specific holding of *McCarty* that had forbidden the states to treat retirement pay as marital or community property. While Congress promptly reversed *Hisquierdo* and *McCarty*, it has never overturned the ruling in *Mansell* that veteran's disability may not be treated as marital or community property and divided upon divorce. However, the fact that disability pay itself is not divisible property does not necessarily mean that courts may not consider it when dividing other property or setting alimony.[968] In fact, the U.S. Supreme Court has upheld state court jurisdiction to hold a disabled veteran in contempt for failing to pay child support, even though the only income he had from which to pay child support was his exempt veteran's disability pay.[969] So courts in the United States generally distinguish retirement and other earning or earning-replacement assets from disability compensation assets, and allow division of the former but treat the latter as belonging exclusively to and as the personal non-divisible asset of the injured former military member. Complications arise with the military member must elect either military retirement (which is divisible) or disability pay (which generally is not), and elects the latter. Some courts have tried to treat such as divisible property on grounds that it replaces divisible property. But as early as *Mansell* (in 1989) the Supreme Court has held that under federal law states may not treat "as property divisible upon divorce military retirement pay that has been waived to receive veterans' disability benefits."[970]

5. Personal Injury Recovery

785. States are divided between two alternative approaches to categorizing *personal injury* recoveries, also. Under the prevailing replacement (or analytical) approach, personal injury awards are classified according to the nature of the assets they replace. Thus, compensation for wages lost during coverture is marital property, but compensation for wages lost after marriage and for pain and suffering, is separate property. A minority of states characterize personal injury recovery on the basis of a mechanical reading of the marital property statutes (the mechanistic view). Since all property that does not fall within the definition of separate property (gift, bequest, devise, or inheritance) is marital property, personal injury awards are,

---

968. Driscoll, *supra*, pp. 97–113.

969. *Rose v. Rose*, 481 US 619 (1987).

970. *Mansell v. Mansell*, 490 U.S. 581 (1989). *See also Military Retirement Pay—Postdivorce Elections*, 1999 National Legal Research Group, available at http://www.divorcesource.com/research/edj/military/99apr37.shtml (seen Jul. 7, 2015).

mechanically, deemed marital property. The states reportedly are divided over whether pain and suffering awards are marital or separate property. Sometimes the award compensates for joint inconvenience and damage (marital property), sometimes solely for personal pain (separate property), sometimes to cover attorney's fees (presumably marital depending on when the fees were accrued).[971] The non-consideration in most states of tort recoveries in property division does not prevent adjustments and allocations of other kinds. As one insightful observer noted (advocating interspousal tort claims in family law disputes): "Family law … deals primarily with monetary aspects, such as maintenance payments and division of property. Family law rarely deals with the inequalities that are the result of a tort involving non-monetary harm. Here, tort law (particularly the goal of distributive justice) fills the gap. Tort law can complete the picture in those instances where family law provides no response."[972]

6. Workers' Compensation Awards

786. Workers' compensation awards are generally classified by the same method of classification as personal injury awards. The states are split between the analytic approach and the mechanistic approach. Since only economic loss is generally covered in workers compensation awards, they are generally treated as marital property in analytical states to the extent the award represents compensation for lost wages during marriage, or reimbursement for medical expenses paid for with marital funds. States following the mechanistic approach focus on when the injury occurs, as that is when the right to the award is acquired; if the injury occurred during marriage, since it does not fall within the rigid definition of separate property, mechanistic states treat it as marital property. However, some mechanistic states recognize an exception for benefits received after divorce. Thus, under both analytical and mechanistic approaches, workers compensation awards are generally broken into component parts (what the award replaces, what period it covers) and the parts are separately characterized as marital or separate. Some states take a "unitary" approach and characterize the entire workers' compensation award one way or the other, but commentators are generally critical of this minority approach. Some state workers' compensation statutes contain anti-assignment provisions, but they have not been interpreted to prevent classification as marital property and division upon divorce.[973] A summary of a typical state's law regarding worker compensation benefits is from Indiana: "Generally speaking, worker's compensation benefits received after the date of separation are not includable in the marital estate. However, worker's compensation benefits received during the marriage are included in the marital estate if those benefits were to replace earnings prior to the date of separation."[974]

971. ALI, Preliminary Draft No. 4, *supra* §4.08 p. 243.
972. Benjamin Shmueli, *Tort Litigation Between Spouses: Let's Meet Somewhere in the Middle*, 15 Harv. Nego. L. Rev. 195, 207–208 (2010).
973. B.R. Turner, *supra* §6.19 at 399–401; and G.G. Blumberg, *supra*, pp. 1274–1276.
974. Recent Developments: *Indiana Family Law*, 40 Ind. L. Rev. 891, 894–895 (2007).

E. Valuation of "New Property"

787. Determining the value of "new property" for purposes of equitable distribution upon divorce can be extremely complicated and rather subjective. The method of valuation depends upon the kind of property involved. "[F]ew rules of general application can be formulated."[975]

788. For determining the value of contingent future benefits, there are two prevailing methods of establishing current value of such contingent property interests. One is to use the amount the earner spouse would be entitled to take from the fund at the time of divorce. That is the simplest and clearest, but least inclusive. The other method is to determine the value the benefits will have when payable (often involving actuarial computation), and reduce that sum to present value by discounting for mortality and vesting.[976] The question may boil down to a contest between appraisal opinions of the plaintiff's and defendant's hired experts.

F. The Practical Effect of Equitable Division of "New Property"

789. Two classes of interested persons benefit from complex property division of "new property." The issues are complex and professional assistance is usually necessary. The bar's services are in demand. Wealthy divorcing couples find more equity in divorce when "new property" is taken into account. In most divorce cases, however, the economic benefits of considering "new property" for purposes of property division are meager, and the costs are quite high.

790. Professor Marsha Garrison examined property division in cases before (1978) and after (1984) the adoption of New York's liberal Equitable Distribution law. She expected to find that cases decided after the law was adopted would give a greater share of property to women because the Equitable Distribution law increased (at least in theory) the range of property that could be divided. Her study concluded, however, that this assumption was "highly flawed."[977] She found that "[m]ost divorcing husbands did not own significant individual assets" and discovered "the scarcity of marital property and the tendency for it to be in nonliquid assets."[978] While liberal equitable distribution of broadly defined property could make a significant difference in rare cases of wealthy divorcing couples, Professor Garrison concluded: "Overall there was little change in the percentage distribution of marital property after the passage of the marital distribution law," and what change she found was not statistically significant.[979]

975. H. Clark, Jr., *supra* §15.4 at 605.
976. H. Clark, *supra* §15.6 at 616.
977. M. Garrison, *Good Intentions Gone Awry: The Impact of New York's Equitable Distribution Law on Divorce Outcomes*, Brooklyn L. Rev. 621, 667 (1991).
978. *Ibid.*
979. *Ibid.*, p. 671.

791. There may be non-economic benefits from considering "new property" for purposes of property division upon divorce. The message that marriage truly is an equal partnership is an important message to make, especially in light of the history of economic inequality in marriage. The symbolic value of total equality (at least upon divorce—in common law states) embodied in the notion of marital property, extending to all forms of property, should not be underrated.

Chapter 4. Alimony and Maintenance after Marriage

792. Upon termination of the marriage, it is possible for American courts in all states to order one of the spouses to provide support payments for the other spouse for some period of time after divorce.[980] These payments have been called at various times alimony, maintenance, spousal support, and (the currently popular term) compensatory spousal payments; the most recognizable term is "alimony."

§1. Alimony, Maintenance and Support Rationale in History

I. Anglo-American Historical Antecedents

793. The contemporary practice of ordering one spouse to pay alimony to support the other spouse is traceable to the fact that until the middle of the nineteenth century, "divorce" did not terminate the marriage. Rather, "divorce *a mensa et thoro*" was the equivalent to a modern order of legal separation. Since the parties were still married, the common law duty of the husband to support the wife translated into an alimony order when the parties separated under a "divorce" decree.[981]

Historically, alimony could be awarded permanently or pendent lite (during the divorce litigation period). Since divorce historically was available only for marital misconduct the duty to pay alimony and right to receive it were connected to notions of fault. That continues to distinguish alimony from property division in American divorce law.[982]

794. With the adoption of divorce *a vinculo matrimonii* laws that terminated the marriage, the former justification for alimony ceased, but the practice continued. Requiring the husband who divorced his wife to pay alimony to the wife was deemed justified to protect the wife's interest in marriage as a lifetime commitment (including the lifetime support expectation), to compensate the wife for the consequences of the husband's faulty behavior (since divorce was available only on fault grounds), and to protect the needy (since employment opportunities for women were quite restricted).

II. Modern Justifications for Alimony

795. Today those justifications seem to no longer be valid. Divorce is so common that it can be argued that there is no realistic expectation that marriage will last for the lifetime of the parties. Fault-grounds for divorce (as they have been called)

---

980. In 1997, Texas became the last and final state to authorize the award of post-divorce alimony. Before then, Texas law allowed only alimony *pendente lite*. D.C. Haugen, Comment, *Texas and Alimony: The Possibility of a Constitutional Attack*, 34 Houston L. Rev. 477 (1997).

981. C.L. Blakesley, *Alimony and Spousal Support*, in *Contemporary Family Law*, Vol. 3 §32:01, Chapter 32 (L.D. Wardle, C.L. Blakesley & J.Y. Parker eds, Callaghan 1988).

982. Lynn D. Wardle, Mark P. Strasser & Lynne Marie Kohm, *Family Law from Multiple Perspectives* 783 (2014).

have been replaced de jure or superseded de facto by modern no-fault divorce grounds. Indeed, fault has been statutorily eliminated totally as a divorce factor in some states. And with the repudiation and significant elimination of gender-discrimination in market, labor, and commerce it is presumptuous, at least, if not anachronistically stereotypical to suggest that divorced women (at least those who have not assumed or have abandoned child raising responsibilities) are categorically or generally "needy" because they are incapable of being self-supporting or of earning incomes comparable to those earned by men. Thus, the rationale for awarding alimony upon divorce today is a matter of some controversy and confusion.[983] A number of different theoretical and doctrinal bases for allowing courts to order one spouse (usually the husband) to make periodic payments to the other (usually the wife) have been advanced, but there is no consensus in support of any of them yet.[984] Nevertheless, the practice of awarding alimony continues with significant regularity. The doctrinal grounds for alimony awards show that despite its theoretical flaws, the policy underpinnings for current alimony are the same as have existed for the past 100 years, despite the substantial social and economic changes.[985] As Professor Tom Oldham has noted:

> The most controversial aspect of American divorce law remains postdivorce spousal support. There is substantial disagreement about its appropriate function today … . There is substantial disagreement about the general norms that should govern the determination of the frequency, amount, and duration of such awards.[986]

Alimony specialist Laura Morgan explains the current status (and dilemma) of alimony law as: "The problem with alimony today is that there is no intuitive sense of its purpose in the twenty-first century. … [T]oday, it [alimony] often is seen as a relic of earlier times. Our reluctance to abolish alimony entirely shows that at some level, in some cases, it must serve a very important purpose."[987]

§2. Contemporary Sociology of Alimony Awards

796. Alimony is potentially available in any divorce, but given the standards and circumstances of the parties, it is not awarded in most cases. As the authors of one textbook put it: "What does seem clear is that alimony has never been awarded to

---

983. J. Carbone & M.F. Brinig, *Rethinking Marriage: Feminist Ideology, Economic Change, and Divorce Reform*, 65 Tulane L. Rev. 953 (1991).

984. American Law Institute, *Principles of the Law of Family Dissolution: Analysis and Recommendations*, Preliminary Draft No. 4 (9 Sept. 1993) at Chapter Five, Compensatory Spousal Payments; I.M. Ellman, *The Theory of Alimony*, 77 California L. Rev. 1 (1989).

985. L.D. Wardle, *Alimony on the Margins: Protecting Homemaking Services in the Public Interest*, in *Family Finances* 475 (Jan Sramek Verlag KG, Austria, B. Verschraegen eds, 2009).

986. J.T. Oldham, *Changes in the Economic Consequences of Divorces, 1958-2008*, 42 Fam. L. Q. 419, 437–438 (2008).

987. Laura Morgan, *Current Trends in Alimony Law: Where Are We Now?*, GPSolo eReport (April 2012).

most divorced women, and still is not."[988] As more wives remain or become regularly employed outside of the home, it is not unlikely that permanent alimony awards will decrease even further.[989]

The economic, social, and cultural factors that have changed our views of marriage have shattered our once cohesive understanding of alimony. Some courts and commentators, and even a few legislatures, have reasoned that since women now work, alimony should be curtailed drastically or even abolished. This trend was most recently exhibited in Massachusetts, where on September 26, 2011, the governor signed legislation, ending alimony when the payor retires, and generally limiting alimony to a number of years based on the length of the marriage.[990]

797. There are many reasons why alimony is not awarded in most divorces. Most divorces in the United States occur within the first six years of marriage. In that short time, the parties' premarital working skills have not been so significantly impaired that self-support is not reasonably possible. Likewise, the percentage of married women who are working (two-career families) has steadily risen, so the economic impact of divorce is less devastating or life-course changing. While it has been suggested that the percentage of alimony awards has dropped since the adoption of no-fault divorce, the connection between no-fault and non-award of alimony is not clear.[991] It is not unusual for American courts to award a token amount of alimony, such as USD 1.00 per year, so that if circumstances change making a larger alimony award just the court will have jurisdiction to modify the alimony award and alimony will not be deemed to have been waived or denied.

§3. Standard for Awarding Alimony

I. The General Dual Standard

798. The standards for awarding alimony are established by legislation in all states. The details of the standards vary significantly. Some simply award the court discretion to make a just award; others list numerous factors that must be considered.[992] In general, however, the awarding of alimony turns on two key considerations: the *need* of the dependent spouse for support, and the *ability* of the other spouse to provide it. Efforts to systematize and constrain alimony awards have not succeeded. As Professor Oldham writes:

988. I.M. Ellman, P.M. Kurtz & K.T. Bartlett, *Family Law, Cases, Text, Problems*, 265 (2d ed., 1991).

989. *See* M. Garrison, *Good Intentions Gone Awry: The Impact of New York's Equitable Distribution Law on Divorce Outcomes*, 57 Brooklyn L. Rev. 621, 634 (1991); J.T. Oldham, *Changes, supra* at 42 Fam. L. Q. at 431.

990. L. Morgan, *Current Trends in Alimony Law: Where Are We Now?*, 1(9) ABA, GPSolo eReport, April 2012, available at http://www.americanbar.org/publications/gpsolo_ereport/2012/april_2012/current_trends_alimony_law.html (seen Jul. 7, 2015).

991. L. Weitzman, *The Economics of Divorce: Social and Economic Consequences of Property, Alimony and Child Support Awards*, 28 UCLA L. Rev. 1181 (1981).

992. J.D. Gregory, P.N. Swisher, and S.L. Scheible, *Understanding Family Law*, §8.03, (1993).

> [I]n almost all states, rules applicable to spousal support now give courts great discretion … . The lack of clarity of these rules appears to result in substantial variation in spousal support outcomes, even in the same jurisdiction."[993]

American states vary significantly in the availability, amount and period of time in alimony awards. For example, in Georgia and North Carolina, adultery is a bar to alimony, and it is said that alimony awards in California are generally high and those in Texas are generally quite low.[994]

799. The Uniform Marriage and Divorce Act provides a typical example of an alimony statute that embodies the need-ability standard. Section 308 of the UMDA provides:

a. In a proceeding for dissolution of marriage, legal separation, or maintenance following a decree of dissolution of the marriage by a court which lacked personal jurisdiction over the absent spouse, the court may grant a maintenance order for either spouse only if it finds that the spouse seeking maintenance:
   1. lacks sufficient property to provide for his reasonable needs; and
   2. is unable to support himself through appropriate employment or is the custodian of a child whose condition or circumstances make it appropriate that the custodian not be required to seek employment outside the home.
b. The maintenance order shall be in amounts and for periods of time the court deems just, without regard to marital misconduct, and after considering all relevant factors including:
   1. the financial resources of the party seeking maintenance, including marital property apportioned to him, his ability to meet his needs independently, and the extent to which a provision for support of a child living with the party includes a sum for that party as custodian;
   2. the time necessary to acquire sufficient education or training to enable the party seeking maintenance to find appropriate employment;
   3. the standard of living established during the marriage;
   4. the duration of the marriage;
   5. the age and the physical and emotional condition of the spouse seeking maintenance; and
   6. the ability of the spouse from whom maintenance is sought to meet his needs while meeting those of the spouse seeking maintenance.[995]

993. J.T. Oldham, *Changes in the Economic Consequences of Divorces, 1958-2008*, 42 Fam. L. Q. 419, 447 (2008).
994. *See What State/States in the USA Award the Lowest Alimony (Amount and Duration)?*, (Jan. 6, 2014).
995. Uniform Marriage and Divorce Act §308.

II. Need

800. The first thing that must be established is need. If the marriage has lasted a long time, and if the wife has not worked in the marketplace, she may have a need for support. However, if she has sufficient assets that would produce sufficient income for her to live comfortably on, she may not be able to show a need. Likewise, if she has job skills that are in current demand she may not have need for support other than temporary support while she revives those skills. As more married couples become dual-income couples, the "need" factor has shrunken as each spouse has proven capable of pursuing a career and supporting him/herself.

A. Relation to Property Award

801. The amount of support is related to the amount of property awarded to the dependant spouse. If the amount of property is sufficient to produce supporting income, alimony may not be necessary. Likewise, if the type of property awarded can be used to produce a livelihood (such as a farm, an orchard, tools of the recipient's trade) alimony may not be necessary. Thus, even though legally they are separate considerations, property division and alimony are linked in the divorce court consideration of doing "equity" in the overall divorce decree.

B. Standard of Living During the Marriage

802. Many statutes refer to the standard of living the parties enjoyed during marriage as the standard to use in measuring need for alimony. In reality, that is not exactly the way the law is interpreted, nor could it be. In fact, most married couples in America live pretty close to the edge of their income. That is, they spend each month about all that they bring in. (Voluntary savings are not popular in the United States, and the percentage of personal income devoted to such savings is comparatively quite small.) Since two people can live together much more cheaply than they can live separately, it is economically impossible for both of them to maintain the previous standard of living after divorce if they both depend upon the same amount of income they had before the divorce. Thus, the standard of living reference is to the post-divorce approximation of pre-divorce living standard that is economically realistic given the loss of the economies of joint and cooperative living.

C. Duration of the Marriage

803. The duration of the marriage is a factor in alimony awards for two reasons. The first is the economic reason—the general fact that the longer the parties were married the more economically dependent the homemaking spouse would become, as she was longer out of the market, as her job skills became obsolete, and as her health deteriorated with age, etc. The second reason is the expectation-justice reason, the belief that the longer the parties are married, the greater "right" they both have to depend upon the continuation of patterns of marital economic support. For example, Utah's property division statute provides in pertinent part that, absent "extenuating circumstances": "Alimony may not be ordered for a duration longer than the number of years that the marriage existed … ":[996]

> During the past two decades, it appears that in a number of states there has been a reevaluation of whether fixed-term alimony is appropriate when couples divorce with substantially different incomes after a long marriage. There appears to be a greater willingness to award indefinite term alimony [only] when parties are divorcing after a marriage of long duration, the parties' incomes are quite different, and the recipients cannot realistically be retrained.[997]

804. The changing economic and social conditions have rendered both considerations much more tenuous today than they were when the UMDA was adopted nearly thirty years ago. It is now uncommon for wives not to work during marriage. Most families are two-income families. It is no longer reasonable to expect that the wife has more diminished job skills the longer the marriage lasts. Indeed, one common pattern is for women to temporarily leave the job market while their children are young, but to reenter the market as they grow up; in that case, the longer the marriage, the more job experience the wife would have.

805. Likewise, expectations about economic arrangements during marriage have changed significantly. Many married women are demanding and expecting that their husbands support them in their efforts during marriage to abandon homemaking for educational, job-training, and employment opportunities that allow them to individually grow and achieve personal fulfillment. The husband who supports his wife in a comfortable lifestyle during several years of her education and start-up employment years (during which she would have struggled economically if she had not been married) might reasonably expect that he will be able to retire earlier than his wife and enjoy a few years doing things he likes to do for his own personal fulfillment and growth. Thus, he might have the expectation of support, rather than she, even though he has the greater earning capacity. Nevertheless, duration of the marriage remains a common and important factor in assessing alimony need.

D. Fault

806. The UMDA provisions do not allow for the court to consider marital misbehavior in awarding alimony. The drafters of the UMDA were staunchly against "fault." Among academicians, that is still a popular position and is the trend of law-reform decisions (more fault states are moving to no-fault in alimony than no-fault

996. Utah Code Annot. § 30-3-5 (8)(h) (2009).
997. J.T. Oldham, *Changes in the Economic Consequences of Divorces, 1958-2008*, 42 Fam. L. Q. 419, 432 (2008).

states are moving back to fault). Nevertheless, nearly one-half of the states allow marital misconduct to be considered in awarding alimony. Since alimony is deemed to be "earned" to some degree by marital commitments and expectations, it is in those states also deemed fairly forfeited or reducible because of serious breach of those commitments and reasonable expectations. The drafters of the American Law Institute's Principles of the Law of Family Dissolution recommended total elimination of consideration of fault in awarding alimony.[998] But that recommendation has not been accepted or endorsed or implemented by lawmakers. In at least thirty states, "fault" still may be considered by courts in making alimony (spousal support) awards upon divorce, and in about half of the American states the consideration of fault in awarding alimony is not uncommon.[999]

E. Gender

807. Both historically and in current practice, alimony is awarded overwhelmingly to women, not men, upon divorce. But as a matter of constitutional law, the alimony statutes must be gender neutral. The U.S. Supreme Court has held that alimony statutes must allow men to seek and obtain alimony on the same grounds as women.[1000] In fact, cases do arise from time to time in which men seek and obtain alimony.[1001] As more and more wives work more and more during their marriages, it is possible that more men will seek and obtain alimony.[1002]

III. Ability to Pay

808. The other factor is the ability of the defending spouse to pay alimony. That must be determined with reference to his property, his income, his health, and his standard of living during marriage, as well. Most of the issues regarding ability to pay arise in connection with motions to modify alimony awards and are considered hereafter in that section.

§4. Types of Alimony Awards

809. There are four types of alimony awards. They all derive from the same statutes and incorporate the same basic principles but the purposes and contexts vary.

998. American Law Institute, *Principles of the Law of Family Dissolution: Analysis and Recommendations*, in *Compensatory Spousal Payments* Chapter 5 (2002). *See also* L.D. Wardle, *Beyond Fault and No-Fault in the Reform of Marital Dissolution Law*, in *Reconceiving the Family* 9 (R.F. Wilson ed., 2006).

999. K.A. Portuan Miller, *Who Says Muslim Women Don't Have the Right to Divorce?—A Comparison Between Anglo-American Law and Islamic Law*, 22 N.Y. Int'l L. Rev. 201, 240 (2009).

1000. *Orr v. Orr*, 440 US 268 (1979).

1001. *Pfohl v. Pfohl*, 345 So.2d 371 (Fla. App. 1977).

1002. For psychological reasons relating to American men's pride of self-sufficiency and independence, men probably will never become as willing to seek alimony as women.

I. *Pendente Lite* Alimony Awards

810. The first type of alimony is alimony during the pendency of the divorce litigation. This is called *pendente lite* alimony, and it is temporary, limited in duration to the pendency of the divorce proceedings. The purpose is to insure that the economically dependant spouse is not "starved into submission" during the pendency of the divorce proceedings. It also allows her to hire and pay her lawyer during the divorce litigation, if her husband has all or most of the wealth and income.

811. Until 1997, Texas allowed only *pendente lite* alimony awards, not allowing permanent alimony. Now, however, Texas permits permanent alimony as well.

II. Permanent Alimony

812. The typical kind of alimony that most people have thought of in America is permanent alimony. That is an order that compels the husband (usually) to pay a periodic amount (usually monthly) to the wife permanently—until she dies or remarries or is no longer dependent upon spousal support. Unless modified, the duty to pay alimony continues until her death or remarriage. All states now allow for alimony awards, though the trend of recent years in most states is toward time-limited alimony awards.

813. Permanent alimony has been compared to a pension. Like a retirement benefit, it provides income stream (or supplements income) until the death of the payee or payor. In days when full-time homemaking was the model for marriage, this type of alimony was the common and prevalent form of alimony. Today, it is much less common.

III. Rehabilitative Alimony

814. Rehabilitative alimony is intended to provide support for an economically dependent or disadvantaged former spouse for a limited period of time. The purpose is to provide her with a decent standard of living while she acquires self-supporting skills or education, or while she refurbishes her job experience and finds appropriate employment. It is a means of equalizing the income-producing consequences of marriage and divorce. It also provides her with incentive to become self-supporting, because the alimony will not be paid indefinitely, but only for a specific term considered by the court to be adequate to allow her to rehabilitate her income-producing abilities. Today, some version of rehabilitative alimony may be the most common form of alimony.[1003]

1003. J.D. Gregory et al., *supra* at §8.04[C].

IV. Compensatory Alimony

815. In some states, compensatory alimony may be awarded. This provides compensation for services rendered during marriage by the recipient which allowed the other spouse to comfortably enhance income-producing abilities, for which the recipient received no permanent economic income-producing enhancements.

816. A common scenario in which compensatory alimony may be awarded involves a couple who marries in college; the wife works to support the family by taking relatively low-paying jobs while husband pursues and obtains a medical degree and training. Upon completion of medical training, after eight or ten years of marriage, just before or after he begins to earn the huge income doctors may earn, he divorces his wife. The husband leaves the marriage with the ability to earn USD 200,000 or USD 300,000 per year, while the wife leaves the marriage with the ability to earn USD 15,000 or USD 20,000 per year. This allows the court to order the husband to reimburse his wife for her contribution to his dramatically increased income-producing ability.[1004]

V. Lump-Sum Alimony

817. Lump-sum alimony is paid in one payment. Unlike ordinary alimony, it is not paid periodically, over time. However, it could provide for the purchase of an annuity which would be payable in installments, over time. From the perspective of "clean break" divorce, it is desirable. It allows the parties to avoid further financial entanglements with each other. But most divorcing parties are not in a position to pay alimony in one lump-sum. And it is possible that if the recipient of lump-sum alimony wasted the amount awarded, and became a public charge, the court could order the payor to subsequently provide more alimony.

§5. Modification and Termination of Alimony Awards

I. Modification of Alimony

818. Alimony awards are generally modifiable. However, the standard for modification is generally a high standard. The party seeking modification generally must show a substantial change of circumstances. As the UMDA puts it, there must be "a showing of changed circumstances so substantial and continuing as to make the terms [of the existing alimony award] unconscionable … ."[1005]

1004. Arizona Revised Statutes §25-319(a)(3) (1991); *Mahoney v. Mahoney*, 453 A.2d 527 (1982).
1005. Uniform Marriage and Divorce Act §316.

A. Retroactive Modification

819. Alimony modification is presumptively prospective—that is, it alters future alimony payments. However, a minority of American states allow retroactive modification of past-due alimony obligations. The reason for this is that often the parties informally modify their continuing post-divorce relations. In reliance upon an informal agreement or understanding, alimony might be suspended or paid at a reduced rate while the payor provides some other consideration for the payee. Later, if the payee insists on compliance with the terms of the formal alimony decree, the payor will seek modification of the alimony obligation. If retroactive modification is not possible, injustice may be inflicted. Likewise, to disallow retroactive modification would force the parties to return to court too often, every time the economy drops, or someone gets sick, or is laid off, or temporary conditions arise that affect income substantially.

B. Factors in Modification

820. Many factors can influence income and expenses after divorce. Apart from death of either party, three of the most common are retirement or job change, remarriage, and cohabitation.

821. If the payor retires voluntarily, or changes his job and his income substantially drops, is that ground for modification of alimony? The American jurisdictions are split. The general rule is that if there is evidence of an intent to financially disadvantage the other party, no modification is permitted. If the motive is vindictive or hostile, modification is inappropriate. If the retirement is normal and usual, or the job change reasonable, on the other hand, modification may be granted. If it is involuntary, a modification is likely to be granted. However, courts are naturally suspicious of job changes or early retirements that result in income reductions to the payor and immediate petitions for modification of alimony, especially if the party petitioning has some other source of income that makes up the salary loss or reduction.[1006]

822. Remarriage by the alimony obligor may result in his assumption of greater financial obligations than existed at the time of the alimony award, detrimentally affecting his "ability to pay." In extraordinary cases, this could result in a reduction of alimony. Nevertheless, most courts are unwilling to reduce alimony because of voluntarily assumed increased financial obligations of the alimony obligor. The effect of this in some cases is to mandated economic inferiority for the second family of the alimony obligor. As between the first and second families, the policy choice has been made (deliberately or by inertia) in favor of the former. It might be

1006. J.D. Gregory et al., *supra* at §8.05.

best to eliminate any preference as a matter of rule, and leave the matter to judgment on a case-by-case basis. But that clearly is not the rule in American states today.

II. Termination of Alimony

823. Remarriage by the alimony recipient (payee) is ground in every state for termination of alimony. Likewise, just as remarriage of the alimony recipient is ground for termination of alimony, in many states nonmarital cohabitation by the recipient is also ground for termination. Thus, for example, the Utah alimony statute provides: "Unless a decree of divorce specifically provides otherwise, any order of the court that a party pay alimony to a former spouse automatically terminates upon the death or remarriage of that former spouse," and also "upon establishment by the party paying alimony that the former spouse is cohabiting [in a sexual relationship] with another person."[1007] Alimony terminates upon remarriage or its equivalent because that act signifies a new economic partnership. The new partner is expected to assume the burden of reciprocal economic support of his or her new partner. There is also a residual concern that alimony should not provide a windfall for the recipient to live a lifestyle that puts the alimony obligor in the position of financing the affair of his former wife and her new boyfriend, or that is contrary to social well-being.

824. Of course, alimony also terminates upon the terms set forth in the court order. Since most alimony decrees are for rehabilitative alimony, alimony terminates upon the expiration of the period indicated in the alimony order. (Of course, the recipient may petition for continuation or extension of the alimony, but the standards for modification are high, as noted above.) Alimony is not dischargeable in general Chapter 7 bankruptcy liquidation.[1008]

§6. Jurisdiction to Award Alimony

825. It is possible that a court may have jurisdiction to grant a divorce, but not jurisdiction to award alimony or divide property. Thus, the basis for alimony jurisdiction must be considered.

1007. Utah Code Annot. § 30-3-5 (9) (2009); *ibid.* at 30-3-5(10).

1008. *See generally* Janet Leach Richards, *A Guide to Spousal Support and Property Division Claims Under the Bankruptcy Abuse Prevention and Consumer Protection Act of 2005*, 41 Fam. L.Q. 227 (2007).

I. Divisible Divorce

826. The basis for asserting jurisdiction to alter marital status is the domicile of either party to the marriage. That is because both parties carry the marital relationship with them. Thus, wherever either one goes, the *res* of the marriage is there and the court can assert jurisdiction over the marriage to adjust the marital status (grant divorce, legal separation).[1009]

827. However, personal jurisdiction over the alleged obligor is necessary for a court to have the power to order a person to pay alimony. Alimony is an economic debt and while it grows out of the marriage, it is a personal obligation so in personam jurisdiction over the defendant is required.[1010] This distinction is the crux of the doctrine of "divisible divorce."[1011]

828. Thus, in order to award alimony, a court must have personal jurisdiction over the defendant. That means the defendant must be served with process in the jurisdiction, or must submit voluntarily to jurisdiction, or must be subject to the "long-arm" jurisdiction of the court on the basis of his actions which created minimum contacts with the jurisdiction such that the assertion of jurisdiction is consistent with traditional notions of fair play and substantial justice. In most cases, this poses no problem, but it cannot be overlooked.

II. Continuing Jurisdiction

829. Once a party is subject to the court's alimony jurisdiction, and once the court enters an alimony order, the court has continuing jurisdiction over the parties regarding payment, enforcement, modification, or termination of alimony. That is, alimony is deemed a continuing obligation under the order and jurisdiction or the court. The court retains jurisdiction to ensure compliance with the order and to ensure that equity is done.[1012]

1009. *Williams v. Williams*, 317 US 287 (1942).
1010. *Vanderbilt v. Vanderbilt*, 354 US 416 (1957).
1011. *Estin v. Estin*, 334 US 541 (1948).
1012. J.D. Gregory, et al., *supra* at §8.02[A].

Part IV. Succession Law

830. Succession law is the law of administering and distributing the estate of a dead person, who is referred to as the decedent. A dead person's estate, consisting of both real and personal property, is commonly called the probate estate.[1013] In community property states, the probate estate consists of the decedent's separate property and half of the community property. In common law states, the probate estate is property owned solely by the decedent, which would be the equivalent of separate property in community property states.[1014]

831. Although there is much commonality among the states, each state enacts, interprets, and administers its own family succession law. Therefore, one must reference the law of a particular state on any subject of family succession law.

1013. For federal and state taxation purposes, the decedent's estate may include non-probate property.

1014. There are two property regimes in the United States; nine states are based upon the civil law, one state where the married couple can opt for either the civil law or the common law, and the remaining states are based upon the English common law.

Chapter 1. Intestate Succession

832. Intestate succession law administers and distributes a decedent's property which neither passes by the terms of his or her will nor was properly disposed of prior to death by an *inter vivos* transaction. The decedent who dies without a will is said to have died intestate; one who dies with a will is said to have died testate. A decedent may have both intestate and testate property because all of his or her property may not pass by a will.

833. Each state has its own intestate succession statute. This statute sets forth the procedure for the administration and the distribution of the decedent's property, including a scheme designating the successors to the property.

§1. The Opening of the Succession

I. Death

834. Whether the decedent's estate passes by intestate succession law or by a valid and operative will (testamentary succession) or by both, death is a jurisdictional requirement. Death is either proved by a death certificate, issued by a state's Bureau of Vital Statistics, or established by a court proceeding, finding a presumption of death.[1015] If the alleged decedent is later found to be alive, most states consider the proceedings administering the estate void. In such states, the alleged decedent may proceed to recover the property.[1016] In other states, the proceedings are binding on all parties if the estate has been closed.

835. About half of the states have adopted the Uniform Determination of Death Act. This Act defines death as "either (1) irreversible cessation of circulatory and respiratory functions or (2) irreversible cessation of all functions of the brain."[1017] If there is no statute defining death, the state has adopted a judicial test for the determination of death, similar to the Uniform Act.

II. Missing Persons and Absentees

A. *Presumptive Death*

836. Each state provides a procedure to determine whether a missing person or an absentee should be presumed dead so that the opening of his or her succession

1015. The court also makes out and signs a certificate of presumptive death, which is also filed with the Bureau of Vital Statistics for that state. *See*, e.g., Alaska Stat. §09.55.050 (1994).

1016. *See*, e.g., Tex. Civ. Prac. & Rem. Code Ann. §133.003 (West 2005) (restoration of the estate). Before distribution, the beneficiary may be required to post a surety bond for a period of years. Ill. Rev. Stat. ch. 755, para. 5/24–5 (Smith-Hurd 1995).

1017. Unif. Determination of Death Act §1, 12A ULA 593 (1980).

might proceed. At common law, there was a presumption of death when a person had been continuously absent and unheard of for seven years. The person's death is presumed to have occurred at the end of that period unless there is sufficient evidence that the death occurred earlier.[1018] The presumption has been codified by most states, but many of them changed the time to five years for succession purposes.[1019] Several states have abolished the presumption, and proof of death is one of fact to be determined at any time upon the evidence.[1020] States may also have specific statutes raising the presumption of death under certain circumstances.[1021]

837. In all states, if there is sufficient evidence that the person has died, a court may proceed immediately to determine whether the person should be presumed dead, without the aid of the presumption.[1022]

838. Courts conduct similar proceedings when the beneficiary of the decedent's property is missing or absent.[1023]

B. Missing or Absent Person

839. If a person is missing or absent but has not been presumed dead, a court should hold a proceeding to appoint a guardian of that person's estate.[1024] The guardian is responsible for managing and conserving the estate until the person is found or presumed dead.

840. All states have statutes providing that property that is unclaimed after a term of years *escheats* to the state. The property of a missing or absent person may eventually become unclaimed property and will *escheat* to the state.

§2. The Heir

841. The heir is the person named in the intestate succession statute to succeed to the intestate property. Historically, "heir" was used to refer to the person, who took the intestate's real property, and "next of kin" or "distributee" was used to refer to the person, who took the intestate's personal property. Today, the term heir is commonly used to refer to either taker.

1018. *See*, e.g., N.D. Cent. Code §30.1-01-04 (1995).
1019. *See*, e.g., Cal. Evid. Code §667 (West, 1995).
1020. *See*, e.g., Md. Code Ann., Cts. & Jud. Proc. §3-102 (2006).
1021. *See*, e.g., W.Va. Code §44-9-1a (2007) (raising a presumption of death in circumstances regarding persons in military service presumed to be dead).
1022. *See*, e.g., Fla. Stat. Ann. §731.103 (West, 1987); N.J. Stat. Ann. §3B:27-1 (West, 2001).
1023. *See*, e.g., S.C. Code Ann. §62-3-914 (Law. Co-op., 1993).
1024. In many states, the guardian of the estate is called a "conservator" or a "committee."

I. Capacity to Succeed

A. *Requirement of Survivorship*

1. Meaning of Survivorship

842. The heir must be living at the death of the intestate or be born alive during the normal period of gestation after the decedent's death, from 280 days in some states to 300 days in others, with some statutes using the term "within 10 lunar months."[1025]

2. Posthumous Children Born from Assisted Reproduction Technology

843. Posthumous children may not only be born but may also be conceived after the traditional period of gestation because of modern technology used in assisted conception. Definitive law in this area of decedent's estates continues to develop. The Uniform Status of Children of Assisted Conception Act was promulgated by the Uniform Commissioners of Laws to suggest guidelines in this area, but was superseded by the Uniform Parentage Act in 2000 and amended in 2002.[1026] The Uniform Parentage Act (2002) provides that the individual who furnishes the egg or sperm for posthumous conception is not a parent of the resulting child, but further provides that if a spouse dies before placement of eggs, sperm, or embryos, the deceased spouse is not a parent of the resulting child unless the deceased spouse consented in a record that if assisted reproduction were to occur after death, the deceased spouse would be a parent of the child. Very few states have enacted legislation dealing with this problem.[1027]

3. Additional Statutory Survivorship Requirement

844. The Uniform Probate Code[1028] has modified the common law rule of survivorship and requires an heir to survive for a longer period of time. The Code requires an heir to survive the decedent by 120 hours. The additional allotted time for survivorship prevents reducing the value of the estate by requiring the estate, in a very short period of time, to pass through two estates for administration instead of one. Most states impose longer periods of survivorship than the common law rule.

1025. N.C. Gen. Stat. §29-9 (1959); *Byerly v. Tolbert*, 108 S.E.2d 29 (NC 1959).
1026. Uniform Status of Children of Assisted Conception Act §1, 9B ULA 86 (Supp. 1996), superseded by the Uniform Parentage Act (UPA) (amended 2002)9B U.L.A. 295 (2001 & Supp. 2003).
1027. *Ibid.* Case law is sparse as well. Most cases that have raised the issue of inheritance by posthumously conceived children have been in the context of social security benefits.
1028. UPC §2-702 (1990) (amended 1997).

B. Type of Kinship Requirement

845. Most states have also abolished the common law distinction between heirs related by the whole-blood and by the half-blood. The majority of the states making this distinction exclude half-blood relatives from inheriting real property, which the decedent inherited from an ancestor who was *not* related to the half-blood relatives.[1029]

846. Relatives by the affinity (step-relatives) are usually excluded altogether under the intestate statute. If they do take at all, it is after all other classes of heirs have been exhausted.[1030]

C. Abolishment of Gender and Order of Birth Requirements

847. Unlike the common law, no intestate statute makes a distinction between male and female heirs or the order of birth.

D. The Effect of the Doctrine of Advancements

848. A decedent, during his or her lifetime, may advance to the potential heir part of his or her inheritance. At the death of the decedent, the doctrine of advancement provides the means for accounting for advances so that the heir's share will be reduced by the advances when the estate is distributed. All states have statutes providing for advances.

849. The central issue in advancement cases is determining the intent of the decedent, i.e., whether the decedent intended the property to be an inheritance, a lifetime gift, or a loan. Most modern statutes either create a presumption that the decedent did not intend the gift to be an advancement or create a presumption against advancements, such that the presumption can be rebutted only by a writing. A few states require a writing to establish the advancement.

850. If the lifetime gift is found to be an advancement, the heir cannot be forced to account to the estate for what he or she has received. The heir, however, cannot participate in the decedent's estate unless he or she accounts for the advancement.

1029. Conn. Gen. Stat. Ann. §45a-439 (2016); Fla. Stat. Ann. §732.105 (2016).

1030. Fla. Stat. Ann. §732.103 (5) (2008); *See generally*, M.M. Mahoney, *Step-families in the Law of Intestate Succession and Wills*, 22 UC Davis L.Rev. 917 (1989).

E. The Effect of Releases, Assignments and Disclaimers

1. Releases and Assignments

851. Although an heir is determined only at the death of the decedent, during the lifetime of the decedent, however, a potential heir may be referred to as the "presumptive heir" and the "heir apparent." The presumptive heir is one who will inherit if the decedent dies immediately, but who may be excluded if kin closer in kinship to the decedent are born. An heir apparent is one who is certain to take unless excluded by a valid will. Although the interests of a potential heir in the estate are mere expectancies, the heir may release such expectancies to the decedent while the decedent lives or may assign them to third parties. A court of equity will enforce such releases and assignments as contracts if the heir has received adequate consideration for the release or the assignment.

852. A valid assignment of the potential heir's expected inheritance bars the heir from keeping the inherited property once the heir receives the property. However, a valid assignment to a third party provides no additional protection for the third party (the assignee) if the decedent decides to give the property to another through a lifetime or testamentary gift because the decedent is not a party to the assignment.

853. A valid release is binding on both the heir and the heir's descendants. They are treated as if they had predeceased the decedent. Some courts have been willing to construe the release as an advancement to prevent collateral relations to inherit over the decedent's children if the testator did not make a will.

2. Renunciation/Disclaimers

854. At common law, an heir could not renounce (modern term: disclaim) his or her right to succeed to the decedent's property because title vested in the heir by operation of law. Therefore, the heir could not refuse to accept title to the inheritance. Title automatically vested in the heir. Beneficiaries under a will may, however, renounce. The theory of gift law is applied to property passing by will from the decedent to the beneficiary. The receiver of a gift must accept the gift before title passes to the receiver.

855. In states where there is a statute abrogating the common law rule, an heir may renounce his inheritance. Renunciation treats the heir as having predeceased the decedent.

856. Renunciation must be distinguished from an heir assigning his or her inheritance after the decedent's death. Once the heir inherits the property, the heir is its owner. The owner of property may assign it to a third party.

F. The Effect of "Negative Will" Statutes

857. Since the heir takes by operation of law, the wishes of the decedent have been irrelevant. The judiciary has not enforced provisions in a will that would disinherit an heir under the intestate succession statute. The Uniform Probate Code of 1990, (amended in 1993), however, recognizes the concept of the "negative will." This concept allows a decedent to state in his or her will that a person will not inherit the property if it should pass under the intestate succession statute.[1031]

II. Commorientes

858. Most states have enacted statutes, based on the Uniform Simultaneous Death Act, to provide for the administering of estates of persons who perish at the same time. This Act provides that if there is insufficient evidence that the persons died otherwise than simultaneously, the property of each person shall be administered as if he had survived.[1032]

III. Unworthiness to Succeed

A. Aliens

859. State laws pertaining to succession rights of aliens are subject to scrutiny under the United States Constitution because of the following reasons: (1) the federal government has exclusive responsibility to conduct foreign affairs, (2) the war and commerce powers, and (3) the equal protection clause of the Fourteenth Amendment if resident aliens and citizens are involved. Therefore, federal law and treaties may supersede any state law.

860. At common law, aliens were extremely limited in their ability to take a decedent's estate by intestate or testate succession, especially regarding real property. Just about all American states have removed all restrictions. The others have various restrictions, with the majority of such restrictions taking the form of "reciprocity" or "retention" statutes. A typical reciprocity statute allows a non-resident alien to inherit in that state if an American citizen can also inherit in the country of the non-resident. A typical retention statute places the burden on the non-resident alien to prove that he or she will have full ownership rights to the inherited property once that property is transmitted to the foreign country.

1031. UPC §2-101(b) (1990). *See generally*, J.A. Heaton, The *Intestate Claims of Heirs Excluded by Will: Should Negative Wills Be Enforced*, 52, U. Chi. L. Rev. 177 (1985).

1032. Uniform Simultaneous Death Act §2, 8B ULA 258 (1993). If the decedent has a will, he or she may provide for a different distribution.

B. Felons

861. Unlike the common law, a felon does not forfeit his or her succession rights unless he or she is guilty of feloniously and intentionally killing the decedent. If he or she murdered the decedent, a majority of the states require forfeiture by case law or by statute.[1033] States, which do not have a forfeiture statute, usually will not interpret their succession law as implying forfeiture. A number of these states are, however, willing to allow the felon to take the property, but will immediately impose a constructive trust over the property so that the felon, as the constructive trustee, is obligated to hold the property for the estate.[1034] A constructive trust is a remedial device, designed to prevent the wrongdoer from benefitting from the wrongdoing and unjustly enriching him or herself. The court has power to impose the constructive trust under its equity powers.

C. Misconduct

862. Marital misconduct may bar a spouse from inheritance. Several states have statutes patterned after The English Statute of Westminster II, which barred dower to a wife who deserted her husband and committed adultery.[1035] Other states bar the spouse for abandonment.[1036] In addition, several states may bar a parent from inheriting from the deceased child if the parent has failed to support the child.[1037]

§3. The System of Descent

863. Each state has enacted a statutory system of descent, the intestate succession statute. For the most part, intestate succession statutes are rooted in the English Canons of Descent and the English Statute of Distribution. Eight of the community property states, however, were influenced by Spanish and French civil law. Wisconsin, the most recent state to become a community property state, was influenced by the Uniform Married Property Act. Alaska allows married couples to hold their property as community property if they so choose. The community property states, except for Arizona and Wisconsin, have a system of descent for separate property distribution and another system for community property distribution.

1033. The law does not usually differentiate between murder and manslaughter, but it may differentiate between involuntary and voluntary manslaughter and allow no forfeiture for involuntary manslaughter. *See* J.C. Sherman, *Mercy Killing and the Right to Inherit*, 61 University of Cincinnati L. Rev. 803 (1993) (arguing that there should be an exception to the slayer rule if the intent of the killing was to relieve the decedent's suffering attributed to the affliction).

1034. *In re Estate of Mahoney*, 220 A.2d 475 (Vt. 1966).

1035. NC Gen. Stat. §31A-1(a) (2001).

1036. NY Est. Powers & Trusts Law §5-1.2(a) (5) (McKinley, 1995); and NC Gen. Stat. §31A-1(a) (3) (1995).

1037. NY Est. Powers & Trusts Law §4-1.4(a) (McKinley, 2007).

864. A descent statute classifies heirs according to the priority in which they are to inherit. This order of priority is followed until there is a taker. If there is no living person who may take, the property *escheats* to the state. The classes of takers, except for the surviving spouse, are related by blood to the intestate. The classes are the intestate's descendants, ancestors, and collateral relations. Some statutes will include relations by the affinity (step-relations) if there are no blood relations before allowing the property to *escheat* to the state.

865. There is generally no distinction, as it was at common law, between real property and personal property distribution. As a general rule, personal property passes under the law of the intestate's domicile and real property under the law of the *situs* of the property.

866. With the exception of the surviving spouse, the intestate succession statutes are partially based on the *parentelic* system of inheritance, where there is a preference for persons who are in the nearest *parentala* to the intestate. The *parentelic* system is evidenced by the specific classes of heirs enumerated in the statutes. A *parentala* consists of an ancestor and that ancestor's surviving descendants. For example, typically, in these statutes, the first *parentala* is the intestate and his or her descendants; the second *parentala* is the intestate's parents and their descendants; the third *parentala* is the intestate's grandparents and their descendants, and so forth. Each *parentala* must be exhausted before proceeding to the next one.

I. The Classes of Heirs

A. Surviving Spouse

867. The definition of spouse has changed with the recognition of same-sex marriage. A number of states give spousal rights for inheritance to persons who have entered into domestic partnerships and persons who have entered into civil unions.[1038]

1. Common Law States

868. Unlike the common law tradition, the surviving spouse is an heir of the intestate and, in many states, the primary heir. The ongoing trend in the United

1038. Oregon has enacted a statute that defines spouse for intestate succession purposes to also include a person, who cohabitated with the decedent for a period of at least 10 years and was capable of entering into a valid contract of marriage with the decedent. During this period of cohabitation, the decedent and the person mutually assumed marital rights, duties and obligations, held themselves out as husband and wife, and acquired a reputation as a marital couple. During the last two years of the 10-year period, both were domiciled in Oregon. The 10-year period ended not earlier than two years before the death of the decedent. Oregon Revised Statutes §112.017 (1995).

States has been to increase the share of the intestate estate passing to the surviving spouse. The Uniform Probate Code has been influential in this trend, both in common law and community property states.

869. Many variations exist among the states regarding the surviving spouse's share. In the common law states, the surviving spouse generally inherits the entire estate if the intestate is not survived by descendants or parents. If there are descendants, the surviving spouse generally shares the property with them. If there are no descendants, but the intestate's parents survive, the spouse may have to share the estate with them or their survivor. If the spouse must share the property, the typical statute may give the surviving spouse a particular fractional share of the property, such as one-third or one-half, or a lump-sum amount plus a fractional share of the remaining balance. A statute which provides for a lump-sum amount plus a fractional share allows the surviving spouse to inherit the entire estate if its value is small. Some states give all the property to the surviving spouse if the descendants are the joint descendants of the decedent and the surviving spouse.

2. Community States

870. In community property states, the intestate estate consists of the intestate's separate property and one-half of the community property. Except for Arizona and Wisconsin, there is a different distribution system for community property and for separate property in the other states. The intestate's share of the community property passes to the spouse under the intestate statutes of California, Idaho, Nevada, New Mexico and Washington.[1039] The distribution of the separate property in these states varies.

871. In Arizona,[1040] the surviving spouse receives the intestate's separate property and the intestate's share of the community property if the only surviving descendants are joint descendants of the intestate and the surviving spouse. If any of the descendants are only related to the intestate, the surviving spouse receives one-half of the separate property and none of the intestate's share of the community property.

872. In Louisiana, the descendants receive both the intestate's separate property and the intestate's share of the community property. The intestate's share of the community property is, however, subject to *usufruct* by the surviving spouse. The *usufruct* is similar to a life estate. The spouse receives the intestate's share of the community property if there are no descendants.

1039. California Probate Code §6401-6402 (West, 1991); Idaho Code §15-2-201 (1995); Nevada Revised Statutes Annotated §123.250 (West, 1999); New Mexico Statutes Annotated §45-2-102 (Michie, 1978); and Washington Revised Code Annotated §11.02.070 (West, 1987).

1040. Arizona Revised Statutes §14-2102 (1995).

873. If there are no descendants but the intestate is survived by a parent and siblings or their descendants,[1041] the separate property passes to the siblings or their descendants, but is subject to the *usufruct* of one or both parents. If there are no siblings or their descendants, the parents or parent succeeds to the property. If only the spouse survives, then the spouse, if not judicially separated from the intestate, succeeds to the property to the exclusion of ascendants and collaterals.

874. In Texas, the intestate's half of the community property passes to his issue who survive him by right of representation. The surviving spouse takes this property if there is no surviving issue. If the intestate is survived by issue, the surviving spouse receives one-third of the personal property and a life estate in one-third of the realty. If the intestate dies without issue, the surviving spouse receives all of the separate personal property and one-half of the separate real property. The other half of the separate real property passes to the parents equally or to their survivor, or if there are no parents, to the parents' issue by right of representation. If there are no parents or none of the parents' issue survive, the surviving spouse takes.[1042]

875. California developed the concept of "quasi-community property" to apply to property of persons arriving in California with property that was accumulated in a common law state. This property is reclassified as quasi-community property if such property would have been community property if it had been accumulated in a community state. At the death of the intestate, without this reclassification, the property would be administered as the intestate's separate property. The surviving spouse would fail to have his or her interest protected as it might have been protected in a common law state with the forced share statute. "Quasi community property" descends in the same manner as community property.[1043] Idaho also recognizes the concept of "quasi community property."[1044]

3. The Uniform Probate Code

876. In large estates, the Uniform Probate Code (1990) has attempted to protect adult children of the intestate's prior marriage and their issue from disinheritance if they are the intestate's only descendants, but there is a surviving spouse. The surviving spouse's share, in such a situation, is a graduated sum, based upon the number of years he or she was married to the intestate.

1041. Louisiana differentiates between whole and half-blood siblings and their descendants. The property is divided between the paternal and maternal lines of the deceased; whole siblings take from both lines and the half-blood take in their own line. If there are only half-blood siblings, they take to the exclusion of all relations in the other line. Louisiana Civil Code Annotated Art. 893 (West, 1995).

1042. Texas Probate Code Annotated §155 (West, 1995)(When either spouse dies intestate and the community property passes to the survivor, no administration of the intestate community property is necessary).

1043. California Probate Code §§6101, 6401, 6402.5 (f)-(g) (West, 2003).

1044. Idaho Code §15-2-201 (1995).

B. Descendants

877. Descendants are the intestate's children and the descendants of these children. All states give the entire estate to the decedent's descendants if there is no surviving spouse. No distinction is made between male and female descendants or on the order of birth. If there is a surviving spouse, the descendants take, but subject to that spouse's share. The statutes generally provide a fractional share for the surviving spouse or a lump-sum amount plus a fractional share of the remaining balance. The remaining balance is divided equally among the intestate's descendants by right of representation. Similarly, in the community property states, the descendants receive the remaining balance of the property after the surviving spouse receives his or her share. In many of these states, the descendants succeed to the separate property.

C. Ascendants

878. Ascendants are the persons from whom one is descended: parents, grandparents, great-grandparents, and so forth. At common law, ancestors were excluded from inheriting land under the Canons of Descent, but they were not excluded under the English Statute of Distribution of 1670. If the intestate is neither survived by descendants nor a spouse, most states give the property to the parents or their survivor. If there are no descendants but a surviving spouse, most states allow the parents to take, but subject to the inheritance rights of the surviving spouse. Grandparents of the intestate are usually not heirs unless the intestate's parents left no descendants, that is, the intestate's brothers and sisters and their descendants. Usually, parents and their descendants are specifically listed as a category. Grandparents and their descendants are often specifically listed in the statutes following the category of parents and their descendants. Grandparents and their descendants would take priority over more remote ancestors and their descendants.

879. If more remote ancestors are not listed as a specific category in the intestate statute, they fall under the general category of next of kin if they are to inherit. Many states do not allow remote ancestors to inherit, but do allow their descendants to inherit.

D. Collaterals

880. Collaterals are the intestate's kin who are not ancestors or descendants.[1045] Collaterals inherit only if the intestate does not have a surviving spouse, or surviving descendants, or a surviving parent. A few states may allow collaterals to inherit if there is only a surviving parent.

1045. They are the descendants of the intestate's ancestors, but excluded from this group are the intestate's own descendants and ancestors.

881. Many of the intestate succession statutes set forth the order in which specific categories of collaterals will succeed. Typically, the category of the intestate's siblings and their descendants is one of these ordered categories, usually following the category designating the intestate's parents.[1046]

882. Collaterals who do not fall within one of the specific classes designated in the intestate succession statute fall within the general category of next of kin. The term next of kin refers to the intestate's nearest surviving blood relation, which may be a descendant, an ancestor, or a collateral, although all statutes include the intestate's spouse.[1047] The next of kin is determined by a computation method based upon degrees of kinship. This method is called the civil law method.[1048] The degree of kinship for an intestate and a claimant collateral relation is calculated by counting the number of generations up from the intestate to the closest common ancestor of the intestate and the claimant and down from this common ancestor to the claimant. The total of these two numbers represents the degree of kinship. The next of kin is the claimant collateral with the lowest numerical degree.

II. Representation

883. The Doctrine of Representation, derived from England's Canons of Descent and the Statute of Distribution, pertains to the concept that lineal descendants may represent their deceased ancestors for inheritance purposes. That is, a deceased person in one generation of heirs who leaves a living descendant is represented by that living descendant at the time of distribution. The deceased person serves as a stock through which his lineal descendant, more remotely related to the intestate, may represent him and succeed to the property. All American statutes have some form of representation.[1049] Unlike inheritance by representation, a per capita (by the head) distribution system is concerned with the individual, taking in his or her own right.

884. The Doctrine of Representation is not uniformly applied among the states. The oldest representation system is the English *per stirpes* system (literally meaning "by the stocks"). This system is derived from the Statute of Distribution. If this

1046. The children of the intestate's parents are the siblings (brothers and sisters) of the intestate. The siblings' descendants would be the nieces and nephews of the intestate, great-nieces and nephews, and so forth.

1047. Problems of determining next of kin arise after the exhaustion of the specific categories delineated in the statute. The specific categories list in order the next of kin, usually starting with the intestate's spouse, followed by the intestate's children, etc.

1048. Most statutes are based upon the civil law method of determining degrees of kinship. From one generation to the next generation is a degree of kinship. The degree of kinship for a decedent and a claimant ancestor is calculated by counting the number of generations up from the decedent to the claimant ancestor. The degree of kinship between a decedent and his parent is one; between his grandparent is two, and so forth.

1049. Louisiana defines representation as a "fiction of the law, the effect of which is to put the representative in the place, degree, and rights of the person represented." Louisiana Civil Code Annotated Art. 881 (West, 1995).

system is applied to the intestate's descendants, one would divide the intestate's property into as many shares as there are living children of the intestate and his or her deceased children who have descendants living. Each child, whether living or dead, is a stock. The initial division always starts at the level of the intestate's children, even if all of them are dead at that generational level. After the initial division, the share to a deceased child passes to his or her nearest living descendant. This nearest living descendant represents the deceased child. A small number of states continue to follow this pattern.

885. The majority of the states have modified the English *per stirpes* system. This modified system merely changes the generation at which the initial division is first made. The initial division is made at the nearest generational level where the deceased person has at least one living descendant. This modified system changes the "stocks" from always being at the intestate's children's level to being at the nearest level where someone is living.

886. The Uniform Probate Code (1990) adopted a different system of representation, known as *per capita per generation.* The basis of this system is to allow those persons, who are equally related to the deceased to share equally. Under this system, the initial division is made at the nearest generational level where the deceased person has at least one living descendant. Each living descendant at this level is allocated his or her share. The remaining shares that would be allocated to deceased persons at that generational level leaving descendants, if any, are combined and divided among the representatives on the next generational level. This process continues until all the property has been distributed.

887. Diagram illustrating examples of representation.

	[X]	
	1	
	1	
(A)	**(B)**	**(C)**
__1__	_1_	_1_
D (E) F	**(G)**	**(H)**
___1__	_1__	_1___
I (J)	**(K)**	**L (M)**
__1__	_1__	___1_
N O	**P**	**Q**
-1-		
R		

[X] – The Intestate
() – The person is dead at X's death.

A, B, and C are X's children; all of them predeceased X, the intestate. A has two living children, D and F, and a deceased child E. E has a living child I and a deceased child J. J has two living children, N and O. N has a living child, R. B has a deceased child G. G has a deceased child K. K has a living child, P. C has a deceased child H. H has a living child L and a deceased child M. M has a living child Q.

A. *Distribution of the Intestate's Property under the Common Law Statute of Distribution: The English "Per Stirpes" System*

888. The initial division of the property is at the generation of the intestate's children, even if there are no living children. The property is divided into as many shares as there are living children and deceased children, who have living descendants. Using the diagram, the initial division is made into thirds. All three of X's children leave living descendants to represent them. A, B, and C receive a one-third share, each. A's one-third share is divided into thirds, so that D and F receive a one-ninth share, each. E's one-ninth share is divided by half because his two children, I and J, represent him and take his share. Each of them receives a one-eighteenth share. Since J predeceased the intestate, his share is divided by one-half because he is represented by his two children, N and O. N and O receive a one-thirty-sixth share, each. N's child, R, receives nothing because N is living.

B's one-third share passes to P by representation since both P's grandparent, G, and his parent, K, are dead.

C's one-third share is divided into half because C's child H is dead, but H leaves one living child, L, and one deceased child, M, who has a living descendant. L receives a one-sixth share. M's one-sixth share passes to M's child, Q.

B. *Distribution of the Intestate's Property by the Modern, Modified "Per Stirpes" System*

889. The initial division of the property is made at the nearest generation where there is at least one living descendant of the intestate. The initial division is at the level of X's grandchildren because D and F are living. E, G, H predeceased the intestate, but each has living descendants. The initial division is made into fifths, with D and F, each receiving a one-fifth share of the Intestate's property.

E's one-fifth share is divided into half because he has one living child, I, and a deceased child, J, who has living descendants. I receives a one-tenth share. J's one-tenth share is divided into half, between J's two children, N and O. N and O, each receives a one-twentieth share of the property. N's child, R, shares nothing because N is living.

G's one-fifth share passes to P by representation since his child, K, is dead.

H's one-fifth share is divided into half because he has one living child, L, and a deceased child, M, who has a living descendant, Q. L and Q receive a one-tenth share, respectively.

C. Distribution of the Intestate's Property by the Uniform Probate Code (1990): "Per Capita Per Generation" System

890. The initial division of the property is at the nearest generation where there is at least one living descendant of the intestate. The initial division is at the level of X's grandchildren because D and F are living. The initial division is divided into fifths because D and F are living and the other three grandchildren (E, G, and H) have living descendants to represent them. D and F receive a one-fifth share, each.

The remaining three one-fifth shares are combined and divided among the descendants at the next generational level. The next generational level is the level of X's great-grandchildren. The three remaining one-fifth shares are combined. This three-fifths combined share is divided by five because the division is made into as many shares as there are living great-grandchildren and deceased great-grandchildren, who have living descendants. I and L are living, and J, K and M have living descendants. I and L receive a three-twentieth-fifths share, each.

The three remaining three-twentieth-fifths shares are combined and divided among the descendants at the next generational level. The next generational level is the level of X's great-great-grandchildren. All the descendants at this generational level are living. The three combined three-twentieth-fifth shares represent a combined nine-twentieth-fifth share. This share is divided into fourths because N, O, P, and Q are living. Each of them receives a nine-hundredth share. N's child R receives no share because N is living.

891. Until the first half of this century, the states usually allowed blood relatives to inherit from the intestate no matter how remote their relationship. Many states now exclude more remote collaterals and ancestors. The typical modification cuts off remote collaterals beyond a certain degree of relationship.[1050] All states, however, allow descendants of the decedent to inherit no matter how remote.

III. Succession Rights of Children Born Out of Wedlock (Nonmarital Children)

892. At common law, children of unmarried parents were labeled as *filius nullius*, the child of no one.[1051] They had no right to inherit from either parent. All states have modified the common law and now grant some inheritance rights to them. All states allow nonmarital children to inherit from and through their mothers.

893. Differences still remain among the states as to the rights of nonmarital children to inherit from their fathers. States following the Uniform Parentage Act[1052]

1050. New Hampshire Revised Statutes Annotated §561:1(II) (f) (2003).
1051. W. Blackstone, *Commentaries*, No. 1 *454 (Cooley, 3d ed., 1884).
1052. Uniform Parentage Act §4, *Uniform Laws Annotated*, No. 9B, 295 (2002).

based the rights and obligations between parent and child on the "parent and child relationship," not on the parents' marital relationship. Such a statute requires only proof of paternity.

894. States, not following the Uniform Parentage Act, allow inheritance rights based on one or more of the following circumstances: (1) the legitimation of the child by the child's father marrying the child's mother and acknowledging or recognizing the child as his child; (2) the legitimation of the child through a court proceeding; (3) the father has openly and notoriously acknowledged the child as his own; (4) a court has made an order of filiation; and (5) the father or the father and the mother have followed a specific procedure in executing an instrument, in which the father acknowledges the child.

895. Inheritance rights for nonmarital children are subject to validation under the Equal Protection Clause of the Fourteenth Amendment to the Constitution of the United States. A total statutory bar to inheritance rights is unconstitutional.[1053] A statutory scheme that is not a total bar but serves substantial state interests as related to proof of paternity and efficient administration of a decedent's estate has been found to be valid.[1054]

896. States have modified the common law so that children born to parents, whose marriages are later found to be void or voidable, are legitimate. Similarly, children of a married couple conceived by artificial insemination, where the sperm is not that of the husband, are deemed legitimate if the husband has agreed to the procedure. Many states allow nonmarital children to prove paternity even after the death of the accused father, but the standard of proof for paternity is usually higher than if paternity had been adjudicated prior to death of the accused father.

IV. Adoption

897. All states allow adopted children to inherit from their adoptive parents. Statutes of most states now treat the adopted person as the child of the adoptive parents, which means that the adopted child is treated as a biological child, inheriting from and through his adoptive parents and, similarly, the adoptive family members inheriting from and through the adopted child.[1055]

898. Adoption issues still arise in many states as to whether an adopted child inherits from his or her natural parents and *vice versa*. State legislation is incomplete and case law has not resolved these issues. Many statutes put the adopted child exclusively in the adoptive family for all purposes, however, making an exception

1053. *Trimble v. Gordon*, 430 US 762 (1977).
1054. *Lalli v. Lalli*, 439 US 259 (1978).
1055. J.E. Rein, *Relatives by Blood, Adoption and Association: Who Should Get What and Why?*, 37 Vanderbilt L. Rev. 711 (1984).

for stepparent adoption. Under the stepparent exception, the adopted child inherits from his or her natural parent as well as from the stepparent, who has adopted the child.

899. Adult adoption is usually allowed. Adult adoption may, however, come under attack as a sham or fraudulent adoption or against public policy.[1056]

900. Foster children who have not been legally adopted may obtain inheritance rights in states that recognize the doctrine of equitable adoption (sometimes referred to by the courts as virtual adoption, de facto adoption, or adoption by *estoppel*). The court requires evidence that there was an intent to adopt, but the adoption lacked formality.[1057] The most typical factual context involves the decedent who has agreed to adopt the child but has not completed the formal process. A few states have codified the doctrine.[1058]

901. Conflicts-of-law problems may arise if the adoption occurs in one state and the decedent lives in another. These states may have conflicting laws regarding the inheritance rights of adopted children. Traditionally, the law of the place of the adoption has controlled, but states are not bound by this rule.

§4. The Rights of the State on the *Bona Vacantia*

902. If no heir, as designated in the state's intestate succession statute, claims the intestate's property, the property *escheats* to the state.[1059] The *escheat* provision is part of the intestate succession statute. This provision or a similar one specifies which state agency will receive the property. If a person has received a gift from an ascendant, either by inheritance or by an *inter vivos* gift, and then dies, but has no surviving spouse and children, the gift does not return to the estate of the ascendant. The gift will pass by the intestate succession law as it applies to the deceased person. If the deceased person is survived by grandchildren or great-grandchildren, these descendants would take the property by right of representation. If no descendants survive, most states allow the surviving parents of the deceased person to take.

1056. *In re Adoption of Robert Paul P.*, 471 N.E.2d 424 (N.Y. Ct. App. 1984) (a man was not allowed to adopt his partner).

1057. J.C. Jeffries, Jr., Note, *Equitable Adoption: They Took Him Into Their Home and Called Him Fred*, 58 Virginia L. Rev. 726, 727 (1972).

1058. Cal. Probate Code §6455 (West 1993).

1059. Any unclaimed personal property, including abandoned property, is subject to *escheat* to the state. *See*, e.g., *Delaware v. New York*, 507 US 490, 497 (1993) (states may take custody of abandoned personal property as *bona vacantia* through a process known as *escheat*); Cal. Civ. Proc. Code §1510 (West, 1982) (*escheat* of intangible personal property). In the case of inheritance, real property also *escheats*.

Grandparents of the deceased person are usually not heirs unless the deceased person's parents left no descendants. Collaterals inherit only if the deceased person does not have a surviving spouse, or surviving descendants, or a surviving parent. If there is no heir, the property *escheats* to the state.

903. Statutes of limitations for the *escheat* of an intestate's property to the state are five years and more. *Escheat* proceedings vary among the states.

Chapter 2. Testamentary Succession

904. Americans enjoy liberal testamentary powers, which allow them to dispose of much of their property at death as they wish and to avoid a state's intestate succession law. State limitations on testamentary powers usually concern protection for the surviving spouse and protection for children who are unintentionally disinherited. Notwithstanding these limitations, a testator may act quite capriciously unless such capriciousness violates public policy.[1060]

905. Each state grants testamentary power by statute. These statutes are referred to as the "Wills Act" or the "Statute of Wills." Except for a few states, testamentary power has been considered to be subject only to regulation by state government. It has not been considered a natural right.[1061] The United States Supreme Court's decision in *Hodel v. Irving*, 481 US 704 (1987), however, suggested that a complete abolishment of descent and devise of a particular class of property may be a taking of property without just compensation in violation of the Fifth Amendment to the Constitution of the United States.

906. A will is a device used to set forth the plan for disposing of one's property according to one's wishes. A will may dispose of real and personal property. Most states have a different statute for disposing of the decedent's body parts although it may be part of the Wills Act.[1062] A will may or may not follow the intestate succession statute. A decedent who dies with a valid will is said to have died testate. Historically, if the maker of the will was male, he was called the testator; if female, the testatrix. Today, "testator" is the term generally used regardless of gender. A will is not effective until the death of its maker and can be revoked until the maker's death.

§1. Capacity to Make a Will

I. Testamentary Capacity

907. In order to make a valid will, the testator must have testamentary capacity. Testamentary capacity includes capacity of age, intellect, and freedom from undue influence, duress, coercion and fraud. Capacity to make a will on the basis of gender or marital status or conviction of a crime or alienage is not prohibited in any jurisdiction.

1060. *See*, e.g., *Eyerman v. Mercantile Trust Co.*, 524 S.W.2d 210 (Mo. Ct. App. 1975).

1061. A few states may protect testamentary power as a natural right. *In re Estate of Beale*, 113 N.W.2d 380, 383 (Wis. 1962); *Shriners Hospitals for Crippled Children v. Zrillic*, 563 So. 2d 64, 67–68 (Fla. 1990).

1062. These statutes are modeled after the Uniform Anatomical Gift Act §8, 8A ULA 15 (1987). The will may be one of the instruments for this purpose.

A. Age

908. All states have statutes setting a minimum chronological age requirement. Almost all states set 18 as the minimum age. A few states set the age at majority without defining majority. Georgia and Louisiana set minimum age requirements of 14 and 16, respectively.[1063] Several states allow minors who are married, in the armed service, or emancipated to make a will. If the will is executed below the minimum age requirement, the will is not valid unless it is re-executed or republished by codicil when the maker attains the required age.

B. Mentality

909. All states require that the testator have mental capacity. State statutes usually define mental capacity as "being of sound mind." The judiciary has developed various standards for interpreting "being of sound mind." A testator may lack mental capacity because of mental deficiency or mental derangement.[1064] Mental deficiency means impaired intellect as a result of sickness or advanced age, or a lack of intellect due to mental disability. Mental derangement may mean total insanity of the mind, or it may mean a specific or narrow form of insanity, such as an insane delusion. Not all mental deficiencies or mental derangements will invalidate a will. During periods of sanity, one has the mental capacity to make a will. An insane delusion will invalidate a will if the will or a particular provision of the will was itself the product of the delusion. The parts of the will which were not part of the delusion are valid.[1065]

910. The degree of mental capacity, which is needed to execute a will, is less than that degree, which is required to execute a contract or transact business. The typical standard for defining when one has mental capacity to execute a will has been stated as follows: "If at the time of its execution the testatrix was capable of recollecting her property, the natural objects of her bounty, and their claims upon her, knew the business about which she was engaged, and how she wished to dispose of her property, that is sufficient."[1066] A decline in mental ability may result because of the natural process of aging. The older a person is when he or she executes a will may result in its challenge of validity on the basis of mental capacity.

II. Factors Affecting Testamentary Capacity

911. A testator does not have testamentary capacity to execute a will if the will was procured because of fraud, undue influence, duress or coercion. The purpose of

1063. Ga. Code Ann. §53-2-22 (1996); La. Civ. Code Ann. Arts. 1476, 1477 (1992).
1064. *See generally*, T.E. Atkinson, *The Law of Wills* (2d ed., 1953).
1065. *In re Hargrove's Will*, 28 N.Y.S.2d 571, 573 (NY App. Div. 1941).
1066. *Tabb v. Willis*, 156 SE 556, 564 (Va. App. Div. 1931).

avoiding these factors is to further the policy of freedom of testation. A will must be voluntarily made by the maker. These factors, if present, prevent the testator from voluntarily executing a will.

A. *Fraud*

912. A will is invalid to the extent that it was procured by fraud. Fraud consists of false statements, which are material and known to be false by the person making them, which are made to deceive the testator, and which in fact do deceive the testator and cause the testator to execute the will in reliance upon them.

913. There are two types of fraud. "Fraud in the execution" (also called "fraud in the *factum*") occurs when the testator is deceived as to the nature or the contents of the document that the testator signs. "Fraud in the inducement" occurs when the testator knows the contents of the will, but the will or parts of it were procured by the testator's reliance on false representations.

B. *Undue Influence*

914. A will is invalid to the extent that it was procured by undue influence. The key to this doctrine is the distinction between "influence" and "undue influence" because all wills result from some degree of influence. Undue influence occurs, however, when the influence is such that it not only destroys the free will of the testator but substitutes the volition of another person for that of the testator. Undue influence is rarely proved by direct evidence. If the will or any part of the will was procured by undue influence, the will or that part of it is invalid.

915. There are two primary approaches for proving undue influence. The first approach requires the party alleging undue influence to raise a presumption of undue influence, which then shifts the burden of proof to the other party to prove there was no undue influence. To raise the presumption, the party alleging undue influence has to prove the existence of (1) a confidential relationship between the testator and the influencer and (2) suspicious circumstances surrounding the execution of the will. The majority of the cases that prove undue influence follow this approach. There are variations of this approach among the states.

916. The second approach for proving undue influence requires the party alleging undue influence to prove the elements of undue influence. In some jurisdictions the elements have been stated to be the following: (1) the susceptibility of the testator to undue influence, (2) the opportunity to influence, (3) the disposition to influence, and (4) the desired result.[1067]

1067. *In re Will of Leisch*, 267 NW 268, 271, 272 (Wis. 1936).

C. Duress/Coercion

917. A will or any part of it is invalid if a testator executed the will under duress or coercion. Duress may take a physical or mental form; for example, a testator may be prevented from making a will if he or she is physically restrained.[1068]

D. Remedies

918. If a will or any of its parts were procured by fraud, undue influence, coercion, or duress, the will or its part is invalid and is not admitted to probate.

919. If a will was prevented from being executed or a provision was omitted because of fraud, undue influence, duress or coercion, remedies are more problematic because a probate court cannot write a will for the testator or restore an omitted provision.[1069] The most feasible remedy is the equitable remedy of the constructive trust. The purpose of this remedy is to prevent the wrongdoer from being unjustly enriched. If a constructive trust is imposed, the wrongdoer holds the property in trust for the proper person. If the wrongdoer is not enriched and an innocent party benefits from the wrongdoing, courts differ as to whether to impose a constructive trust over the innocent party's benefits. Courts, which do impose the constructive trust, impose it on the theory that the innocent party would not have benefitted but for the wrongful behavior.[1070] The tort, tortious interference with inheritance, may be another remedy.[1071]

III. Wills Procured by Mistake or Negligence

920. Unless there is a statute to the contrary,[1072] the general rule is that if the will is procured by negligence or by mistake either made by the testator or by a third party, there is no relief. The will is probated. Extrinsic evidence will not be admitted to show the mistake or the negligence. Policy considerations for this rule are based on concern for fraud, on the parole evidence rule, and on the general rule that a will must be in writing.

921. Where there is no applicable statute, some states may provide relief under certain circumstances. The leading case that gives relief where there is a mistake in

1068. *Pope v. Garrett*, 211 S.W.2d 559, 560 (Tex. 1948).
1069. W.H. Page, *Of Forbidding or Hindering the Testator to Make Another Testament*, 1951 Wisc. L. Rev.474, 481 (1951).
1070. *Pope v. Garrett*, 211 S.W.2d 559 (Tex. 1948).
1071. *Peralta v. Peralta*, 131 P.3d 81 (2005).
1072. The attorney who drafted a will may be liable for malpractice under certain circumstances to a third party. Of course, the decedent's estate would have a cause of action if damages were proved.

the inducement is *Gifford v. Dryer*, 2 RI 99, (1852). That case held that both the mistake and what the testator would have done but for the mistake must appear on the face of the will. Recently, there has been a movement to relax this rule.[1073]

§2. Different Types of Wills

I. General Principles

922. The Wills Act of each state defines the types of wills that are valid and the requirements for their execution or revocation.[1074] Except for Louisiana, all states have statutes based upon the English Statute of Frauds, 1677, or the English Wills Act, 1837. Louisiana's Wills Act is derived from the civil law.

923. All states recognize the formal or attested will. About half of the states recognize the holographic will. Historically, the holographic will must be written entirely in the handwriting of the testator, but required no attestation. About twenty states recognize oral wills, which, to be effective, must be reduced to a writing. Several states have promulgated a statutory will. A state statute provides the form, which is the statutory will, and the instructions for its execution.

924. No will, written or oral, is valid unless the testator intended such to be his or her will. The issue of testamentary intent usually arises when an informal document is presented as the testator's will, but it is difficult to determine whether the document was intended to be testamentary. For example, letter wills are often litigated on this point. Testamentary intent must appear on the face of the document. Most jurisdictions, therefore, do not allow extrinsic evidence be used to prove that the document is testamentary.[1075] The issue of testamentary intent also arises in connection with conditional and sham wills.

II. Attested Wills

925. The attested will is the basic will used in the United States. The Wills Act enumerates certain formalities, which must be followed for a will to be valid. These formalities provide greater security that a particular document is in fact the will of the decedent. These formalities serve important security functions, including those

---

1073. J.H. Langbein & L.W. Waggoner, *Reformation of Wills on the Ground of Mistake: Change of Direction in American Law*, 130 U. of Pennsylvania L. Rev. 521 (1982); *In re Matter of Snide*, 418 N.E.2d 656 (NY Ct. App. 1981) (mistake in signing wrong will).

1074. The jurisdiction over will formalities is left to the states; however, the federal government of the United States must approve the Wills Act of the District of the Columbia. The federal government also approves wills of tribal Indians who are disposing of allotted land. (25 USC §373.) *See also* M. Taylor, *Modern Practice in the Indian Courts*, 10 U. of Puget Sound L. Rev. 231 (1987). The United States has not ratified the International Wills Act convention.

1075. *In re Kauffman's Estate*, 76 A.2d 414 (Pa. 1950); *In re Larin's Estate*, 424 A.2d 1290 (1981).

of ritual, evidentiary, protection, and procedure.[1076] The formalities of the attested will require that the will be in writing, signed by the testator, and attested to by witnesses.

A. Writing

926. The writing may be in any form, in any language if someone can translate it, and upon some reasonably permanent record. No court has accepted videotaped and recorded wills as forms, meeting the writing requirement, except Nevada has enacted a statute authorizing wills to be documented by electronic records.[1077]

B. Signature

927. All statutes require that a testator sign the will. In most states, a testator may sign by mark. The testator must have intended that whatever he or she writes as a signature is intended to be his or her signature. The signature requirement is satisfied if the testator is assisted in writing the signature. Assistance must not be confused with signature by proxy. A signature by assistance occurs if the testator holds the writing instrument while another guides the testator's hand. Some courts recognize signature by assistance if the testator touches the writing instrument while another is writing the signature.

928. Most state statutes provide that the signature requirement may be satisfied by allowing the signing be by proxy, that is, by another person. These statutes usually require that the proxy sign the testator's name only at the direction of the testator and in the presence of the testator.

929. The vast majority of states following the English Statute of Frauds do not designate any particular location for the testator's signature. The other states, following the English Statute of Wills, designate that the signature be "subscribed" or "signed at the end." The majority of the latter states do not follow a literal interpretation of "the end" but follow the "logical end" interpretation, that is, wherever the end of the will logically appears on the paper.

C. Attestation

1. Number and Competency of Witnesses

930. The will must be attested to by the number of witnesses designated in the Wills Statute. With the exception of Vermont which requires three witnesses and

1076. J.H. Langbein, *Substantial Compliance With the Wills Act*, 88 Harvard L. Rev. 489 (1975).
1077. Nev. Rev. Stat. 133.085 (2001)(setting out the requirements of the electronic will).

Louisiana, the other states require at least two witnesses. Some statutes require that the witnesses be "credible;" other statutes use the terminology "competent." The witness must be competent at the time of the execution of the will. First, the witness must be mentally competent. Second, unless an age is specified in the statute, a minor may be a witness as long as he or she is competent to testify in court. No prudent testator should choose a witness who is a minor.

931. At common law, a witness was not deemed competent if the witness was an interested witness, meaning that the witness was a beneficiary under the will. Most states have enacted "purging statutes," which eliminate the witness's interest in the will and thereby making the witness competent. The majority of these purging statutes do not eliminate the share altogether, but only to the extent that the share exceeds what the witness either would take as an heir of the testator or would take under the testator's prior will.

932. At common law, a witness was also disqualified if his or her spouse was a beneficiary under the will. Some of the purging statutes extend to the spouse of the witness although most states do not disqualify the witness if the witness's spouse is a will beneficiary.

2. To What the Witnesses Attest

933. Witnesses attest to the testator's acts, which are required in the execution of the will, and also to the testator's testamentary capacity. The testator's acts authenticate the fact that the will is the testator's will. The witnesses do not have to know that the document is a will unless the Wills Statute requires the formality of publication. The publication formality requires the testator to indicate to the witnesses that the document is a will. Disclosure of the contents of the will is not necessary in any state, except in Louisiana.

934. The witnesses also attest to the testator's capacity to execute a will, including his or her capacity in age and mentality, and being free of fraud, undue influence, and duress.

3. The Presence Requirement

935. Some states have relaxed the formality, requiring the witnessing of the testator's signing of the will. These states allow the testator to acknowledge his or her signature to the witness as well. Many statutes, however, require the testator to sign the will in the "presence" of the witnesses or acknowledge his or her signature in the "presence" of them or that the witnesses attest in the "presence" of the testator and each other. The interpretation of "presence" varies. The majority of states which did not enact the pre-1990 Uniform Probate Code follow the line-of-vision test. This test does not require that the testator actually see the signing but he or she must be in a position to see if he or she cared to look. Other states follow the conscious presence test, which all states follow for blind testators. This test allows the testator to use any of his or her senses to comprehend that a witness is in the act of signing.

936. States following the pre-1990 Uniform Probate Code eliminate the presence requirement and require the witnesses to "witness" the testator's act of "signing" or "acknowledging," which requires them to observe the act. The current Uniform Probate Code codified the conscious presence test.

937. Statutes, eliminating the presence requirement in the attestation formality, may focus the issue on whether attesting and signing by the witnesses are contemporaneous acts. Attestation is the mental act of observing. Signing the will is certifying that attestation occurred. If attesting and signing are contemporaneous acts, there can be no time lag between them. If they are not contemporaneous acts, however, the issue becomes: how much time lag may be between them. One court interpreted its statute to require signing by the witnesses to be within a reasonable time, even after the death of the testator so long as it was reasonable.[1078] The current Uniform Probate Code codified the reasonable standard.

4. The Request Requirement

938. A few states require that the testator request the witnesses to attest to the will. The courts have interpreted a request to include words, gestures, or a request by another if the testator agrees. A prudent testator would request the witnesses to attest even if there were no statutory requirement.

5. The Order of Signing

939. The majority of states require no order of signing between the testator and witnesses as long as they all sign as part of a single, continuous transaction. A minority of states, however, requires the testator to sign first. The testator should, as a prudent matter, sign the will before the witnesses sign.

6. Signature Requirements of the Witnesses

940. Witnesses may sign any place on the will unless the statute requires signing at the end or subscription. The form of the witnesses' signatures follows the same requirements as applied to the signature of the testator. Although the statutes do not provide for signature by proxy, the majority of courts allow the witness to

---

1078. *In re Estate of Peters*, 526 A.2d 1005, 1012–1013 (NJ 1987).

sign by proxy. As a prudent matter, witnesses should sign beneath the attestation clause if there is one; or, in the absence of such a clause, to the left of the testator's signature.

7. Purpose of the Attestation Clause

941. Although no state requires one, an attestation clause sets forth the formalities to which the witnesses attest. The formalities stated in the attestation clause should repeat those required in the Wills Act. This clause is important legally because it raises a rebuttable presumption that the formalities enumerated in the clause took place.

D. Self-Proving Affidavit

942. The majority of the states provides for self-proving affidavits although no state requires this affidavit as a formality for execution. The purpose of the self-proving affidavit differs among the states. The initial purpose of the affidavit was to preserve the testimony of the witnesses. Thus, the witnesses were the only ones to sign (before a notary public or similar officer) the affidavit, detailing the formalities followed at the execution of the will. The affidavit is used instead of the personal testimony of the witnesses. Some states may use the self-proving affidavit to raise a conclusive presumption that the formalities for execution were followed.

943. A second form of the affidavit has also developed, which provides for the testator and the witnesses to sign the affidavit, which details the formalities that were followed at the execution of the will. This self-proving affidavit is viewed as a separate instrument from the will even though it could be executed at the same time as the will is executed and even be on the same paper as the will. In some states, the purpose of the second form of the self-proving affidavit is not only to preserve the testimony of the witnesses but also to raise a conclusive presumption that the formalities for execution were followed.

944. A third form of the affidavit has also developed. The testator's and witnesses' signing of the affidavit also serves as the testator's signature to the will and the attestation by the witnesses. This third form combines in one step, both the signing and attesting of the will and the execution of the self-proving affidavit. It may raise a conclusive presumption that the formalities of the Wills Act were properly followed.

E. The Ordinary Attested Will in Louisiana

945. Louisiana has modified its former law providing for three types of ordinary attested wills, designated as the statutory will, and has combined them into one will, which is now called the notarial testament. In Louisiana, in addition to attestation, the ordinary attested will, now the notarial testament, requires execution before a notary public. The notarial will provides specifically for persons who are literate and able to sign their name, for persons with sight impairment or who are illiterate, and for persons who are literate but use braille.[1079] Wills executed before the revision remain valid.

III. Holographic Wills

946. Holographic wills are recognized in over half of the states. The important features of the traditional holographic will are: it must be written entirely in the testator's handwriting, be signed by the testator, and requires no witnesses (unattested). The handwriting must be established to be that of the testator at the time the will is offered for probate. A few jurisdictions require a certain number of witnesses to prove that the testator's handwriting is authentic. Some states require the will be dated. A few states require that the signature be "at the end" of the will and interpret "at the end" the same as they do for attested wills. The holographic will in Louisiana is called the olographic testament.

947. Some jurisdictions have relaxed the requirement of the will being "entirely" in the testator's handwriting and thus, have validated holographic wills whose material parts are in the testator's handwriting, although the testator must still personally sign the will. Other jurisdictions will ignore the non-handwriting parts if they can be construed as superfluous. If the handwriting requirement is not satisfied, the will must be attested to as any other formal will is required to be attested to in order to be valid.

IV. Oral Wills

A. Nuncupative Wills

948. A nuncupative will, as defined in this section, is an oral will that is not limited to testators who are soldiers and sailors. Statutes in fifteen states authorize the nuncupative will. Such wills are usually limited to persons in their last sickness, usually requiring them to be at home. The oral statements, made by the testator witnesses, must be meant to be his or her will and not just oral instructions for drafting a will. The number of witnesses that must witness the testator's oral statements are designated in the state statute; usually, the number is two. The time period in which the witnesses must put their testimony in writing is also designated by statute. Most statutes only allow the testator to dispose of personal property, often limited in value to USD 1,000.

1079. La. Stat. Ann. Civ Code §1576-1580.1 (West, 1999).

B. Soldiers' and Sailors' Wills

949. Nine states statutorily recognize oral wills if they are made by soldiers in actual military service or by sailors at sea. These wills are limited to the disposal of personal property, whose value is generally not limited. They are not as important now because of the current military practice to provide for the execution of wills as part of the induction procedures. There has been no litigation challenging these military testamentary instruments.

V. Statutory Wills

950. A statutory will is a state-authorized form for a will. It is intended to be used by people who will not be using the services of an attorney. The execution requirements are similar to the state's attested will requirements. California was the first state to authorize the statutory will. Michigan, Wisconsin, and Maine have also enacted statutory will statutes.

VI. Louisiana: Civil Law Wills

951. Louisiana has extensively reformed the types of wills it recognizes. It now recognizes only two types of wills: the notarial testament and the olographic testament.

A. The Nuncupative Will (Repealed)

952. Louisiana has repealed the recognition of the nuncupative will. The notarial testament provides in its provisions for the former nuncupative will.

953. The "nuncupative testament by private signature" is no longer recognized.

B. The "Mystic," "Secret", or "Closed" Will (Repealed)

954. The "mystic," "secret", or "closed" will is no longer recognized as being obsolete and unnecessary. Recognized today only in Louisiana under limited circumstances, a mystic will is secretly drafted and signed, then given by the maker to a notary public who endorses it on the envelope in the presence of at least three witnesses.

VII. Unattested Documents

A. *Substantial Compliance*

955. The formalities (writing, signing, attesting) required to execute the attested will are meant to be strictly complied with. They serve important functions to ensure that the document is in fact the testator's will. Strict compliance, however, invalidates wills that have very slight imperfections.[1080] In 1990, the Restatement (Second) of Property took a position, favoring the doctrine of substantial compliance. New Jersey has judicially adopted the doctrine of substantial compliance.[1081] The interpretation of what is meant by substantial compliance is still unsettled because of the scarcity of cases. One approach would be to apply the doctrine if the defect was minimal, that is, near perfect compliance. A second approach would be to apply the doctrine "if the testator's conduct served the purposes of the Wills Act."[1082]

B. *Dispensing Power*

956. The 1990 Uniform Probate Code[1083] adopted the dispensing power approach to validate wills which did not strictly comply with the formalities of the Wills Act. This approach follows the approach of several of the Australian States. The dispensing power approach dispenses with a required formality, such as attestation, and validates the defective document as the testator's will if it is established by clear and convincing evidence that the decedent intended that the document be the decedent's will. A number of states have enacted a dispensing power statute based on the Uniform Probate Code.[1084]

C. *Incorporation by Reference*

957. Most states recognize the doctrine of incorporation by reference. This doctrine allows an unattested document to be incorporated into a validly executed will if the following requirements are satisfied. First, the will must describe the unattested document with certainty, refer to the document as being in existence at the time of the execution of the will, and show the intent to incorporate. Second, the document must in fact be in existence at the time of execution of the will and must

---

1080. Several academicians have advocated that the states should adopt a substantial compliance doctrine or a dispensing power policy, following several Australian federal states. *See*, e.g., J.H. Langbein, "Excusing Harmless Errors in the Execution of Wills: A Report on Australia's Tranquil Revolution in Probate Law", No. 87, *Columbia Law Review*, (1987), p. 1; but *see*, W.F. Ormiston, *Formalities and Wills: A Plea for Caution*, 54 Austrl. L. J. 451 (1980).

1081. *In re Will of Ranney*, 589 A.2d 1339, 1342–1344 (NJ 1991).

1082. J.H. Langbein, *Excusing Harmless Errors in the Execution of Wills: A Report on Australia's Tranquil Revolution in Probate Law*, 87 Columbia L. Rev. 1, 41–45 (1987).

1083. UPC §2-503 (1990), amended by UPC §2-503 (1993) (1996 pocket part).

1084. MT. Code Ann §72-2-523 (1993); Estate of Hall, 51 P.3d 1134 (2002)(admitting will under the dispensing power statute).

be shown as the document described in the will. The provisions in the incorporated document are valid to distribute property as if the document had been validly executed as a will.[1085]

D. *Doctrine of Facts of Independent Significance*

958. The Doctrine of Independent Significance allows a will to dispose of property by reference to unattested documents or acts, as long as these documents or acts have a purpose independent of only disposing of the testator's property at his or her death. If a document's only purpose is to dispose of the testator's property at death, then that document will fail to dispose of the property unless it has met the requirements of the Wills Act.[1086] For example, a provision in a will devising property to a trustee of an *inter vivos* trust would be valid under this doctrine because the *inter vivos* trust has significance as a trust, which is independent of its being used only to dispose of the testator's property at death.[1087] The doctrine is also known as Acts or Events of Independent Significance or the Doctrine of Nontestamentary Acts.

VIII. Sham and Conditional Wills

A. *Sham Wills*

959. Sham wills are not intended to be valid wills when they are executed. Since they lack testamentary intent, they should not be probated. However, without extrinsic evidence showing that they are shams, the documents appear to be valid wills. The danger of permitting extrinsic evidence to show that a will is a sham puts all wills in jeopardy of being challenged by extrinsic evidence. Most courts will not allow extrinsic evidence to prove the will is a sham unless the evidence is clear and convincing.

B. *Conditional Wills*

960. The continued validity of a will may be conditioned upon certain circumstances. Depending upon the circumstances, the will ceases to be the valid will at the testator's death. If the words of the will are ambiguous as to whether the will is a conditional will, the favored rule of construction is to construe the words, if they can be so interpreted, as those of motive or inducement for making the will, and not

---

1085. *Bryan's Appeal*, 58 A 748 (Conn. 1904).
1086. *Hastings v. Bridge*, 166 A 273 (N.H. 1933).
1087. Most states do not have to rely solely on this doctrine in order for a testator to transfer property to an *inter vivos* trust. They have enacted statutes called "pour over" statutes, which permit a devise to a trust. These statutes are modeled after the Uniform Testamentary Additions to Trusts Act.

as those of condition. For example, a testator may execute a will on the condition that it is to be valid only if the testator dies under certain circumstances.

IX. Codicil

961. A codicil is a subsequent will that amends a prior written will. It is usually not meant to supplant the prior will altogether. A will and a codicil are separate instruments for execution purposes. A codicil is executed in the same manner as prescribed by the state's Wills Act for attested or holographic wills. A will may have more than one codicil.

§3. The Joint Will and the Mutual Will

962. A joint will is one document executed by two or more persons as the will of each of them. A joint will is probated and administered at the death of each testator. Litigation may arise in the context as to whether the joint will implies a contract so that all of the testators are bound not to revoke the will.[1088]

963. Mutual wills are the separate wills of different persons, but each of the wills contains reciprocal provisions. Unless there is a contract not to revoke, these wills are revocable just as any other will is revocable. However, if mutual wills are not carefully drafted, they may be vulnerable to a court implying that the wills were executed pursuant to a contract. Such an interpretation would require that the property be distributed according to these wills. Revocation of either of these wills would then be a breach of contract. Frequently, spouses execute mutual wills.[1089] To assure that mutual wills will not be vulnerable to attack as a will contract not to revoke either of the wills, the drafter should draft a provision specifically stating that fact in each will.

964. A joint and mutual will is a joint will which contains reciprocal provisions. Courts may refer to mutual wills as joint and mutual wills. Joint wills or joint and mutual wills should be cautiously undertaken. Invariably, they invite litigation.

§4. Revocation of a Will

I. General Principles

965. Wills may be revoked by (1) operation of law, (2) by a physical act to the will, either to the paper or to the writing, or (3) expressly or impliedly by a subsequent writing. Each state's Wills Act sets forth the formalities for the latter two

1088. *Shimp v. Huff*, 556 A.2d 252 (Md. Ct. App. 1989).
1089. *O'Connor v. Immele*, 43 N.W.2d 649, 653 (ND 1950).

methods of revocation. Unless the formalities are satisfied, the revocation is ineffective. Except for Louisiana, the formalities for revocation are derived either from the English Statute of Frauds (1677) or the English Wills Act (1837).[1090] A revocation by a physical act or by a subsequent writing must be done with the intent to revoke. A will may be revoked entirely or partially.

966. The same requirements for testamentary capacity that are required for the execution of a will must be satisfied for a valid revocation by physical act or by a subsequent writing. The revocation must be of the testator's own free choice. If the revocation is procured by undue influence, fraud, duress, or coercion, the revocation is invalid.[1091]

II. Methods of Revocation

A. Operation by Law

967. With the increase of divorce, almost all states have enacted statutes revoking the provisions of a will in favor of a spouse upon divorce. Many of these statutes also apply to the annulment of a marriage. Most statutes allow the testator to prevent revocation by operation of law at divorce or annulment if the will expressly has such a provision. About half of the states revive the will if the spouses remarry. The remaining states provide for revocation by operation of law if the divorce is accompanied by a property settlement.

968. At common law, a woman's will executed before marriage was revoked by operation of law upon marriage, while a man's will executed before marriage was revoked by operation of law upon the marriage and the birth of a subsequent child. Very few states still revoke a will upon marriage, but they do allow the testator to prevent the revocation by a provision in the will.

B. By Physical Act

969. All states allow revocation by physical act.[1092] The physical act must be accompanied by the intent to revoke. Each state's Wills Act must be consulted for the required formalities. Typically, the physical acts include tearing, burning, canceling, destroying, or obliterating. Canceling and obliterating are typically construed to mean acts done to the writing on the paper. Difficulties have arisen when the testator writes a statement of cancellation on the margin or back of the will. This type of revocation cannot be sustained as a writing because it does not satisfy all

1090. Louisiana's wills act is derived from the civil law.

1091. *See* Part 4, Chapter 2, s. 1.

1092. The Louisiana Code contains no provision enumerating physical acts although it refers to tacit revocations. La. Civ. Code Ann. Art. 1607 (West, 1997). Case law has recognized revocation of a will by destruction. *Rivette v. Moreau*, 341 So. 2d 459, (La. Ct. App. 1976).

the formalities required for revocation by a subsequent writing. The majority of jurisdictions will not uphold this type of writing as the physical act of canceling because the statement itself does not touch the writing of the will.

970. Revocation by physical act by another person is allowed if the act is done at the direction of and in the presence of the testator. Similar problems of interpretation of direction and presence arise as they do in the execution of the will.[1093]

971. About half of the states allow for the partial revocation of a will by physical act. In these states, partial revocation by physical act may be problematic in interpreting as to whether the act revokes the will entirely or partially. If the required formalities and intent to revoke are satisfied, the partial revocation is effective. If the partial revocation of the words of a provision changes the construction of the remainder of the provision, the revocation is ineffective.

972. If the revocation of a will, either entirely or partially, is ineffective, the entire or partial will clause remains in effect and is probated unless it cannot be read because the attempted act has made it unreadable. An attempt shall be made to prove what the prior writing was before the ineffective revoking act took place. If the prior writing cannot be proved, the result is the same as if the revocation had been effective.

973. A codicil is a subsequent will that amends a prior will; it is not meant to replace the prior will. For execution purposes, a will and a codicil are separate instruments. However, revocation by physical act to a will revokes its codicil unless it is proved that the codicil is not dependent on the will. Revocation of a codicil, however, does not revoke the will.

C. Subsequent Writing

974. All states allow revocation by a subsequent writing. The writing may be a later will, a codicil to a will, or an informal writing revoking the will. The subsequent writing may revoke a will entirely or partially. The writing may revoke a previous will expressly or by inconsistency. The writing must be properly executed, and executed with the intent to revoke. The formalities are usually the same as those that are required for executing a will. The writing may be signed by proxy if done at the direction and in the presence of the testator.

975. Even if there is no express revocation clause in the later will, all states allow wills to be revoked by a later inconsistent will. The provisions in the wills that are not inconsistent are probated as part of the testator's will. The inconsistent provision in the wills that was executed last in point of time prevails over earlier ones. There may be difficulty in determining whether a later inconsistent will is supplementary to or a replacement of the previous will. The 1990 Uniform Probate

1093. *See* paras. 890–892.

Code tries to resolve this difficulty by creating several rebuttable presumptions to be rebutted by clear and convincing evidence. The UPC raises a rebuttable presumption that a subsequent will replaces a previous will if it makes a complete disposition of all of the testator's property. A rebuttable presumption is also raised that a subsequent will is supplementary to a previous will if the latter one contains provisions that do not make a complete disposition of the testator's property.[1094]

D. Substantial Compliance and UPC Section 2-503

976. Unless the formalities required for revocation are strictly complied with, the attempted revocation is void. If, however, a state has adopted the substantial compliance doctrine or the dispensing power approach adopted by the Uniform Probate Code (1990), the imperfect compliance may still revoke the will. These doctrines are interpreted in the same manner as they are interpreted in the execution of a will.[1095]

III. Revalidation of a Revoked Will

977. A testator may want to revalidate a revoked will. If the will was revoked by a physical act, the usual procedure is to draft and execute a new will. If the will has not been revoked by a physical act, the will may be revalidated by republication by codicil or revived under the revival doctrine. A will that was revoked by a writing or a physical act may also be revalidated under the doctrine of dependent relative revocation.

A. Republication by Codicil

978. A codicil may republish and revalidate a revoked will. The codicil must be executed, satisfying all the formalities required in the Wills Act. The revoked will must, in fact, be in existence. The codicil must be executed with the intent to republish the revoked will and must describe the revoked will with reasonable certainty and as being in existence. A revoked will is republished and revalidated as of the date of the execution of the codicil. A will that has never been valid is validated for the first time at republication of that will by codicil. Intervening invalid codicils are also validated if the codicil specifically refers to them.

B. Revival Doctrine

979. The doctrine of revival arises under the following circumstances: Will #1 has been revoked by Will #2, either expressly or by inconsistency. Will #2 is then

1094. UPC §2-509 (1993) (1996 pocket part).
1095. *See* Part 4, Chapter 2, s. 2, Part VII.

revoked by physical act. All states recognize that revocation by physical act is instantaneous. Does Will #1 remain revoked or is it now revived by the revocation of Will #2 by physical act? Many states do not recognize revival under these circumstances and require that Will #1 be re-executed or republished by codicil. The remaining states recognize revival under either of the following circumstances. States, following the common law rule, always permit revival of Will #1 under these circumstances on the theory that revocation by a written instrument is effective only at the death of the testator. If the revoking instrument (Will #2) is no longer in existence, it cannot revoke Will #1. States, following the civil law rule, do not recognize the automatic revival of Will #1 under these circumstances, but permit revival of Will #1 if it can be proved that when the testator revoked Will #2 it was with the intent that Will #1 be revived.

980. Many states that revoke a will or a portion of a will by operation of law upon divorce or annulment automatically revive the will upon the remarriage of the former spouses to one another.

C. Dependent Relative Revocation

981. The doctrine of dependent relative revocation is an equitable doctrine, based upon a theory of mistaken revocation. This doctrine may be best described as "a fictional process which consists of disregarding revocation brought about by mistake on the feigned ground that the revocation was conditional."[1096] Unlike revival, where there was a revocation, the doctrine of dependent relative revocation holds that there was no absolute revocation, but rather a conditional one. The courts usually limit the application of the doctrine to situations where there is an alternative will that is either valid or invalid, or where the mistake physically appears on the face of the revoking instrument.

982. Most courts apply the doctrine of dependent relative revocation to revocation by a subsequent instrument as well as revocation by a physical act. When the revocation is by a physical act, courts liberally admit extrinsic evidence to prove the mistake and to show the conditional intent of the testator. If the revocation is by a subsequent instrument containing an expressed revocation clause, extrinsic evidence is not admitted unless the mistake appears on the face of the will.

983. This doctrine should be applied to carry out the testator's presumed intent and not as a rule of substantive law. Even if the circumstances are those in which the doctrine would usually apply, the court should make further inquiry as to whether the testator would have wanted the application of this doctrine.[1097]

1096. T.E. Atkinson, *The Law of Wills* §88, 454 (2d ed., 1953).

1097. If the testator revokes a will under the mistaken belief that an earlier will may be revived, but the earlier will may not be revived because the state does not recognize revival, the doctrine would recognize the later will as having never been revoked absolutely, but only conditionally, upon the

§5. PROVISIONS IN A WILL

984. A will generally contains introductory and revocation clauses, diverse administrative provisions, dispositive provisions, and executory provisions. A will should include a heading, identifying the document as the testator's last will and testament.

I. The Introductory and Revocation Clauses

985. The first provision in a will is usually the introductory clause, often called the exordium clause. In this clause, the testator identifies him or herself by name, identifies his or her domicile, and declares that this instrument is his or her will. The testator usually declares his or her competency to make a will in this clause. The next clause is usually the revocation clause, which revokes all prior wills. Often, the introductory and revocation clauses are combined. A revocation clause is not required, but every will should contain one so that it is clear that all previous wills are revoked.[1098]

II. Administrative Provisions

A. Burial Provisions

986. The will usually has a provision providing for payment of burial expenses and the erection of a grave marker. Many state statutes limit these expenses to a statutory amount unless a will provision provides for a payment in excess of this limit. In many states, a general provision for the payment of burial expenses is not sufficient to override the statutory limit, but a provision must be specifically drafted, stating that burial expenses are not to be limited by the statutory requirement.

B. Debts and Taxes

987. The will usually contains a provision requiring the payment of the testator's debts. Unless the property is exempt from satisfying debts, this clause is redundant in the sense that the testator's debts must be paid before any property is disbursed to the beneficiaries.

---

revival of the earlier will. Before applying the doctrine, a court should determine whether the testator would rather die intestate than having the later will not be revoked. For example, if the beneficiaries are very different under the later will from those under the will that the testator thought would be revived, the court may presume that the intent of the testator would be not to apply the doctrine. The testator would rather die intestate under such circumstances. (*In re Callahan's Estate*, 29 N.W.2d 352, 355 (Wis. 1947)).

1098. If the instrument is a codicil to amend an existing will, the introductory clause should clearly identify the instrument as a codicil and identify the will and other codicils that it is amending.

988. The will may contain a clause directing the payment of inheritance and estate taxes. Inheritance taxes are imposed by most states on the property passing to the beneficiaries. Without a direction in the will, each beneficiary is directly responsible for paying this tax levied on his or her inherited property. The direction in the will may provide that the taxes be paid by the decedent's estate or by the beneficiaries who receive the property. If there is no direction, the beneficiaries receiving the property pay the inheritance taxes.

989. The federal government and many states also impose an estate tax on both probate and non-probate property. A provision, allocating how these federal and state estate taxes should be paid, may be an important part of estate planning in determining whether the estate should bear the tax burden, which would mean that probate assets would be used to pay the tax; or, whether the estate tax burden should be apportioned among all the assets, i.e., both probate and non-probate.

C. Personal Representative

990. A will usually contains a provision appointing a personal representative, who will administer the estate. The older term for personal representative and still used is "executor" if male or "executrix" if female. The will usually appoints a successor to the personal representative if the original personal representative does not qualify under state law or does not accept the appointment or resigns. If the will does not appoint a personal representative, the probate court will appoint one. The will usually sets forth the duties and powers that the testator confers on the personal representative. Such duties and powers are in addition to those imposed by law. A will often waives the statutory requirement for a bond for the personal representative. Many jurisdictions recognize this provision by requiring a nominal bond.

D. Guardian

991. If the testator has a minor child, the will usually appoints a guardian for the person of the child and a guardian for the property of the child. The guardian of the person and of the property may be the same person or institution. A financial institution is often appointed as the guardian of the child's property. The guardian of the person is referred to as the testamentary guardian. In many states, the appointment by the will of the testamentary guardian is binding on the court.

E. Testamentary Trust

992. If the will provides for a testamentary trust, there will be provisions appointing a trustee or trustees and setting forth the trustee's duties and powers. A will often waives the statutory requirement for a bond for the trustee.

993. If the will contains a trust, a savings clause should also accompany the trust. The trust will be invalid if it violates the Rule Against Perpetuities. The savings clause "saves" the trust in case there is a violation.

F. "No Contest Clause" or In Terrorem Clause

994. Many jurisdictions recognize an "*in terrorem*" or "no contest" clause, which conditions the beneficiary's share in the will on the basis of not contesting the will. If the beneficiary does contest the will and wins the contest, the no contest clause has no effect because the will is defeated as the will of the testator. Even if the beneficiary does not succeed in defeating the will in the contest, some jurisdictions will give no effect to the no contest clause if the contest was entered into in good faith.

G. Planning for the Unified Credit and the Marital Deduction

995. A will may contain provisions to take advantage of federal estate tax savings by using the unified credit and the marital deduction.[1099]

H. Miscellaneous Administrative Provisions

1. Simultaneous Death and Survivorship Provisions

996. The testator may decide not to rely upon statutory provisions defining simultaneous death and survivorship. In that case, the will provides the definition of these terms.

2. Definitions

997. A will may provide definitions which might be useful if the will needs to be construed and interpreted. It may define such terms as *per stirpes*, representation, or child. It may also provide that certain gender, singular, or plural words are not to be construed as words of limitation.

3. The Negative Will

998. The purpose of a negative will clause is to override the intestate succession statute so that if property fails to pass under the will, it will not pass to the heir. The provision may apply to an individual or to a class. Negative will provisions have

1099. *See* Part 4, Chapter 3, s. 1, Part III.

usually been unenforceable. The 1990 Uniform Probate Code has, however, embraced the concept of the negative will. New York also recognizes this concept in its Wills Act.[1100]

III. Dispositive Provisions

A. Non-residuary Personal Property

999. Personal property passing under a will is classified as a bequest. If it passes in the form of a cash gift, it is usually classified as a legacy. Personal property can be further classified as a specific bequest if the property can be specifically identified from all of the other personal property. If it cannot be specifically identified and is not part of the residuary, it is classified as a general bequest. A legacy is usually classified as general and not specific unless it is to be satisfied from a specific source.

B. Non-residuary Real Property

1000. Real property is classified as a devise. A devise may be classified as a specific devise if the real estate can be specifically identified from all of the other real property. A devise may be classified as a general devise if it is not specifically defined nor part of the residuary.

C. Exoneration

1001. At common law, the Doctrine of Exoneration provided that the devisee of real property was entitled to have the land pass to him or her free of any debt unless the will showed a contrary intent. This doctrine is now limited to specific devises and not to general or residuary ones. Many jurisdictions have abolished the doctrine following the Uniform Probate Code. The will provision should clearly indicate whether the property should pass with any indebtedness to the beneficiary or whether the indebtedness should be paid by the estate.

D. The Residuary Clause

1002. If the estate is disposed of by several clauses, the will usually contains a catch-all clause disposing of the remaining estate, which is called the residuary clause. The purpose of the residuary clause is to make certain that all the property

1100. UPC §2-101(b) (1990) as amended, UPC §2-101(b) (2008 Electronic Pocket Part); and NY Est. Powers & Trusts Law §1-2.18 (McKinney, 1996).

is disposed of by the will so that none of it will pass by intestate succession. However, a will may not have a residuary clause and still dispose of all the property by the will. All of the estate may be disposed of in a single clause.

E. Outright Gifts, Trusts and Pour over Provisions

1003. Beneficiaries under a will may receive property as an outright gift. Outright gifts may be made to minors. However, because minority is a legal disability, distribution must be made to the child's guardian. Statutes based on the Uniform Transfers to Minors Act and the Uniform Gift to Minors Act provide a simplified method for making such gifts and appointing a custodian.

1004. Beneficiaries under a will may receive property as beneficiaries under a trust created in the will. The trust, called a testamentary trust, usually allows the court to continue to supervise the management of the trust until it terminates. The testamentary trust is often used when the beneficiaries are minors or legally disabled.

1005. A trust created during the lifetime of an individual (called living or *inter vivos* trusts) may itself be a beneficiary under a will in most states. Statutes have been enacted to allow the will disposition to "pour over" into the living trust. In addition to "pour over" statutes, many states recognize the validity of a living trust as a beneficiary of a will under the doctrine of independent significance, where the trust is considered as an entity independent of the will.

F. Charitable Gifts

1006. Almost all states have eliminated restrictions on charitable or religious gifts under *mortmain* statutes. These statutes limit or prohibit such gifts if the death of the testator occurred within a certain period of time after the execution of the will or the amount of the gift.[1101]

G. Anatomical Gifts

1007. All states have modified the common law's nonrecognition of a decedent's property rights in his or her body. Any direction in a decedent's will as to the disposition of his or her body or any of its parts was merely unenforceable requests. All jurisdictions have enacted statutes modeled after the Uniform Anatomical Gift Act.[1102] These Acts provide that any competent person of a certain age may donate

1101. *See*, e.g., Ga. Code Ann. §53-2-10 (1996) (limitation on power to devise to charity to exclusion of spouse or child).

1102. Uniform Anatomical Gift Act §1, 8A ULA 31-33 (1987).

any portion or all of his or her body to certain institutions or individuals for scientific advancement, research, therapy, education, or transplantation. The gift may be made by will or by other *inter vivos* instruments as well.

H. Gifts to Pets/Animals

1008. Gifts to animals are void because animals are incompetent to take and hold title to property. A state may recognize the concept of the honorary trust, where the transferee of the property is given a power to apply the property for the designated purpose: to care for the animal. The rule against perpetuities applies to this arrangement so that the duration of the honorary trust must be tied to human lives.[1103] A legacy or bequest may have an equitable charge attached to it. The equitable charge, used in connection with pets, would require the legatee to care for the pets if the legatee accepts the gift. Presently, over thirty-six states have enacted statutes, which specifically recognize honorary trusts for pets, or have enacted similar types of legislation protecting and caring for pets after the death of the owner.

IV. Execution Provisions

A. Testimonium Clause and Testator's Signature

1009. In a designated area, preceding the testator's signature, most wills contain a testimonium clause, where the testator formally declares that he or she signed the will and declares the date of the signing. Although a testimonium clause may be omitted, every will should contain one to help to alleviate issues of proper execution. This clause is followed by the testator's signature.

B. Attestation Clause

1010. The attestation clause, describing the formalities that the witnesses attested to in the execution of the will and their opinion of the testamentary capacity of the testator, should follow the testator's signature. No state requires a will to contain an attestation clause, but an attestation clause raises a rebuttable presumption that the formalities recited therein actually occurred. These formalities described in the attestation clause are the requirements for the execution of a valid will as prescribed by the Wills Act. The witnesses' signatures follow the attestation clause.

1103. Restatement (Second) of Trusts §124 (1959); and *In re Searight's Estate*, 95 N.E.2d 779, 783-84 (Ohio 1950). The Uniform Probate Code, UPC §2-907, provides for both pet and non-pet honorary trusts.

§6. RESTRICTIONS

I. The "Legitime"

A. *Louisiana: The Principle of "Legitime"*

1011. Louisiana recognizes a form of the civil law principle of the *legitime*, which protects the testator's children from complete disinheritance. This protection extends to the issue of the testator's deceased children. In 1989 and 1990, Louisiana enacted legislation to limit disinheritance of children to children under the age of 23 and to those who had been interdicted or were subject to being interdicted because of mental incapacity or physical infirmity. In 1993, however, the Supreme Court of Louisiana held this legislation unconstitutional under Louisiana's constitution[1104] and restored the original protection from disinheritance to all of the testator's children,[1105] unless just cause is shown.[1106] The just cause must be stated in the will. The child will be disinherited unless he or she proves that the just cause, as stated, did not exist or a reconciliation had occurred.[1107] The Louisiana Constitution was amended in 1995 to extend the forced share only to the testator's children, twenty-three years of age or younger.[1108]

B. *The Other States*

1012. All states, except Louisiana, permit parents to disinherit their children. Such a will, however, may be more vulnerable to contest, especially if all of the testator's children are disinherited. The common law, unlike the civil law, places more importance on testamentary freedom than in protecting the surviving family members.[1109]

C. *The Pretermitted Heir*

1013. All states have statutes that protect the testator's children from unintentional disinheritance due to oversight, forgetfulness, or mistake when they are omitted from the will. These pretermitted heir statutes vary among the states as to the degree of protection. The majority of the statutes apply to children born after the execution of the will.

1104. *Succession of Lauga*, 624 So.2d 1156, 1170 (La. 1993).

1105. La. Civ. Code Ann. Art. 1495 (West, 1996) (if one child, 25% of the parent's estate; two or more, then 50% of the parent's estate).

1106. La. Civ. Code Ann. Art. 1621 (West, 2001) (lists eight just causes).

1107. La. Civ. Code Ann. Art. 1624 (West, 1995); and R.C. Brashier, *Disinheritance and the Modern Family*, 45, Case Western Reserve L. Rev. 83, 120 & 121 (1994).

1108. La. Const. Art. XII, §5(B).

1109. R.C. Brashier, *Disinheritance and the Modern Family*, 45 Case Western Reserve L. Rev. 83, 121 (1994).

1014. Other states also extend these statutes to include children born before the execution of the will, but who are unintentionally omitted. Children may include adopted children. The statutes usually extend only to the testator's children, but some statutes include grandchildren if their parent predeceased the testator.

II. Maintenance Provisions

1015. All states have some form of protection for the surviving spouse, which takes priority over the will provisions and often takes priority over creditors. The effectiveness of the protection varies both according to the different types of protection provided by the state and to the form of the protection itself. The protection for the surviving spouse is usually based upon the marital status, and not on need.[1110] In those states that recognize same-sex marriages or authorize inheritance rights for domestic partners or civil unions, the term spouse would include them.

A. The Common Law States

1016. Many states recognize or have versions of the common law marital estates of dower and curtesy. At common law, dower gave the wife a life estate in one-third of her husband's real property. Curtesy gave the husband a life estate in one-half of his wife's property if a child was born to the marriage. Most states now have modified these common law estates to reflect the change in society from wealth based upon land to wealth based upon personalty. The forced shared statutes in most states give the surviving spouse ownership of a fractional share of both real and personal property of the decedent's probate estate.[1111] States, following the Uniform Probate Code, have enlarged the forced share to include certain of the testator's non-probate property. This additional property is referred to as the augmented estate.[1112]

1017. The surviving spouse has a choice to elect to take his or her statutory forced share estate[1113] or to elect to take under the will. Statutes, typically, provide a one-year time limit for the election. The election is usually personal to the surviving spouse, which means only the spouse can make the election. In other states, if the surviving spouse dies before making the election, his or her personal representative may make the election. If the surviving spouse does not make a timely election, the will governs.

1110. *See*, La. Civ. Code Ann. Arts. 2432–2434 (West, 1995); and UPC §2-202 et seq. (1990).

1111. R.C. Brashier, *Disinheritance and the Modern Family*, 45, Case Western Reserve L. Rev. 83, 99–102 (1994).

1112. UPC §2-201 et seq. (1996).

1113. The forced share may be referred to as the elective share since the surviving spouse must elect to take the share.

B. The Community Property States

1018. Community property has a built-in protection for the surviving spouse since one-half of the property is owned by the surviving spouse. The decedent may only dispose of his or her one-half share of the community property by will. However, under certain circumstances, the testator may put the surviving spouse to an election of his or her share of the community property or of renouncing his or her half of the community property and receive what the testator has provided for the surviving spouse under the will. This is known as the doctrine of election.[1114]

1019. In Louisiana, a testator's community property is subject to *usufruct* by the surviving spouse. The *usufruct* is an estate that is more or less the equivalent of a life estate. A surviving spouse may also claim a marital portion if the testator dies rich in comparison to the surviving spouse. The marital portion is one-fourth if the testator died without children and to a *usufruct* of a certain portion depending on the number of the testator's surviving children.[1115]

C. The Uniform Code and the Augmented Estate

1020. In 1969, the Uniform Probate Code introduced the concept of the augmented estate to include certain of the testator's non-probate property. The probate estate and the augmented estate are both subject to the forced share. Several states have enacted statutes adopting the concept of the augmented estate. The extension of the forced share to non-probate property provides greater protection to the surviving spouse and alleviates the problem of determining whether the non-probate property is a fraudulent or illusory transfer.

1021. In 1990, the Uniform Probate Code continued the augmented estate concept but changed the concept of the forced share to an accrued share concept. The surviving spouse's forced share increases for each year of marriage up through the fifteenth year, to a maximum share of 50%. Certain properties of the surviving spouse may offset the forced share.[1116] The Code also introduced the concept of a supplemental forced share for the needy spouse.[1117]

1114. This doctrine may apply in both community and common law states and requires any beneficiary under the will to elect to take the gift under the will and give up the beneficiary's own property over which the testator has no testamentary power. In community property states this doctrine is a useful estate planning technique. For example, the decedent may want to place all the community property in a trust for the surviving spouse for life and then to leave the property to their children.

1115. La. Civ. Code Ann. Arts. 2432–2434 (West, 1995). The share cannot exceed USD 1,000,000.

1116. UPC §2-202 et seq. (1990).

1117. UPC §2-202 et seq. (1990).

D. Fraud on the Spouse's Forced Share

1022. Unless the state has adopted the concept of the augmented estate, the statutory forced share usually applies only to the decedent's probate property and not to the non-probate property. The surviving spouse receives little protection if most of the decedent's property is comprised of non-probate assets. The majority of the states limit the surviving spouse's protection to probate property. Some common law states have, however, offered some relief if most of the property is non-probate by determining whether the decedent's lifetime gratuitous transfers to third parties were made with the intent to defraud the surviving spouse of his or her statutory share.[1118] If the transfer is fraudulent, the property remains in the decedent's estate. Other states have examined the gratuitous transfers to determine whether they are illusory transfers because the decedent continued to keep control over the property as if he or she were the owner. If it is an illusory transfer, the property is still the decedent's probate property.[1119] In addition to the remedy of transfers of community property to defraud the surviving spouse, some of the community property states remedy this problem by not allowing unilateral gratuitous transfers of community property without both spouses either consenting to the transfer or joining in the transfer.[1120]

E. Homestead, Exemption and Quarantine

1023. The concepts of homestead and exemption developed in American law[1121] primarily to protect an insolvent debtor's residence and certain items of personal property from his or her creditors. These protections are also extended to a decedent's spouse and minor children against his or her creditors.[1122] Exemption and homestead protections do not include exemption of the decedent's estate from the administrative expenses, funeral expenses, or expenses of the last illness.

1024. Homestead and exemption laws differ among the states. The homestead statutes usually protect the home or residence by exempting a certain fixed amount of the value of the home from being available for the creditor's execution, or in rural areas by exempting a fixed acreage of the family home from being available for the creditor's execution.

1025. Exemption laws exempt certain personal property from creditors, usually clothing, furniture, and certain tools of trade. In rural areas they may extend to livestock. The statute may enumerate certain items of personal property that are exempt, or may allow the spouse to choose personal property of a certain fixed value, or may provide the spouse with an allowance of a fixed sum of money.

1118. *National Shawmut Bank of Boston v. Cumming*, 91 N.E.2d 337 (Mass. 1950).
1119. *Newman v. Dore*, 9 N.E.2d 966 (NY Ct. App. 1937).
1120. La. Civ. Code Ann. Art. 2347 (West, 1995); and Wash. Rev. Code §26.16.030 (2) (1994).
1121. *See generally*, *American Law of Property* §§5.75–5.120 (A.J. Casner ed., 1952).
1122. Homestead and exemption statutes apply whether the decedent dies with or without a will.

1026. Several states have laws similar to the common law concept of quarantine, which allowed a widow to occupy her husband's house for forty days.[1123] In these states, the surviving spouse may occupy the house for a period of time, usually one year.[1124]

F. The Family Allowance

1027. Most states provide an allowance to be paid to the spouse and dependent children for maintenance during the administration of the estate and before the property is distributed. The allowance is usually not charged against any share the spouse or children will receive under the will or by intestate succession. This allowance takes priority over creditors.

G. Putative Spouse Doctrine

1028. A surviving spouse must be the legal spouse of the decedent, that is, the marriage must be a valid ceremonial or common law marriage. Some states recognize the concept of the putative spouse doctrine to provide relief to a person who believed in good faith that his or her marriage was valid, but the marriage was in fact invalid. This doctrine gives rights to the putative spouse to share in the decedent's estate. This doctrine, initially recognized in some of the community property states, is also recognized in a few common law states.[1125]

III. Prenuptial (Antenuptial) and Nuptial Agreements

1029. Every state allows a spouse to enter into prenuptial agreements, waiving property rights, such as the forced share, at the death of the other spouse. These agreements may also include certain provisions pertaining to the acquisition of property during the marriage.[1126] The agreements are based upon contract law, but are considered to be special contracts because the parties are considered to be in a confidential relationship and not bargaining at arms' length. The trend among the states is to require full disclosure between the would-be spouses of their property before the execution of the prenuptial agreement. If this requirement is not satisfied, the agreement is invalid.

1123. 4 J. Kent, *Commentaries on American Law* 61, 901 (1st ed., 1830).

1124. Ohio Rev. Code Ann. §2106.15 (Baldwin, 1995) (a surviving spouse may remain in the mansion house for one year); Cal. Prob. Code §6500 (West 1995) (right of surviving spouse to remain in family dwelling); and Ark. Code Ann. §28-39-102 (Michie 1995) (a surviving spouse may remain-...for two months).

1125. Cal. Fam. Code §225-2252 (West, 2008); La. Civ. Code Ann. Art. 96 (West, 1996); Ill. Rev. Stat. Ch. 750, para. 5, §5/305 (1995); and Minn. Stat. Ann. §518.055 (West, 1995).

1126. In community property states, for example, the state may allow spouses to contract for the transmutation of the character of separate and community property.

1030. Prenuptial Agreements must be consensual. The parties must be free from duress, coercion, undue influence, and fraud. Many states require consideration for the agreement. The consideration is either the promise of marriage or the marriage itself. Courts usually validate agreements that are fair and free from overreaching.

1031. Most states allow spouses to enter into similar agreements after marriage, the nuptial agreement. Nuptial agreements are different from separation agreements, entered into by spouses as they agree to separate from the bonds of matrimony.

§7. INTERPRETATION OF A WILL

I. General Principles

A. Interpretation and Construction of a Will

1032. Even with the most skillful drafting of a will, circumstances often arise requiring the court to interpret the meaning of the words. The interpretation of a will is the process, whereby the court actually tries to determine the intent of a specific testator. The construction of a will, on the other hand, is the application of rules, which courts have constructed to apply in specific circumstances when the intent of a specific testator cannot be ascertained. Although the interpretation of a will and the construction of a will are technically different, these terms are used interchangeably. Courts apply rules of construction more frequently because of the impossibility of determining the "true" intent of a specific testator.

1033. Courts may follow a strict approach in interpreting and construing the meaning of a will. Under this approach, emphasis is placed on the meaning of the words of the will as they are usually used, that is, their plain meaning. The court will only look to the "four corners" of the will to obtain its meaning. The intent of the testator must be found within the will itself. The court may look to court opinions to aid its search, but the court limits these opinions to those involving the same issue. Courts following the strict approach may consider extrinsic evidence if there is an ambiguity, but restricts the scope of the type of evidence that may be admitted.

1034. Courts may also follow a liberal approach. Under this approach, the court seeks to find the testator's intent but is willing to look beyond the "four corners" of the will and consider relevant extrinsic evidence in order to find the testator's intent.

1035. The same court may be inconsistent as to which approach it follows: in one case following the strict interpretation approach, and in another case following the liberal approach.

B. Common Rules of Construction

1036. Each jurisdiction has developed its own rules of construction. These rules may be based upon public policy. For example, rules of construction may favor the spouse because of the public policy of protecting the spouse. They may also be based upon the court's presumption of what the typical testator would want. For example, rules may favor the spouse and children over strangers because the assumption is that the former are the natural objects of a testator's bounty.

1037. The fundamental rule of construction focuses on the determination of the testator's intent. This rule is stated frequently in court opinions. A typical statement of this rule is the following: the testator's intent is the polar star in construing a will. Other common rules of construction include: (1) A will is presumed to dispose of all of the testator's property, (2) Intestacy is disfavored, (3) Words should be given their ordinary or technical meanings, (4) Disinheritance is disfavored, (5) There is a presumption in favor of the spouse and heirs, (6) There is a presumption that the will speaks at the date of death, (7) There is a presumption in favor of early vesting, (8) A will operates as of the death of the testator, but it is interpreted as of the date of its execution, (9) Legacies in different instruments are presumed to be cumulative instead of substitutionary, and (10) A court will not reform a will.

II. Ambiguities

A. General Principles

1038. Ordinarily, a court will not resort to extrinsic evidence to interpret a will if it follows the plain meaning approach. Many courts will resort to extrinsic evidence if an ambiguity appears during the process of interpreting and construing the will, but the court is limited as to what extrinsic evidence it may consider. The court is usually limited to the circumstances surrounding the execution of the will. The declarations of the testator are usually inadmissible on the grounds that the testator's will must be in writing or because of the parol evidence rule. The testator's declarations are oral statements; and, therefore, they are not written and attested statements as required by the Wills Act. The parol evidence rule prevents introduction of evidence to alter the meaning of written instruments. Some courts may deny the decedent's declarations because of the Dead Man's Statute or the hearsay rule. The testator's declarations made before the execution of the will may be an exception to the hearsay rule if they are only to show the testator's state of mind.

1039. The prevailing rule in this country is that unless there is a statute to the contrary, a court will not reform either a will induced by mistake or a will in which the testator was mistaken as to the contents or the instrument.

B. Mistakes: Misdescription

1040. As a general rule, the states are more liberal in admitting extrinsic evidence when the testator makes a mistake in describing persons and property if the mistake raises a latent ambiguity than when the will is induced by mistake or negligence.

1. Latent Ambiguities

1041. Courts will reform wills if a misdescription can be characterized as a latent ambiguity. A latent ambiguity occurs where the meaning of the words of the will are clear but become unclear when applied to the extrinsic facts to which they refer. When there is a latent ambiguity, it is unlikely that extrinsic evidence will be fraudulent or a product of perjury. There are several types of latent ambiguities. One type, called an equivocation, occurs when the words describe exactly two or more persons or properties. In order to interpret these words, courts liberally admit extrinsic evidence to clear up the ambiguity, including the declarations of the testator.

1042. A second type of latent ambiguity partially describes one person or thing and also partially describes another person or thing, but neither is described fully. As a general rule, except for the testator's declarations, extrinsic evidence is admitted in an attempt to clear up the ambiguity.

1043. A third type of latent ambiguity is a description that is accurate in part and erroneous in part. Courts will ignore the erroneous part under the doctrine of *falsa demonstratio non nocet*, and then will attempt to interpret the remaining part.[1127] Often, cases involving misdescription of land falls under this type of latent ambiguity.

2. Patent Ambiguities

1044. A patent ambiguity is apparent from the face of the will. Because a court will not reform a will, a long standing rule in the United States is that courts will not correct a misdescription if it is a patent ambiguity unless it can be cleared up from the "four corners of the will." Some states will allow extrinsic evidence to interpret patent as well as latent ambiguities.

3. Perfect Description

1045. A provision in a will may perfectly describe a person or thing, but it is still a result of a mistake. This type of mistake is a classical example of the general

1127. T.E. Atkinson, *Law of Wills* 283 (2d ed., 1953).

rule that a court will not reform a will. If extrinsic evidence were admitted, it would reveal the provision is a mistaken description.

1046. Some states do allow reformation of the will under these circumstances. Under the personal-usage doctrine, courts will correct mistakes of accurate description where a person is generally known by one name, but it is not his or her proper name. Extrinsic evidence is allowed to show the name of the beneficiary really refers to another person. Other states have become liberal in allowing extrinsic evidence when there is no ambiguity on the face of the will. These states will admit extrinsic evidence to show that a perfect description is ambiguous.[1128]

III. Other Mistake Problems

1047. Issues of mistake as to the contents of a will often arise during its interpretation. The issues concern mistakes of words, mistakenly either included in the will or omitted from the will. The prevailing principle of construction applicable to both issues is that the court will not reform a will.

A. *Mistake as to the Contents of the Will*

1048. If a provision were mistakenly included in the will, typically through drafting and typographical errors by an attorney, the provision lacks testamentary intent and should not be admitted to probate. Two principles of law usually prevent relief. First, there is a rebuttable presumption that a testator who signs a will knows the contents of the will. Second, extrinsic evidence to show that the inclusion was a mistake is usually inadmissible if the provision is clear on its face. There may be relief if the provision raises an ambiguity, which permits the admission of extrinsic evidence, or if the jurisdiction has relaxed its rule against reformation of a will.

B. *Mistake in Omissions*

1049. If a provision is mistakenly omitted from a will, there is generally no relief because a court will not reform a will unless an applicable ambiguity rule of exception exists.[1129] Courts are more reluctant to relax the no-reformation rule in omission cases because inserting words in a will violates the policy that a court cannot write the testator's will.

1128. New Jersey has further departed from the no reformation doctrine for a perfect description and has developed the doctrine of probable intent. "A court not only examines the 'entire will' but also studies 'competent extrinsic evidence'; it attributes to the testator 'common human impulses' and seeks to find what he would subjectively have desired had he in fact actually addressed the contingency which has arisen." *Engle v. Siegel*, 377 A.2d 892, 893–894 (NJ 1977).

1129. *Knupp v. District of Columbia*, 578 A.2d 702 (DC Ct. App. 1990).

C. Mistake in Signing Wrong Will/Mistake in the Factum

1050. If a testator signs the wrong will by mistake, almost all jurisdictions will not reform the will. The will that the testator signed lacks testamentary intent because the testator did not intend the document to be his or her will. This type of mistake usually occurs when spouses are executing their individual wills at the same time and sign each other's will. *Matter of Snide* [1130] is the leading case to the contrary. In this case, the New York Court admitted extrinsic evidence and reformed the will that the decedent had mistakenly signed. The Court reasoned that under the facts of the case, the primary policy reason for not reforming a will was not present. There was no danger of fraud. The wills were the identical, mutual wills of a husband and his wife. The husband had mistakenly signed his wife's will, and *vice versa.*

IV. Integration

1051. Integration is the process of determining what is the "will" of the testator. This process involves both external and internal integration. This process may require interpretation and construction of the will. Although there may be several instruments, the testator's "will" may include all, some or none of them.

1052. External integration is the process of determining which pages constitute the will. The testator must have intended the pages to be his or her will, and the pages must have been present when the testator executed the will. Courts have developed rules of construction in the form of presumptions to aid them in external integration. For example, courts raise a rebuttal presumption that the document is the testator's will if the pages are connected by logical language or are sequentially numbered or are fastened together.

1053. Internal integration is the process of determining which writings compose the will when there are different writings. As long as the writings are not inconsistent with one another, they operate together. If they are inconsistent, the last one executed in point of time prevails. There is a construction preference, however, that if the testator gives legacies to the same person by different instruments, it is presumed the legacy in the later instrument is in addition to the one in the prior instrument.

§8. Rule Against Perpetuities

1054. The Rule Against Perpetuities concerns the vesting of ownership of property, both real and personal, within a fixed period of time. The classic statement of

1130. *In re Snide*, 418 N.E.2d 656 (NY Ct. App. 1981).

the Rule Against Perpetuities as developed in America is the following: "No interest is good unless it must vest, if at all, no later than twenty-one years after some life in being at the creation of the interest."[1131]

1055. The Rule Against Perpetuities serves several public policies. It restricts the dead hand so that the living can have control over the property. It also serves the policy of limiting the alienability of property for too long of a period of time. It supports these policies by limiting the time in which interests must vest. Interests must vest either at their creation or within twenty-one years after a life in being at the creation of the interest.[1132] The rule applies specifically to the following future interests: the contingent remainder, a contingent executory interest, and the vested remainder subject to open. The rule applies to property interests created in both *inter vivos* and testamentary instruments and to powers of appointment.

1056. Under the traditional application of the Rule, a provision that violates the Rule is invalid and fails altogether. In order to alleviate the possibility that a provision will violate the Rule, a savings clause is usually included in the instrument. The purpose of the savings clause is to make certain that the Rule will not be violated although the savings clause may not implement the provision as originally intended.

1057. The Rule has been reformed in many jurisdictions to lessen its harshness. By statute or case law, some jurisdictions apply a wait-and-see rule. The Rule is not applied until the actual time has expired for vesting. If vesting actually occurs in that time period, the interest is valid; if not, it is void.[1133] Other jurisdictions will apply a *cy pres* doctrine to reform the provision so that it will come within the rule.[1134] Other jurisdictions apply a combination of the wait-and-see rule and the *cy pres* doctrine. Other jurisdictions have adopted the Uniform Statutory Rule Against Perpetuities.[1135] The Uniform Statutory Rule adopts the traditional Rule, but it provides both a ninety-year wait-and-see period and a *cy pres* reformation if the interest violates the ninety-year wait-and-see period. Nearly half of the states have completely abolished or substantially reformed the Rule when applied to trusts. These states allow settlers to create trusts, known as dynasty trusts, which may last indefinitely.

1131. J.C. Gray, *The Rule Against Perpetuities* §201 191 (4th ed., 1942).
1132. L.M. Simes, *Public Policy and the Dead Hand* 36–60 (1953).
1133. *Merchants National Bank v. Curtis*, 97 A.2d 207 (NH 1953).
1134. *Edgerly v. Barker*, 31 A 900 (NH 1891).
1135. Uniform Statutory Rule Against Perpetuities §1, 8B ULA 333 (1993).

§9. POWERS OF APPOINTMENT

I. Definition and Purpose

1058. Historically, the law of powers of appointment was developed by the judiciary. Today, many jurisdictions have enacted statutes to govern powers of appointment. A power of appointment is a power one holds to appoint property. The donor is the creator of the power of appointment. The donee is the holder of the power. A primary purpose of the power of appointment is to allow the donee to decide who should receive the property. This purpose greatly adds flexibility to estate planning. It allows the donor to postpone the final decision as to who should take the property, delegating that decision to the donee, who may be in a better position to deal with unforeseen circumstances. Powers of appointment have also become important in estate planning because of federal estate and gift tax rules.[1136]

II. Classification

1059. A power may be classified according to the scope of the appointment. The traditional classification according to scope are general, special, and hybrid powers. A power is a general power if the donee may appoint to anyone, including the donee, the donee's estate, or the donee's creditors. A power is a special power if the donee may appoint to a specific group, excluding the donee, the donee's estate, or creditors. If the appointment is a general power but excludes certain appointees, the power is known as a hybrid power.

1060. The Restatement (Second) of Property classifies powers as general and non-general powers, following the Internal Revenue Code. A general power is one that may also be exercised in favor of the donee, his estate, his creditors, or creditors of the estate.[1137] All other powers are non-general powers. The traditional special power would be classified as a non-general power under this classification.

1061. Special powers (non-general) are further classified as to whether they are exclusive or non-exclusive. If exclusive, the appointment may exclude one or more of the appointees in the class. If non-exclusive the appointment must include all the appointees. If the appointment is made to appointees outside of the class, the appointment is invalid. If the special power is non-exclusive and the appointment excludes one or more of the class, the appointment is invalid.

1136. Powers that are classified as general powers may be used to qualify property for the marital deduction. Property over which the donee has a general power of appointment as defined by the tax code, but not property over which the donee has a special power, is included as part of the donee's estate for federal estate purposes. IRC §§2041(b) (1), 2514(c) (West, 1996).

1137. Restatement (Second) of Property §11.4 (1986); and IRC §§2041(b) (1), 2514(c) (West, 1996).

1062. A power may be classified according to the time of its exercise. If the power may be exercised only by will, it is a testamentary power; if it may be exercised at any time, it is a presently exercisable power. A general power is either a testamentary general power or a presently exercisable general power. A special (non-general) power is either a testamentary special power or a presently exercisable special power.

III. Creation

1063. A power of appointment may be created in either a will or an *inter vivos* instrument. In creating a power of appointment, the donor names the donee and the appointees, states when and how the power is to be exercised, and names the taker in default if the donee does not exercise the power. The donee need not accept the power of appointment, that is, the donee may disclaim or renounce the power. If the donee has accepted the power, the donee may release the power.

IV. Exercise

1064. A power of appointment usually needs not be exercised because there is no duty to appoint. If the power must be exercised, however, it is classified as a power in trust.

1065. The donee must intend to exercise the power of appointment. If the intent to exercise a testamentary general power of appointment is not clear, most states will raise a rebuttable presumption that the residuary clause of the donee's will did not exercise the power.

1066. If there is no exercise of the power or an ineffective appointment, the property usually passes to the takers in the default clause. If there is no default clause, however, there are several possibilities as to who should receive the property. If the power is a general power, the property usually reverts to the donor or the donor's successors in interest. If there is an ineffective appointment of a general power, some courts make a further inquiry to determine if the donee intended to take the property "out of the instrument conferring the power for all purposes or only for the limited purpose of giving effect to the particular disposition expressed."[1138] If the intent was for all purposes, the property becomes part of the donee's estate.

1067. If the donee of a special power fails to exercise the power or the exercise is ineffective and there is no default clause, the property usually reverts to the donor or the donor's successors in interest. Some courts, however, give the property to the persons named as the appointees[1139] under either (1) the theory of presuming that the intent of the donor would have been to make the appointees the takers in

1138. *Talbot v. Riggs*, 191 NE 360, 361 (Mass. Sup. Jud. Ct. 1934).
1139. *Daniel v. Brown*, 159 SE 209 (Va. Ct. App. 1931).

default[1140] or (2) the theory of a power in trust. A power is construed to be a power in trust if the language of the donor's instrument mandated the donee to make the appointment instead of leaving the appointment to the donee's discretion.

V. Creditors, Surviving Spouse and Federal Tax

A. Donor's Creditors, Surviving Spouse and Federal Tax

1068. If the donor reserves a general power of appointment, even if it is not exercised, the donor's creditors may reach the property. If the donor reserves a power of appointment, whether general or special, but the power of appointment was created to defraud creditors, the creditors may reach the property.

1069. The general rule is that the surviving spouse has no right to property over which the donor has reserved a general power of appointment. A few states have begun to modify this rule, following the Uniform Probate Code.[1141]

1070. If the donor reserves a power of appointment, federal tax law generally treats the property as that of the donor for tax purposes.

B. Donee's Creditors, Surviving Spouse and Federal Tax

1071. Generally, the creditors of a donee may reach the appointed property only if the donee exercises a general power of appointment. A minority of jurisdictions deny the creditor's reach even if the donee exercises the power.[1142]

1072. Generally, a donee's surviving spouse's forced share does not extend to the appointed property. The Uniform Probate Code includes property over which the decedent solely holds a presently exercisable power of appointment as part of the augmented estate, which is subject to the surviving spouse's forced share.[1143]

1073. Since federal tax law treats the donee of a general power of appointment as the owner of the property, there are tax consequences for the donee. Federal tax law, however, does not treat the donee of a special (non-general) power as the owner of the property. Hence, there are no federal tax consequences for the donee of a special (non-general) power.

1140. Under the first theory, the court construes the instrument to determine whether the intent of the testator can be presumed that the testator would have made the appointees the takers in the default clause.

1141. UPC §2-202(b) (1996) (any interests that are part of the donee's will that can be appointed by general powers become part of the donee's estate).

1142. *St. Matthews Bank v. DeCharette*, 83 S.W.2d 471 (Ky. 1935).

1143. UPC §2-202(b) (2) (I) (1996); Michigan also subjects the appointive property to the forced share if the donee's will exercised the power or manifested an intent to do so. Mich. Comp. Laws Ann. §556.116 (West, 1996).

§10. Ethical and Malpractice Issues

1074. In recent years, the legal community has focused more attention on estate planning attorneys in the areas of legal ethics and legal malpractice.[1144] Both areas protect the client from the attorney's legal and ethical misconduct.[1145] These areas are also important to the courts and the bar in maintaining both the integrity of the legal profession and the public's confidence in the legal profession.

I. Ethical Considerations

1075. The relationship between attorney and client is a fiduciary relationship. This relationship imposes a higher standard of conduct on the attorney while he or she is acting on behalf of the client. Even though there may be no finding of wrongdoing, an attorney's conduct may raise ethical considerations. Standards, governing ethical conduct between attorneys and their clients, are either based upon the American Bar Association Rules of Professional Conduct (Model Rules) or the American Bar Association Code of Professional Responsibility (Code of Professional Responsibility), depending upon which one a state has adopted. Violations of these rules may result in disciplinary action by the state bar. In recent years, two important areas of legal ethics have become more pronounced in estate planning. They involve either issues of conflict of interest or issues of an attorney benefitting from the will.

A. Multiple Client Representation

1076. The attorney, as a fiduciary, has a fundamental duty of loyalty to the client. The attorney is, therefore, ethically bound to avoid conflicts of interests between or among clients. The rules governing ethical standards require the attorney not to represent multiple clients when their interests are adverse to one another unless the attorney believes the representation will not adversely affect the other client, and, additionally, if each client agrees to the representation after consultation. Furthermore, if the representation of one client may be materially limited by the attorney's responsibilities to another client or to the attorney's own interest, the attorney must not continue representation. The attorney may continue the representation if the attorney believes the representation will not adversely affect the client,

1144. Estate planning includes both testamentary and *inter vivos* instruments.

1145. *See generally* E.D. Spurgeon & M.J. Ciccarello, *The Lawyer in Other Fiduciary Roles: Policy and Ethical Considerations*, 62 Fordham L. Rev. 1357 (1994); and G.P. Johnston, *An Ethical Analysis of Common Estate Planning Practices—Is Good Business Bad Ethics?*, 45 Ohio St. L. J. 57 (1984).

and if the client consents after full disclosure.[1146] Estate planning is especially vulnerable to potential conflict-of-interest issues. Because of the nature of estate planning, family members often use the same attorney. Typically, they include husband and wife or other closely related family members.[1147]

1077. Multiple representation may also raise the ethical problem of confidentiality. An attorney is under the duty not to disclose information to others without the consent of the client. The duty of confidentiality continues after representation ends.[1148] In the context of estate planning, the issues of confidentiality may be compounded because disclosing information for estate planning is different from disclosing information for litigation. Disclosing information for estate planning may in fact be helpful since the present planning will certainly have future significance to others. The present rule of conduct focusing on confidentiality does not take into consideration the difference between litigation and estate planning.[1149]

B. The Drafting Attorney Acting as the Personal Representative and/or the Attorney for the Personal Representative

1078. Many parts of this country follow the general rule that as long as an attorney did not solicit the testator to nominate the attorney as the Personal Representative in the will, the attorney has not violated the ethical conduct of conflict of interest or of solicitation or of the appearance of impropriety if he or she is so nominated. Such nomination may, however, prompt will contests on the basis of undue influence and overreaching on part of the attorney.[1150] If the attorney suggests that he or she be nominated, this conduct does violate the Code of Professional Responsibility. Its EC 5-6 rule against solicitation specifically deals with "consciously" influencing a client to name the attorney as a fiduciary in an instrument. The Model Rules have no comparable provision, but its rules against conflict of interest would apply. Such a nomination may also conflict with the attorney's duty to provide independent legal advice as well as the duty not to promote an attorney's own self-interest. The general rule that a drafter of the will should not nominate him or herself in the will as the attorney to represent the personal representative is similar

1146. Model Rules of Professional Conduct Rule 1.7 (2007) (client-lawyer relationship: general conflict of interest).

1147. J.R. Wade, *When Can A Lawyer Represent Both Husband and Wife In Estate Planning*, 1(2), *Probate & Property* 12 (1987).

1148. Model Rules of Professional Conduct Rule 1.6 (2007) (client-lawyer relationship: confidentiality of information).

1149. G.P. Johnston, *An Ethical Analysis of Common Estate Planning Practices—Is Good Business Bad Ethics?*, 45 Ohio St. L. J. 57, 86–101 (1984); and E.D. Spurgeon & M.J. Ciccarello, *The Lawyer in Other Fiduciary Roles: Policy and Ethical Considerations*, 62 Fordham L. Rev. 1357 (1994).

1150. J.W. de Furia, *A Matter of Ethics Ignored: The Attorney Draftsman as Testamentary Fiduciary*, 36 U. Kansas L. Rev. 275 (1988); G.P. Johnston, *An Ethical Analysis of Common Estate Planning Practices—Is Good Business Bad Ethics?*, 45 Ohio St. L. J. 57, 86–101 (1984); and E.D. Spurgeon & M.J. Ciccarello, *The Lawyer in Other Fiduciary Roles: Policy and Ethical Considerations*, 62 Fordham L. Rev. 1357 (1994).

to the rule regarding nominating the drafter of the will as the personal representative. If the attorney solicits the nomination, the ethical rules of solicitation, duty to provide independent legal advice, and conflict of interest are violated. Even so, such conduct may be less offensive than naming the drafting attorney as the personal representative because in most jurisdictions the personal representative is free to choose the attorney to represent him or her and is not bound by the will. This practice is widespread in some states.

1079. The modern trend in these circumstances is to hold the attorney to a higher standard even if no solicitation provoked the nomination. Since the Model Rules of Professional Conduct do not deal with these issues directly, legal commentaries generally agree that there needs to be clarity.[1151] Some of them suggest there should not be total prohibition of either, but a process should be in place for the attorney to prove that the nomination was not a product of undue influence.[1152]

C. The Drafting Attorney Named as Will Beneficiary

1080. Even if there is no wrongdoing, ethical issues of conflict of interest and of the appearance of impropriety arise when the drafting attorney is named as a beneficiary in the will. In most states, the presumption of undue influence arises as well. Both the Code and the Rules address this issue. The Model Code of Professional Responsibility, EC 5-5, provides that the drafting attorney should not suggest to the client that the attorney be named as a beneficiary of the will. If the client voluntarily offers to name the attorney as a beneficiary, the attorney should urge the client to get disinterested advice before accepting the gift. Unless there are extraordinary circumstances, the attorney must insist the instrument be prepared by another. In the Model Rules of Professional Conduct, Rule 1.8(c) provides that the attorney shall not prepare an instrument that gives a substantial gift to the attorney or to his family unless the attorney is related to the client.

1081. Another general rule is that there is no violation of ethical conduct if there is no solicitation and the attorney's gift is reasonable; e.g., if the drafting is for family members or the gift is a modest one if drafting for close friends or clients.[1153]

1151. G.P. Johnston, *An Ethical Analysis of Common Estate Planning Practices—Is Good Business Bad Ethics?*, 45 Ohio St. L. J. 57, 86–101 (1984); E.D. Spurgeon & M.J. Ciccarello, *The Lawyer in Other Fiduciary Roles: Policy and Ethical Considerations*, 62 Fordham L. Rev. 1357 (1994); *Developments Regarding the Professional Responsibility of the Estate Planning Lawyer: The Effect of the Model Rules of Professional Conduct*, 22 Real Property Probate & Trust J. 1 (1987).

1152. E.D. Spurgeon & M.J. Ciccarello, *The Lawyer in Other Fiduciary Roles: Policy and Ethical Considerations*, 62 Fordham L. Rev. 1357, 1385 (1994).

1153. G.P. Johnston, *An Ethical Analysis of Common Estate Planning Practices—Is Good Business Bad Ethics?*, 45 Ohio St. L. J. 57, 67 (1984).

II. Malpractice Issues

1082. There is no question that an attorney owes a duty of care to the client, arising from their estate planning contract. The traditional rule arising from this duty states that the attorney is liable only to his or her client for malpractice. The intended beneficiary could not sue on the theory of lack of privity between the attorney and the beneficiary. This rule is being quickly eroded. Malpractice suits by disappointed beneficiaries are rapidly increasing and are being resolved in their favor.

1083. Most states allow the beneficiary to sue on a tort theory or a contract theory or both. On the tort theory, some courts have found a duty of care owed directly to the beneficiary.[1154] Other courts have found the beneficiary's tort claim to be derivative from the breach of duty created by the contract between the testator and the attorney.[1155] On the contract theory, the beneficiary is considered to be the third-party beneficiary of the contract between the testator and the attorney.

1154. *Ogle v. Fuiten*, 466 N.E.2d 224, 227 (Ill. 1984).
1155. *Hale v. Groce*, 744 P.2d 1289, 1290 (Or. 1987).

Chapter 3. Acts *Inter Vivos* Related to the Estate

§1. Estate Planning

I. Meaning

1084. Estate Planning is a process of arranging one's property for both testamentary and lifetime goals. These goals usually focus upon maximizing and conserving the estate for the benefit of specific persons and causes.[1156] Estate Planning has evolved from the simple goal of planning for death by using a will instead of dying intestate to planning for lifetime property management to planning for incapacity.

1085. The impetus for the development of estate planning as a defined profession was the need for federal estate tax planning for death and lifetime transfers. In large and middle size estates, careful planning is typical to minimize the effect of this tax on the decedent and on the beneficiary of the decedent's property. This tax planning is sometimes referred to as post mortem estate planning.

1086. The desire to avoid probate administration by having one's assets in the form of non-probate assets was another factor in the development of estate planning. Avoiding probate often lessens administration costs and protects privacy.

II. Estate Property Planning Devices

1087. The process of estate planning integrates both death and lifetime transfer devices. The will is the most common device used in all of estate planning. At death, property is transferred according to the terms of the decedent's will. The goal of many persons in estate planning is to avoid the will for distribution by probate administration, but to accomplish this same distribution by other means. These other means are known as will substitutes, whereby the decedent creates rights of other persons in the property by various lifetime transactions. The most frequently used will substitutes are the contract, the living trust, the beneficiary deed in some states, and the *inter vivos* gift (donation). If the will substitute device fails to create a property right in another person, at the decedent's death the property remains in the decedent's estate as probate property.

1088. In the past will substitutes were subject to intense scrutiny by a court at the decedent's death to determine whether the decedent intended to create a property right in another so that at death it would not be probate property, or whether the decedent intended to continue his or her own sole right in the property until death. If the intent was not to create a property right in another, the transaction is

1156. Estate Planning is an ongoing process because goals change. The goals, for example, of a young married couple with children may be very different when that couple is middle aged or has divorced or has retired.

testamentary in nature and not a valid *inter vivos* one. A common test used to determine the decedent's intent is the measure of control the decedent retained after the transaction. Under this test, the greater the control retained the more likely the transaction is testamentary. Today, will substitutes have become acceptable and useful devices in estate planning although some of them may be subject to the surviving spouse's elective share.

III. Tax Implications

1089. An important part of estate planning concerns tax implications. The goal is to minimize, defer, or avoid taxation. There are two types of taxes connected with succession law. The first type is the estate tax, which is the privilege of transferring property. The second type is the inheritance tax, which is a tax levied on the recipient of the property for the privilege of receiving a gratuitous gift. The federal government levies an estate tax, the federal estate tax. States levy inheritance taxes, estates taxes, or both. The federal government also has a federal gift tax, which levies a tax on *inter vivos* (lifetime) gifts. Most states have similar taxes on *inter vivos* (lifetime) gifts.

A. *The Federal Gift Tax*

1090. The federal gift tax is a tax on the transfer of property through *inter vivos (lifetime)* gifting. The federal gift tax is a separate tax system and is presently no longer unified with the federal estate tax system as a result of the enactment of the Economic Growth and Tax Relief Reconciliation Act of 2001. Presently, the lifetime gift tax credit is USD 345,800, which is equivalent to allowing an individual to give away during his or her lifetime USD 1,000,000 before the gift tax is applied.[1157]

1091. No gift tax is due until the gift credit has been exceeded. The maximum rate of the gift tax is 45% on the amount exceeding the credit in 2009 and will be 35% in 2010 and will return to 55% in 2011, with an additional 5% tax on all transfers between USD 10 million and USD 17,184,000 unless the U.S. Congress enacts new legislation.

1092. Federal gift tax law provides an annual exclusion, which, if used properly, becomes an effective planning tool to reduce federal gift and federal estate taxes. Presently, the exclusion allows one to give USD 10,000, as adjusted by inflation, worth of property per donee per year without being taxed as a gift or without this amount being accumulated towards the gift credit.[1158] A spouse may give an annual exclusion of USD 20,000, as adjusted by inflation, per donee per year if his or her spouse agrees to split the gift with the donor, amounting to contributing his or her

1157. IRC §2010(2001) and IRC §2502(2001) (unified credit against the gift tax.
1158. IRC §2503(b) (2001) (taxable gifts and exclusion).

USD 10,000, as adjusted by inflation.[1159] The usefulness of the gift splitting occurs when one spouse does not have the USD 10,000, but the other spouse has USD 20,000. Gift splitting may apply to any amount as long as the other spouse agrees. Beginning in 1998, the USD 10,000 annual gift exclusion is indexed to inflation so that the amount will be rounded to the next lowest multiple of USD 1,000. As of 2009, the annual exclusion is USD 12,000, which means the annual exclusion for gift splitting by spouses is USD 24,000.

1093. Gifts may be made to minors. As a general rule, donors do not give outright gifts of substantial value to minors. State law imposes legal disabilities so that minors are not competent to manage property. Such gifts may be given to minors by establishing formal guardianships or to a custodian authorized by state law following either the Uniform Gifts to Minors Act or the Uniform Transfers to Minors Act. A trust may also be established for the gift to a minor, but it must conform to the Internal Revenue Code.[1160] Most states have enacted statutes modeled on the Uniform Transfers to Minors Act.

1094. Gifts between spouses are exempt from federal gift taxation if the donee spouse is a U.S. citizen. If not, a marital deduction for gifts is denied. An annual exclusion for the non-citizen spouse is, however, allowed up to USD 100,000 as long as the transfer is not a nondeductible terminable interest.[1161]

B. The Federal Estate Tax

1095. The federal estate tax system is no longer unified with the federal gift tax system so that lifetime and death transfers are taxed at the same rate and share a unified credit.[1162] In 2001, the United States Congress enacted the Economic Growth and Tax Relief Reconciliation Act of 2001, which implemented a ten-year phase-in of lower estate tax rates and increased the estate credit through 2009 as well as separating the federal gift tax credit for lifetime gifts from the federal estate tax credit. It also repealed the estate tax for the year 2010. In 2015, individual estates valued under USD 5,430,000 were not taxable.

1096. The gross estate for federal estate tax purposes includes the decedent's probate property and non-probate assets as defined by the Internal Revenue Code.[1163] The gross estate also includes any *inter vivos* gifts that were made within

1159. IRC §2513 (2001) (gift by spouse to third party).
1160. IRC §2503(c) (1996) (taxable gifts, transfer for the benefit of a minor).
1161. IRC § 2523(a) (1996) (gift to spouse; disallowance of marital deduction where spouse is not a citizen).
1162. IRC §§2010, 2505 (2001).
1163. IRC §2033 (property in which the decedent had an interest); §2034 (dower and curtesy); §2035 (transfers of life insurance policies and certain interests within three years of death); §2036 (transfers with retained life estates or retained control; §2037 (transfer taking effect at death); §2038

three years of death.[1164] The gross estate is reduced by certain deductions. These deductions include expenses,[1165] casualty losses,[1166] charitable deductions,[1167] and the marital deduction.[1168] The taxable estate is the gross estate minus these deductions. The tentative estate tax is calculated on the taxable estate.[1169] The tentative estate tax is furthered reduced by certain credits, including the unified credit.[1170] The federal estate tax is, therefore, the tentative estate tax reduced by the credits.

1. Unified Credit (Repealed by the Economic Growth and Tax Relief Reconciliation Act of 2001)

1097. The federal estate and federal gift tax rates are no longer unified. Each has its separate rates and credits. Currently, the federal estate credit for 2009 is USD 1,455,800, which is the equivalent of allowing an individual to leave property worth USD 3,500,000 if no lifetime gifts triggering the federal gift tax have been made. The federal estate tax is repealed for 2010. Unless Congress enacts more legislation, 2011 the tax rates will return to the 2001 level, with the estate credit being, USD 345,000, the equivalent of excluding USD 1,000,000 before the federal estate tax applies and the maximum tax rate of 55% in excess of USD 3,000,000, with an additional 5% imposed on estates in excess of USD 10,000,000.[1171]

2. Marital Deduction

1098. There is no federal estate tax on property passing to the surviving spouse if the property meets the requirements of the marital deduction.[1172] The marital deduction applies to property that passes from the decedent to the surviving spouse in a prescribed form. The property, if not consumed, must be taxable in the spouse's estate. One of the purposes of the marital deduction is to defer taxes until the death of the second spouse. In addition, the decedent must be a citizen or resident of the United States. The surviving spouse must also be an American citizen. If she or he is not, the property must pass to a "qualified domestic trust."[1173] The spouse must in fact be the decedent's lawful spouse and survive the decedent. The property must

---

(revocable transfers); §2039 (annuities and employee benefits); §2040 (survivorship property); §2041 (general powers of appointment); §2042 (life insurance); and §2043 (transfers for insufficient consideration) (1996).

1164. IRC §2035 (1996).
1165. IRC §2053 (1996) (expenses, indebtedness, and taxes).
1166. IRC §2054 (1996) (losses).
1167. IRC §2055 (1996) (transfer to charitable uses).
1168. IRC §2056 (1996) (bequests to surviving spouse).
1169. The tax rates range from 18% to 55%.
1170. IRC §2010 (unified estate tax credit); §2011 (credit for state death taxes); §2012 (credit for pre-1977 gift taxes on property included in gross estate); §2013 (credit for taxes on prior transfers); and §2014 (credit for foreign death taxes) (1996).
1171. IRC §2001 (1996) (estate tax rate schedule).
1172. IRC §2056 (2001).
1173. IRC §2056 (d) (2001).

have also been included in the decedent's federal gross estate. The property must be transferred from the decedent to the surviving spouse, and the interest must not be a nondeductible terminable interest.

1099. There are five basic forms in which property may be transferred to the surviving spouse to qualify for the marital deduction so that at the death of the surviving spouse the property is in the surviving spouse's estate for federal estate tax purposes: (1) Property may be transferred absolutely, in fee simple. A trust can also be used to accommodate this transfer in fee simple. (2) The spouse may receive a life estate, coupled with a general power of appointment. Often a trust is used, but is not necessary.[1174] (3) The surviving spouse may receive a life estate with the remainder limited to the spouse's estate.[1175] (4) The transfer may be a qualified terminal interest property arrangement. This arrangement may also take the form of a trust.

1100. These kinds of property arrangements are popularly called "QTIP" transfers or "QTIP" trusts.[1176] Under this transfer, the surviving spouse has only an interest for life but with an absolute right to the income for life, paid at least annually. No person has a power of appointment to appoint any of the property to any person other than the surviving spouse. The personal representative of the decedent must affirmatively elect the "QTIP" for the marital deduction.

1101. Finally, if the surviving spouse has a life interest in a charitable deduction annuity trust or in a unitrust, this interest would satisfy the marital deduction requirement. The spouse must be the only noncharitable beneficiary. There are other rules as to payments, which must be satisfied.

1102. The "QTIP" arrangement is frequently used in estate planning, especially in second marriages where the surviving spouse is not the parent of all the children of the decedent. The "QTIP" qualifies for the marital deduction, but also allows the decedent to determine who will ultimately receive the property because the "QTIP" does not require giving the surviving spouse a power of appointment over the property. In such an arrangement, the surviving spouse may be given a life income interest while the decedent's children will be the ultimate takers. The "QTIP" trust is usually used when the surviving spouse is given a terminal life interest and the children are the ultimate takers.

1103. The marital deduction is an effective estate planning tool if the estate is greater than USD 600,000 since the first USD 600,000 is nontaxable because of the unified credit.

1174. IRC §2056(b) (6) (1996).
1175. IRC Reg. §20.2056(e)-2(b) (1) (1996).
1176. IRC §§2056(b) (7); 2053(f) (1996).

3. Coordinating the Estate Credit and the Marital Deduction

1104. The estate credit and the marital deduction, if coordinated, will reduce federal estate taxes for a married couple. Although all the property could be tax exempt in the estate of the first spouse to die because the marital deduction allows for a 100% deduction, this arrangement would not take advantage of the estate credit. Property qualifying for the marital deduction, if not consumed, however, must be included in the estate of the surviving spouse. A common arrangement provides for two trusts. One trust is created to preserve the estate credit. This trust is often called the "credit shelter" trust or the "bypass trust." The other trust, called "the marital deduction trust," qualifies for the marital deduction. Under this arrangement, the "credit shelter trust" is not part of the surviving spouse's estate at death although the surviving spouse may be a beneficiary of the trust, but not the ultimate beneficiary.

1105. Frequently, these trusts are expressed in terms of a formula, either a "pecuniary" or a "fractional" formula. Their purpose is to put the right amount of property in each of the trusts.[1177]

4. Generation-Skipping Transfer Tax

1106. The purpose of the generation-skipping transfer tax is to require the payment of transfer taxes once per generation and not to bypass a generation. When property is transferred so that it bypasses a generation, this tax is imposed on a skipped generation. This tax is in addition to the federal estate and federal gift taxes.

1107. A generation-skipping transfer occurs when there is a direct skip, a taxable termination, or a taxable distribution.[1178] The tax code defines a "skip person" as a person assigned to a generation that is two or more generations below the transferor's generation.[1179] The skipped generation is created by blood, adoption, or years of seniority if applied to nonrelatives, defined as more than thirty-seven and one-half younger than the transferor. An example of a direct skip is that of a grandparent giving a gift outright to a grandchild. The grandchild's generation is two generations below that of the grandparent, the transferor. A transfer to the grandchildren bypasses the transferor's children's generation for taxation purposes.

1108. There was a USD 1,000,000 exemption per transferor.[1180] The Economic Growth and Tax Relief Reconciliation Act of 2001 ties the exemption rate to that of the federal estate tax until 2009, with the exemption amount equivalent to USD 3,500,000 in 2009 and no generational-skipping tax due in 2010. If the United States

---

1177. A "pecuniary" formula states a fixed dollar amount. The "fractional" formula states a fractional share of the residue.
1178. IRC §2611(a) (1996) (definition of generation-skipping transfer).
1179. IRC §2613(a) (1996) (definition of skip person and non-skip person).
1180. IRC §2631(a) (1996) (GST exemption).

Congress does not enact more legislation, the exemption for 2011 and years thereafter will be USD 1,060,000 plus the inflation amount. This tax is, therefore, imposed on the very wealthy. The provisions of the Internal Revenue Code for the definition and the imposition of this tax are quite complex. Beginning in 1998, this exemption will be indexed, rounded to the next lowest multiple of USD 10,000.

5. Charitable Deductions

1109. Transfers for public, charitable, or religious purposes are exempt from federal gift and federal estate taxation[1181] if they satisfy the requirements of the Internal Revenue Code.[1182] As to the transfer of a remainder interest to a charity, the Internal Revenue Code imposes special requirements. The remainder must be in an annuity trust, unitrust, or a gift to a pooled income fund unless it is a remainder in a personal residence or in a farm, not in trust.[1183]

C. State Estate Taxes

1110. State death taxes take the form of an inheritance tax or an estate tax or both. An inheritance tax is a tax on the privilege to receive property. In many states the tax rate on inheritances depends on the identity of the beneficiary. The closer the family relationship between the decedent and the beneficiary, the lower the rate. For example, the surviving spouse and the children would be taxed at a lower rate than would collateral relations.

1111. An estate tax is a tax on the privilege to transfer property. The focus of this tax is on the estate rather than on the beneficiaries. Many states have estate taxes instead of inheritance taxes. Others have both.[1184]

IV. Estate Planning for Incapacity

1112. Planning for incapacity is a growing aspect of the field of estate planning. Incapacity includes both physical and mental incapacity. Estate planning for incapacity may or may not require transfers of property. Such planning often requires the individual, while competent, to create the devices to manage property and to

1181. IRC §2055 (1996).
1182. As defined by IRC §501(c)(3) (1996) (tax exemption for trusts, corporations, etc.).
1183. IRC §§664(d) (charitable remainder trusts); and 2055(e) (2); 2522(c) (2) (charitable and similar gifts) (1996).
1184. Some of those with both the inheritance and the estate tax. They enacted the estate tax in order to take advantage of the federal estate tax credit, which the federal estate tax system permits the deduction of state estate taxes. Many states no longer tie their state credit with the federal estate credit because the federal estate credit is too great since the enactment of the Economic Growth and Tax Relief Reconciliation Act of 2001.

make health care decisions when the individual becomes incapacitated. The revocable trust and the durable power of attorney are common devices used in providing for the management of property during incapacity. The living will and the durable power of attorney for health care are common tools used to direct health care during incapacity.

A. *Revocable Trust and Durable Power of Attorney*

1113. The revocable trust and the durable power of attorney are several alternatives to guardianship.[1185] These devices must be arranged when the person is competent.

1. The Revocable Trust

1114. The revocable trust allows a person to plan for incapacity because the trustee manages the trust property for the benefit of the beneficiary, who is the incapacitated person. In the typical arrangement, the creator of the trust is the trustee or co-trustee until he or she becomes incapacitated. Then, the successor trustee or co-trustee automatically takes over the management of the property.

2. Durable Power of Attorney

1115. A durable power of attorney is authorized by statute in all states. It provides that a power of attorney will continue throughout incapacity and not terminate as would the ordinary power of attorney. It is therefore "durable." The creator of the durable power of attorney is termed the principal, and the holder of the power is termed the attorney-in-fact. In order to create a durable power of attorney, most state statutes require the durable-power-of-attorney instrument to contain specific language, expressing that the power of attorney will endure during incapacity. In a few states, there is a presumption that any power of attorney is durable. The durable power of attorney ends at the death of the principal. The durable power of attorney may be effective immediately upon execution or effective when the principal becomes incapacitated. The latter is described as a "springing power."

1116. The durable power of attorney sets forth the powers granted to the holder of the power. The managerial powers may be broadly or narrowly stated. These powers are in addition to any statutory powers. This device is not very helpful unless third parties will recognize the durable power of attorney and interact with

1185. If alternative devices have not been put in place for incapacity, a guardianship proceeding must be initiated. A guardianship requires a court proceeding to determine that a person is incapacitated. If the person is found to be incapacitated, the court appoints a guardian. The incapacitated person is referred to as the ward. Guardianship proceedings may be voluntary or involuntary. Frequently, in involuntary guardianships, the court appoints the guardian without the ward's consent.

the agent as if he or she were the principal. More states are considering alternatives in encouraging third parties to recognize and follow the durable power of attorney.

B. Health Care Directives

1117. A competent person usually has the right to accept or refuse medical care. Many states allow incompetent persons to direct their medical treatment if they have, while competent, executed a health care directive. Since 1991, federal law has required every person, admitted to a hospital which receives federal funding, to be advised of his or her right to sign an advance directive. This written directive states the person's wishes as to the withdrawal or continuing of medical treatment under certain circumstances, usually in connection with life sustaining medical treatment. The use of health care directives has continued to increase in estates of all sizes.

1. The Living Will

1118. All states authorize some form of the living will, which may also be called an advance directive, directives to physicians, or natural death statement. It is not a "will" in the common usage of that term, but a document setting forth a person's wishes as to whether or not to receive life sustaining medical treatment when he or she is incapable of making such a decision. Life-sustaining medical treatment usually refers to artificial life-sustaining procedures, such as a ventilator. Many of the states also extend the living will to include artificial nutritional feeding and hydration as well as artificial life-sustaining procedures.

1119. The living will must conform to statutory requirements. Many states have their own statutory form that the person may execute. Execution requirements frequently do not require the document to be notarized. The individual's signature is required, and that signature is required to be witnessed, usually by two witnesses. The witnesses are required to sign their names as witnesses.

1120. It is unclear as to how effective living wills are in carrying out the wishes of the individual. Their effectiveness depends upon the medical profession's adherence to the document and that the document is readily available. There are few empirical studies on their effectiveness.

2. Durable Power of Attorney for Health Care

1121. The durable power of attorney for health care is authorized in most states. This power of attorney allows the creator to name a person to make health care decisions for the creator, when the creator becomes incapacitated. They are similar to the durable power of attorney for the management of property. The creator is termed the principal, and the holder of the power is termed the attorney-in-fact. It is durable because it continues during the principal's incapacity. Each state's statute requires that the document specifically contain language expressing that it is durable. The document may be effective upon execution or only at the time when the principal becomes incapacitated.

1122. The powers given to the attorney-in-fact may be broadly stated in order to give more flexibility to the attorney-in-fact in carrying out the wishes of the principal. The principal may limit the attorney-in-fact's powers to specific instructions.

§2. DONATIONS

I. General Principles

1123. As a general rule, the basis of American donative law is that of the individual's freedom to dispose of one's property, whether during one's lifetime or at death.

1124. *Inter vivos* (lifetime) donations (gifts) may be made of any property that is transferrable. The transferor is usually referred to as the donor and the transferee as the donee. There are three requirements for an *inter vivos* gift. The donor must have a present intent to make the gift, must actually or symbolically deliver the gift, and the donee must accept. A third party may accept the gift on behalf of the donee. A donee may decline a gift. The delivery requirement for personal property is satisfied with actual delivery of the property or a symbolic delivery if actual delivery is impracticable, but the transfer must eventually occur. Delivery of a gift of real property is the actual delivery of the deed.

1125. The gift may be given outright or in trust. If a substantial gift is made to a minor, the gift is given to the minor's guardian or custodian.[1186] The gift may be given as a gift to co-owners. The co-owners may hold the property as tenants-in-common[1187] as joint tenants,[1188] or as tenants by the entirety,[1189] if husband and wife are the co-owners. If co-owners hold title as joint tenants or as tenants by the entirety, the surviving tenant owns the property absolutely.

1126. There is a federal gift tax on gifts currently that are greater than USD 12,000 per donee per annum. Gifts of USD 12,000 or less per donee per annum, however, are tax exempt.[1190] A gift to a spouse is tax exempt[1191] as well as gifts to

1186. *See* para. 1048.
1187. Each co-owner owns outright a prescribed share.
1188. The co-owners own the property together as a whole while living. When a co-owner dies, his or her share ends and the surviving co-owners own the property as a whole. This type of ownership is called "survivorship."
1189. This is the form of joint tenancy when the owners are married. There are additional rules attached to ownership by the entirety.
1190. Beginning in 1998, the USD 10,000 annual gift exclusion will be indexed to inflation so that the amount will be rounded to the next lowest multiple of USD 1,000. At the time of the revision of the monograph the amount is USD 12,000.

charitable organizations if they satisfy the requirements of the Internal Revenue Code. The federal gift tax exemptions stimulate using lifetime donations as part of estate planning.

II. Gifts *Causa Mortis*

1127. Gifts, given in contemplation of death, are called gifts *causa mortis*. The donor must be in imminent peril of death when the gift is made. If the contemplated death does not occur, the gift is revoked. A gift *causa mortis* applies only to personal property. The same requirements for a completed *inter vivos* gift are required for a completed gift *causa mortis*.

III. Will Substitutes

1128. Lifetime gifts may be manipulated so that transfers during life have the effect of passing property at the death of the donor. Such transfers are often referred to as will substitutes because the donor continues to own or control or have the option to control the gift until death. Often, the determination of whether such a transaction is an *inter vivos* gift depends upon the degree of control that the donor continues to have over the property. If the transaction is deemed not to be a valid *inter vivos* gift, it remains part of the donor's probate estate. It may also be invalid only for certain challengers' claims, such as a surviving spouse's claim.

1129. Will substitutes are purposely used to avoid the probate process. At the death of the donor, the property is not in the probate estate because the transfer is recognized as a valid *inter vivos* transfer. The revocable trust, a joint tenancy, and the manipulation of delivery of deeds are examples of will substitutes.

IV. Limitations on *Inter Vivos* Transfers: Spousal Rights

A. Common Law States

1130. As a general rule in common law states, one spouse has no immediate right in the property of the other, except in the case of dower.[1192] Each spouse is, usually, free to make gratuitous transfers during life. At death, the spouse has a right to share in the probate estate of the other spouse through the state's elective forced share statute or dower.

1191. If the spouse is a noncitizen, the donor spouse may give up to USD 100,000 as an annual gift exclusion. The gift must not be a terminal interest transfer.

1192. If the state has common law dower, the spouse has a right in the real estate because of the marriage. Dower is not defeated if the property is disposed of prior to death.

1131. If there is no property in the probate estate, the elective share is meaningless. Several states have developed doctrines to protect the surviving spouse's elective share by limiting *inter vivos* gifts under certain circumstances. The doctrine of fraud on the spouse's elective share voids such gifts when made with the intent to defeat the surviving spouse's elective share. Those states following this doctrine have not developed a standard rule as to what constitutes fraud. Other states have developed the concept of the illusory transfer, especially in the context of the revocable trust. The degree of control that the donor retains makes the transfer a mere illusion. If the transfer is determined to be illusory, the property remains in the donor's estate at death. The concept of the illusory transfer eliminates the finding of intent as would be necessary in the doctrine of fraud on the spouse's elective share. Some states may limit the illusory transfer concept only to the surviving spouse.[1193]

1132. The Uniform Probate Code has developed the concept of the augmented estate where the elective forced share would also apply to certain of the decedent spouse's non-probate property. Several states have legislatively adopted the concept of the augmented estate. In this approach, a spouse may make *inter vivos* gifts, but they may be subject to the surviving spouse's elective share.[1194]

B. Community Property States

1133. Community property states follow the concept that property acquired during the marriage except for inheritance, devises, and gifts is equally owned by the spouses. Prior to the 1970s, the husband was the manager of both halves of the community. In that role, he could unilaterally transfer the wife's half. Since the 1970s, all of the community property states have modified the system of management. Texas essentially has a two-spouse management system, where both spouses jointly manage the community. The other community property states essentially have a one-spouse-management system, where either spouse may manage the community.

1134. Gifts made to third parties with intent to defraud the other spouse may be set aside. There is, however, no common standard for determining fraud.[1195] Several states further restrict gifts made by either spouse alone by requiring the other spouse to consent to the transfer. California requires a written consent for personal property sold for less than fair value,[1196] Nevada and Washington require an express

1193. *Seifert v. Southern National Bank of South Carolina*, 409 S.E.2d 337 (SC, 1991), *Montgomery v. Michaels*, 301 N.E.2d 465 (Ill. 1973).

1194. NY Est. Powers & Trusts Laws §5-1.1 (McKinney, 1996); Minn. Stat. Ann. §524.2-201, §524-2.207 (West, 1996); and 20 Pa. Cons. Stat. Ann. §2203 (1996).

1195. California and Wisconsin have a good faith rule for management. *See In re Marriage of Reuling*, 28 Cal. Rptr. 2d 726 (Ct. App. 1994); and Cal. Fam. Code §1101, §5127 (1996).

1196. Cal. Family Code §1100 (1996).

or implied consent,[1197] and Louisiana requires the concurrence of the spouses.[1198] Wisconsin requires joint consent of gifts over USD 1,000 per donee per year.[1199]

1135. If the gift is made in violation of these rules, the gift is voidable by the injured spouse. The injured spouse may bring the entire gift back to the community if the community still exists, but only his or her half of the gift if the community does not exist.

V. Limitations on *Inter Vivos* Transfers: Children

1136. Louisiana recognizes the principle of the *legitime*. This principle provides a forced share for the testator's children when the testator dies. The testator's estate that is subject to this forced share is the testator's probate estate and any property disposed of by certain gifts *inter vivos* and *causa mortis*.[1200]

VI. Limitations on *Inter Vivos* Transfers: Creditors

1137. Creditors may set aside gratuitous transfers, made either while the donor is insolvent or to make himself or herself insolvent.

1138. The settlor's share of a trust in which he or she is also a beneficiary is subject to the settlor's creditors. Generally, a settlor's creditor has no right to a trust in which the settlor has reserved a power to revoke, unless there is a statute. Such statutes are of two types. One type deems the settlor the owner of the trust property because the power to revoke is tantamount to ownership; and, therefore, the trust is subject to creditors' rights. The other type allows the creditor to compel the settlor to exercise the power to revoke to the extent to satisfy the claim.

§3. Trusts

I. General Principles

A. *Definition*

1. The Express Trust

1139. A trust is a property arrangement where one person (the trustee) takes, holds, and manages property for the benefit of another (the beneficiary). This

1197. Nev. Rev. Stat. §123.230 (1996); and Wash. Rev. Code Ann. §26.16.030(2) (West, 1996).
1198. La. Civ. Code Ann. Art. 2349 (West, 1996).
1199. Wis. Stat. §766.53 (1996).
1200. La. Civ. Code Ann. Art. 1495 (West, 1995). These lifetime gifts may not exceed 3/4 of the estate if there is one forced share; may not exceed 1/2 if 2 or more forced shares.

arrangement creates a fiduciary relationship between the trustee and the beneficiary. The trustee takes legal title of the property. The beneficiary's interest is described as an equitable interest or equitable title. Almost all trusts created in the United States are gratuitous.

2. Trusts by Operation of Law

a. The Resulting Trust

1140. The resulting trust is a trust that the law will imply under any one of the following circumstances. If an express trust fails,[1201] the trustee holds the property on a resulting trust for the settlor or the settlor's successors in interest. If the property is in excess of the purposes of the express trust, the trustee holds the excess on a resulting trust for the settlor or the settlor's successors in interest. Finally, if the purchase money is given to another on an oral express trust to purchase real property and the purchaser takes title to the property, a purchase money resulting trust is presumed for the donor of the purchase money.

b. The Constructive Trust

1141. The law employs the constructive trust as an equitable remedy, particularly in circumstances to provide restitution and to prevent unjust enrichment. The law converts the holder of the legal title of the property to that of a trustee, whose duty is to deliver the property to whoever should have the beneficial use of the property.

B. Purposes

1. Allowable Purposes

1142. Trusts may be created for various purposes. They may be created to secure expert management of the property for the beneficiary, to conserve the property for the beneficiaries where there are beneficiaries with successive interests, to allow more than one generation to benefit from the property, to avoid probate, to minimize or defer federal estate tax, to be used as an estate planning device, to be used as a business entity, or to benefit the public for an indefinite period of time.

1201. If the express trust is a charitable trust which fails, a court may apply the *cy pres* doctrine to allow the trust to continue for a similar purpose instead of allowing it to pass as a resulting trust to the settlor or the settlor's successors in interest.

2. Prohibited Purposes

1143. A trust may not be created for purposes deemed contrary to public policy. Such policies include criminal purposes, fraud on creditors' rights, restraints on marriage, and restrictions on the longevity of trusts.

C. Creation of a Trust

1. Settlor

a. Definition

1144. The creator of a trust is usually called the settlor although other terms used are trustor, donor, or creator. The settlor must manifest the intent to create the trust. The settlor, who owns the property, must transfer this property to the trustee so that the trustee holds the legal title.[1202]

1145. Unless the settlor maintains some interest in the trust or is a trustee or beneficiary of the trust, the settlor has no standing to enforce the trust. There may be more than one settlor. A settlor may be the trustee and/or the beneficiary of the trust. A settlor cannot, however, be both the sole trustee and the sole beneficiary because there would be no one to enforce the trust, and the equitable and legal interests would merge, terminating the trust.

1146. If the settlor creates a trust while living, the trust is called an *inter vivos* or living trust. If the settlor creates the trust by will, it is called a testamentary trust. If the settlor creates a trust for private purposes, it is called a private express trust. If the settlor creates a trust for public purposes, it is called a charitable trust. If the settlor creates a trust to carry out a private objective but not to benefit a specified human, it is called an honorary trust.

b. Settlor's Intent

1147. The settlor must intend to create a trust. This intent must be manifested to impose mandatory duties. There are no specific words that must be used. The issue of intent often arises under circumstances where precatory words are used in making a gift, but typically without the words "trust" or "trustee." It is unclear under such circumstances whether the gift is an absolute gift or one in trust. Precatory words are words requesting, suggesting, or advising. The law in most states presumes that precatory words do not create a trust.

1202. The transfer is accomplished either by declaration or transfer. Using the declaration method, the settlor declares he or she is holding the property in trust, becoming the trustee as well as the settlor. Using the transfer method, the settlor must use the appropriate method for transferring title of property to another. For example, a deed is the method for transferring real estate.

1148. The issue of intent also arises where the settlor continues to control the property (even after it has been transferred to the trust) as if he or she were still its absolute owner. The amount of control that is retained by the settlor may render the trust illusory and invalid.

2. Trustee

1149. The trustee must be capable of taking, holding and managing property. The trustee may be an individual or a corporation or a combination of both. There may be more than one trustee. The trustee may also be the settlor or a beneficiary of the trust. The trustee cannot, however, be the sole trustee and the sole beneficiary. A court will appoint a trustee if the settlor fails to name a trustee. The trustee must voluntarily accept the trusteeship. If the trust does not provide for a successor trustee, a court will appoint one if the trustee does not accept the appointment, is removed, resigns, or dies.

3. Beneficiary

1150. The beneficiary must be capable of taking and holding property. The beneficiary does not have to be capable of managing property because the trustee manages the trust property. The beneficiary's interest in the trust is an equitable interest, which gives the beneficiary a claim against the trustee for breach of trust. A beneficiary may be the settlor of the trust or a trustee. The beneficiary cannot simultaneously be the sole beneficiary and the sole trustee.

4. Trust Property

1151. Trust property (also called the trust *corpus* or the trust *res*) may be any interest that presently exists and is transferable. Unless there is a statute to the contrary, a trust does not come into existence without trust property. Many states have recognized unfunded trusts in the pour-over will context if they meet the standard of the Uniform Testamentary Additions to Trusts Act. The settlor may transfer property into the trust by declaring himself or herself the trustee of the property so long as there is a clear manifestation that the property is now held in trust. If there is a transfer of the property to a third party as trustee, the required method of transferring legal title must be used. A deed, for example, transfers ownership in land.

5. Requirement of a Written Instrument

a. Statute of Wills and Statute of Frauds

1152. The Statute of Wills requires all testamentary trusts to be in writing. The Statute of Frauds, in effect in most states, requires all *inter vivos* trusts of real property, even if the trust was created by declaration, to be in writing.[1203] *Inter vivos* trusts in personal property do not require a writing unless there is a state statute to the contrary. A prudent settlor would not create a trust without a writing.

b. Oral Trusts

1153. The Statute of Frauds and the Statute of Wills prevent extrinsic evidence from being admitted to prove *inter vivos* oral trusts in real property or oral testamentary trusts.[1204] They may, however, be proved and enforced under certain circumstances. The courts will enforce an oral trust as a constructive trust or a resulting trust. These trusts are trusts implied by operation of law. The Statute of Frauds does not apply to trusts that are created by operation of law.

i The Constructive Trust

1154. An oral trust, whether *inter vivos* or testamentary, can be proved if it meets the condition of a constructive trust. A constructive trust is raised if "(a) the transfer was procured by fraud, misrepresentation, duress, undue influence or mistake of such a character that the transferor is entitled to restitution, or (b) the transferee at the time of the transfer was in a confidential relationship to the transferor, or (c) the transfer was made as security for an indebtedness of the transferor."[1205] The transferee holds the property on a constructive trust for the transferor or the beneficiaries. The majority of courts will not raise a constructive trust on the basis of constructive fraud (a broken promise) if the trust was an oral *inter vivos* trust, but the majority of states will raise a constructive trust on the basis of constructive fraud if the trust was an oral testamentary trust.

ii The Resulting Trust

1155. If an oral trust can be classified as a purchase money resulting trust, it will be enforced as a resulting trust since the Statute of Frauds does not apply to trusts created by operation of law. If purchase money is given to a person on an oral trust to purchase real estate and the purchaser takes title to the property, a purchase money resulting trust is presumed for the donor of the purchase money. Many jurisdictions have abolished the purchase money resulting trust.

1203. If there is part performance of the trust by going on the land, the trust may be taken out of the Statute of Frauds so that its proof may be made without a showing of a writing.
1204. Such trusts are sometimes referred to as secret trusts.
1205. Restatement of Restitution and Unjust Enrichment §182 (1937).

D. Administration of a Trust

1. Duties of the Trustee

1156. The trustee is held to a very high standard of conduct in managing the trust because the trust arrangement creates a fiduciary relationship between the trustee and the beneficiary. The law imposes duties on the trustee, which may be altered by the trust document.

a. Duty to Carry Out the Terms of the Trust

1157. The trustee must carry out the intent of the settlor as stated in the terms of the trust. The terms of the trust take precedence over the wishes of the beneficiaries. The trustee may possibly deviate from the trust terms, with court approval, in situations of illegality, impossibility, or a change of circumstance.

b. Duty of Loyalty

1158. The duty of loyalty is often described as the most fundamental duty owed by the trustee to the trust and the beneficiary. The duty of loyalty requires the trustee to administer the trust only for the benefit of the beneficiary. There can be no conflict of interest between the trustee and the beneficiary. If there is such a conflict, it must be resolved in favor of the beneficiary. There can be no self-dealing even if done in good faith. Co-trustees of a private express trust must act in unison, unless the trust provides otherwise. In charitable trusts, however, action by the majority of the trustees is only required.

c. Duty of Impartiality

1159. There may be multiple beneficiaries to a trust. They may have conflicting interests. The trustee has the duty to deal with the beneficiaries impartially. Such conflicts, for example, may arise between an income beneficiary, who wants investments that produce high income, and the remainder beneficiary, who wants investments that will increase in value since he or she will eventually receive the principal.

d. Duty to Use Reasonable Care

1160. The trustee has the duty to manage the property so that it is productive unless the trust provides otherwise. In the past the standard of care followed in the majority of the states in judging the trustee's conduct in the management of the trust was that of a reasonable and prudent person standard or its variations.[1206] "[T]he trustee is bound to employ such diligence and such prudence in the care and management as in general, prudent men of discretion and intelligence in such matters,

1206. *Originated in Harvard College v. Amory*, 26 Mass. (9 Pick.) 446, 461 (1830).

employ in their own affairs."[1207] Accordingly, trustees, such as investment banking corporations, would be held at a higher standard than trustees with no special investment skills. The trust agreement may modify this standard to hold the trustee to the standard of willfulness or negligence. State law may also limit what type of investments may be made by the trustee.

1161. Most states have modified the standard from the reasonable prudent person standard to the reasonable prudent investor or portfolio standard. A trustee must "exercise reasonable care, skill and caution to make and implement investment and management decisions as a prudent investor would for the entire portfolio."[1208] This standard shifts the emphasis from each individual investment in isolation to the portfolio as a whole.[1209]

e. Duty to Collect and Protect the Property

1162. The trustee must, as soon as it is reasonably possible, collect, protect, and conserve the trust property. This duty may require the trustee to initiate or defend against lawsuits. The trustee has no duty to personally bear the litigation expense.[1210]

f. Duty to Earmark the Trust Property

1163. The trustee has the duty to safeguard and earmark the property as trust property. Earmarking requires the trustee to identify and reregister the property as trust property.

g. Duty Not to Commingle

1164. The trustee must keep the trust property separate from the trustee's own personal property and other property that is not trust property. Many states have laws regulating commingling. In some states, commingling may also be a crime. State law may, however, allow commingling of various trusts for a better return on investment and/or to conserve trust property by reducing administrative costs.

h. Duty Not to Delegate

1165. The trustee is under a duty to the beneficiary not to delegate to others acts, which the trustee can reasonably be required personally to perform. The traditional test to determine if there has been a breach has been in terms of distinguishing between discretionary versus ministerial duties. If the duty involves discretion, the trustee cannot delegate; if ministerial, the trustee may delegate if the trustee uses

1207. *King v. Talbot*, 40 NY 76 (1869).
1208. NY Est. Powers & Trusts Law §11-2.3(b)(2) (McKinney, 1993).
1209. The Restatement (Third) of Trusts §227 (1992), Art. 9 of the Uniform Trust Code, and the Uniform Prudent Investor Act adopt this standard.
1210. Bogart, Trusts and Trustees §582 (2d ed., 1959).

reasonable care in selecting the agents and in supervising them. This traditional test has been modified in some jurisdictions in terms of what a prudent person might delegate to others.[1211]

i Duty to Account

1166. The trustee has the duty to account to the beneficiary. This duty requires the trustee to provide information to the beneficiary, to keep a written and accurate account of administration matters, and render the account to the beneficiary. Most states require trustees of testamentary trusts to render a written account annually. Failure to keep an accurate account results in all questions being resolved against the trustee.

j. Duty of Confidentiality

1167. The trustee is under the duty to keep the affairs of the trust in confidence from third parties and disclose to them only what the law requires or what furthers the interests of the beneficiaries.[1212]

2. Powers of the Trustee

1168. The administrative powers of the trustee to carry out the intent of the settlor are to be determined initially from the trust instrument. They may be expressly stated in the instrument or implied as necessary to carry out the purpose of the trust. Many states have enacted statutes based on the Uniform Trustees' Powers Act (1964) to bring certainty in the law as to the scope of the powers and to broaden them.

3. Breach of Trust

1169. The trustee is liable to the beneficiary for negligent and intentional breach of trust unless the trust instrument contains an enforceable exculpatory clause. A trustee may be liable even if the breach is in good faith, for example, breaching the duty of loyalty. Exculpatory clauses are usually strictly construed.[1213] Most courts will not enforce such clauses if the breach was in bad faith, intentional, or willfully reckless.[1214]

1170. The relief to the beneficiaries for breach may take several forms, depending upon the nature of the breach. The beneficiaries may be able to recover the property through equitable remedies of tracing and constructive trust. Money damages

1211. Restatement (Third) of Trusts §171 (1992).
1212. Restatement (Third) of Trusts §170 (1992).
1213. *Hatcher v. United States National Bank of Oregon*, 643 P.2d 359 (Or. Ct. App. 1982).
1214. Restatement (Second) of Trusts §222 (1959).

may be appropriate relief if the property is not recoverable. Other equitable relief may include injunctive relief, specific performance, general accounting, restitution, appointment of a receiver, or removal of the trustee. Historically, punitive damages were not assessed because at common law the court of equity did not have jurisdiction to award such damages. Several courts, however, have upheld punitive damage awards.[1215]

4. Tort and Contract Liabilities

1171. At common law, the trustee was deemed the owner of the trust property as far as third parties were concerned, making the trustee personally liable on contracts and torts regarding the trust estate. Most states have modified the common law. The trustee is personally liable on contracts if he or she does not reveal the fiduciary relationship, and on tort only for his or her own personal torts. If, however, the trust property is not sufficient to indemnify the trustee, the trustee is responsible for the insufficiency.

II. The Private Express Trust

A. *General Principles*

1172. A trust is a private express trust if the beneficiaries are private individuals.[1216] Private trusts may be *inter vivos* (created during life) or testamentary (created by will). *Inter vivos* trusts may be either irrevocable or revocable, depending on whether the settlor retains a power to revoke.

1173. A beneficiary of a private trust must be definite and identifiable. The beneficiary need only be identified by description. Usually, the beneficiary is either identified by name or by a class identification. The identification must have a definite meaning, such as children, and not an indefinite meaning, such as friends. Beneficiaries may be unborn at the time the trust is created as long as they are definitely within the period of the rule against perpetuities.

1174. The beneficiaries of a private trust often have successive interests. A typical successive interests arrangement would provide a beneficiary with an interest for life to receive the income generated by the property. On the death of the life beneficiary, another beneficiary would receive the trust property outright.

1215. Bogert, *Trusts and Trustees* §862 n. 12 (2d ed., 1959).

1216. The private express trust may be a business trust. In many parts of the country, a deed of trust is used when real property is bought on credit. Many of the employee benefit plans for retirement are trust arrangements.

B. Protective Provisions

1175. Generally, a beneficiary may assign, alienate, or devise his or her interest in the trust unless there are provisions in the trust limiting those rights, and which are also enforceable at law. Similarly, a beneficiary's creditors can reach the equitable interest unless such provisions exist. These protective provisions permit the settlor of the trust to protect the beneficiary from his or her own harmful actions and to protect the trust property from the beneficiary's creditors. A trust may contain more than one of these provisions.

1. Spendthrift Trusts

1176. The great majority of states recognize the spendthrift trust. A spendthrift provision restrains the beneficiary from voluntarily or involuntarily assigning his or her interest in the trust.[1217] The beneficiary's creditors cannot reach the trust property while it is in the hands of the trustee. A spendthrift provision allows a trustee to disperse trust funds to the beneficiary even if the creditor has levied against the trust. The creditor can reach the property only when it reaches the hands of the beneficiary.

1177. Most states do not enforce spendthrift provisions if the debt is for child support or alimony and frequently if the debt is for necessaries. A federal tax lien is also enforceable. Spendthrift provisions are unenforceable against creditors if the beneficiary is also the settlor of the trust unless the state has enacted an asset protection trust. At present eight states have enacted such trusts in competition with foreign countries that have created similar-type protected settlor-asset protective trusts, commonly called "off shore trusts."

2. Discretionary Trusts

1178. A discretionary trust is created when the settlor gives the trustee absolute discretion to apply or not to apply the trust funds for the benefit of the beneficiary. The beneficiary has no right to compel the trustee to disperse trust funds until the trustee acts unless there is an abuse of discretion.

1179. The beneficiary is, however, not barred from assigning his or her interest. Neither the beneficiary's assignees nor creditors have rights to the trust funds until the trustee decides to act on its discretion. Their rights are the same as those of the beneficiary. It is, therefore, the nature of the beneficiary's interest in the trust that gives the protection to the trust property. The discretionary trust gives the trustee

1217. *Broadway National Bank v. Adams*, 133 Mass. 170 (1882) is the seminal case, holding that such provisions are not against public policy.

flexibility of determining when or when not to distribute trust funds. The discretionary trust is often used when there are several beneficiaries. The trustee may act on its discretion to disperse to some beneficiaries and not to others.[1218]

1180. If the trustee decides to act on its discretion, the trustee will be personally liable if it does not make the disbursement to the creditor or the assignee if it has notice of the assignment or of the creditor's attachment. Even with notice, there may be no disbursement to the creditor or assignee if there is a spendthrift provision.

1181. Discretionary trusts are unenforceable against creditors if the beneficiary is the settlor of the trust. Some states will enforce support claims of spouses and children.

1182. A court will review the trustee's decisions for abuse of discretion. Some courts follow a standard of good faith. This standard requires the court to determine whether the decision was made in good faith, not the quality of the decision itself.[1219] Others follow a standard of judging the prudence and reasonableness of the decision itself.[1220]

3. Support Trusts and Discretionary-Support Trusts

1183. A support trust is created when the trustee is required to apply the trust funds for the support and maintenance of the beneficiary. Support may include education. The beneficiary's interest in the trust is then limited to support. It is, therefore, the nature of the beneficiary's interest that prevents it from being alienable or attachable. Only creditors who have supplied the beneficiary with necessaries can reach the trust.

1184. A discretionary-support trust is created when the trustee is required to apply the trust funds for the support of the beneficiary, but only in the trustee's absolute discretion. The discretionary-support trust is more frequently used than the pure support trust. The support is contingent upon the trustee's discretion.

1185. Support and discretionary-support trusts are unenforceable against creditors if the beneficiary is the settlor of the trust. In some states, claims for support of spouses and children will be enforced.

1186. In a pure support trust the standard for the trustee's decision as to the level of support, if not defined in the instrument, is that of the beneficiary's accustomed standard of living at the time the trust was created. A discretionary-support trust

1218. A blended trust is a form of a discretionary trust where the interests of the beneficiaries are so blended that individually their interests are inalienable or unattachable. *St. John v. Dann*, 34 A 110 (Conn. 1895); and Restatement (Second) Trusts §160 (1959) ("To A and his family").

1219. Scott on *Trusts* §187.

1220. *Boyden v. Stevens*, 188 NE 741 (Mass. Jud. Ct. 1934).

gives the trustee more discretion in determining the support standard. The trustee's decision in either of these trusts is also subject to review for abuse of discretion. Similar to the discretionary trust, some courts follow a standard of good faith. This standard turns upon whether the decision was made in good faith, not the decision itself.[1221] Other states follow a standard of judging the prudence and reasonableness of the decision itself.

4. Other Protective Provisions

1187. A trust may contain a provision that if the beneficiary attempts to alienate his or her interest or if a creditor attempts to attach the trust, the beneficiary's interest ceases. This forfeiture provision protects only the trust property and not the welfare of the beneficiary.

1188. A trust may provide that when alienation or an attachment is attempted, the trust converts to a discretionary trust or support trust.

C. Modification/Termination

1. The Settlor

a. The Irrevocable Trust

1189. Unless the settlor has retained a power to modify or terminate a trust or unless there is a statute to the contrary, the settlor, acting alone, has no power to modify or terminate the trust unless the settlor can prove that the trust was created due to fraud, undue influence, duress, or mistake. The standard of proof required to prove these grounds is usually the clear and convincing standard.

1190. A settlor and all the beneficiaries may modify or terminate a trust if they all consent. In order to be able to consent, the beneficiaries must be in existence (i.e., born) and competent (sui juris) unless a statute provides for the appointment of a guardian *ad litem* to represent them and give the consent for them. Some states allow unborn and incompetent beneficiaries to be represented by competent beneficiaries under the doctrine of virtual representation. Under this doctrine, the interests between the representative beneficiaries and those of the beneficiaries they represent must be identical, not conflicting.[1222] This doctrine allows unborn and incompetent beneficiaries to be bound by the lawsuit judgment.

1191. If the settlor is also the sole beneficiary of the trust or if the settlor's estate is the sole beneficiary, the settlor may terminate or modify the trust under the rule that no one has any interest in this trust except the settlor/beneficiary.

1221. Scott on *Trusts* §187.
1222. *Lowe v. Taylor*, 2 S.W.2d 1042 (Ky. 1928).

b. The Revocable Trust

1192. If the settlor retains a power to revoke or to modify the trust, the settlor may act on this power. Most courts require that the revocation follow the procedure as set forth in the trust document. The rationale for this requirement is to provide the maximum protection for the trustee.

2. The Trustee

1193. The trustee has no inherent power to modify or terminate a trust unless the trust instrument contains that power. The trustee may, however, illegally terminate a trust by transferring all the property from the trust. In such an event, the trust terminates because there is no trust property. Such action would be a breach of trust and the trustee would be liable for breach.

1194. The trustee may acquiesce to the demands of the beneficiaries and illegally terminate the trust. Such acquiescence is breach of trust. If, however, all the beneficiaries are ascertained, are competent, and have indefeasibly vested interests in the trust when the trustee acquiesces to their demand to terminate the trust, the beneficiaries may be prevented from seeking damages under the doctrine of unjust enrichment.

3. The Beneficiary

1195. The beneficiaries of a trust may modify or terminate a trust without the consent of the settlor if all the beneficiaries are in existence, are competent, do consent to the modification or termination, and all the material purposes of the trust are accomplished. This rule favors upholding the settlor's intent so long as there is a material purpose.

1196. Although there is disagreement as to what constitutes a material purpose, there are several general rules regarding certain types of trusts. Trusts are considered to state a material purpose if they are spendthrift, discretionary, or support trusts. The majority rule in this country is that a trust has a material purpose, where the beneficiary is sui juris and has an indefeasibly vested interest in the trust, and the trust fund is to be paid out at intervals.[1223] However, a minority of the states do not follow the majority rule, but the English rule. They allow the beneficiary to terminate the trust on the basis of rights of absolute ownership of the trust property and not on the basis of the intention of the settlor. The beneficiary cannot terminate a trust with a material purpose unless the settlor agrees, which becomes impossible if the settlor is dead.

1223. This rule is referred to as the Claflin Doctrine, originating in the case of *Claflin v. Claflin*, 20 NE 454 (Mass. 1889).

1197. Trusts which provide for only the successive enjoyment of the property are not considered to be trusts with a material purpose. A trust with one beneficiary with a life estate and another who will succeed to the trust property after the life estate ends is such an example of a trust without a material purpose.

1198. Notwithstanding these general rules, statutes and judicial action in a few states may give some relief to a destitute beneficiary. This relief may come in the form of allowing termination of a trust when the trust property falls below a minimum amount. A court may appoint guardians to represent unborn beneficiaries and may allow them to give consent for the unborn to terminate or modify the trust.

1199. The majority of courts will not permit testamentary trusts to be terminated by a will compromise agreement.[1224] A minority of courts will, nevertheless, permit such trusts to be terminated by a court-approved will compromise agreement.[1225]

4. Passive Trusts

1200. A trust that imposes no active duties on the trustee is called a passive or naked or dry trust. This trust terminates by operation of law because there is no purpose for its continuation.

5. Deviation and Illegality

1201. Courts will often modify trusts if the deviation pertains to trust administration and does not terminate or reduce the interests of the beneficiaries.

1202. If the purpose of the trust is or becomes illegal, the trust terminates. If the purpose of the trust becomes impractical, the court may modify or terminate the trust. In both situations the trustee usually holds the property on a resulting trust for the settlor or the settlor's successor in interests unless the intent of the settlor is to give the property to the trustee.

D. Use of Trusts in Estate Planning

1203. The trust is frequently used in estate planning because of its versatility and flexibility. The trust provides the means to allow expert property management. This is especially useful for beneficiaries who do not have such expertise or who are incapable or who do not want the responsibility or who are incompetent at law to manage property.

1224. *Adams v. Link*, 145 A.2d 753 (Conn. 1958).
1225. *Budin v. Levy*, 180 N.E.2d 74 (Mass. 1962).

1204. The trust will conserve and control property through successive generations. This arrangement is superior to the legal life estate and legal remainder arrangement.

1205. The *inter vivos* trust allows the settlor to retain ownership and control of his or her property while alive and competent. Under this arrangement, the settlor may be the trustee and one of the beneficiaries. Upon incapacity, the successor trustee succeeds as trustee. Such an *inter vivos* trust with a durable power of attorney adds even more flexibility during incapacity.

1206. The *inter vivos* trust is usually a better arrangement for incapacity than guardianship. The trustee will manage the property for the incapacitated person. The incapacitated person, while competent and not the court, will have appointed the person of his or her choice to manage the property.

1207. The *inter vivos* trust serves as a will substitute. The settlor creates an *inter vivos* trust so that upon his or her death the trust property bypasses probate administration and costs and is dispersed directly to the trust beneficiaries. The *inter vivos* trust can also accept property from the will or from other sources. This arrangement may save additional probate expense if the bulk of the decedent's property is from life insurance. The *inter vivos* trustee is named as the beneficiary of the life insurance policy. At the death of the policy holder, the life insurance proceeds go directly to the *inter vivos* trust and are dispersed directly to the trust beneficiaries.

1208. Instead of creating an *inter vivos* trust, the settlor may prefer a testamentary trust because most states supervise testamentary trusts. The trustee is usually required to make an annual accounting to the court. Such an accounting is expected to further safeguard against breach of trust. The settlor's will creates the trust.

1209. Trusts may provide federal estate and gift tax advantages. Trust property transferred to an irrevocable trust is valued at the date of transfer. A married couple may use trusts to take advantage of the marital deduction. Property, qualified for the marital deduction, is deductible from the decedent's estate. Successive-generation trusts may save considerable estate tax by using the generation skipping tax exemption.

III. Charitable Trusts

A. *The Nature of Charitable Trusts*

1210. A charitable trust is an express trust. Unlike the private express trust, a charitable trust is to benefit the general public or promote the public good. A charitable trust must have a charitable purpose. The meaning of the nature of the charitable purpose in this country evolved from the English Statute of Charitable Uses, which delineated categories of charitable purposes. In the United States, common charitable purposes are for the relief of poverty, the advancement of education, the advancement of religion, the promotion of health, governmental or municipal purposes, and other purposes, the accomplishment of which is beneficial to the community.[1226]

1211. If the purpose is merely benevolent or philanthropic, the purpose is not charitable. Most courts determine whether the trust is for a charitable purpose by examining the purpose against the categories of purposes the state has deemed to be charitable. Some courts interpret charitable purposes very narrowly within these general categories. Other courts view charity as an expanding concept that keeps pace with the contemporary views of society.

B. The Beneficiary

1212. The beneficiary of a charitable trust need not be definite as required by the private express trust. The beneficiary may be as uncertain and indefinite as a gift "to charity" or for a limited number of persons. The ultimate beneficiary of the charitable trust is the public. The designated beneficiary is merely a conduit.

1213. A charitable trust may last in perpetuity. The vesting of the interests, however, must be according to the Rule Against Perpetuities. The common law rule allows trust income to accumulate indefinitely, but subject to the supervision of the court under the standard of reasonableness.

C. Modification and Termination: The Cy Pres *Doctrine*

1214. The charitable trust instrument should provide an alternative plan if the trust purpose becomes impractical, unlawful, or impossible. If there is no such direction, most states will apply the doctrine of *cy pres* or an equivalent doctrine before allowing the trust to fail and revert back to the settlor or the settlor's successors on a resulting trust. The court attempts to ascertain what the intent of the settlor would have been if the settlor had thought of these contingencies.[1227] The court ascertains whether the intent of the settlor was more general than the particular purpose, as stated in the instrument. If the court determines that the settlor's intent was general, the court should apply the trust to a purpose as near as possible as the one stated in the trust instrument. If the intent was for the particular purpose as stated in the trust, the trust fails and is held on a resulting trust for the settlor or the settlor's successors in interest.

1226. The Restatement (Second) of Trusts §368 (1959).

1227. The Restatement (Second) of Trusts §399 (1959) states the doctrine as follows: If property is given in trust to be applied to a particular charitable purpose, and it is or becomes impossible or impracticable or illegal to carry out the particular purpose, and if the settlor manifested a more general intention to devote the property to charitable purposes, the trust will not fail but the court will direct the application of the property to some charitable purpose which falls within the general charitable intention of the settlor.

1215. Until recently, charitable trusts favoring certain groups were valid. Discrimination on the basis of race or gender may now render the charitable trust illegal under the Equal Protection Clause of the Fourteenth Amendment to the United States Constitution. It is unsettled now if all charitable trusts would be affected by the Equal Protection Clause since the clause requires the state to be acting (state action). If the trust is administered by public trustees, state action is usually present. Such trusts discriminating on the basis of gender and race are illegal and fail. The *cy pres* doctrine has been applied to cases where the trustees have been public trustees.

1216. There is uncertainty, however, whether state action is involved if the charitable trust is administered by private trustees. All charitable trusts may be within the scope of state action, even with private trustees, because the state's attorney general enforces all charitable trusts.

D. Enforcement of the Charitable Trust

1217. The law of fiduciary administration applies to the trustee of a charitable trust.[1228] The Attorney General of each state, however, enforces the charitable trust. Most states have adopted statutes based upon or similar to the Uniform Supervision of Trustees for Charitable Purposes. The statutes require the trustees to register with the office of the Attorney General and submit reports. The Attorney General is also given investigatory powers.[1229]

1218. A co-trustee may also enforce the trust. A person with a special interest as a beneficiary or the settlor may also have standing to enforce the trust. Special interest has been defined as an interest that is not available to the public at large or to the average beneficiary.[1230] Individual states may have statutes enlarging the categories of enforcers.[1231] Some states are following the trend as set forth in the Uniform Trust Code that permits the settlor of a charitable trust even without a special interest to enforce the trust.

E. Liabilities

1219. Many states have modified the common law, now permitting trust property to be used to satisfy claims against the charitable trust.[1232]

1228. Part 4, Chapter 3, s. 3, Part I(D) (1). All charitable contributions, whether as an outright gift, as a trust or as a charitable corporation, must be used for the purpose for which they were donated.
1229. The Internal Revenue Service also investigates charitable trusts to some extent. The Service investigates charitable trusts to assure they continue to meet their definition of charitable.
1230. *Gray v. St. Matthew's Cathedral*, 544 S.W.2d 488 (Tex. Ct. App. 1976).
1231. Wis. Stat. Ann. §701.10 (1996).
1232. R. Chester, *The Lawyer as Charitable Fiduciary: Public Trust or Private Gain?*, 25 Pacific L. J. 1353 (1994); and Ward, *The Charitable Fiduciary Liability Question*, 17 Real Property, Probate & Trust J. 700 (1982).

F. Tax Status

1220. A charitable trust is exempt for federal tax income purposes if it meets the requirement of the Internal Revenue Code.[1233] If a substantial part of its work is "carrying on propaganda, or otherwise attempting to influence legislation," it is not a charitable trust for federal tax purposes.[1234] The gift is tax deductible for the donor. A charitable trust is tax exempt in most states for property tax.

1221. If a donor wants to give a remainder in property to charity, the Internal Revenue Code requires the trust form be used if the property is not a farm or residence.[1235] These trusts are identified as the "charitable remainder annuity trust," the "charitable remainder unitrust," and the "pooled-income" fund. They must follow the requirements of the Code. The first two may be used to qualify property for the marital deduction as well.

G. Other Charitable Organizations

1222. A charitable organization may also take the form of a nonprofit corporation. Unlike the charitable trust, the laws of most states do not restrict the purposes of a charitable corporation. Nevertheless, the rules pertaining to charitable trusts usually apply to the charitable corporation.

IV. Honorary Trusts

1223. Honorary trusts are not trusts in the true sense. The honorary trust is a device created to carry out a specific noncharitable purpose of the settlor, where there is no human beneficiary. Honorary trusts are frequently used for the care of pets, the care of a burial plot, or the recital of masses for the soul of a designated person. The Rule Against Perpetuities applies to honorary trusts unless the state has exempted them from the effect of the Rule. Most states have now enacted statutes which codify the honorary trust for pets or similar type of legislation.

1233. A trust may meet the requirement for charitable under state law but not federal law. The aim is to have the trust be charitable under both laws.
1234. A charitable organization may satisfy the requirements of the Internal Revenue Code, but violate a public policy so that its exempt tax status is eliminated. *See*, e.g., *Bob Jones University v. United States*, 461 US 574 (1983).
1235. IRC §2055(e) (2) (A) (1996).

§4. Insurance Contracts

I. General Principles

1224. Generally, contracts are *inter vivos* transactions even if they are performed upon death. Life insurance contracts are based upon this principle. The owner of the policy contracts with the insurance company to pay the proceeds at the death of the insured to a designated beneficiary.

1225. If the proceeds are not paid to the decedent's estate, they are not part of the probate estate and are distributed to the beneficiary. If there are no augmented estate and community property issues, the proceeds are usually free of the claims of the insured's creditors and of the surviving spouse.

1226. Life insurance allows the decedent to increase the value of his or her estate at minimum investment.[1236]

II. Use in Estate Planning

A. As a Will Substitute: Generally

1227. Life insurance serves various purposes in estate planning. It is also an effective will substitute. The owner may reserve incidents of ownership until death, such as the rights to designate the beneficiary, borrow against the policy, or surrender the policy. The proceeds bypass the decedent's estate, if the decedent is the owner and the insured, and go directly to the beneficiary.

1228. In a typical family, the owner of the life insurance policy is also the insured. At the death of the insured, the insurance proceeds are paid to the beneficiary. There are several options for payment of the proceeds. They may be paid in a lump sum or retained by the company on a settlement option. The interest option allows the insurance company to retain the proceeds and to pay the interest that is earned on the proceeds. Under the fixed payment option, periodic payments of principal and income are paid until the proceeds are exhausted. Under the life income option, periodic payments are made over the life of the beneficiary as calculated by actuarial tables. There may be variations with all of the options.

1236. It is especially attractive to a young couple with minor children, but who have little property. The insurance proceeds will provide the protection for the family in case of death.

B. As a Will Substitute: Trust

1229. The insurance trust is a useful estate planning device. It has the advantages of a will substitute and of an *inter vivos* trust device. Many states have specifically given the insurance trust further usefulness in estate planning by allowing the trust to be set up without being funded until the insurance proceeds are paid to the trustee.

1230. Insurance proceeds paid to an *inter vivos* trust may provide liquidity to a decedent's estate without the proceeds being paid to the estate. In this situation, the trust provisions may allow the trustee to lend money to the estate or buy assets from the estate.

1231. The trustee, as the beneficiary of the insurance policy, would have the same options to select from for payment of the proceeds as would any other beneficiary. The trustee may select a lump sum payment or one of the settlement options.

III. Special Problems in Community Property States

1232. Determining whether life insurance is separate or community property becomes problematic when both separate and community sources are used to pay the premiums. Community property states follow three theories in determining the character of the policy and its proceeds. States following the inception of title theory characterize the insurance policy and its proceeds upon the basis of the character of the source of the property used to make the first premium payment. Any subsequent payments made from a different source of property do not change the character of the property, but create a right for reimbursement. States following the apportionment theory characterize the property according to the proportion of the contribution from each of the sources. States following the annual policy theory characterize the policy and its proceeds based upon the character of the source of the final payment.

§5. OTHERS

I. Survivorship Interests

1233. Property held by co-owners may be in the form of survivorship ownership. Such property is usually classified as non-probate property. If recognized as non-probate property, at the decedent's death, the co-owner's share in the property avoids probate and is usually not available to the decedent's surviving spouse or creditors.

1234. At common law, real property could be held as survivorship ownership. There were the joint tenancy and the tenancy by the entirety, if owned by husband

and wife. Under the survivorship theory of ownership, at the death of one of the parties, his or her interest ceases, resulting in the surviving owner or owners owning the property. Survivorship ownership may now extend to include personal property as well as real property.

1235. State and federal law determines which property can be held as survivorship property as well as the method for its creation. The type and method vary among the states and the federal government.

1236. Joint tenancy may be a form of ownership of separate property in community property states. Placing community property in joint tenancy ownership may transmute the property to separate property. Joint tenancy property is not subject to probate because the surviving spouse succeeds to the whole by operation of law. Joint tenancy by the entirety is not recognized in the community property states; however, several states allow the creation of survivorship in community property. Nevada, expressly, by statute allows the creation of survivorship in community property.[1237] Idaho allows spouses to enter into a written agreement to pass community property as survivorship property at the death of either spouse.[1238] Washington allows spouses to create survivorship in community property by a properly executed and recorded community property agreement. Wisconsin allows the holding of marital property in the survivorship form.[1239]

1237. Survivorship property is included in the decedent's gross estate for federal estate tax purposes. Many states will also include survivorship property for state estate tax purposes.

II. Contract Interests

1238. Contracts, other than life insurance, may be used as will substitutes. The decedent's interest passes according to the contract terms at his or her death. Multiparty bank accounts may be valid will substitutes under contract law. Under contract principles, a bank agrees with the parties to a multi-party account that when a party dies the bank will pay the proceeds of that account to the surviving co-party or to a named beneficiary. Problems have often arisen in interpreting whether joint bank accounts were intended to be convenience accounts only and not will substitutes, to be survivorship accounts, or to be payable on death accounts (POD), where the other party has no right to the property until the decedent dies and the agreement with the bank is to pay the balance to the named beneficiary. Many states have enacted statutes to clarify the establishment of such accounts. If the accounts fail as valid will substitutes, the proceeds will be probate property.

1237. Nev. Rev. Stat. §111.064 (2) (1996).
1238. Idaho Code §15-6-201(c) (1996).
1239. Wis. Stat. §766.60(4) (a) (1996) (this property is available to the creditors of the community).

1239. Bonds may also be held in will substitute forms. Bonds may be jointly owned or "payable on death" to a named beneficiary.

1240. Retirement benefits are usually in the form of a contract. These contracts are often used as will substitutes to provide for survivorship payments to beneficiaries after the death of the retiree or take the form of a payable-on-death account to a named beneficiary. Federal law requires most pension plans to provide a survivorship annuity for the surviving spouse unless waived, but in the form of an annuity trust. Most private pension funds are governed by federal law.[1240]

1241. The Social Security System is the public retirement system that provides retirement benefits, survivorship benefits, and disability benefits for most employees, their spouses and dependent children. Employees and their employers make mandated payments based on employee earnings.[1241] The employee's spouse also qualifies for retirement benefits based on the employee's record, generally about half of what the retired employee is receiving.[1242] At the death of the decedent, the spouse receives survivorship benefits.

1240. Employee Retirement Income Security Act of 1974 (ERISA).

1241. A self-employed person pays as both employee and employer.

1242. The spouse may have worked and is eligible on his or her own record. If divorced spouses were married for ten or more years, an unmarried, divorced spouse is eligible for social security on the former spouse's record.

Chapter 4. Acquisition and Administration of the Estate

§1. The System of Acquisition

1242. A general principle of American property law is that the character of property is determined at the time of acquisition. This character does not change when property is moved from one state to another. This principle applies to both common law and community property states. California, however, was the first state to reclassify property acquired in common law states as "quasi community" property if such property would have been community property if it had been acquired in California. "Quasi community property" is treated as community property in order to protect a married couple whose property would be separate property in California. Without this reclassification, the protection of the forced share that is built into the regime of the common law state would be lost.[1243]

I. The Common Law System

1243. Acquisition of property in the common law states is based upon the theory that property is acquired through the individual's own labor and efforts. This theory carries over into marriage. Each spouse acquires his or her property through his or her own labor and efforts.[1244] The property is usually titled in the acquiring individual's name. Spouses may agree to title property as co-owners. One form of co-ownership is the tenancy in common, where each owns a specific portion of the property. That portion becomes part of his or her probate estate. The other form of co-ownership is the tenancy by the entirety. At the death of one of the spouses, his or her interest in the property ceases and the surviving spouse becomes the owner of the entire property.

1244. Property may be gratuitously acquired through gift, inheritance, and by will.

II. The Community Property System

1245. In the nine community property states,[1245] property is acquired as separate property or as community property. If the property is acquired prior to the marriage or after the marriage or during the marriage as a gift or inheritance or by will, the property is classified as the separate property of the individual. During marriage

1243. Cal. Prob. Code §28 (West, 1996); Idaho and Wisconsin also recognize "quasi community" property for probate administration.

1244. *See*, e.g., Ark. Code Ann. §9-11-503(b) (1996).

1245. The nine community property states are Arizona, California, Idaho, Louisiana, Nevada, New Mexico, Texas, Washington, and Wisconsin. Alaska permits spouses to choose either system.

property acquired through the labor and efforts of either of the spouses is classified as community property. Each spouse is deemed owner of half of the community property.

1246. Separate property and community property remain as such even if they are exchanged for other property so long as the exchange is separate for separate and community for community. They do not remain as such if there are the occurrences of transmutation or of commingling.

1247. Transmutation occurs when separate property is changed to community property and *vice versa*. Transmutation of community property to separate property or *vice versa* may occur by agreement between the spouses and by gifts between them. Some states may require a writing to prove that transmutation has occurred.

1248. Commingling occurs when separate property and community property are commingled. Commingling may be of such a nature that the property is both community and separate property. Separate property, however, becomes community property if, after the commingling, the separate property cannot be identified as such.

1249. The earnings from community property is community property. The earnings from separate property, however, vary among the states as to whether they are classified as separate or community property.

§2. The Administration of the Estate

I. Purpose

1250. There are several purposes served by the formal administration of a decedent's estate. Administration safeguards an orderly process in distributing the decedent's estate, establishes which property should pass by will or by intestate succession, provides a process for creditors to present claims against the estate, protects the property for beneficiaries until the property is dispersed, provides for an orderly transfer of title from the decedent to the beneficiary, and finally, in the case of a will, provides assurance that the intent of the testator will be adhered to.

II. The Administration Process

1251. The administration of decedents' estates has historically been a court-supervised process. This process is not uniform among the states although there is much commonality. The trend among the states is to reduce the formal steps to a minimum. Many states allow the Office of the Register of Wills to supervise the process unless the court needs to be involved. Other states require no supervision by the Office of the Register of Wills unless someone initiates the process.[1246] Other states have moved to a summary proceeding if there are no disputes. Most states retain both formal and informal proceedings. Louisiana follows the civil law system of universal administration, where the heirs or the residuary devisees succeed to the title of the decedent's property and assume the decedent's liabilities and the obligation to pay them off. The court is not involved until there is a dispute. The 1990 Uniform Probate Code approves universal succession as an alternative process.[1247] Several states have adopted legislation modeled after the Uniform Probate Code.

1252. The administration of decedents' estates applies to probate property, the property that the decedent individually owns at death. There is no administration of non-probate property unless for purposes of the augmented estate. In those states which enforce an estate tax on non-probate assets, the personal representative may, however, be responsible for inventorying the non-probate property for the court.

A. *Jurisdiction*

1253. Each state gives a particular court jurisdiction over decedents' estates. This court is usually called the probate court. It may also be called the orphans' court or the surrogate's court or some other name. The primary place for the administration is at the decedent's domicile (domiciliary administration). Each state has discretion to determine the decedent's domicile. If the decedent has assets in a non-domiciliary state, an administration of those assets may be required in that state. A non-domiciliary state administration is called an ancillary administration, and with some states using the term supplemental administration. If the assets are personal properties, they are usually administered in the domiciliary administration. Real property is usually administered in the state where it is located.[1248]

1254. The court, having venue over the decedent's estate for domiciliary administration, is usually located in the county where the decedent was domiciled; for ancillary jurisdiction, the court is located where the assets are.

B. *Starting the Administration Process*

1255. The administration process is not automatic. Someone must initiate the process by filing a petition to probate the will or to make a finding of intestacy.

1246. The Office of the Register of Wills accepts and safeguards the various documents filed in a decedent's estate, including the will if there is one.

1247. UPC §§3-312 to 3-322 (1990).

1248. If real property has been placed in an *inter vivos* trust, the trust would be treated as nonprobate property and not require administration proceedings in the state where the real property is located. This is a technique to avoid ancillary administration.

1. Testate

a. Probating the Will

1256. "Probate" means determining whether the instrument offered as the decedent's will is in fact the decedent's valid will.[1249] The process[1250] begins with the filing of a petition (1) to probate the will and (2) to grant administration to the personal representative.

1257. Historically, two types of probate proceedings exist: the common form and the solemn form. The common form proceeds ex parte, without giving notice to anyone or without having an hearing. There is much doubt as to whether ex parte probate is valid under the Constitution of the United States, which requires proper notice and a hearing to satisfy the due process clauses of the fourteenth and fifth amendments. The United States Supreme Court has not decided a recent case on this issue since its modern jurisprudence regarding due process, notice, and fairness evolved. Many states have eliminated the common form.

1258. The solemn form requires notice to all interested persons and a hearing. In many jurisdictions, the solemn form is not before the probate court unless there is a will contest. The Office of the Register of Wills, in those jurisdictions, would supervise the probate process.

1259. Other states have modified the solemn form so that notice is given to all interested parties, but a hearing to probate the will is not formally held unless an interested party requests the hearing.

1260. If the court accepts an instrument to be the decedent's will, the will is now "probated." The court grants administration to the personal representative. The personal representative is the person or institution named[1251] in the will to serve in that capacity. The court will appoint another to succeed as the successor personal representative if the personal representative so named cannot serve because of non-acceptance or disqualification. The court issues official documents, called letters testamentary, authorizing the personal representative to act on behalf of the estate. If a will is not probated, the matter proceeds as an intestacy proceeding.

1261. If a will cannot be found at the decedent's death or is found in a mutilated condition, there is a presumption that the testator has revoked the will by physical act if the will can be traced to have been in the testator's possession. If the presumption is rebutted by clear and convincing evidence, the will is considered to be a lost will. Many states have statutes determining the procedure for proving lost wills. If the contents of the lost will cannot be proved, the testator dies without a will, i.e., dies intestate.

1249. The testator's will may be filed with the court before the petition is filed. While the testator is living, the will may be filed with the court for safekeeping.

1250. The personal representative named in the will is usually the person who files the petition.

1251. The older terms for personal representative are executor (male) and executrix (female).

1262. There is a time limit for probating a will, but it varies among the states. If no will is offered during the prescribed period, a finding of intestacy by the court becomes final. If an additional will is offered during the prescribed period, but after the probating of a previous will, some courts view the second will as a challenge to the first will. The hearing will then proceed as a will contest. Other courts view this subsequent will not as an attack on the previous will, but a proceeding to determine whether the subsequent will should be probated. If the subsequent will is probated, its legal effect will revoke the previous will. Most states have statutes protecting bona fide purchasers of property from the personal representative, the devisees, or heirs of the previous will.

b. Will Contests

1263. Any interested party whose interest will be adversely affected if a will is probated has standing to contest the will. The object of the contest is to prove to the court that the instrument being offered for probate is not the decedent's valid will. There is a time limit in which to bring a will contest proceeding. A will contest proceeding starts with the filing of a petition, containing the grounds for objecting to the will. In some jurisdictions, the proceeding is called a *caveat* and the petitioner is called a *caveator.*

1264. There are several grounds for contesting a will. The will may be challenged on grounds that the will was not properly executed or properly revoked, that the testator did not have testamentary capacity or intent, or that the will was procured by undue influence, fraud, coercion, or duress.

1265. Many states allow the parties to enter into will settlements, usually if there is no testamentary trust involved. The public policies of promoting family harmony and favoring settlements over litigation take precedence over carrying out the intent of the testator. These states also reason that once the property has been distributed to the parties, they are free anyway to redistribute the property. The settlements are enforced as contracts and are binding upon the parties. The settlements may be unenforceable if they are not approved by the probate court.

1266. Some states may recognize and enforce a will's "no contest clause" (frequently referred to as "*in terrorem* clause"), which requires a will beneficiary to forfeit his or her gift if the will contest is unsuccessful. Other states will enforce a no contest clause only if the contest was not made in good faith. "No-contest provisions are valuable will devices. They serve to protect the estates from costly and time-consuming litigation. They tend to minimize family bickering over the competence and capacity of testators, and over the various amounts bequeathed. However, the function of the court is to effect the testator's intent to the greatest extent possible within the bounds of the law."[1252]

1252. *In re Estate of Seymour*, 600 P.2d 274 (NM 1979).

2. Intestate

1267. An intestacy proceeding begins with the filing of an application for the finding of intestacy and the granting of administration. Parties entitled to file an application are determined by statute. All interested parties to the estate are given notice and a hearing is held on the application.[1253] If the court makes a finding of intestacy, an administrator is named to administer the estate. A statute determines whom the court may appoint as the administrator. The court issues official documents, called letters of administration, authorizing the administrator to act on behalf of the estate. The administrator acts in the same manner as the personal representative for testate estates and will be hereinafter referred to as the personal representative.

3. Small Estates

1268. Every state has statutes simplifying the administration of probate estates of small sizes, typically those under USD 50,000. These proceedings are informal, summarily conducted, and without court supervision. Typically, states may have a specific process, in addition to the small estate proceedings, for the administration of small estates, where there is essentially only one asset of value, such as an automobile.

C. Principal Steps in the Process

1269. The personal representative is authorized to act on behalf of the decedent's estate once the will has been probated or upon the finding of intestacy. The personal representative is required to post bond, representing the value of the estate unless waived or required to be nominal. The purpose of the bond is to provide tangible security for the faithful discharge of the personal representative's duties.

1270. The letters testamentary or the letters of administration provide identification to third parties that the personal representative is the official person to act on behalf of the estate. The personal representative is required to locate, take control of, and protect the probate property. The personal representative must appraise the estate and file an inventory. The personal representative must manage and wind up the decedent's business affairs.

1271. The personal representative must notify the creditors of the decedent. A United States Supreme Court case[1254] requires the personal representative to give actual notice to known or reasonably ascertainable creditors and to give notice by

1253. Many jurisdictions do not hold formal hearings unless an interested party requests a hearing. The Office of the Register of Wills often administers the estate until the probate court's involvement is needed.

1254. *Tulsa Professional Collection Services, Inc. v. Pope*, 485 US 478 (1988).

publication to unknown creditors. After notification, creditors must present their claims to the personal representative within a time period authorized by the non-claim statute.[1255] The personal representative accepts or rejects these claims. If a claim is rejected, the creditor may file a petition for a hearing on the rejection.

1272. The personal representative also marshals the estate assets. Marshaling determines in which order a creditor may proceed against the assets to satisfy a claim.

1273. The personal representative files with the court an accounting of the estate from time to time, usually in six month intervals until the final accounting is filed. The accounting depicts all of the property received and the expenses paid, including the estate's court costs, taxes, and fees. Notice of the filing of the accounting must be given to all interested parties.

1274. The personal representative files a plan for distribution. Thereafter, the court issues a decree of final distribution. The personal representative distributes the property according to the court decree to the beneficiaries. Each beneficiary gives a receipt for each distribution, which the personal representative files with the court. The personal representative makes a final accounting and petitions the court to be discharged as the personal representative. The court approves the final accounting and discharges the personal representative. The modern trend in many jurisdictions is to reduce the formal supervision of such actions unless a party specifically requests.

1275. During the administration of the estate, the personal representative may also petition the court for construction or interpretation of the will or for other guidance.

D. Personal Representative

1. Duties and Powers

1276. Personal Representatives act in the capacity of a fiduciary because they are responsible for property that does not belong to them. They owe duties both to the beneficiaries and the creditors of the estate. Their duties are temporary because they are limited to the period of administering the estate. Most of the duties are imposed by law and are the same ones as those imposed upon other fiduciaries, such as the trustee of a trust.[1256]

1277. The will or a statute contains the administrative powers allowing the personal representative of a will to carry out the duties. Such powers are either

1255. The surviving spouse in community property states may be a creditor for reimbursement for funds used to improve the decedent's separate property.

1256. *See*, Part 4, Chapter 3, s. 3, Part I(D) (1).

expressly stated or implied. The administrator of an intestate estate must look either to a statute or to the court for his or her administrative powers.

2. Breach of Duties

1278. The personal representative is liable to the beneficiaries and creditors for negligent and intentional breach of his or her duties. The relief for a breach may take several forms, depending upon the nature of the breach. The bond which the personal representative posted may be used. The property may be recovered through the equitable remedies of tracing and constructive trust. Money damages may be appropriate relief if the property is not recoverable. Other equitable relief may include injunctive relief, specific performance, general accounting, restitution, appointment of a receiver, or removal of the personal representative or administrator.

3. Liabilities to Third Parties

1279. Traditionally, the personal representative and the administrator were personally liable for expenses incurred in the administration of the estate even though they had a right to indemnity from the estate for all properly incurred expenses. Some states have modified this rule so that they are not personally liable on the contract if the contract is entered into in their fiduciary capacity and the estate is identified. Likewise, they are not liable personally for torts committed in the course of the estate's administration if they are without fault. They are, however, personally liable for improperly incurred expenses as well as for their own personal tort and negligent actions to third parties.

4. Compensation

1280. The personal representative may be compensated out of the estate for serving as the personal representative. Many states have abandoned the fee schedule and have adopted the standard of reasonable compensation. Even under this standard, some jurisdictions set a limit. As a general rule, all compensation must be court approved. A personal representative may engage an attorney to represent the estate during administration. Attorney fees must also be approved by the court.

III. Abatement

1281. The doctrine of abatement applies when there is not enough property in the decedent's estate to satisfy both the bequests and devises in the will and the claims made against the estate. Claims made against the estate take priority over gifts under the will or by property passing by intestacy. Claims may arise not only because of creditors but also for such reasons as excessive estate expenses, or the surviving spouse's forced share, or the pretermitted heir's share. To determine the order in which the property will be used to satisfy these claims, the court construes the will to ascertain the testator's intent as to this order. If the testator's intent cannot be found, a statute or case law provides the abatement scheme.

1282. Although abatement schemes vary among the states, common elements to all of them are the abatement of intestate property first, then residuary bequests and devises, then general bequests and devises, then demonstrative bequests and devises, and finally specific bequests and devises. Most states make no difference between bequests and devises within the same category as the older view did, which abated bequests before devises. Usually, within a class, bequests and devises abate ratably. Some schemes protect the surviving spouse and abate his or her share under the will after all of the other bequests and devises in that class have abated.

IV. Ademption by Extinction and Ademption by Satisfaction

A. Ademption by Extinction

1283. If property is specifically identified in the will but at the death of the testator the property is no longer in the estate, the property is said to have "adeemed by extinction." The majority of the states follow the identity doctrine, sometimes called the *in specie* test. Under this theory, if the property is not in the will as specifically identified, there is an ademption by extinction regardless of the testator's intent. A minority of the states follow the intent theory. Even though the property as described in the will cannot be identified, no ademption by extinction results unless it was the intent of the testator.

1284. States following the majority view (the identity doctrine) soften the harshness of the doctrine by applying the "form and substance rule." If the specific property has substantially changed in its nature and character, there is an ademption. If the change has merely been a nominal or formal change, there is no ademption. For example, if a bank account specifically identified in a will no longer exists because the bank has consolidated with another bank and at the testator's death is known by the other bank's name, the bank account has not adeemed because the change is a formal change, not a substantive change.

1285. Courts may also avoid the harshness of this doctrine by construing the property as a demonstrative or general gift and not as a specific gift. Ademption by extinction applies to specific gifts.

1286. Statutes may have modified this doctrine so that it does not apply to condemnation awards, proceeds from fire or casualty insurance on the property, or balances from the sale of the property.

B. Ademption by Satisfaction

1287. The doctrine of ademption by satisfaction applies when a testator makes an *inter vivos* gift of a general or residuary bequest or devise in his or her will to the named beneficiary with the intention that the gift is to satisfy the will provision.[1257] One of the difficulties in applying this doctrine is proving the testator's intent when the evidence is circumstantial. Many states will raise a presumption that the *inter vivos* gift was intended as a gift in satisfaction of the will provision if the testator stands *in loco parentis* to the beneficiary. Other states, following the Uniform Probate Code, require that there be a writing in order to raise the doctrine. The writing directly expresses the testator's intent that the *inter vivos* gift is meant to satisfy the will provision. The writing may be made by the testator or the beneficiary.

V. Lapse and Void Gifts

1288. A lapse occurs when a beneficiary under the will was alive when the will was executed, but predeceased the testator. A void gift occurs when a beneficiary under the will was dead when the will was executed. At common law, both lapse and void gifts failed.

1289. The intention of the testator controls as to whether a gift lapses. Most jurisdictions will not allow extrinsic evidence to aid the court in determining the testator's intent. The testator's intent must be found in the will. Usually, the testator's intent for a gift not to lapse is expressed by the will providing for a substitute gift or for a class gift.

1290. All states have enacted legislation, called anti-lapse statutes, to prevent lapse under certain circumstances. The statute identifies the circumstances and the person who will take the deceased beneficiary's share. Typical statutes prevent lapse only if the deceased beneficiary has kinship ties to the testator. Most anti-lapse statutes also apply to void gifts, to class gifts, and to residuary gifts.

1291. If a non-residuary gift lapses, it becomes part of the testator's residuary estate if there is no other will provision determining its disposition. If a residuary gift lapses, it passes as intestate property. In most jurisdictions under anti-lapse statutes, the lapsed gift passes directly by operation of law to the substituted statutory beneficiary and not through the deceased beneficiary's estate.

VI. Accretion

1292. The increase or growth in property specifically identified in the will between the time of the execution of the will and the death of the testator is called *inter vivos* accretion or accession. States vary as to whether the beneficiary receives

1257. This doctrine is the equivalent to the doctrine of advancements in intestate succession.

this growth or whether the decedent's general estate receives it. Generally, the beneficiary receives any increase in the market value and any improvement of the property. If there are no specific statutes, the intent of the testator governs or the courts apply specific rules.

1293. Postmortem accretion is the increase or growth in property specifically identified in the will between the moment of the death of the testator and distribution. This growth passes to the beneficiary of the property unless the testator has determined differently in the will.

Selected Bibliography

§1. Treatises

American Law Institute. *Restatement, Second, of Conflict of Laws,* 1972.
Thomas Edgar Atkinson. *The Law of Wills.* 2nd ed. 1953.
Black's Law Dictionary. West Publishing Co., 1968.
W. Blackstone. *Commentaries On the Law of England.* 3rd ed. Cooley, 1884.
Bogart. *Trusts and Trustees.* 2nd ed. 1962.
H. Clark, Jr. *The Law of Domestic Relations in the United States.* 2nd ed. West Publishing Co., 1988.
David Orgon Coolidge. *The Hawai'i Marriage Amendment: Its Origins, Meaning and Fate.* 22 U. Haw. L. Rev. 19 (2000).
W. DeFuniak & M. J. Vaughn. *Principles of Community Property.* §227 (1971).
Frederick Pollock & Frederick Maitland. *The History of English Law.* 405–406 (1898 ed., reprinted 1968).
A. Scott. *Trusts,* edited by W. Fratcher 4th ed. 1987.
B.R. Turner. *Equitable Distribution of Property.* 2d ed. Shepard's/McGraw-Hill, 1994.
C. G. Vernier. *American Family Laws.* Greenwood Press, 1932, 1971 reprint.
L.D. Wardle, C.L. Blakesley & J.Y. Parker (eds). *Contemporary Family Law.* Callaghan, 1998.

§2. Books

A. de Tocqueville. *Democracy in America.* 1945 ed.
D.M. Blair & M.H. Weiner *International Family Law.* 2d ed. 2009.
A. L. Milne, J. Folberg & P. Salem. *The Evolution of Divorce and Family Mediation.* In *Divorce and Family Mediation,* 2004.
M.A. Glendon. *The New Family and the New Property.* Butterworths, 1981.
J. Goldstein. A. Freud, & A. Solnit, *Beyond the Best Interests of the Child,* 1973.
J.D.W. Gregory, P.N. Swisher & S.L. Scheible. *Understanding Family Law.* Matthew Bender, 1993.
L.J. Harris, L.E. Teitelbaum & C.A. Weisbrod. *Family Law.* Little, Brown & Co., 1996.
B.M. Hoggett & D.S. Pearl. *The Family, Law and Society.* Butterworths, 3rd ed. 1991.

N. Lowe & G. Douglas (eds). *Families Across Frontiers.* Martinus Nijhoff, 1996.
Marie-Therese Meulders-Klein (ed.). *Families & Justice.* Bruylant, 1997.
W, A. Reppy & C. A. Samuel. *Community Property in the United States.* 11-1 3rd ed. 1991.
U.S. Bureau of the Census. *Statistical Abstract of the United States 2010.* U.S. Department of Commerce, 2010.
L.D. Wardle & M.Q. Wood. *A Lawyer Looks at Abortion.* BYU Press, 1982.
L.D. Wardle. *Contemporary Family Law, Principles, Policy and Practice.* Callaghan & Co. 1988.
L.D. Wardle, Mark P. Strasser & Lynne Marie Kohm. *Family Law from Multiple Perspectives, Cases and Commentary.* West Academic Publishing, 2014.
L. Weitzman. *The Marriage Contract,* 1981.
L. J. Weitzman & M. Maclean. *Economic Consequences of Divorce, The International Perspective.* Clarendon Press, Oxford, 1992.

§3. Uniform Acts (in "Uniform Laws Annotated" orU.L.A.)

Uniform Adoption Act 9 U.L.A. 1 (1997 Cumulative Supplement).
Uniform Anatomical Gift Act, 8A U.L.A. (1987).
Uniform Child Custody Jurisdiction Act, 9 U.L.A. 115 (1988).
Uniform Civil Liability for Support Act, 9 U.L.A. 333 (1954).
Uniform Disclaimer of Property Interests Act, 8A U.L.A. 149 (West 1978).
Uniform Disclaimer of Transfers by Will, Intestacy or Appointment Act, 8A U.L.A. 161 (1978).
Uniform Durable Power of Attorney Act, 8A U.L.A. 309 (1979).
Uniform Gifts to Minors Act, 8A U.L.A. 367 (1966).
Uniform Guardianship and Protective Proceedings Act, 8A U.L.A. 439 (1982).
Uniform Interstate Family Support Act, 9 U.L.A. 272 (1996 Cumulative Supplement).
Uniform Marital Property Act, 9A U.L.A. 97 (1983).
Uniform Marriage and Divorce Act, 9A U.L.A. 174 (1970).
Uniform Parentage Act, 9B U.L.A. 296 (1987).
Uniform Paternity Act, 9B U.L.A. 347 (1960).
Uniform Premarital Agreement Act, 9B U.L.A. 369 (1983).
Uniform Probate Code 8 U.L.A. 22 (West 1969).
Uniform Reciprocal Enforcement of Support Act, 9B U.L.A. 381 (1968).
Uniform Status of Children Assisted Conception Act, 9B U.L.A. 154 (Supp. 1994).
Uniform Simultaneous Death Act, 8B U.L.A. 258 (1991).
American Law Institute, *Principles of the Law of Family Dissolution: Analysis and Recommendations, Preliminary Draft No. 4* (ALI, Philadelphia Sept. 9, 1993).
American Bar Association Model Rules of Professional Conduct.
American Bar Association Code of Professional Responsibility.

§4. Law Review Articles

G. G. Blumberg. "Marital Property Treatment of Pensions, Disability Pay, Workers' Compensation, and Other Wage Substitutes: An Insurance, Or Replacement, Analysis." *U.C.L.A. Law Review* 33 (1986): 1250.

L. D. Elrod & R. G. Spector. "A Review of the Year in Family Law 2007-2008: Federalization and Nationalization Continue." *Fam. L. Q.* 42 (2009): 713.

J.H. Ely. "The Wages of Crying Wolf: A Comment on Roe v. Wade." *Yale Law Journal* 82 (1973): 920.

B.C. Hafen. "The Constitutional Status of Marriage, Kinship, and Sexual Privacy—Balancing the Individual and Social Interests." *Michigan Law Review* 81 (1983): 463.

LeAnn Larsen LaFave. "Origins and Evolution of the 'Best Interests of the Child' Standard." *S. D. L. Rev.* 34 (1989): 459.

C.E. Schneider. "Moral Discourse and the Transformation of American Family Law." *Mich. L. Rev.* 83 (1986): 1803.

J. B. Singer. "The Privatization of Family Law." *WIS. L. REV.* (1992): 1443.

L. D. *Wardle.* "A Critical Analysis of Constitutional Claims for Same-Sex Marriage." *BYU L. Rev.* 1 (1996).

L.D. Wardle. "Adoption: Upside Down and Sideways? Some Causes of and Remedies for Declining Domestic and International Adoptions." *Regent U. L. Rev.* 26 (2013–2014): 209, 215.

L.D. Wardle. "No-Fault Divorce and the Divorce Conundrum." *BYU Law Review* 73 (1991).

L. D. Wardle. "The Merit of Modesty: Abduction, Relocation, and the Hague Abduction Convention." *J. Compar. L.* 9 (2014): 89–110.

§5. Other Articles

Kempe et al., *The Battered Child Syndrome*, 181 J.A.M.A. 17 (1962).

§6. Cases

U.S. Supreme Court

DeShaney v. Winnebago, 489 U.S. 189 (1989).

Eisenstadt v. Baird, 405 U.S. 438 (1972).

Garska v. McCoy, 278 S.E.2d 357 (W.Va. 1981).

Gomez v. Perez, 409 U.S. 535 (1973).

Griswold v. Connecticut, 381 U.S. 479 (1965).

Lawrence *v.* Texas, 539 U.S. 558 (2003).

Levy v. Louisiana, 391 U.S. 68 (1968).

Meyer v. Nebraska, 262 U.S. 390 (1923).

Michael H. v. Gerald D., 491 U.S. 110 (1989).

Parham v. J.R., 442 U.S. 584 (1979).

Pierce v. Society of Sisters, 268 U.S. 510 (1925).
Planned Parenthood v. Casey, 505 U.S. 833 (1992).
Planned Parenthood v. Missouri, 428 U.S. 2 (1976).
Roe v. Wade, 410 U.S. 113 (1973).
Stanley v. Illinois, 405 U.S. 645 (1972).
Zablocki v. Redhail, 434 U.S. 374 (1978)

STATES

Goodridge v. Dep't of Pub. Health, 798 N.E.2d 941 (Mass, 2003).
In re Baby M., 537 A.2d 1227 (N.J. 1988).
In re Marriage Cases, 183 P.3d 384 (Cal. 2008).
Varnum v. Brien, 763 N.W.2d 862 (Iowa 2009).

§7. STATUTES

FEDERAL

The Indian Child Welfare Act of 1978, USC (§§1901–1923) (1994).
Parental Kidnapping Prevention Act of 1980, P. L. 96-611, Sec. 7 (a), codified at 28 USCA. §1738 A.
Internal Revenue Code, 11 USC 1 et seq.

Index

The numbers here refer to paragraph numbers.

Index

Index

Made in the USA
Monee, IL
13 September 2026

62974259R00234